THE DRONE DEBATE

THE DRONE DEBATE

A Primer on the U.S. Use of Unmanned Aircraft Outside Conventional Battlefields

Avery Plaw, Matthew S. Fricker, and Carlos R. Colon

ROWMAN & LITTLEFIELD
Lanham • Boulder • New York • London

434 /349

Published by Rowman & Littlefield
A wholly owned subsidiary of The Rowman & Littlefield Publishing Group, Inc.
4501 Forbes Boulevard, Suite 200, Lanham, Maryland 20706
www.rowman.com

Unit A, Whitacre Mews, 26-34 Stannary Street, London SE11 4AB

British Library Cataloguing in Publication Information Available

Library of Congress Cataloging-in-Publication Data

Plaw, Avery, author.
    The drone debate : a primer on the U.S. use of unmanned aircraft outside conventional battlefields / Avery Plaw, Matthew S. Fricker and Carlos R. Colon.
      pages cm
    Includes bibliographical references and index.
    ISBN 978-1-4422-3058-3 (cloth : alk. paper) — ISBN 978-1-4422-3059-0 (pbk. : alk. paper) — ISBN 978-1-4422-3060-6 (electronic)   1. Drone aircraft—Moral and ethical aspects—United States.   2. Drone aircraft—Government policy—United States.
3. Drone aircraft—Political aspects.   4. War—Moral and ethical aspects—United States.   5. United States—Military policy.   I. Fricker, Matthew S., author.
II. Title.   III. Title: Primer on the U.S. use of unmanned aircraft outside conventional battlefields.
UG1242.D7P53   2015
358.4—dc23   2016034956

♾ ™ The paper used in this publication meets the minimum requirements of American National Standard for Information Sciences—Permanence of Paper for Printed Library Materials, ANSI/NISO Z39.48-1992.

Printed in the United States of America

Contents

Acknowledgments

WE WOULD LIKE TO EXPRESS our gratitude to the University of Massachusetts at Dartmouth for its generous support of this research, and Marie-Claire Antoine for encouraging us to undertake this particular project. We would also like to thank Brian Williams and Peter Sandby-Thomas for kindly taking time to comment on specific chapters. Gordon Aronoff deserves special recognition for working through the entire manuscript with us, helping us to make improvements in every area. And our very deepest, humblest, and most emphatic thanks go our own in-house researcher, fact checker, and editor, Barbara Gurgel, who always demanded more and better, and always delivered the very best.

Introduction

The Drone Debate

THE U.S. GOVERNMENT's covert use of armed drones to hunt and kill suspected terrorists outside of conventional battlefields is a strikingly new departure in American defense policy, and to many people a terrifying one. As recently as July 2001, American ambassador Martin Indyk sharply criticized Israel for a terrorist targeting policy that was in many respects similar to the United States' policy (although drones were not Israel's weapon of choice): "The United States government is very clearly on record as against targeted assassinations. . . . They are extrajudicial killings, and we do not support that."[1] But there can no longer be any doubt that the United States has adopted its own policy of targeted killing, and on a massive scale. Since November 2002, the United States is credibly reported to have carried out at least five hundred covert drone strikes in Pakistan, Yemen, and Somalia, killing in excess of 3,500 people, including civilians.[2] Indeed, targeted killings by drone strikes have come "to define the War on Terror" under President Obama, in the apt formulation of a *New York Times* cover story on April 7, 2013.[3]

These U.S. drone strikes have generated growing attention and controversy, as indeed they should, and this book is devoted to providing an overview of the debate around them. This is an important project for two main reasons.

I. The Importance of Debating Drones

First, Americans need to be better informed about this program. According to a March 2013 Gallup poll, 49 percent of Americans report that they are not following U.S. drone strikes closely (25 percent say "not at all"), and only 14 percent report that they are following "very closely."[4] Yet the stakes of the policy are enormous, and not only in the obvious sense of the blood that is being shed. If, on the one hand, critics of the program are right, it may involve war crimes, or even a "crime against humanity that verges on genocide."[5] It may also be undermining the entire system of international law and traditional ethics governing the use of force.[6] It may be inspiring a new generation of terrorists to attack the United States while undermining America's ability to cooperate with its allies to prevent such attacks.[7] It may, finally, be damaging American moral authority and popularity around the world, and with them its prospects of ever isolating and containing violent extremism aimed at the West.[8]

If, on the other hand, defenders of the program, including the president and his senior officials, are right, then the program may be "legal," "ethical," and "wise."[9] Indeed, drone strikes may be an indispensable tool for protecting America and its allies from the violence that terrorists would visit on their civilian populations.[10] Drones may also offer a unique means to deliver justice to those planning, preparing, and carrying out terrorist attacks from remote bases and to disrupt and degrade their organizations.[11]

Obviously the considerations at stake on both sides of this issue are important. That is one good reason for examining the debate over drones.

The second reason is that the important arguments in this debate are not easily assembled or, in some cases, understood. They relate to different areas of policy and are discussed and debated in different public and private forums. They appear in popular and scholarly literature, court cases and legal opinions, news reports, and documentaries, among others. In some cases the language and concepts used can be technical, as in legal briefs, or scholarly articles on the ethics of autonomous weapon systems. Given the covert nature of most operations, public information is very limited. By consequence, assessment must rely on partial information and a degree of speculation, and it is not always obvious what is or is not plausible given what is known. Given these difficulties, it is perhaps not surprising that so many Americans report that they are not well informed about the drone program.

Yet given the stakes of what is being done, and for Americans what is being done in their name, it is crucial that the public be informed. This is especially true in a liberal democracy like the United States where the fundamental basis for political legitimacy is popular consent. The people cannot be said to consent to a policy of which they are ignorant.

This book aims to better inform people about what is known about the U.S. drone program, and of some of the key debates that have emerged around it, so that they can come to their own, independent judgments about it. It avoids technical language where possible, and where it is unavoidable it explains and illustrates obscure terms. It is divided into six chapters, each devoted to a major aspect of the program—history, strategy, ethics, law, politics, and future implications. A short case study is included in each chapter in which we examine key issues in more detail, including drone strike impacts in particular regions (like Pakistan or Yemen), specific types of operations (such as signature strikes), and individual aspects of the targeting process (including accountability and oversight mechanisms). A final case study provides an overview of drone development and use by two other leading drone powers, Israel and China, as points of comparison with the U.S. program.

II. The Structure of the Book

The first chapter opens with an historical overview of drones in warfare. In it we review the evolution of the drone from its remote origin as a mobile practice target before World War II, through the early unarmed Predators used by the United States in Bosnia and Kosovo, to its initial weaponization in 2001 and through the deployment of the MQ-9 Reaper, the Predator's bigger and more deadly cousin, in 2007. The chapter then provides an overview of the U.S. drone campaigns outside of conventional battlefields (in Pakistan, Yemen, and Somalia), reviews the fatality statistics from these campaigns as reported by various open-source databases, and discusses how the various databases tracking strikes differ in their methodology and results. The chapter culminates with a detailed case study of the covert U.S. drone campaign in Pakistan.

The second chapter covers the debate over whether targeted killing operations are strategically wise. It discusses the positive strategic dimensions of the drone campaigns, such as terrorist leadership decapitation, the neutralization of threats while in the operational phase, and the provocation of internal divisions in terrorist organizations. It also addresses the negative consequences of drone use, including increased sympathy for, and recruitment by, terrorist organizations, and the increased strain with U.S. allies instigated by the perceived illegality and disproportionality of drone strikes. The chapter culminates with a case study of U.S. drone strikes in Yemen. We discuss how Yemen's government permitted U.S. drone operations on its territory and how they succeeded in killing a number of prominent leaders, but also how these strikes may have strengthened the local branch of al-Qaeda, and indeed may have contributed to the toppling of the government of President Hadi.

The third chapter explores the debate over whether the drone campaigns are permissible under domestic and international law. It begins with a discussion of the compliance of drone strikes overseas with Executive Order 12333, prohibiting U.S. participation in assassinations. This is followed with a brief review of the constitutional issues raised on the rare occasion in which U.S. drones target an American citizen. We then turn to issues of international law, and first examine the *ad bellum* questions of whether U.S. drone strikes have generally taken place in the contexts of armed conflict (even if they occur away from conventional battlefields) or can be justified by appeal to the right of self-defense. We then consider whether drone strikes adhere to the *in bello* principles of distinction, proportionality, and necessity. In all of these areas we illustrate both arguments supportive of, and critical of, the U.S. uses of drones away from conventional battlefields. The case study of chapter 3 examines signature strikes and the debate over whether they violate the principle of distinction and/or result in increased civilian casualties.

The fourth chapter examines the ethical debate surrounding the U.S. use of drones outside conventional battlefields. Drawing on leading contemporary theorists of the just war tradition, the chapter first explores the controversial claim that there is an ethical obligation to use drones under certain circumstances (for example, where they do not increase the danger to civilians) because they better protect pilots. We then examine how the U.S. use of drones to track and kill suspected terrorists comports with just war criteria like just cause, last resort, and probability of success. We also consider arguments over whether drones are likely to increase the temptation for states possessing them to resort to armed force, including whether they might increase the willingness of states to undertake humanitarian interventions. Finally, we briefly examine arguments over fully autonomous drones and whether these might ever be ethically permissible. The chapter ends with a case study focused on whether the United States is meeting its obligations to assure oversight and accountability in the conduct of drone strikes. This debate provides an opportunity to delve into detail on what is known of U.S. procedures in planning and conducting drone strikes.

The fifth chapter provides an overview of how political factors appear to be shaping the use of drones today, and how these factors are evolving over time. We review, for example, surveys of U.S. attitudes about the use of drones, how the results have changed since the beginning of the drone campaigns, and how these attitudes may be impacting back on the use of drones. We also consider global attitudes and some of the ways that U.S. drone use has been challenged, such as in UN reports and by resolution of the EU Parliament. The case study in this chapter considers some additional polling on drone strikes with a focus on what factors appear to influence people's attitudes.

The final chapter focuses on the proliferation of drones, especially armed ones, and considers whether or not the U.S. use of drones outside of conventional battlefields is setting dangerous precedents for the use of force by other states and armed groups around the world. The chapter focuses in particular on arguments over whether the most dangerous types of drones (i.e., long-range strategic armed drones) are likely to proliferate quickly and whether existing international agreements will be sufficient to control which countries develop the capacity to project power using drones. We consider, in particular, whether other states are likely to resort to using armed drones to carry out strikes beyond their borders citing U.S. precedents. We then turn to debates over whether drones are really revolutionizing the conduct of warfare and whether they will tend to escalate conflicts and promote instability. The chapter ends with a case study examining the record of drone use by Israel and China, which has to date attracted comparatively little attention.

The books ends with a brief conclusion that explores some possible points of agreement that are often obscured in the give and take of the drone debate, and possible reasons this debate has attracted so much passion and public attention. In it we try to isolate a central point of dispute, which helps to explain the wide-ranging disagreements around drones.

III. Strategy and Approach

Since the purpose of this book is to inform readers about the issues surrounding the U.S. drone campaigns, we have generally endeavored to avoid taking sides or advancing our own views. We do sometimes refer to our own published writings that engage with the debates we discuss, but without trying to defend or elaborate those contributions. However, some readers may understandably suspect that even if they are not explicitly advanced, our views nonetheless bleed into the text of this book in a number of indirect ways, such as the arguments we choose to highlight, the order in which we present them, and the quotes that we choose. At times the very language we employ may be thought to reflect a bias.

Perhaps such suspicions are warranted. Some unconscious bias may be inevitable. We can only add that we've consciously tried to avoid it, and if it is any assurance to readers, we are by no means of one mind ourselves in regard to any of the key questions relating to the use of drone strikes outside of conventional battlefields. Indeed, it is out of our arguments among ourselves that the idea for this book emerged. Nonetheless, it is also fair to say that we share at least some basic points of agreement, and those include that drone strikes are an option that the United States should keep in its arsenal. Where we are apt to disagree is on when and where the United States should exercise that option. Still, even in saying this much we will put ourselves in disagreement with many smart, well-intentioned people—probably most people, although not perhaps most Americans.

We would encourage readers to engage critically with this book, with an alert eye to unconscious bias. But we would also ask readers to try to see past any bias they may find to grasp the forceful arguments on both sides of the debates that we cover in the most generous terms and see how they fare in the light of the readers' own sustained, critical examination. That is where we hope that the book can be useful, and we hope that any unintended, residual bias is not so obnoxious as to prevent the book being used in this way.

While we have refrained from critical engagement with the arguments that are canvassed in the book, we have tried to supply historical background and statistical data where possible that should inform readers' deliberations. For example, we include many tables presenting data on drone strikes. Here we try to always draw on multiple credible sources. For example, in presenting data on casualties resulting from drone strikes, we generally use four open-source databases that are all available on the Web: The Bureau of Investigative Journalism, the New America Foundation, The Long War Journal, and the Center for the Study of Targeted Killing (formerly UMass Drone). We are each part of the team that maintains the Center for the Study of Targeted Killing database and website. We hope that by presenting a range of data sources, with some explanation about how their approaches and methodologies differ, that we can take advantage of the different strengths and emphases of these data sources, and put readers in a position to navigate their way through the data in an informed way.

In writing the text we've tried to adopt the common terms of debate and to avoid formulations that tend to effectively prejudge questions. In talking about drone strikes, for example, we neither call them "extrajudicial assassinations" (which would indicate illegality from the start) or "preemptive self-defense operations" (which would tend to suggest their legitimacy), but simply "drone strikes" or "targeted killings." These formulations seem to us to have two main advantages: first, they are plainly descriptive, and second, they are the terms that are most often accepted by both sides in the debates we are describing.

In general, we have tried to use short, clear, colloquial terms. For example, we usually talk about "drones" rather than uninhabited aerial vehicles (UAVs) or remotely piloted aircraft (RPAs) or unmanned aerial systems (UAS), or any of the other cumbersome formulations or diverse acronyms that are sometimes used. These terms may appear in quotations we use, and we occasionally use the acronym UAV (as the most familiar of them) in the text just for purposes of stylistic variation, but no more than we deem necessary.

We choose *drone* because it is the term commonly used in conversation, and people generally know exactly what is being referenced.[12] *Drone* refers to a machine subject to an "external form of control."[13] So drones are just machines that are remotely controlled, and can therefore in principle take a wide variety of forms, as Peter W. Singer memorably dramatizes in his book *Wired for War*. There are tank drones and submarine drones, for example. But current debates over U.S. policy are focused overwhelmingly on aerial drones, and when people argue about drones, that is what they are presumed to mean, at least first and foremost. Indeed, what people usually mean when they argue about drone policy is even more specific—that is, long-range strategic armed drones or what are more technically referred to as unmanned combat aerial vehicles (UCAVs) such as MQ-1 Predators and MQ-9 Reapers. It is these "weapons platforms" that we are generally talking about when we use the term *drone*, unless context or stipulation indicates aerial drones more generally.

Of course, there are many other types of aerial drones currently in use in the United States and elsewhere—indeed, even within the U.S. military the Predators and Reapers represent only a small minority of drones in use. Drones come in a variety of sizes, some as small as insects and others as large as small commercial airliners. Drones also vary in range, payload, and complexity. For instance, the U.S. Government Accountability Office (GAO) distinguishes three types of drones (mini, tactical, and strategic) based on three performance categories (altitude, endurance, and range—see table I.1).

Strategic drones are those that have the capacity to travel long distances at medium to high altitude to attack targets.[14] Drones that fall within the tactical category primarily conduct local, lower altitude surveillance and reconnaissance missions.[15] Minidrones like the RQ-11 Raven can be carried and hand launched by soldiers to perform local surveillance (looking over a hill or around a corner and down the street). According to the analysis by GAO, mini and tactical drones have long comprised the vast majority of the drone systems in operation.[16] Furthermore, the majority of drones acquired by other countries fall within the tactical category.[17] In order to avoid confusion, we clearly indicate when we shift from using *drone* in our usual, narrow, "strategic" sense to one that also includes "tactical" and "mini" categories.

Another set of terms that deserve some brief comment are *war, armed conflict,* and *conventional battlefields*. We use *armed conflict* in the narrow legal sense of meeting the standards of international law for applying the *lex*

TABLE I.1
The GAO's Three Major Categories of UAVs[1]

Category	Mini	Tactical	Strategic
Altitude	Low	Low to Medium	Medium to High
Endurance	Short (about an hour)	Medium (up to several hours)	Long (ranges from hours to days)
Range	Close range	"line of sight" (meaning a direct communication and control link) approximately 300 kilometers or less (about 186 miles)	Long range
Examples	RQ-11 Raven	RQ-7 Shadow	MQ-1 Predator

1. This is a modified version of the table appearing in Government Accountability Office, *Nonproliferation: Agencies Could Improve Information Sharing and End-Use Monitoring on Unmanned Aerial Vehicle Exports* (Washington, DC: GAO, 2012), 4.

specialis or the law of armed conflict (LOAC) to the conduct of hostilities. We employ the term *war* more broadly to refer to situations in which there is violence persistently arising between at least two parties and where the parties believe themselves to have belligerent rights against one another (i.e., that they may use deliberate armed force to attack one another's forces). In other words, we use *armed conflict* as more closely bound up with objective, legally established criteria, and *war* as a broader, more subjective condition in which parties are attempting to conduct hostilities against one another. So there is an armed conflict in Afghanistan (involving the Afghan government and its ISAF allies fighting against an insurgency led by the Afghan Taliban), and it makes sense to talk about a war between the United States and al-Qaeda, although this does not necessarily establish whether LOAC legally applies (for that depends on whether the legal conditions of armed conflict are met).

We also use the term *conventional battlefield* in a significant way. By this we mean military operations within clear-cut cases of armed conflict (such as in Afghanistan, Iraq, Libya, and more recently Syria). The main context in which we use this term is in defining the scope of this book as limited to "U.S. drone strikes outside of conventional battlefields." So by this we mean that we are concerned with attacks carried out by American armed drone aircraft that do not occur within clear-cut armed conflicts and/or are not carried out by the military (which generally means that they are conducted under the authority of the CIA, a civilian agency).

It might be objected that this subject matter is rather narrowly circumscribed. To this we would reply that we construe the framework of "outside conventional battlefields" (i.e., armed conflict) broadly to include cases of serious doubt, uncertainty, or rapidly shifting circumstances. Moreover, when in doubt, we generally err toward inclusion. For example, we include all U.S. drone strikes in Yemen and Somalia without trying to determine in each case whether a temporary situation of armed conflict may have arisen, or in each case whether a strike occurred under the authority of the CIA or the military. On the other hand, we do exclude drone strikes that occurred in Afghanistan, Iraq, Libya, and Syria, as we think these occur in clearer cases of conventional armed conflicts, with international coalitions of states coordinating their forces in sustained military operations. Admittedly, this way of distinguishing drone strikes is crude, and it may well result in excluding some cases that could be included and vice versa. Nonetheless, given the limited information available on drone strikes and the disagreements over where and when the threshold of armed conflict is crossed, it provides a useful approximation of drone strikes outside of conventional battlefields. It is also the U.S. campaigns in Yemen, Somalia, and Pakistan that have generated the most critical reaction and debate, and so can provide the best guidance on the general issues at stake. Moreover, focusing on these three campaigns also produces a robust set of cases, including over five hundred strikes that have killed over 3,500 people. The scope of this violence alone calls for careful, critical attention, especially as many of these strikes have been conducted covertly.

Finally, we invoked at the beginning of this introduction a further reason for focusing on this particular class of lethal operations that we think is compelling—the stakes in play. If, as critics have suggested, the strikes are illegal and kill mainly civilians, then they may well amount to crimes against humanity. If, on the other hand, they are legal, ethical, and wise, as U.S. officials and defenders have maintained, and primarily target terrorist leaders, then the strikes may represent the single most effective weapon in the struggle against international terrorist networks operating from remote locations in failed (or failing) states. The stakes of drone strikes outside conventional combat are thus high for American policy, its reputation, and its future (and as drones begin to rapidly proliferate, for everyone's future). And yet most Americans (and probably most people) are not yet taking an active interest, and likely lack the knowledge to make an informed judgment about the policy.

This book is intended to make a contribution to rectifying the situation by providing an overview of the key issues of debate in a short, clear, accessible, and affordable form. It makes the case that while its subject may be somewhat narrowly defined, the issue that it does address is one of particular importance on which we badly need more information and more reflection.

Notes

1. Jane Mayer, "The Predator War," *New Yorker*, October 26, 2009, accessed March 20, 2015, http://www.newyorker.com/magazine/2009/10/26/the-predator-war.
2. The Center for the Study of Targeted Killing Database (http://targetedkilling .org/strikes) records 535 U.S. drone strikes in Pakistan, Yemen, and Somalia as of March 18, 2015, resulting in 3,712 deaths.
3. Scott Shane, "Targeted Killing Comes to Define War on Terror," *New York Times*, April 7, 2013, accessed June 3, 2015, http://www.nytimes.com/2013/04/08/world/targeted-killing-comes-to-define-war-on-terror.html?_r = 0.
4. Specifically, "not too closely" or "not at all." Alyssa Brown and Frank Newport, "In U.S., 65% Support Drone Attacks on Terrorists Abroad," Gallup, March 25, 2013, accessed March 20, 2015, http://www.gallup.com/poll/161474/support-drone -attacks-terrorists-abroad.aspx?utm_source = Less%20than%20half%20of%20Ameri cans%20are%20closely%20following%20&utm_medium = search&utm_campaign = tiles.
5. Sherwood Ross, "Obama Drone Campaign 'Verges on Genocide,' Legal Authority Says," Global Research, February 16, 2014, accessed July 28, 2015, http:// www.globalresearch.ca/obama-drone-campaign-verges-on-genocide-legal-authority -says/5369027.
6. Philip Alston, "The CIA and Targeted Killing Beyond Borders," *Harvard National Security Journal* 2 (2011): 446; Daniel Brunstetter and Megan Braun, "The Implications of Drones on the Just War Tradition," *Ethics and International Affairs* 25, no. 3 (2011): 338–40, 344–46, 350, 355–56.
7. Ibrahim Mothana, "How Drones Help Al Qaeda," *New York Times*, June 13, 2012, accessed March 15, 2015, http://www.nytimes.com/2012/06/14/opinion/how -drones-help-al-qaeda.html; Audrey Kurth Cronin, "Why Drones Fail: When Tactics Drive Strategy," *Foreign Affairs* (July/August 2013): 52; General John P. Abizaid and Rosa Brooks, *Recommendations and Report of the Task Force on US Drone Policy* (Washington: Stimson Center, 2014), 28–29.
8. Michael J. Boyle, "The Costs and Consequences of Drone Warfare," *International Affairs* 89, no. 1 (2013): 3, 12–22; Cronin, "Why Drones Fail," 46–52; Vivian Salama, "Death from Above: How American Drone Strikes Are Devastating Yemen," *Rolling Stone*, April 14, 2014, accessed August 3, 2015, http://www.rollingstone.com/ politics/news/death-from-above-how-american-drone-strikes-are-devastating-yem en-20140414.
9. Mary Bruce, "Drone Strikes on US Terrors Suspects 'Legal,' 'Ethical,' 'Wise' White House Says," ABC News, February 5, 2013, accessed July 28, 2015, http://abc news.go.com/blogs/politics/2013/02/drone-strikes-on-us-terror-suspects-legal-ethi cal-wise-white-house-says/; John Brennan, "The Efficacy and Ethics of U.S. Counterterrorism Strategy," Wilson Center, April 30, 2012, accessed July 28, 2015, http:// www.wilsoncenter.org/event/the-efficacy-and-ethics-us-counterterrorism-strategy.

10. Steven Simon, "In Defense of Drones," *MSNBC: National Security*, April 25, 2015, accessed August 3, 2015, http://www.msnbc.com/msnbc/defense-drones.

11. Brennan, "The Efficacy and Ethics of U.S. Counterterrorism Strategy"; Harold Koh quoted in Tara McKelvey, "Defending the Drones: Harold Koh and the Evolution of U.S. Policy," in *Drone Wars: Transforming Conflict, Law and Policy*, edited by Peter Bergen and Daniel Rothenberg (Cambridge: Cambridge University Press, 2015), 203.

12. Richard Whittle, *Predator: The Secret Origins of the Drone Revolution* (New York: Henry Holt and Company, 2014), 310–11.

13. Bill Yenne, *Birds of Prey* (North Branch, MN: Specialty Press, 2010), 7.

14. There are several other systems of classification that are used in discussing drones. For example, a 2014 report by researchers at RAND suggested a more nuanced system of classification for drones. In their work, they separated the types of drones into four major categories, making distinctions based on range and the technology required to develop them. The four types are as follows: (1) long range, high technology; (2) long range, low technology; (3) short range, high technology; and (4) short range, low technology. In this system of classification, it is the (1) long-range, high-technology vehicles that we primarily mean when we use the term *drone*.

15. Government Accountability Office, *Nonproliferation: Agencies Could Improve Information Sharing and End-Use Monitoring on Unmanned Aerial Vehicle Exports* (Washington, DC: GAO, 2012), 9. These statistics cover 2005 to 2011. See further discussion in chapter 6.

16. Government Accountability Office, *Nonproliferation*, 3.

17. Government Accountability Office, *Nonproliferation*, 11.

1

A Brief Overview of Aerial Drones and Their Military Use by the United States

THE USE OF ARMED DRONES after 9/11 is transforming the way that wars are waged, counterterrorism is pursued, and militaries are structured. In December 2001, with the War on Terror in its opening stages, President George W. Bush declared that "before the war, the Predator had skeptics, because it did not fit the old ways. Now it is clear the military does not have enough unmanned vehicles. We're entering an era in which unmanned vehicles of all kinds will take on greater importance."[1]

Today it seems that President Bush's prediction has come true. Since 2001, drones have become America's signature means of conducting wars and counterterrorism around the globe, and they currently represent the most rapidly growing area of military research and development worldwide. Whereas virtually no drone pilots were being trained in 2000, the majority of U.S. pilots being trained today are being trained to fly drones rather than manned planes, which makes sense, since the majority of planes being procured are drones rather than traditional manned aircraft.[2] From possessing only a few dozen drones at the outbreak of the "War on Terror," the U.S. Department of Defense reported owning some 7,500 drones (of all sizes) by 2010 and close to 11,000 by 2013.[3] From virtually none at the turn of the millennia, the number of U.S. personnel working with drones is anticipated to be as high as 9,900 by 2017, up from 2,100 in 2005.[4] Moreover, it was reported in 2011 that the Pentagon was planning on nearly doubling its annual purchase of medium- and high-altitude drones by 2021 (from 340 to 650 per year).[5] Indeed, the increase in the drone fleet has been so rapid that it has drawn some criticism from within the Pentagon, which suggested that the U.S. Air Force was buying too many armed Reaper (hunter-killer) drones in 2015.[6]

Though it is apparent that we are already in a drone revolution, the consequences of which are still not fully understood, few observers are aware of how this change in aerial warfare came about. This chapter aims to fill in this gap by beginning with a brief, historical introduction to the American development of aerial military drones and to the distinctive capabilities that they offer.[7] It then turns to how these drones are being used today outside of conventional battlefields. In particular, it provides a general overview of the drone campaigns that the United States has waged in Pakistan, Yemen, and Somalia. The discussion surrounding the impact of strikes will make use of data obtained from four leading databases tracking the drone campaigns, whose statistics will be compared against one another. The chapter closes with a case study examining the CIA's drone campaign in Pakistan.

I. A History of Drone Development

The development of drone aircraft can be traced to World War I and the development of "aerial torpedoes."[8] More akin to cruise missiles than to the drones of today, these remotely controlled aircraft were not intended to fly multiple missions. The Curtiss-Sperry Aerial Torpedo, for example, was loaded with TNT and designed to crash into its target after a preset timer killed its engine.[9] It took its maiden test flight just months before World War I ended and was never used on the battlefield.[10] In World War II, however, drones would play a more significant role, and the term *drone* would begin to refer to a multirole aircraft rather than simply a remotely controlled missile.

WWII and Its Aftermath

The Second World War saw drones being used in several ways, including as assault weapons in their own right. Most often, however, antiaircraft personnel used them for target practice.[11] Prior to the introduction of drones as practice targets, antiaircraft gunners had trained on "sleeves" being towed by friendly aircraft flying only in straight lines.[12] Unlike these sleeves, the most popular target drones, the OQ-2 Radioplane and its successors, resembled aircraft, and could even simulate strike maneuvers.[13] These radio-controlled aircraft were in great demand during the war, with nearly fifteen thousand sold to the army, air force, and navy.[14]

In addition to drones used for target practice, the U.S. Navy also had a drone in its arsenal that would do some targeting of its own.[15] The TDR-1, introduced to combat in 1944, was guided by a primitive television camera and radar system and was capable of carrying an explosive of up to two thousand pounds.[16] In contrast to the drones of today, which can be flown from ground control stations literally thousands of miles away, the TDR-1 was much more limited. It used a control aircraft, the TBM (or TBF) Avenger, for guidance.[17] The Avenger was able to control the drone while viewing the image from its television camera up to thirty miles away.[18]

In March 1944, two squadrons of the Special Air Task Force were sent to the Pacific Theater to gauge the capabilities of the aircraft. While the TDR-1 was initially tested and used as a guided missile, flying into positions held by the Japanese, in October 1944 it also briefly assumed a role as an assault aircraft that dropped bombs on enemy positions.[19] On October 19, a TDR-1 dropped a combination of five-hundred- and one-hundred-pound bombs on Japanese gun positions on Ballale Island.[20] However, while the plan called for the drone to return to its base after its bombing run, it wound up crashing on its return trip due to antiaircraft fire.[21] In the following days a slightly amended plan was implemented: drones were used to drop bombs and then to intentionally crash into their targets.[22] However, just eight days after the TDR-1 was first used as an assault drone, the navy cancelled the program and used the remainder of the drones for target practice.[23] While the cameras aboard these WWII assault drones were originally intended to facilitate navigation, the imagery collected by drones would become a primary utility in the coming decades.

Vietnam and the Lightning Bugs

Interest in aerial drones rose again in the early 1960s. After multiple manned U-2 spy planes were shot down, the U.S. military explored the possibility of an unmanned spy plane.[24] One of the drones developed was called the Lightning Bug. It was first used for surveillance purposes over China in 1964.[25] The Lightning Bugs, which were launched from the air by "motherships," did not land on a runway.[26] Instead, the aircraft would fall to the ground with a parachute system, or in some cases, would be snatched up in midair by specially equipped helicopters.[27] Like all military aircraft, however, the Lightning Bugs did not always reach the end of their mission. One of the drones, for example, was reportedly shot down by China in November 1964.[28] Despite the loss of the aircraft, the incident illustrated one of the key advantages of drones. In contrast with the situation that arose with the Soviets in 1960, when they put captured U-2 pilot Gary Powers on trial after they shot down his aircraft, the Chinese government had to celebrate its "major victory" without a pilot in captivity.[29]

The Lightning Bugs' spying was not limited to China. They also flew 3,435 missions in the Vietnam War.[30] Initially, these high-altitude drones had some difficulty in conducting surveillance through the dense cloud that often filled Vietnam's sky.[31] In short order, however, a low-altitude version of the drone was developed.[32]

Some of the Lightning Bugs' biggest successes in the Vietnam War were finding the SA-2 surface to air missile (SAM) command link signals and inadvertently causing the destruction of Vietnamese MiG fighter jets.[33] This inadvertent destruction was caused by the MiG jets themselves, which would sometimes crash while trying to intercept the drones, or would get struck by SAMs intended to strike the drones.[34]

Of course, the Lightning Bugs' primary purpose was to collect intelligence. However, the intelligence garnered from the Lightning Bugs was a far cry from the virtually instantaneous transmission of images today. The film from the drone needed to be flown out of Vietnam to be developed and analyzed before being flown back into the war zone, a process that generally took days to complete.[35] Fortunately, the Lightning Bugs also survived in combat over Vietnam longer than was originally projected, returning from an average of 7.3 missions before being destroyed, nearly tripling the initial estimate of 2.5 missions.[36] However, due in part to the difficulty of their use and the delay in accessing their surveillance data, they were not seen as a great success, and military drones would not again play a really prominent role in U.S. combat until Operation Desert Storm.

Drones in the 1990s: Pioneers to Predators

In the Gulf War of the early 1990s, the United States used drones in a variety of ways.[37] The drone of choice was the Pioneer, which was the result of collaboration between U.S. and Israeli companies.[38] The U.S. Navy purchased Pioneers secondhand from the Israeli military and used them for surveillance and reconnaissance.[39] In fact, the U.S. Navy reported that there had been at least one drone in the sky at all times throughout Desert Storm.[40] In one well-publicized case, the Pioneers sent to survey the aftermath of an attack found surviving Iraqis who waved sheets at the drones in an effort to surrender.[41]

The Pioneer played an especially important role in helping the various military branches identify targets. While the navy used it to discern targets for their battleship guns, the marines made use of its infrared sensors to find enemy positions for aerial raids.[42] General Walter Boomer of the marines has asserted that "the single most valuable intelligence collector" during Operation Desert Storm was the Pioneer.[43] Despite its many successes, however, the Pioneer failed in many cases to locate mobile Scud missiles, eighty-eight of which were successfully fired into Israel, Bahrain and Saudi Arabia during the conflict.[44] Similar limitations persisted two years later and prompted the Clinton administration to seek new technology to monitor conflicts in the Balkans.[45] So while the Pioneer lived up to its name in contributing to Operation Desert Storm, it was also quickly replaced by the Predator, which became the U.S. military's drone of choice and the trailblazer both for increased surveillance capacity and ultimately for a new capability to launch attacks.

In the mid-1990s, the ethnically charged civil war in Bosnia in particular created a need for new U.S. surveillance capability. Clear images of the region were hard to come by even from U-2 spy planes and satellites due to formidable cloud covering.[46] Serbian forces also foiled U.S. intelligence gathering by moving their weapons at night, and by hiding them when satellites were scheduled to pass overhead.[47] In early 1994, the CIA began flying the precursor of the Predator, the Gnat 750, over Bosnia.[48] The Gnat 750 was a long-endurance tactical surveillance drone manufactured by General Atomics based on a design by Abe Karem, who has been described as the "Moses of modern drones" and "the Dronefather."[49] The Gnat 750 was sixteen-and-a-half feet long with a wingspan of just over thirty-five feet. It could fly as high as twenty-five thousand feet and stay aloft for as long as forty-eight hours without needing additional fuel.[50] While the Gnat would prove its worth by providing valuable intelligence in the Bosnian conflict, engineers also began a cycle of refinements to its communication and payload capabilities. These improvements culminated in an upgraded drone with a new name, Predator, which made its fourteen-second debut test flight in July 1994 at the El Mirage airfield in California.[51]

Enter the Predator

The Predator, produced like the Gnat by General Atomics, retained some of the distinct features of its predecessor, including its odd "inverted V" tail distinguished by two rectangular stabilizers jutting downward.[52] It also had the same long wings reminiscent of gliders. Indeed, its long wingspan, at 48.7 feet, greatly exceeded its length of 27 feet.[53] But what clearly differentiated Predator from its earlier relations was its bulging head containing its satellite dish and a "chin turret," which directed the daylight and infrared cameras with which it surveilled the world around it. The Predator also came equipped with a 115-horsepower engine.[54] The engine, as Lieutenant Colonel Lawrence Spinetta aptly put it, "literally sips gas. It is exceedingly 'wimpy' compared with other modern Air Force aircraft . . . it is the same type of engine commonly used on snowmobiles."[55] While it may not have made the Predator as powerful or swift as other aircraft (it could reach speeds of up 135 miles per hour), it was precisely the wimpy engine that was the key to some of its most formidable capabilities. For one thing, it was the Predator's abstemious gas sipping in combination with its long wingspan that allowed it to stay in the air for potentially up to forty hours (although in many practical configurations this would be reduced to around a day), gathering intelligence and relentlessly tracking targets.[56] The combination of a small engine and large wingspan also gave the Predator a rare capacity to "loiter" over an area or target, maintaining continuous observation.

Meanwhile, the Predator's crew (or rotating crews) remained safely in a ground control station (GCS) some distance away (although throughout the 1990s the GCS remained in or near the theater of operations). The GCS was typically a rectangular, three-axle trailer, thirty-six feet long, eight feet wide, and eight feet tall, similar to those that NASCAR teams used to haul stock cars between races.[57] The crew consisted of at least a pilot and sensor operator (sometimes accompanied by data analysts) who sat in faux leather chairs and manipulated control sticks, like those in a conventional aircraft, to fly the plane.[58] Before them lay a console, with computer keyboards and communication equipment, including a radio that could be used to talk to radio air traffic control towers. Above the consoles, screens provided a normal pilot cockpit display, sensor status data, video stream from the drone, and a route and/or map display (in later years with GPS tracking the drone's movement), and more.[59]

Three other features of the Predator helped to enhance its attractiveness to policymakers. First, it was relatively cheap, often in the range of $1.5 to $4.5 million, as compared to the manned F-22 Raptor, for example, at $137 million per aircraft, or the F-35 Joint Strike Fighter at $110 million per aircraft ("flyaway costs").[60] Second, low fuel consumption helped to keep the cost of operating the machine down, especially as compared to more conventional manned military aircraft (although savings would be increasingly offset by the large number of personnel required, especially analysts to review the growing surveillance data provided).[61] Third, by cycling crews in the GCS, drone surveillance could be maintained for the aircraft's entire flight time of potentially up to forty hours (minus transit time from and back to base), and if another drone was ready to replace the first, close surveillance could be maintained continuously.

In light of these potential advantages, it is not surprising that the new Predator was rushed into service over Bosnia starting in July 1995 even before some of the aircraft's components were fully ready. For example, the three drones that arrived at Gjader Airbase in Albania on July 8 relied on

UHF satellite dishes, which offered so little bandwidth that it proved impossible to both control the aircrafts and stream live video from their cameras.[62] As a result, the Predators could only provide live video when they had a direct line of contact with the GCS, permitting them to use their C-band antennas, and this was only guaranteed to 115 miles, assuming that no major natural obstacle (like a mountain) blocked the signals.[63] Moreover, even when live video was transmitted back to the GCS, initially intelligence analysts working at Gjader converted it into still photos before disseminating it to command centers.[64]

Nonetheless, ad hoc solutions to these challenges were quickly developed in the field, and the Predator flights soon began making a significant contribution to operations. Predator operators discovered that if they flew at certain altitudes over Sarajevo, the besieged capital of Bosnia and Herzegovina, they could maintain C-band links with the drone and so receive a live video feed.[65] At the same time, a way was patched together to share the video feed with the Combined Air Operations Center in Vicenza, Italy, and other command centers.[66] By August, a powerful Ku-band satellite dish was substituted for the poorly performing UHF model, resulting in vastly improved satellite communications and permitting the drones to broadcast video from a far wider area.[67]

At this point, the results being obtained began to attract widespread attention across allied commands, and despite the loss of two drones, the deployment was extended to support Operation Deliberate Force, during which drones played a key role in exposing Serbian duplicities.[68] In a now declassified 1996 Pentagon report on the performance of the Predator, Major General Kenneth R. Israel wrote: "This single resource gave NATO commanders the key piece of intelligence that underlay their decision to resume the bombing campaign that, in turn, led to the Dayton Accords."[69] As military aviation historian Richard Whittle summarizes, "the Predator played a key role in the success of Operation Deliberate Force,"[70] and overall, "the new drone had made a big and positive impression."[71] At the end of 1995 it was decided to send Predators back to the Bosnian theater to help enforce the Dayton Accords, this time flying out of Taszár Air Base in southern Hungary.[72]

The Predator's success in Bosnia marked the beginning of what Peter W. Singer characterizes as Predator's " 'magic moment' . . . when it really came together."[73] Singer lays particular emphasis on the integration of GPS into the Predator system. GPS, which stands for Global Positioning System, is a constellation of military satellites that allows users to know their exact location, velocity, and direction. At this point Singer reports that "drones began to be more intuitive to fly, while the information they passed on to the generals and troops in the field became ever more detailed."[74]

The Predator also "played a valuable role in the Kosovo conflict," particularly in gathering surveillance that permitted the United States to anticipate Serbian actions.[75] In the waning days of the conflict a laser designator was added to the Predator's sensor ball that allowed it to "light up" or "paint" targets that could then be struck precisely with laser-guided munitions from other aircraft.[76]

The next important step in the Predator's development came during the "Summer Project" (also known as "Afghan Eyes"[77]) in 2000 as the United States began to fly drones over Afghanistan in search of Osama bin Laden and his senior lieutenants.[78] In essence, the U.S. Air Force achieved "split operations," meaning that they figured out how to fly Predator missions over Afghanistan from a GCS at Ramstein Airbase in Germany. Local crew at an airfield in Uzbekistan flew takeoffs and landings using the line-of-sight C-band link.[79] The main missions, however, were flown via satellite from Germany using the Ku-band dish (with roughly one second of "latency" or delay in communications).[80] On September 27, one of the drones spotted Osama bin Laden at the al-Qaeda training camp at Tarnak Farms and tracked him for some time.[81] For reasons that have never been entirely clear, but probably related to the time that would be required to program and fire cruise missiles and for them to arrive on target, no action was taken against bin Laden.[82] Two weeks later, al-Qaeda struck again, with a suicide bombing in Aden Harbor that ripped a forty-by-forty-foot hole in the side of the destroyer USS *Cole*, leaving seventeen sailors dead.[83]

Arming the Predator

The next and perhaps most decisive step in the Predator's development came the following fall, in the immediate aftermath of the 9/11 attacks, when drones were armed before being sent back to Afghanistan. The decision to attempt this innovation dated back to May 1, 2000, when Air Combat Command chief John Jumper had sent out an order to his subordinates to proceed with "the next logical step for USAF UAVs . . . weaponizing UAVs."[84] The 645th Aeronautical Systems Group (nicknamed "Big Safari"), which had since 1997 taken the lead in Predator's development, started testing a Predator (tail number 3034) armed with two Hellfire antitank missiles in January 2001, after government treaty experts determined that arming a drone would not violate the 1987 Intermediate-Range Nuclear Forces Agreement.[85] An upgrade that contributed critically to the success of this project was the adoption of a new sensor turret on the Predator's chin, Raytheon Corporation's new Multi-Spectral Targeting System (or MTS ball) in April 2001.[86] The MTS ball combined, for the first time, a daylight camera and a long-range laser designator, so that the Predator could simultaneously provide live color video and designate a target from as much as five miles away.[87] After airborne testing at Naval Air Weapons Station China Lake in early June 2001 (seven of thirteen missiles fired struck their target), Big Safari reported to Washington on June 9 that the armed Predator was ready to deploy.[88] However, bureaucratic wrangling between the CIA and the air force, neither of which wanted to pay for the deployment or assume responsibility for pulling the trigger in a bin Laden strike, and a cautious National Security Council, delayed deployment until after September 11.[89]

By September 18, a week after the 9/11 attacks, an armed drone was in the sky over Afghanistan.[90] Even more impressively, it was employing an experimental extension of the previous summer's "split operations," which permitted it to be flown all the way from Washington, D.C.—to be precise, from a doublewide trailer parked behind CIA headquarters in Langley, Virginia.[91] The United States was now hunting bin Laden with a drone armed with laser-guided Hellfire missiles being flown from virtually around the world.

The original designation of the Predator was the RQ-1, with the Q signifying that the aircraft was a drone and the R that it was for reconnaissance and surveillance purposes. When a Predator was armed, its name was changed to the MQ-1, with the M denoting that it could be used in multiple missions, such as reconnaissance and attack.[92]

Unfortunately, after the 9/11 attack the drones proved unable to locate and target Osama bin Laden, who had wisely gone into hiding. It would be more than a decade until bin Laden was killed, and ultimately it would not be by means of a drone but by a team of Navy SEALs. Still, drones would play a significant role in preparations for the operation. Stealth drone aircraft surveilled the bin Laden compound dozens of times "because [U.S. officials] needed to see more about what was going on" prior to the targeted killing operation.[93] The stealth drones were also used during the raid that killed bin Laden, both to provide imagery to President Obama and other decision makers, as well as to listen to Pakistani communications as they responded to the attack.[94]

First Strikes

The first ever Predator strike occurred southwest of Kandahar, Afghanistan, on the night of October 7, 2001, the first night of Operation Enduring Freedom.[95] The attack killed several members of the Taliban leader Mullah Omar's security detail in an attempt to flush him out of a nearby building.[96] The decision to target the security detail is believed to have been made by

General Tommy Franks, who passed on the opportunity to target Omar directly, thinking that he was located in a mosque.[97] A few weeks later, a drone aided in the targeted killing of Mohammed Atef, a prominent al-Qaeda leader.[98] The use of armed drones would not be isolated to Afghanistan for long, however; less than a year later the Predator would also fire missiles at a target in Yemen.

The first drone strike outside of a recognized conflict zone (as Afghanistan was after October 7, 2001) was launched by the U.S. Central Intelligence Agency (CIA), which used a Predator to target and kill Ali Qaed Sunian al-Harithi and five of his associates in Yemen in early November 2002.[99] Harithi was the leader of a group of al-Qaeda members in Yemen that was believed to have undertaken the bombing of the USS *Cole* in 2000.[100] While the CIA's drone strike successfully killed its target, it would also cause unanticipated tension between the United States and Yemen.

In the ensuing days after the attack that killed al-Harithi, it became abundantly clear that Yemen had expected the United States to remain silent about its involvement.[101] Then, just two days after the attack, the Deputy Secretary of Defense Paul Wolfowitz suggested that it had in fact been the United States that launched the strike.[102] This admission from a ranking U.S. official left the president of Yemen, Ali Abdullah Saleh, "highly pissed"; he told General Tommy Franks "this is going to cause me major political problems."[103] The United States would not launch another drone strike in Yemen for more than seven years.

Still, in less than two years, the Predator had gone from being an unarmed spy plane focused on intelligence, surveillance, and reconnaissance (ISR) to a machine not just capable of, but being used to, track, target, and kill human beings. The drones would also quickly become a serious threat to the Taliban in Afghanistan and Pakistan, coming to be referred to by the Pashtun tribesmen who make up the Taliban as *machay*, or "wasps," due to their distinct buzzing noise.[104]

Moreover, the Predator's evolution was not yet complete. By March 2005, a new and improved version of the Predator was ready to be deployed, the MQ-1B Predator, which featured an upgraded turbo-charged engine, fuel injection, longer wings, dual alternators, an ice mitigation system, and improved communication equipment (see table 1.1 for details). In early 2009, the Predator was equipped with smaller Scorpion missiles, weighing approximately thirty-five pounds and coming with the option of being fitted with four different types of guidance system.[105] The Scorpion caused less explosive damage than the Hellfire and reportedly increased the precision of strikes.[106]

The Coming of the Reaper

In late 2010, U.S. Air Force spokesman Lieutenant Colonel Richard Johnson announced that the military branch would purchase no more Predator drones. Instead, they would focus their acquisitions on the more technologically advanced (but also more expensive) MQ-9 Reaper, which carried a price per aircraft of around $20 million (or $56.5 million for a group of four aircraft and GCS).[107] In the words of General T. Michael Moseley, who had served as the Air Force Chief of Staff, "We've moved from using UAVs primarily in intelligence, surveillance, and reconnaissance roles before Operation Iraqi Freedom, to a true hunter-killer role with the Reaper."[108] The Reaper was bigger, faster, and considerably more lethal than the Predator even in its upgraded MQ-1B form (see table 1.1 for details). The Reaper could carry over eight times the payload of the MQ-1B Predator, including not only AGM-114 Hellfire missiles,[109] but also larger GBU-12 Paveway II laser-guided bombs and GBU-38 Joint Direct Attack Munitions (i.e., satellite-guided bombs).[110] These armaments were more characteristic of attack aircraft than those used by the smaller Predator, which was limited to two Hellfire missiles.[111] The military describes the Predator as a surveillance aircraft with weapons capability. In contrast, the Reaper was an aircraft whose main responsibility was to join the "kill chain," with conducting ISR (intelligence, surveillance, and reconnaissance) considered an ancillary capability.[112] While the Reaper's base endurance time was just fourteen hours when equipped with a full array of weapons, the aircraft could also be equipped with two external fuel tanks that tripled this flight time to forty-two hours.[113]

In addition to its improved capacity to bear arms, the Reaper has also benefited from significant improvements in regard to its surveillance capabilities. The most advanced camera system for the MQ-9 Reaper, for example, has been upgraded multiple times in recent years. In 2009, then Secretary of Defense Robert Gates became impatient with poor aerial surveillance in Iraq and Afghanistan, prompting the development of Gorgon Stare, a system that aimed to increase the surveillance area of video captures.[114] In 2011, the first iteration of Gorgon Stare was tested on whether it could cover an area of sixteen square kilometers with its one camera system. In 2014, the second iteration of Gorgon Stare increased that coverage up to one hundred square kilometers from a single drone, allowing those monitoring the drone's video capture to view everything happening in that area in high resolution.[115] The volume of data being collected from this system was enormous. The 368 cameras captured video at the rate of twelve frames per second, and the 1.8-billion-pixel composite image took up several terabytes of data every minute.[116] With such exponential increases in the technology with which

TABLE 1.1
Predator and Reaper Main Features

Feature	MQ-1B Predator[1]	MQ-9 Reaper[2]
Primary Function	Armed reconnaissance, airborne surveillance, and target acquisition	Intelligence collection in support of strike, coordination, and reconnaissance missions
Contractor	General Atomics Aeronautical Systems, Inc.	General Atomics Aeronautical Systems, Inc.
Power Plant	Rotax 914F four-cylinder engine	Honeywell TPE331-10GD turboprop engine
Thrust	115 horsepower	900 shaft horsepower maximum
Wingspan	55 feet (16.8 meters)	66 feet (20.1 meters)
Length	27 feet (8.22 meters)	36 feet (11 meters)
Weight	1,130 pounds (512 kilograms) empty	4,900 pounds (2,223 kilograms) empty
Maximum Takeoff Weight	2,250 pounds (1,020 kilograms)	10,500 pounds (4,760 kilograms)
Fuel Capacity	665 pounds (100 gallons)	4,000 pounds (602 gallons)
Payload	450 pounds (204 kilograms)	3,750 pounds (1,701 kilograms)
Speed	Cruise speed around 84 miles per hour (70 knots), up to 135 miles per hour	Cruise speed around 230 miles per hour (200 knots)
Range	Up to 770 miles (675 nautical miles)	1,150 miles (1,000 nautical miles)
Ceiling	Up to 25,000 feet (7,620 meters)	Up to 50,000 feet (15,240 meters)
Armament	Two laser-guided AGM-114 Hellfire missiles	Combination of AGM-114 Hellfire missiles, GBU-12 Paveway II, and GBU-38 Joint Direct Attack Munitions
Crew (Remote)	Two (pilot and sensor operator)	Two (pilot and sensor operator)
Unit Cost	$20 million (includes four aircraft with sensors, ground control station, and Predator Primary satellite link) (fiscal 2009 dollars)	$56.5 million (includes four aircraft with sensors, ground control station, and Predator Primary satellite link) (fiscal 2011 dollars)
Initial Operating Capability	March 2005	October 2007
Inventory	Total force, 164 as of July 2010	Total force, 104 as of August 2010

1. "MQ-1B Predator," *U.S. Air Force Fact Sheets*, July 20, 2010, accessed July 10, 2015, http://www.af.mil/AboutUs/FactSheets/Display/tabid/224/Article/104469/mq-1b-predator.aspx.
2. "MQ-9 Reaper," *U.S. Air Force Fact Sheets*, August 18, 2010, accessed July 10, 2015, http://www.af.mil/AboutUs/FactSheets/Display/tabid/224/Article/104470/mq-9-reaper.aspx.

drones are equipped, they are poised to continue changing the way conflicts are viewed and carried out. At the same time, the stress placed on their human operators by some of these innovations, for example as they begin to collect exponentially more data, is proving formidable.

Current Plans

In April 2014, it was reported that the air force would reach the goal of sixty-five combat air patrols (CAPs), which had been set by former secretary of defense Robert Gates.[117] Also referred to as an orbit, each CAP includes (up to four) drones, GCS, and crew to keep a mission going without interruption.[118] The air force intended to divide the CAPs relatively evenly, with thirty-three by the Predator and thirty-two by the Reaper.[119] However, the U.S. Air Force planned to cut the number of CAPs by nearly a third (to forty-five) in 2015, stating that sixty-five patrols did not make sense with the war in Afghanistan drawing down.[120]

However, the belief that the number of active drones could be reduced with the pullout of troops from Afghanistan proved mistaken, especially in the wake of the conflict with the Islamic State of Iraq and the Levant (ISIL). This new conflict has generated increased demands for drones.[121] In light of renewed demand, the air force has abandoned plans to reduce the number of CAPs and budgeted instead to continue at sixty-five for 2016.[122] Acquiring and sustaining this number of CAPs has been challenging, however, as each drone that flies over Syria and Iraq requires approximately thirty ground crew members for its operation and more than eighty analysts to go over the footage.[123] Indeed, in congressional testimony, Martha McSally, a retired U.S. Air Force colonel now in Congress, reported that "it takes over 200 operations and intelligence personnel to sustain an RPA [i.e., Remotely Piloted Aircraft] like the Predator or Reaper in an orbit for 24 hours."[124]

As the Pentagon reflects on future procurement, development, and deployment of combat drones, and the degree to which it should rely on them in preference to manned aircraft, it will doubtlessly consider, in addition to the important capabilities outlined above, some of the problems and/or difficulties associated with the use of drones. A few of these important concerns are briefly described below.

Concerns about Drones: Adequate Manpower

In January 2015, the secretary of the U.S. Air Force noted that there was a shortage of drone pilots.[125] At the time of her statement, Secretary of the Air Force Deborah Lee James noted that the air force had only 80 percent of the drone pilots that they needed, with 988 of the 1,232 that the military branch should have.[126] In addition to pulling crew members from the national guard, reserves, and manned aircraft groups, the air force has also moved to offer pay incentives that can potentially almost double the pay of a pilot.[127] On the issue, Secretary James stated:

> The airmen who perform this essential mission do a phenomenal job, but talks with the RPA pilots and the sensor operators, and their leaders certainly told me—suggested to me—that this is a force that is under significant stress— significant stress—from what is an unrelenting pace of operations.[128]

The air force has clearly had issues maintaining the necessary personnel for its growing drone needs. In one striking instance sometime between late 2005 and the beginning of 2006, drone crews that had been involuntarily moved from fighter jets to drones "were just so bitter and so angry" that they booed their commander.[129] General Mark Welsh offered the following observation while discussing the drone pilots in January 2015:

> They're just worn out, because this is not a new problem. It's been going on since 2007, as the requirement keeps increasing and all our solutions to it keep lagging the requirement change.[130]

As Welsh suggested, drone pilots are working longer hours than the pilots of manned fighter jets. According to Secretary James, drone pilots operate their vehicle for between 900 and 1,100 hours per year, as opposed to the two-hundred- to three-hundred-hour range of those who fly a manned aircraft.[131] When active, these drone pilots fly six days in a row for an average of fourteen hours per day.[132] These tough conditions have led to a shrinking force of drone pilots. While the air force is in need of around 300 new drone pilots a year, it is only able to train 180 new pilots, and recently lost approximately 240 over the same span.[133] Evidently, the drone program faces substantial continuing demand that is contributing to serious, and perhaps growing, internal challenges today.

Drone Accidents

Drones, and especially combat drones, have also been shown to be especially prone to accidents as compared to traditional manned aircraft. For example, Predators are reported to have a mishap rate of 7.6 per 100,000 flight hours as compared to 2.36 for an F-15.[134] The Reaper, too, has exhibited a worrying tendency to crash. Two high-profile mishaps with the aircraft occurred in

U.S. airspace in 2013 alone, including the crash-landing of a Reaper into Lake Ontario in November.[135] Other drones, including the much larger surveillance drone, the Global Hawk, also appear to be prone to accident. Data compiled by Bloomberg in 2012 showed that the combined accident rates of the Predators, Reapers, and Global Hawks in the air force fleet were more than three times higher than the rate for manned aircraft.[136] In 2014, the *Washington Post* published a study that found there had been over four hundred crashes of large U.S. drones since 2001.[137] The study described a 2010 crash involving an armed Predator that resulted from the pilot inadvertently flying the drone upside down over Afghanistan.[138] Another incident hit closer to home in April 2014 when a 375 pound RQ-7 Shadow surveillance drone operated by Pennsylvania's Army National Guard crash-landed near a school shortly after students had left for the day.[139]

Combat Limitations and Sundry Costs

A number of other concerns, beyond their tendency to crash, have also been raised about the rapidly expanding use of drones, especially by the military. For example, in late 2013 General Mike Hostage, the chief of the Air Combat Command, stated that "Predators and Reapers are useless in a contested environment."[140] The slow speed of the current drones and their limited altitudes have made them easy targets for even the most basic air defense systems or air forces.[141] In other words, there will be no reason to keep as many slow-moving Predators and Reapers if the United States faces an enemy that has even basic air defenses. In those situations, the United States will need aircraft that are faster and stealthier than existing drones.

It is also important to recognize that despite the relatively low cost of procuring drones and even flying them, maintaining sixty-five orbits of combat drones in continual circulation does involve very significant costs, particularly once the two hundred operations and intelligence personnel described by Martha McSally are factored in. Lieutenant Bob Otto, the air force's deputy chief of staff for ISR, explicitly recognized this difficulty in 2013, stating "my argument would be, we can't afford to keep all of this capability, so we're going to have to bring some of it down."[142]

However, the difficulties and challenges that confront drones today should not be viewed in isolation, but should rather be contextualized within an account of the accomplishments and failings of drones since 2001. The following sections are devoted to framing that more general context with emphasis on their most iconic use—that is, to hunt, track, and kill suspected terrorists outside of conventional battlefields.

II. Impacts of the U.S. Drone Campaigns

Since 2002, both the U.S. military and the CIA have used drones to launch airstrikes in several countries. While both the CIA and the U.S. military's Joint Special Operations Command (JSOC) have used drones for targeted killing operations outside of conventional battlefields, the military has also used them for close air support in the context of more conventional armed conflicts.[143] Each of these programs and the differences between them will be discussed in more detail below. One key feature that they have in common is that little is officially reported to the general public about their effects on the ground. Due to this lack of transparency, the public has been forced to rely on media reports and investigative journalism in order to get a glimpse into the actual impact of the drone programs.

Using these unofficial sources of information, a few organizations have assembled databases tracking U.S. drone strikes in places like Pakistan, Yemen, and Somalia and have made them available on open-source online websites. Each of these databases employs a different approach and methodology, and reports somewhat different results, at least in some key categories—most notably perhaps in regard to the civilian casualties resulting from the attacks. In the following section, we present the findings of the four most complete and credible online open-source databases tracking U.S. drone strikes, specifically the New America Foundation (NAF),[144] The Long War Journal (LWJ),[145] The Bureau of Investigative Journalism (TBIJ),[146] and the Center for the Study of Targeted Killing (CSTK).[147] While the contents of the following section are useful in understanding the different sources for statistics relied upon by the media, various governments, and scholars alike, it is also dense with statistics that some readers may prefer to skim over.

Data Collection on U.S. Drone Strikes

These databases cataloging the drone campaigns are similar to one another in the respect that they are largely based on freely available media sources, and many of the specific sources on which they rely are the same. Unfortunately, it must be emphasized that this reliance infuses a degree of uncertainty into all of their results, because the credibility of the public media sources on which they all rely is open to question. In essence, it is difficult to know how much confidence one should have in the raw numbers being reported. On the one hand, news reports often rely on numbers provided by anonymous government officials, and they may have an interest, for example, in underestimating civilian casualties. On the other hand, the groups being targeted by drones, and particularly the Taliban, often quickly take control of the site of a drone strike and control the reporting of casualties, which they have an interest in exaggerating.[148] The latter concern is well articulated by Farhat Taj, a research fellow at the University of Oslo, who has written extensively about the drone campaign in Pakistan:

> The reason why these estimates about civilian "casualties" in the US and Pakistani media are wrong is that after every attack the terrorists cordon off the area and no one, including the local villagers, is allowed to come even near the targeted place. The militants themselves collect the bodies, bury the dead and then issue the statement that all of them were innocent civilians.[149]

The problem is also nicely summarized by C. Christine Fair, assistant professor at Georgetown's Center for Peace and Security Studies, who stresses that "no one has independently verified the Taliban's reports—journalists cannot travel to FATA to confirm the deaths."[150] Even in Yemen, where there is better access to strike sites, the government has been known to mislead the media over whether attacks were carried out by American drones or the Yemeni Air Force, as well as concerning details of the attacks and resulting casualties.[151] Still, without official statistics or comprehensive investigations, these databases are the best available sources for getting an estimate of fatalities caused by the U.S. drones.

At the same time, it is worth noting that there are some significant differences in the sources the various databases use. Some of them, for instance, draw occasionally on special sources. TBIJ, for example, sometimes relies on leaked documents and reports from government and/or nongovernment organizations. The Long War Journal occasionally relies on unnamed U.S. intelligence officials. NAF and CSTK rely more exclusively on publicly available news sources.

Another important difference among the databases is that while TBIJ and CSTK clearly distinguish between drone strikes and other targeted killing operations in Yemen and Somalia, NAF and LWJ differ in two key ways. First, they merge their drone strike data with other types of airstrikes in their statistical breakdowns, and second, they do not include aggregate statistics for Somalia. In light of these differences, we have separated the data provided by these two pairs of sources (TBIJ and CSTK on one side, and NAF and LWJ on the other) and presented them on two separate tables. The first table presents data compiled by TBIJ and CSTK, which pertains solely to casualties inflicted by drones and includes strikes in Somalia (see table 1.2). The second table, based on data compiled by NAF and LWJ, presents data on U.S. airstrikes in Pakistan and Yemen more generally, regardless of whether they were launched by drones, and excludes strikes carried out in Somalia (see table 1.3).

TABLE 1.2
The Impacts of Drone Strikes in Pakistan, Yemen, and Somalia as Reported by TBIJ and CSTK, 2002 to 2015 (as of March 18, 2015)[1]

Source	Year(s)	Total Strikes	Total Killed	Suspected Militants Killed	Civilians Killed	"Unknowns" Killed	Civilian Deaths as Percentage of Total
The Bureau of Investigative Journalism (TBIJ)*	2002–2008	50	501	—	250	—	49.90%
	2009	54	612	—	155	—	25.33%
	2010	128	932	—	143	—	15.34%
	2011	91	592	—	138	—	23.31%
	2012	96	547	—	49	—	8.96%
	2013	49	254	—	29	—	11.42%
	2014	46	274	—	8	—	2.92%
	2015	12	86	—	6	—	6.98%
	Total 2002–2015	526	3,798	—	778	—	20.48%
Center for the Study of Targeted Killing (CSTK)	2002–2008	48	499	273	82	144	16.43%
	2009	56	607	479	39	89	6.43%
	2010	139	887	701	26	160	2.93%
	2011	92	575	438	21	116	3.65%
	2012	95	590	541	28	21	4.75%
	2013	56	275	240	23	12	8.36%
	2014	50	308	298	4	6	1.30%
	2015	9	43	42	0	1	0.00%
	Total 2002–2015	545	3,784	3,012	223	549	5.89%

*TBIJ's data was calculated by averaging their high and low ranges together.

1. "Targeted Killing Database," Center for the Study of Targeted Killing, accessed April 25, 2015, http://targetedkilling.org/; "Get the Data: Drone Wars," The Bureau of Investigative Journalism, https://www.thebureauinvestigates.com/category/projects/drones/drones-graphs/.
2. TBIJ does not offer separate statistics for "confirmed" drone strikes in Somalia. Instead they integrate those numbers with "possible" drone strikes

As noted above, the databases all rely on many of the same news sources, and so it is not surprising that in some important respects they report similar numbers. For example, in table 1.2, total fatalities resulting from U.S. drone strikes are similar, with TBIJ reporting 3,798 and CSTK reporting fourteen less (3,784). This small divergence is likely explained in part by the fact that we average TBIJ's low and high ranges to get a single (mean) number for the table—an admittedly crude procedure.

CSTK also reports a slightly greater total of nineteen more strikes than TBIJ (545 as opposed to 526). This likely results at least in part from TBIJ's decision to classify double-tap strikes (where drones come back after a pause to strike a site for a second time) as one strike, instead of treating them as two distinct strikes as CSTK does (see the chapter 3 case study for more information on double-tap strikes).

There are also, however, some striking differences in the data reported. This is perhaps most noticeable in the number of civilian casualties reported (CSTK reports 223 while TBIJ reports a total of 778, or at least that is the average of its high and low estimates). Part of the explanation for this divergence is another important methodological difference: CSTK reports a category of "unknowns" (which includes 549 fatalities), whereas TBIJ does not use this category. The "unknown" category encompasses those cases where there is not sufficient evidence to confidently classify an individual into either "civilian" or "suspected militant" categories, or where evidence is conflicting (i.e., some news reports say the dead were civilians and other equally credible/authoritative sources say they were suspected militants). By contrast, TBIJ classifies conflicting or doubtful cases as either civilians or possible civilians (this distinction will be explained below).

Nevertheless, the differences between these databases may not be as sharp as they initially appear. Interestingly, if one combines CSTK's categories of "civilians" and "unknowns," the resulting total of 772 approximately matches TBIJ's civilian total of 778. This suggests that much of the apparent divergence comes down to differences of classification. In order to understand what is going on, it will be helpful to briefly consider the different methodologies and classifications employed by TBIJ and CSTK.

One key difference in the way TBIJ and CSTK interpret and present their data is that TBIJ divides casualties into two main categories, whereas CSTK (like NAF) uses four. TBIJ reports only total killed and civilians killed, whereas CSTK adds the additional categories of suspected militants and unknowns. The TBIJ approach has the obvious virtue of keeping things simple. TBIJ also introduces some nuance, however, by including a very broadly defined subcategory of "possible civilian" casualties. They then present this number, the "possible civilian" casualties, as the top of a range, the bottom end of which is the clear civilian casualties. They explain this way of presenting their results as follows:

> We report all instances where civilians are credibly reported to have been killed or injured, using the 0-X formula . . . where accounts vary as to whether civilians or militants were killed. It is fairly common for reporting to refer to the dead as "people," "local tribesmen" or "family members" rather than specifically referring to civilians. At times the indication of civilian casualties is clearer—such as when reports refer to "militants and local tribesmen" being killed. For all of these formulations, we will include possible civilian casualties in our casualty count using the 0-X formula.[152]

The key points here are that TBIJ records those killed as "civilians" (i.e., the bottom end of the 0-X range) if they are clearly identified as such in news reports. It classifies them as "possible civilians" (i.e., the top end of the 0-X range) if reports vary and at least one news report describes them as such. Moreover, TBIJ considers language like "people" or "local tribesman" or "family members" as possibly referring to civilians, and so if at least one news story uses one of these terms to describe those killed, then they may be included in the possible civilian range (i.e., the X or top end of the civilian range), even if they are persistently described as militants, Taliban, or al-Qaeda in every other news story. This is a sensible methodology if one is primarily concerned with identifying civilian casualties and therefore one's priority is to be certain of counting every possible case where a civilian may have died. It may, however, lead to some people being included in the possible civilian count who were not civilians, especially in light of the issues with the reliability of news reports discussed above.

TBIJ is also distinguished from the other three open-source databases in not including any aggregate count of "suspected militants" (although they do note militants in their case-by-case breakdowns). TBIJ explains their reasoning as follows in their explanation of their methodology:

> As academics at Columbia Law School's Human Rights Clinic noted in a 2012 report on counting drone strike casualties, the term "militant" is politically and emotively charged, yet has no accepted legal definition. Although the Bureau records reports of alleged militant casualties in the narratives describing each strike, we do not keep a specific count of reported "militant" deaths. We keep tallies only of reported civilian deaths and of total casualties.[153]

We therefore leave the category of suspected militant blank in table 1.2 when summarizing their data.

CSTK, by contrast, does report as "suspected militants" those who are persistently described in news reports as "suspected militants," "foreign fighters," "terrorists," "Taliban," or "al-Qaeda"[154]—as indeed do NAF and LWJ as well. As noted above, CSTK also classifies some fatalities into an "unknown" category where there is either insufficient evidence to confidently place the individual into either the "civilian" or "suspected militant" category or where reports conflict on this question. The NAF also uses the same categories on a similar basis. The rationale in both cases is roughly the same, that the additional categories allow a more full and nuanced representation of the often incongruous sources.

In one respect, however, TBIJ does provide a more nuanced categorization than the other databases. TBIJ provides a separate total for number of children killed in drone strikes, which they determine as follows: "When reporting on casualties among children we employ the United Nations–designated age range of 0–17 years inclusive."[155] CSTK does not currently provide a separate aggregate count of children killed but does identify all children killed in its strike descriptions and automatically counts them as civilians. But in contrast to TBIJ's standard of considering everyone seventeen or younger as a child, CSTK considers those who are fourteen or under as children. The rationale here is that this standard is closer to what is generally meant in everyday speech by describing someone as a child and correspondingly better matches the impression (or image) that is conveyed by a report that a child has been killed or injured. Moreover, the Geneva Conventions set fifteen as the legal minimum age for recruitment into armed forces and for participation in hostilities, so it makes sense to allow for at least the possibility that those over the age of fourteen could legally be combatants (although of course many will not be).[156]

In addition to the different categories they use, there are also some important differences in the way TBIJ and CSTK gather their raw data (to then be organized into the categories discussed above). Here TBIJ's key virtues are its comprehensiveness and consistency, whereas CSTK employs a selective strategy designed to extract the best quality data from the diverse mass of reporting. To begin with, TBIJ draws on the widest range of news reports of any of the four databases discussed here and applies a consistent methodology.[157] It looks through each news story for a common baseline of clear civilian fatalities and any indications that any others killed may have been civilians to formulate the "possible civilian" top of their "civilians killed" range. CSTK, by contrast, tries to assess and factor in the quality and timing of news reporting. It begins by identifying in each case the most credible media report on the basis of three criteria: (1) level of detail (including such things as the names, characteristics, and backgrounds of the dead, the precise location of the strike, specific details of the attack, etc.), (2) range of sources cited (such as local witnesses and doctors, local government officials, CIA officials, and militant spokespersons), and (3) how recently the reporting has been updated (with emphasis on newly emergent details and delayed effects, such as when those injured in strikes later die). CSTK then reports strike effects based on this most credible source (which it terms "the primary source"). In the case of Pakistan, CSTK identifies both a global primary source as well as a specifically Pakistani primary source, so that any differences between international reports and local reports can be observed. The rationale for this approach is to try to obtain the most credible and precise data possible from the media reports. It should be noted, however, that attempting to organize the reporting in this way—assessing it on a scale of quality and putting priority only on the best reporting—opens CSTK to concerns about manipulating the data (charges that do not arise on TBIJ's approach). To offset any such concerns, CSTK makes the mechanics of ranking transparent on its database, explaining on a case-by-case basis what distinguishes the primary sources.

The Madrassa Strike: An Illustration of Analysis

The practical differences between the TBIJ and CSTK methods of classification can be illustrated by considering a particular incident. Here we select a particularly controversial case to help dramatize how the different approaches play and produce, at least in some respects, different results. In October 2006, the CIA launched an attack against a madrassa, or a religious school, being run by a radical cleric named Maulvi Liaquat.[158] Liaquat was reportedly the second in command of the Tehreek Nifaz-e-Shariat Mohammadi (TNSM), which has aided the Taliban in its fight against the United States.[159] The spokesman for Pakistan's army, Major General Shaukat Sultan, stated that the location was used as a militant training center and was no longer used as a religious school.[160] Reinforcing the possibility that the targeted location was used to train militants, the *New York Times* quoted a Pakistani intelligence official as follows:

> [These] two local militant leaders, Mr. Liaqat and Maulana Faqir Muhammad, members of the now-banned movement [TNSM], were heavily involved in logistics, recruitment and training of fighters who were sent to fight United States and Afghan forces in Afghanistan.[161]

Liaquat was reportedly advised to stop his training but rejected these calls.[162] Liaquat also had been charged with aiding al-Qaeda operatives and was expected to be pardoned by a peace treaty that was to be signed the day after the strike.[163] After viewing footage of the institution released by the

Pakistani government, the *New York Times* described the events captured as follows:

> The men, who appear as shadowy figures because the camera picks up their body heat and shows it as black, filter out of a building, which an intelligence official said was their living quarters, and line up in rows. Trainers walk among the rows of men, who appear to do stretches, jog in circles and at one point lie motionless on the ground.[164]

Maulana Faqir Mohammad, the TNSM leader in Bajaur, had attended a meeting at the madrassa prior to the strike.[165] After the attack, Mohammad spoke to a crowd in front of the wreckage and called the strike on it a terrorist attack, arguing that those killed were students learning the Koran.[166] At one point in his speech Mohammed challenged the government to prove that those killed were militants, stating, "show us the body of one foreigner killed in the attack. Show us one gun or bullet that has been found in the debris of the Madrassa."[167] Mushtaq Yusufzai of *NBC News*, who was about a mile from the madrassa at the time of the attack and was permitted to film and conduct interviews in the aftermath, reported that despite Mohammed's challenge, the madrassa was in fact used for training militants:

> **"Prior to this attack, what was the reputation of [the] school? Was it known to be a training ground for militants?"**
> Yes, it was. Mohammed, the al-Qaida leader in the area, was one of the first people in the area to publicly support the Taliban and Osama bin Laden. He tells people that it is their responsibility to support the Taliban and Osama bin Laden because he says we are at war with people who are fighting Islam. He has said it is their responsibility to support mujahedeen and war with the West. The school was known as a strong supporter of the Taliban.
> Mohammed's deputy Maulana Liaquat Ali Hussain—a leader of the madrassa—was killed in the attack.
> Mohammed has been accused of providing shelter to militants and even invited bin Laden's deputy, Ayman al-Zawahri, to the madrassa.[168]

Nearly six years later, the Pakistani president at the time of the attack, Pervez Musharraf, similarly argued that the madrassa had been used for training militants, stating:

> It's all bullshit—sorry for the word—that it was a madrasa and seminary and children were studying Quran. They used this as cover . . . In the media, they said it was all children. They were absolutely wrong. There may have been some collateral damage of some children but they were not children at all, they were all militants doing training inside.[169]

Other elements of the Pakistani government did not share the belief that all of those killed were suspected militants, however. In July 2013, TBIJ released a leaked Pakistani document that recorded death tolls in the drone attacks from 2006 to 2009.[170] The document stated that "80 children, 1 men [*sic*] all civilian" were killed.[171] Additionally, an article by *The News International* reported the names, origin, and ages of seventy-nine of the victims in the attack, relating that at least seventy of those killed were under the age of eighteen.[172] In view of these facts, TBIJ reports a total of eighty-one to eighty-three killed, including eighty to eighty-two civilians, including sixty-eight to seventy children. The difference between the total fatality count (eighty-one to eighty-three) and civilian fatalities (eighty to eighty-two) seems to allow the possibility that Liaquat may not be properly counted as a civilian, but it is worth noting that reporting this way does not assure recognition that at least one noncivilian was killed, since they allow for the possibility that the result may simply have been eighty-one civilians killed, or eighty-two civilians killed.

CSTK reported the results of this strike as including one suspected militant (Liaquat) and thirty civilian casualties (counting all the victims under fifteen as civilians).[173] The remaining fifty-two people killed were recorded as "unknowns" due to the conflicting reports regarding whether they were students pursuing education, or people who, despite their age, were training for militant activities. These reported impacts differ in some important ways, but they are largely attributable, as has been shown, to different approaches to classification. It is worth noting that many of the underlying facts are agreed—for example, when and where the strike took place, the number of people killed, the identities and ages of those killed, and more. So while it is often pointed out that there are sharp discrepancies among the databases, there is also a great deal of overlap and agreement. While not ideal, these uncontested facts can provide some understanding of the covert actions being taken in these volatile areas, including northwest Pakistan, where outside reporters are largely prohibited. Much the same can be said of the two other main open-source databases tracking U.S. drone strikes, at least once consideration is given to exactly what is being included in their aggregate counts.

General Airstrike Databases: NAF and LWJ

The two additional databases that collect and report data on drone strikes do so only as part of a broader category of U.S. airstrikes in specific countries. In particular, the New America Foundation (NAF) and The Long War Journal (LWJ) separately track U.S. airstrikes in both Pakistan and Yemen (although not in Somalia). So what they are tracking is not exclusively drone strikes, but rather the effects of the U.S. air war being conducted in both countries, including those produced by manned aircraft and missile strikes. In both the cases of Pakistan and Yemen, however, the vast majority of U.S. strikes have likely been carried out by drones, so these numbers do provide a rough indicator of drone effects. Each database's summary findings (including both Pakistan and Yemen) are summarized in table 1.3 below.

Given the differences in coverage from CSTK and TBIJ[174] (that is, including nondrone strikes and excluding Somalia cases), it is not surprising that the NAF and LWJ data vary from them a little bit. In fact, it's surprising how little they do vary, at least in some respects (which may have led some readers to overlook the important differences in coverage). For example, the NAF strike total of 518 falls just under the TBIJ and CSTK totals (526 and 545, respectively), and the LWJ total (492) is only slightly below the NAF.

Some important similarities are also evident in the way that both the proportional and absolute numbers vary over time. All of the databases show a steep, general reduction in civilian casualties over time. The drop is clearly marked in each case. For example, absolute numbers of civilians killed have fallen sharply in each of the databases. In 2009 TBIJ reported 155 civilians killed, but in 2014 only eight, and six as of March 18, 2015; CSTK reported thirty-nine in 2009 and four and zero in 2014 and 2015 (to March 18); NAF reported 111 in 2009 and four and zero in 2014 and 2015 (to March 18); and LWJ reports eighty-four in 2009 but only six and zero in 2014 and 2015 (to March 18). Each of the databases also shows a sharp corresponding drop in the proportion of civilian deaths to all deaths. TBIJ shows a decline from 49.9 percent in the early years of the program (2002 to 2008) to 2.92 percent in 2014 and 6.98 percent thus far in 2015, while NAF shows a drop in the same periods from 26.71 percent to 1.43 percent and 0 percent, CSTK drops from 16.43 percent to 1.3 percent and 0 percent, and LWJ drops from 9.46 percent to 2.03 percent and 0 percent.

Some differences are apparent, however, in the number and proportion of those killed who are classified as suspected militants. CSTK classifies 79.6 percent (representing 3,012) as suspected militants, NAF classifies 82.88 percent (representing 3,327) as suspected militants, and LWJ classifies 92.67 percent (representing 3,300) as suspected militants. Much of this variation is again explained by the fact that CSTK has a substantial (14.51 percent) category of unknowns, NAF has a smaller (7.90 percent) category, while LWJ classifies each case as either civilian or suspected militant (and so ends up with a slightly higher count and proportion). Similarly, some differences can be found in the reporting of high-value targets (HVTs) killed. LWJ reports 122 HVTs or senior al-Qaeda and Taliban military leaders killed in Pakistan,

TABLE 1.3

The Impacts of Airstrikes, Including Drone Strikes, as Reported by NAF and LWJ, 2002 to 2015 (as of March 18, 2015).[1,2]

Source	Year(s)	Total Strikes	Total Killed	Suspected Militants Killed	Civilians Killed	"Unknowns" Killed	Civilian Deaths as Percentage of Total
New America Foundation (NAF)*	2002–2008	47	483	289	129	65	26.71%
	2009	56	644	441	111	92	17.24%
	2010	123	856	790	21	45	2.45%
	2011	85	629	511	66	52	10.49%
	2012	104	793	719	22	52	2.77%
	2013	53	286	259	17	10	5.94%
	2014	41	279	275	4	0	1.43%
	2015	9	44	43	0	1	0.00%
	Total 2002–2015	518	4,014	3,327	370	317	9.22%
The Long War Journal (LWJ)	2002–2008	47	539	488	51	—	9.46%
	2009	55	561	477	84	—	14.97%
	2010	121	831	811	20	—	2.41%
	2011	74	516	486	30	—	5.81%
	2012	87	529	490	39	—	7.37%
	2013	54	253	222	31	—	12.25%
	2014	47	296	290	6	—	2.03%
	2015	7	36	36	0	—	0.00%
	Total 2002–2015	492	3,561	3,300	261	—	7.33%

*NAF data was calculated by averaging its high-low ranges.

1. "Targeted Killing Database," Center for the Study of Targeted Killing, accessed April 25, 2015, http://targetedkilling.org/; "Get the Data: Drone Wars," The Bureau of Investigative Journalism, https://www.thebureauinvestigates.com/category/projects/drones/drones-graphs/.

while NAF reports ninety-nine HVTs killed in both Pakistan and Yemen to date.[175]

Differences between the databases are sharper (once again) when it comes to *total* civilian casualties. At first glance, TBIJ appears as the clear outlier when it comes to the number of civilian deaths reported (778), with its total just seventy-six below the sum of those reported by the other three databases combined (NAF at 370, LWJ at 261, and CSTK at 223). Here it is worth noting that NAF, like CSTK, also tracks a category of "unknowns" (317 in total, which may account in part for the lower count of civilian casualties), while TBIJ and LWJ do not. Similarly again, the overall proportion of civilian deaths as a percentage of total deaths reported by NAF (9.22 percent) and LWJ (7.33 percent) fall between TBIJ (20.48 percent) and CSTK (5.89 percent)—although again this is excluding the category of "unknowns" used by both NAF and CSTK, which treat them as a separate classification. If one compares, as we did in the discussion of table 1.2, the combination of civilians and unknowns together with TBIJ's civilian proportion (20.48 percent), then you get much closer results, with NAF at 17.12 percent and CSTK at 20.4 percent. In this scenario, which assumes that all unknowns turn out to be civilians, LWJ becomes the outlier, with total civilian casualties at 7.33 percent. If, however, unknowns are all assumed to be suspected militants, then TBIJ at 20.48 percent becomes the outlier in relation to CSTK, LWJ, and NAF, who put the proportion of civilian casualties at 5.89 percent, 7.33 percent, and 9.22 percent, respectively.

The difference between the TBIJ and LWJ counts of civilian casualties (778 versus 261, a difference of 517) is particularly notable given the fact that neither uses the category of unknowns. How can this divergence between the TBIJ and LWJ casualty counts be explained, especially insofar as the databases draw on many of the same sources? One possible explanation is that LWJ does not include the Somalia cases, but since TBIJ counts only 23 to 105 killed in drone strikes in Somalia, it cannot be the full explanation. It could also be that by including nondrone strikes (such as manned airstrikes and missile strikes) in their totals, LWJ ends up diluting the proportion of civilian casualties. But this also seems at best a very partial explanation. First, it would do nothing to explain the discrepancy in absolute numbers (which diverge by 517 lives, with TBIJ's count almost tripling LWJ's); second, operations not involving drones appear to be a distinct minority among all attacks, and so it seems unlikely that their inclusion could fully explain the lower proportion of civilian casualties in the LWJ data.

In this light, we suggest that the primary explanation for the divergence is the same that was identified in comparing the TBIJ and CSTK data—that is, the way that ambiguous cases (the types of difficult cases that CSTK and

NAF classify as "unknowns") are being classified. In essence, TBIJ tends to count ambiguous cases as civilians (or possible civilians), and LWJ tends to classify the majority of them as suspected militants (which explains why its proportion of civilian casualties at 7.33 percent is only a little higher than CSTK's at 5.89 percent, even though LWJ does not have a separate category for "unknowns"). This would also help to explain LWJ's higher total of suspected militants killed (compared with CSTK). If this explanation is right, then the same logic can be applied to explain the NAF results largely on the basis of their taking a slightly more flexible approach to who counts as civilians or suspected militants than CSTK, resulting in a slightly lower count of unknowns (317 in contrast to CSTK's 549) and slightly higher counts of civilians (370 to CSTK's 223) and suspected militants (3,327 to CSTK's 3,012).

If this analysis, which attributes the bulk of the divergence among the databases to different ways of classifying the difficult cases or unknowns, is correct, then one key takeaway is that there is more agreement on the underlying data than there often appears, although it is obscured by some important differences on how best to interpret and present it. If this is so, then the databases as a group seem to suggest that the actual number of civilian casualties is likely somewhere between the low (CSTK) and high (TBIJ) counts of civilian casualties. TBIJ's top estimate of possible civilian casualties (the numbers from table 1.2 are averages of their ranges) stands at 1,063 as of March 20, 2015, out of a total possible casualty count of 4,689 (or 22.67 percent of all casualties). So in sum, the databases as a group seem to suggest that the civilian casualties are likely between 223 and 1,061, and between 5.89 percent and 22.67 percent of all deaths resulting from U.S. drone strikes.

So what do these numbers mean? Those who see the situation with al-Qaeda and its affiliates as something akin to war tend to see the civilian deaths as tragic but not unreasonable in comparison with other wartime scenarios. The most frequently cited statistics on average wartime casualties worldwide between 1990 and 2000 suggest that civilians usually amount to around two-thirds of total casualties.[176] A recent data set, offering an avowedly conservative assessment of civilian deaths in armed conflict around the world, gives a significantly lower assessment. Taking as a basis for analysis the database of battle deaths assembled in 2005 by Bethany Lacina (of the University of Rochester) and Nils Gleditsch (from the Peace Research Institute of Oslo), Kristine Eck and Lisa Hultman of Uppsala University found that over 1989 to 2004, battle deaths exceeded deaths from one-sided violence (a rough indicator of civilian casualties) by a ratio of two to one.[177] In other words, civilian deaths in armed conflict averaged around one-third over that fifteen-year period. From the perspective of the harm visited on civilians in war (including unconventional war), drones appear to be performing comparatively well, especially when it is added that they are doing so in a war where enemy fighters hide among civilian populations, often in relatively remote, difficult-to-reach locations.[178]

By contrast, if considered from a law enforcement/human rights perspective, the number of civilian casualties is staggering—between 223 and 1,061 people killed would be a disaster. As a point of comparison, the Bloody Sunday massacre on January 30, 1972, in Derry, Northern Ireland, involved the killing of fourteen unarmed civilians.

Part of the purpose of this book is to provide an overview of these two perspectives and to help readers come to their own informed judgments on this basic question. Indeed, in many ways this basic issue is at the core of the debate around drones, and finds reflection not only in specific disputes but also in the institutions and practices connected with the drone campaigns. For example, the ongoing struggle over whether the war with al-Qaeda and its affiliates should be seen as a military or civilian enterprise is reflected even in which U.S. departments, agencies, and personnel are asked to lead the fight, as will be shown in the following section.

Divided Authorities

Beyond the distinctions between the various databases reporting the impact of drone strikes on the ground, there is an important division in the U.S. drone program itself that needs to be acknowledged. In essence, lead executive authority for strikes is divided between a civilian agency, the CIA, which runs the drone campaign in Pakistan, and a military one, the Joint Special Operations Command (JSOC)—a subunit of the Department of Defense (DOD) Special Operations Command—which carries out some of the strikes in Yemen and Somalia. One key difference is that the CIA strikes are covert operations, which the U.S. government generally does not specifically acknowledge publicly, although the Obama administration has now recognized in a general way that such operations occur; and in at least one case (the January 15, 2015, strike that killed two Western hostages) provided some details. JSOC strikes, by contrast, can be acknowledged, although again little detail on specific operations is generally provided to the public. Similarly, the government cannot provide information on the procedures, safeguards, and oversight employed by the CIA, but it can in the case of JSOC operations—for example, *Joint Targeting, Joint Publication 3-60*, provides an overview of the authorities, targeting processes, and procedures for mitigation of danger to local civilians (these are discussed in detail in the case study in chapter 4).[179]

It is possible that the CIA's role in targeted killings may come to an end in the coming years, as both the Obama administration and Congress have considered whether the targeted killing operations should stay in part under its authority or be transitioned exclusively to the military. In March 2013, news that the White House wished for targeted operations by drone aircraft to transition away from the CIA to the U.S. military began to surface.[180] The likelihood of this transition was further bolstered by a speech from President Obama in May 2013, in which he intimated that the drone strikes were a military tactic.[181] It was reported in early 2014, however, that Congress had added language to the national budget that would make this transition more difficult.[182] Nonetheless, in April 2015 senior administration officials indicated that "the President plans to make a new push to move the CIA's drone strikes against groups like al Qaeda to the Pentagon."[183] With this transition hanging in the balance, it is important to understand the differences between drone strikes launched by the CIA and those run by the military. This section will first examine CIA drone strikes before turning to the operations launched by the U.S. military.

CIA Strikes

Over the last ten years, the CIA has launched drone operations outside conventional armed conflict against perceived enemies in Pakistan, Yemen, and Somalia,[184] with some reports that strikes have occurred in the Philippines as well.[185] Since at least 2009, it has been reported that pilots located in Creech Air Force Base, Nevada, fly the CIA drone missions,[186] but the specifics of these operations have been unknown. In April 2014, however, former air force drone pilots claimed in a documentary that the air force's 17th Reconnaissance Squadron executes the CIA's drone strikes in Pakistan.[187] One such former pilot, Brandon Bryant, stated that he decided to share this information after hearing that the Obama administration desired to switch control of the strikes from the CIA to the military.[188] Bryant stated:

> There is a lie hidden within that truth. And the lie is that it's always been the air force that has flown those missions. The CIA might be the customer but the air force has always flown it. A CIA label is just an excuse to not have to give up any information. That is all it has ever been.[189]

While the revelation of the air force flying the CIA's missions has offered increased understanding of the attacks, many questions remain unanswered. The opacity of the program has gone beyond the lack of casualty figures, or the specific targets of attacks, and for a long time it impeded public recognition even of its existence. It was not until almost a decade after the first covert drone attack in Yemen that the U.S. president officially acknowledged that the United States was behind the drone strikes.[190] This secrecy has prevented the global community, including UN observers, from being able to assess the impact of the strikes. In 2013, a preliminary UN report concerning the drone campaign in Pakistan stated the following:

> The single greatest obstacle to an evaluation of the civilian impact of drone strikes is lack of transparency, which makes it extremely difficult to assess claims of precision targeting objectively.[191]

Without official data on these attacks, scholars and other members of the public have out of necessity relied primarily on databases such as those summarized above to track the covert strikes.[192]

Air Force Drone Strike Reports

The military is at times a little more transparent than the CIA in reporting on drone strikes. Military-directed drone strikes have played a significant part in the exercise of U.S. air power since 9/11. This has involved performing various roles, including targeting operations and close-air support as well as intelligence, surveillance, and reconnaissance (ISR).[193] While the public must rely on databases based on possibly corrupt media reporting when scrutinizing the CIA's drone campaigns, the same has not been entirely true for strikes launched by military-directed drones, particularly when it comes to theaters of conventional armed conflict. In October 2012, for example, the U.S. Air Force released information concerning the number of weapon releases from aircraft in Afghanistan, segmenting out those carried out by unmanned craft.[194] While the term *weapon releases* is not clearly synonymous with the term *strikes* seen in the previous section, table 1.4 (below) shows a sharp increase in the use of armed drones by the U.S. Air Force until the end of 2012.

While table 1.4 shows an increase in the number of drone strikes year-over-year by the U.S. Air Force, it was in 2012 that the most drastic shift occurred. In that year, as troop drawdowns were in full effect,[195] the percentage of weapon releases carried out by drones more than doubled from 5.4 percent to 12.4 percent of all air force weapons releases for the year. Unfortunately, however, the release of such data on drone strikes has been discontinued since March 2013.[196] U.S. Central Command stated that the numbers were removed because the only data published had been for the small subset of drone missions that launched an attack and consequently were "disproportionately focused" on drone strikes relative to other drone missions.[197] It

TABLE 1.4
Drone Operations in Afghanistan Reported by the U.S. Air Force*

Year	2009	2010	2011	2012
Number of weapon releases by drone	257	279	294	506
Number of weapon releases by all aircraft	4,165	5,102	5,411	4,092
Percentage of weapon releases that were carried out by drones	6.2%	5.5%	5.4%	12.4%

*Data acquired from unclassified U.S. Air Force document as of December 31, 2012.[1]
1. "Combined Forces Air Component Commander 2007–2012 Airpower Statistics."

is worth mentioning that the debate surrounding the U.S. use of drones was especially intense during this period, including a thirteen-hour filibuster from Senator Rand Paul protesting John Brennan's confirmation as the director of the CIA due to his role in the drone program (see chapter 5 for more information on Senator Paul's filibuster).[198]

The military also regularly reports on the impacts of specific air strikes on the ground in Afghanistan, and although at times it may understate harms to civilians, this at least invites dispute, investigation, and correction. For example, the International Security Assistance Force (ISAF) recorded an attack that targeted a vehicle in November 2013 as having killed ten enemy combatants.[199] Afghan officials, however, claimed that between eight and eleven civilians had been killed.[200] Investigations by both ISAF and the United Nations Assistance Mission in Afghanistan (UNAMA) ensued, both reaching the conclusion that civilians had been among those killed.[201] While UNAMA found that six combatants had been killed in the attack along with eleven civilians, it was only after pressing ISAF that they admitted that at least two civilians had been killed.[202]

While ISAF had originally "denied the possibility of civilian casualties,"[203] the release and altering of these figures showed at least some willingness to be held accountable for the strike. Open investigations and official responses do not extend to CIA drone strikes, however. U.S. officials have occasionally voiced their desire for increased transparency regarding drone strikes that occur outside of conventional battlefields, but to date we still lack any official statistics, let alone case-by-case reporting.[204] Some top military leaders have cited strategic reasons for wanting public disclosure, noting that it would allow them to defend the drones against international criticism.[205] The desire for "meaningful transparency" is also reportedly one of the reasons that the government has weighed moving drone strikes away from the CIA to the military.[206] In addition to the ability to publicly oppose false information about the drones, increased transparency may also reflect an increased commitment to the protection of civilians and an increased confidence that the numbers will lend credibility to this commitment. For a more detailed discussion of oversight and accountability in relation to drone strikes, see the case study in chapter 4.

The foregoing discussion has provided a general introduction and background on aerial drones, a brief overview of the U.S. drone campaigns of the last fourteen years, and some points of controversy and agreement concerning their impact on the ground. But to gain a deeper understanding of U.S. drone strikes outside of conventional armed conflict, it is necessary to drill down into the campaigns in specific countries, and the patterns and issues that arise within them. The case studies in this book are devoted to this purpose, beginning with the one that follows, which focuses on the CIA's biggest and most prolonged drone campaign.

Case Study: The U.S. Drone Campaign in Pakistan

The U.S. drone campaign in Pakistan began in June 2004, when Taliban leader Nek Muhammad was killed in South Waziristan by an AGM-114 Hellfire missile.[207] The missile also killed several other individuals and left a thirty-six-square-foot crater.[208] As of mid-March 2015, there have been approximately 410 drone strikes launched in Pakistan, with more than 360 of them attributed to the Obama administration.[209] Disputes surrounding the wisdom and propriety of the aerial campaign have surfaced, including whether the strikes are causing a disproportionate number of civilian deaths, or if they violate Pakistan's sovereignty. Consensus on many of these debates remains elusive, even after more than a decade since the dust settled on that summer night in Waziristan.

Still, there are at least some facts that are commonly agreed upon. For example, it is generally recognized that throughout the years the drones have killed a number of high-value targets in both the Taliban and al-Qaeda as well as affiliated groups.[210] Those who have been killed include the Haqqani Network's head of suicide operations, Abdullah Haqqani;[211] al-Qaeda's second-in-command, Atiyah Abd al-Rahman;[212] another second in command, Abu Yahya al-Libi;[213] Abdullah Said al Libi, the leader of al-Qaeda's paramilitary in Afghanistan (known as its "Shadow Army"[214]); and Osama al Kini, the chief of al-Qaeda's operations in Pakistan, who was also believed to have been involved in the bombing of the U.S. embassies in Kenya and Tanzania.[215]

The deaths of these and many other high-value targets have not been without collateral damage, however, as indicated in table 1.5 below.

The Pakistan drone campaign accounts for the majority of U.S. targeted killings outside of conventional battlefields since 9/11.[216] U.S. drone strikes in Pakistan have also killed more people per strike than in the combined operations in Yemen and Somalia, as Pakistani strikes account for 81 percent of deaths (across all categories) in just 77.5 percent of the attacks. However, when examining the civilian deaths as a percentage of the total (averaging across all four databases), the strikes in Pakistan (table 1.5) are very slightly lower than in all operations combined (tables 1.2 and 1.3). Comparing the average civilian casualties reported on table 1.5 to those on tables 1.2 and 1.3 (for the U.S. air campaigns in total) suggests that 10.59 percent of total deaths in Pakistan were recorded as civilians, compared to 10.77 percent in all strikes. While LWJ and CSTK report a lower proportion of civilian casualties in connection with the Pakistani drone campaign (on table 1.5) than with U.S. strikes outside conventional battlefields in general (on tables 1.3 and 1.2, respectively), NAF and TBIJ indicate the reverse, with a slightly higher proportion of civilians killed in Pakistan than in all operations combined.[217] This would seem to indicate that although the overall average of the database results shows slightly lower civilian casualties in Pakistan, this is not a very reliable data point (as two of the four databases tip slightly in the other direction).

Moreover, the slightly lower proportion of civilian deaths in the Pakistani data (at least when averaging across the databases) may be accounted for by a higher proportion of unknowns in comparison with the U.S. strikes outside of conventional battlefields as a whole (that is, some civilian casualties that might be accurately counted elsewhere are ending up in the "unknown" column in Pakistan). While the strikes in Pakistan account for 81 percent of total deaths, they also account for 92.73 percent of "unknown" deaths (401.5 of 433)[218] reported by CSTK and NAF (the only two databases that track "unknowns"). Since these "unknowns" represent cases where the facts are ambiguous, their concentration in the Pakistan data supports the notion that news reports covering strikes in Yemen and Somalia are more complete and possibly more informed than their Pakistani counterparts.

However, not all followers of the drone campaigns base their judgments on the data presented by these research organizations. Medea Benjamin, cofounder of the activist group CODEPINK, has been one of the most outspoken critics of the drone campaigns in recent years. After a trip to Pakistan, where she researched the effects of drone strikes on civilians, Benjamin wondered whether U.S. officials knew the suffering that she had just learned about.[219] Benjamin decided to figure out where then counterterrorism chief

TABLE 1.5

Drone Strikes in Pakistan According to Four Open-Source Databases 2004 to 2015 (as of March 18, 2015)[1]

Source	Year(s)	Total Strikes	Total Killed	Suspected Militants Killed	Civilians Killed	"Unknowns" Killed	Civilian Deaths as Percentage of Total
New America Foundation (NAF)*	2004–2008	46	477	283	129	65	27.04%
	2009	54	549	387	70	92	12.75%
	2010	122	849	788	16	45	1.88%
	2011	73	517	420	62	35	11.99%
	2012	48	306	268	5	33	1.63%
	2013	27	153	145	4	4	2.61%
	2014	22	151	151	0	0	0.00%
	2015	4	26	26	0	0	0.00%
	Total 2004–2015	396	3,028	2,468	286	274	9.45%
The Long War Journal (LWJ)	2004–2008	46	533	482	51	—	9.57%
	2009	53	506	463	43	—	8.50%
	2010	117	815	801	14	—	1.72%
	2011	64	435	405	30	—	6.90%
	2012	46	304	300	4	—	1.32%
	2013	28	137	123	14	—	10.22%
	2014	24	152	152	0	—	0.00%
	2015	3	22	22	0	—	0.00%
	Total 2004–2015	381	2,904	2,748	156	—	5.37%

TABLE 1.5 (Continued)

Source	Year(s)	Total Strikes	Total Killed	Suspected Militants Killed	Civilians Killed	"Unknowns" Killed	Civilian Deaths as Percentage of Total
The Bureau of Investigative Journalism (TBIJ)*	2004–2008	49	495	—	250	—	50.51%
	2009	54	612	—	155	—	25.33%
	2010	128	932	—	143	—	15.34%
	2011	75	515	—	102	—	19.81%
	2012	50	305	—	38	—	12.46%
	2013	27	152	—	2	—	1.32%
	2014	25	151	—	1	—	0.66%
	2015	6	35	—	2	—	5.71%
	Total 2004–2015	414	3,197	—	693	—	21.68%
Center for the Study of Targeted Killing (CSTK)	2004–2008	47	493	267	82	144	13.79%
	2009	56	607	479	39	89	6.43%
	2010	137	883	701	22	160	2.49%
	2011	78	514	397	17	100	3.31%
	2012	49	306	283	3	20	0.98%
	2013	27	153	141	2	10	1.31%
	2014	23	157	151	0	6	0.00%
	2015	5	31	31	0	0	0.00%
	Total 2004–2015	422	3,144	2,450	165	529	5.25%

*TBIJ and NAF data was calculated by averaging its high-low ranges.
1. "International Security Data Site"; "Pakistan Strikes"; "Covert Drone War"; "Targeted Killing Database."

John Brennan lived in order to pay him a visit.[220] On a Sunday morning trip, she claims to have told him that:

> I had just returned from a delegation to Pakistan meeting with drone victims, how heartbroken I was to hear their stories, how terrible it is that these drone attacks are causing so much suffering to innocent people and turning the entire Pakistani population against us.[221]

In response to this, Brennan informed Benjamin that what she said was untrue and that the strikes were not harming civilians.[222] In June 2011, Brennan had made a similar statement in public, claiming that for nearly a year "there hasn't been a single collateral death because of the exceptional proficiency, precision of the capabilities we've been able to develop."[223] This claim was proven false in April 2013, however, when leaked government documents showed that the United States suspected that civilians had died in a strike in April 2011, just two months before Brennan's public statement.[224]

While Brennan's claim that drone strikes have not caused harm to civilians may have been false, there are many who believe that the drone strikes in Pakistan are very accurate and that they result in relatively few civilian casualties. Contrary to Benjamin's contention that drones are causing a disproportionate amount of suffering, Farhat Taj claimed that "the people feel comfortable with the drone attacks because of their precision and targeted strikes. [People prefer them to] the Pakistan Army's attacks which always result in collateral damage."[225] Avery Plaw, associate professor at the University of Massachusetts, Dartmouth (and one of the present authors), published a study of the four databases and their discrepancies that concluded that "the best available evidence suggests that civilian casualties are moderate to low in relation to suspected militant casualties."[226] Close examination of the aggregate casualty statistics in table 1.5 indeed points to civilian deaths being in a distinct minority of overall fatalities in Pakistan (between 5.25 percent and 21.7 percent), especially in recent years (the average for the period January 1, 2012, through March 18, 2015, inclusive across all four databases is 2.39 percent).

On the U.S. side, drones have also kept casualties low, although perhaps not nonexistent. The biggest loss of life for the CIA in over a quarter century occurred at Forward Operating Base Chapman in Afghanistan in December 2009.[227] Seven CIA agents, including the chief of the base, were killed in the attack executed by a suicide bomber affiliated with the Taliban.[228] Several former intelligence officials claimed that the attack was "devastating" to the CIA, as the Chapman base and its personnel are believed to have had integral roles in maintaining contact with Pakistani informants as well as in the execution of the drone campaign.[229] In response to the attack, an anonymous

U.S. intelligence official reportedly said, "This attack will be avenged through successful, aggressive counterterrorism operations."[230] Whether the bombing served as the primary catalyst or not, 2010 would become the year with the highest number of drone strikes, more than doubling the frequency of strikes in 2009 (see table 1.5).

The United States may not be the only party in the conflict that seeks revenge for its losses, however. While the Chapman attack may have propelled the CIA to expand its targeting campaign in Pakistan, there is evidence that the Taliban and al-Qaeda also retaliate for attacks against their personnel. For example, the leader of al-Qaeda in Afghanistan, Mustafa Abu al-Yazid, stated that the attack against the CIA was in response to the killing of three al-Qaeda and Taliban leaders in drone strikes.[231] Still, it is unclear whether the Taliban's publicly proclaimed motives should be taken entirely at face value. In a May 2011 incident, the Taliban claimed that they had killed eighty-two Pakistani paramilitary soldiers in retaliation for the raid that killed Osama bin Laden.[232] Official sources, however, claimed that it was more likely a response for a Pakistani offensive in the tribal areas.[233]

In November 2011, several months after the raid that killed Osama bin Laden, NATO accidentally killed twenty-four Pakistani troops on the border between Afghanistan and Pakistan.[234] A U.S. investigation of the incident found that both NATO and Pakistan made mistakes that led to the fatal airstrikes.[235] Pakistan rejected these findings and called the attack an intentional act of aggression.[236] As retaliation for the incident, Pakistan shut down NATO's supply routes through the country, which did not reopen until July 2012 after Secretary of State Hillary Clinton negotiated a deal that included an apology.[237] In addition to the closing of NATO's supply routes, Pakistan ordered that the United States abandon the Shamsi Airfield, which had become widely known as a hangar used for drones.[238] The strain on ties between the United States and Pakistan caused the United States to refrain from using drone strikes for a month and a half after the incident.[239] After this pause, U.S. drone strikes returned at a slower pace and with perhaps a more cautious approach.

Indeed, since the renewal of drone strikes at the beginning of 2012, the drone campaign in Pakistan has exhibited two features that may be calculated to temper criticism at least slightly. First, the rate of strikes has diminished considerably. From a peak intensity of between 117 and 137 strikes in 2010 (depending on which database you look at), the numbers have fallen to between twenty-seven and twenty-eight in 2013 and between twenty-two and twenty-five in 2014 (as indicated on table 1.5).

Second, civilian casualties have fallen sharply. In fact, none of the four databases report any clear cases of civilian casualties for 2014 (TBIJ reports zero clear cases, but two possible cases that we average to one for purposes of the table), and there have been none reported so far this year (to March 2015, although TBIJ notes four possible cases). Even in 2013, reported civilian casualties were very low on most counts, with TBIJ reporting no clear cases but four possible cases, and CSTK reporting two and NAF reporting three to five (averaged to four).[240] Finally, there are reports that the Pakistani military is participating more actively in the coordination of drone strikes, particularly with its troops fighting on the ground in North Waziristan.[241]

While these developments may somewhat temper criticism of the United States, they address only a few of the major strategic, legal, and ethical criticisms of the campaign. These concerns demand direct response and have in recent years received some answers. The remainder of this book is devoted to examining these exchanges to help readers to draw their own conclusions as to their adequacy, beginning with the question of whether drone strikes, such as those in Pakistan, are strategically effective.

Notes

1. "U.S. President George W. Bush Addresses the Corps of Cadets," *The Citadel*, last modified December 12, 2001, accessed March 18, 2015, http://www.citadel.edu/root/presbush01; see chapter 6 for details on drone research, procurement, and training.

2. Edward Helmore, "US Now Trains More Drone Operators Than Pilots," *The Guardian*, August 22, 2009, accessed March 21, 2015, http://www.theguardian.com/world/2009/aug/23/drones-air-force-robot-planes; see chapter 6 for details on procurement.

3. *Unmanned Systems Integrated Roadmap FY2013–2038* (U.S. Department of Defense, 2013): 5, http://www.defense.gov/Portals/1/Documents/pubs/DOD-USRM-2013.pdf; http://www.defense.gov/pubs/DOD-USRM-2013.pdf; Jeremiah Gertler, *U.S. Unmanned Aerial Systems* (Congressional Research Service, 2012): 2, http://fas.org/sgp/crs/natsec/R42136.pdf.

4. Brian Everstine, "Report Details Air Force Plans for Future Drones," *Air Force Times*, April 7, 2014, accessed January 19, 2015, http://archive.airforcetimes.com/article/20140407/NEWS04/304070049/Report-details-Air-force-plans-future-drones.

5. Jennifer Rizzo, "Drones Soar in U.S. Plans for Future Aircraft Purchases," *CNN News*, June 10, 2011, accessed July 7, 2015, http://www.cnn.com/2011/US/06/10/pentagon.drones/.

6. Spencer Ackerman, "Pentagon Says Air Force's 'Expanding Drone Fleet' Is Unjustified and Wasteful," *The Guardian*, January 21, 2015, accessed March 21, 2015,

http://www.theguardian.com/world/2015/jan/21/pentagon-air-forces-drones-fleet-reaper.

7. Other countries, most notably Israel, have a fascinating history with military drones and their development, but this lies outside the focus of the current book. For a brief overview see Konstantin Kakaes, "From Orville Wright to September 11: What the History of Drone Technology Says about Its Future," in *Drone Wars*, edited by Peter Bergen and Daniel Rothenberg (Cambridge: Cambridge University Press, 2015), 371–74.

8. Steven Zaloga, *Unmanned Aerial Vehicles: Robotic Air Warfare 1917–2007* (New York: Osprey Press, 2008), 4–6.

9. "Curtiss-Sperry Aerial Torpedo at the Cradle of Aviation Museum," *Cradle of Aviation Museum*, accessed February 19, 2015, http://www.cradleofaviation.org/history/permanent_exhibits/world_war_i/curtiss_sperry_aerial_torpedo.html.

10. Zaloga, *Unmanned Aerial Vehicles*, 6; "Curtiss-Sperry Aerial Torpedo at the Cradle of Aviation Museum."

11. "Radioplane RP-5A Target Drone," *Western Museum of Flight*, accessed February 27, 2015, http://www.wmof.com/rp5a.htm.

12. "Radioplane RP-5A Target Drone."

13. "Radioplane RP-5A Target Drone."

14. "Radioplane RP-5A Target Drone."

15. Zaloga, *Unmanned Aerial Vehicles*, 8.

16. "TDR Assault Drone," *The Pacific War Online Encyclopedia*, accessed August 27, 2014, http://pwencycl.kgbudge.com/T/d/TDR_Assault_Drone.htm; Laurence R. Newcome, *Unmanned Aviation: A Brief History of Unmanned Aerial Vehicles* (AIAA, 2004), 69.

17. Zaloga, *Unmanned Aerial Vehicles*, 8; "TDR Assault Drone."

18. "TDR Assault Drone."

19. Zaloga, *Unmanned Aerial Vehicles*, 8; Newcome, *Unmanned Aviation*, 69.

20. Newcome, *Unmanned Aviation*, 69.

21. Newcome, *Unmanned Aviation*, 69.

22. Newcome, *Unmanned Aviation*, 69.

23. Newcome, *Unmanned Aviation*, 69.

24. Zaloga, *Unmanned Aerial Vehicles*, 11–12.

25. Zaloga, *Unmanned Aerial Vehicles*, 12.

26. Bill Yenne, *Birds of Prey: Predators, Reapers and America's Newest UAVs in Combat* (North Branch, MN: Specialty Press, 2010), 15.

27. Yenne, *Birds of Prey*, 15.

28. "Nation: The Firebee," *Time*, November 27, 1964, http://content.time.com/time/magazine/article/0,9171,871380,00.html.

29. "Nation: The Firebee."

30. Newcome, *Unmanned Aviation*, 83.

31. Zaloga, *Unmanned Aerial Vehicles*, 12.

32. Zaloga, *Unmanned Aerial Vehicles*, 12.

33. Zaloga, *Unmanned Aerial Vehicles*, 14.

34. Zaloga, *Unmanned Aerial Vehicles*, 14.

35. Richard Whittle, *Predator: The Secret Origins of the Drone Revolution* (New York: Henry Holt and Company, 2014), 22.

36. Zaloga, *Unmanned Aerial Vehicles*, 14–15.

37. Zaloga, *Unmanned Aerial Vehicles*, 26–28.

38. Zaloga, *Unmanned Aerial Vehicles*, 25–26.

39. Peter W. Singer, *Wired for War: The Robotics Revolution and Conflict in the 21st Century* (New York: Penguin Books, 2009), 56.

40. "Weapons: Drones (RVPs)," *Frontline*, accessed August 28, 2014, http://www.pbs.org/wgbh/pages/frontline/gulf/weapons/drones.html.

41. Yenne, *Birds of Prey*, 27.

42. "Weapons: Drones (RVPs)."

43. Yenne, *Birds of Prey*, 27.

44. Whittle, *Predator*, 73.

45. Whittle, *Predator*, 73.

46. Whittle, *Predator*, 71.

47. Whittle, *Predator*, 71.

48. Whittle, *Predator*, 81.

49. "The Dronefather," *The Economist*, November 29, 2012, accessed May 1, 2015, http://www.economist.com/news/technology-quarterly/21567205-abe-karem-created-robotic-plane-transformed-way-modern-warfare; Chris Woods, *Sudden Justice: America's Secret Drone Wars* (New York: Oxford University Press, 2015), 30.

50. John Pike, "General Atomic GNAT-750 Lofty View," FAS, last modified November 27, 1999, http://fas.org/irp/program/collect/gnat-750.htm.

51. Whittle, *Predator*, 85–86; Williams reports the first flight in June 1994: Brian Williams, *Predator: The CIA's Drone War on al-Qaeda* (Washington: Potomac Books, 2013), 20.

52. Whittle, *Predator*, 84; Woods, *Sudden Justice*, 31.

53. "MQ-1 Predator," Air Force Reserve: Aircraft, accessed July 31, 2015, http://afreserve.com/about/aircraft/mq-1-predator.

54. Yenne, *Birds of Prey*, 38.

55. Yenne, *Birds of Prey*, 38.

56. Whittle, *Predator*, 98; although reports of maximum duration vary, see "Predator UAS," *General Atomics Aeronautical*, accessed November 20, 2014, http://www.ga-asi.com/products/aircraft/predator.php; Matt J. Martin and Charles Sasser, *Predator: The Remote-Control Air War over Iraq and Afghanistan* (Minneapolis: Zenith Press, 2010), 18–19.

57. Whittle, *Predator*, 84.

58. Whittle, *Predator*, 84.

59. Whittle, *Predator*, 84–85.

60. Williams, *Predator*, 24; Whittle, *Predator*, 108, 124; David Axe, "Buyer's Remorse: How Much Has the F-22 Really Cost?" *Wired*, December 14, 2011, accessed July 23, 2015, http://www.wired.com/2011/12/f-22-real-cost/.

61. "Attack of the Drones," *The Economist*, September 3, 2009, accessed July 28, 2015, http://www.economist.com/node/14299496; Lynn E. Davis et al., "Armed and Dangerous?" RAND Corporation, http://www.rand.org/pubs/research_reports/RR449.html, 2.

62. Whittle, *Predator*, 101, 103.

63. Whittle, *Predator*, 103.

64. Whittle, *Predator*, 100–3.

65. Whittle, *Predator*, 103–4.

66. Whittle, *Predator*, 102–4.

67. Whittle, *Predator*, 104; Martin and Sasser, *Predator*, 19.

68. Whittle, *Predator*, 104–7.

69. Kenneth Israel, *UAV Annual Report FY 1996*, Defense Airborne Reconnaissance Office, November 6, 1996, declassified.

70. Whittle, *Predator*, 108.

71. Whittle, *Predator*, 107.

72. Whittle, *Predator*, 110.

73. Singer, *Wired for War*, 58.

74. Singer, *Wired for War*, 58.

75. Woods, *Sudden Justice*, 36.

76. Woods, *Sudden Justice*, 5, 153; Whittle, *Predator*, 129–30, 136–37, 141–42. The expression "lasing the target" is used when the laser marks the target, "sparking the target" when the infrared marker is used; see, Martin and Sasser, *Predator*, 19.

77. Williams, *Predator*, 22; Whittle, *Predator*, 147, 149, 154.

78. Whittle, *Predator*, 143–63.

79. Whittle, *Predator*, 154–56, 141–53.

80. Whittle, *Predator*, 151, 154–57.

81. Whittle, *Predator*, 157–61.

82. Whittle, *Predator*, 160–61.

83. Whittle, *Predator*, 162.

84. Whittle, *Predator*, 169.

85. Whittle, *Predator*, 125, 183.

86. Whittle, *Predator*, 194–95.

87. Whittle, *Predator*, 195.

88. Whittle, *Predator*, 205, 201–4.

89. Williams, *Predator*, 25–26; Whittle, *Predator*, 205–9, 224–26.

90. Whittle, *Predator*, 243–44.

91. Whittle, *Predator*, 214–17, 237–38, 243–45, 228–29.

92. United States Air Force, "Designating and Naming Military Aerospace Vehicles," *Air Force Instruction 16-401* (The Air Force Departmental Publishing Office, 2014), 23; Williams, *Predator*, 24.

93. Greg Miller, "CIA Flew Stealth Drones into Pakistan to Monitor Bin Laden House," *Washington Post*, May 17, 2011, accessed February 28, 2015, http://www.washingtonpost.com/world/national-security/cia-flew-stealth-drones-into-pakistan-to-monitor-bin-laden-house/2011/05/13/AF5dW55G_story.html.

94. Miller, "CIA Flew Stealth Drones."

95. Whittle, *Predator*, 252–59.

96. Whittle, *Predator*, 252–59.

97. Whittle, *Predator*, 252–59.

98. "U.S. Kills Al Qaeda Leaders by Remote Control," *Fox News*, November 19, 2001, accessed August 28, 2014, http://www.foxnews.com/story/2001/11/19/us-kills-al-qaeda-leaders-by-remote-control/.

99. "CIA Used Pilotless Drone in Yemen Attack: TV," *Dawn*, November 6, 2002, accessed August 28, 2014, http://www.dawn.com/news/65186/cia-used-pilotless-drone-in-yemen-attack-tv.

100. "Al Qaeda in Yemen," *Stanford*, last modified August 2, 2012, http://web.stanford.edu/group/mappingmilitants/cgi-bin/groups/print_view/23.

101. Brian Whitaker and Duncan Campbell, "CIA Missile Kills Al-Qaida Suspects," *The Guardian*, November 4, 2002, accessed August 14, 2014, http://www.theguardian.com/world/2002/nov/05/alqaida.terrorism.

102. "U.S. Missile Strike Kills Al Qaeda Chief," *CNN*, November 5, 2002, accessed August 14, 2014, http://edition.cnn.com/2002/WORLD/meast/11/05/yemen.blast/.

103. Jeremy Scahill, "The Dangerous US Game in Yemen," *The Nation*, March 30, 2011, accessed November 19, 2014, http://www.thenation.com/print/article/159578/dangerous-us-game-yemen.

104. Jane Mayer, "The Predator War: What Are the Risks of the C.I.A.'s Covert Drone Program?" *New Yorker*, October 26, 2009, accessed January 15, 2015, http://www.newyorker.com/magazine/2009/10/26/the-predator-war.

105. Joby Warrick and Peter Finn, "Amid Outrage over Civilian Deaths in Pakistan, CIA Turns to Smaller Missiles," *Washington Post*, April 26, 2010, accessed February 28, 2015, http://www.washingtonpost.com/wp-dyn/content/article/2010/04/25/AR2010042503114.html.

106. Warrick and Finn, "Amid Outrage over Civilian Deaths."

107. Williams, *Predator*, 70; Spencer Ackerman, "Air Force Is Through with Predator Drones," *Wired*, December 14, 2010, accessed August 29, 2014, http://www.wired.com/2010/12/air-force-is-through-with-predator-drones/; John Kaag and Sarah Kreps, *Drone Warfare* (Cambridge: Polity Press, 2014), 24.

108. Andrew Tarantola, "The Terrifying Reaper That Shoots Hellfire from 50,000 Feet," *Gizmodo*, September 7, 2012, accessed August 29, 2014, http://gizmodo.com/5941047/the-terrifying-reaper-that-shoots-hellfire-from-50000-feet.

109. Some sources state that it could carry as many as fourteen Hellfire missiles (Tarantola, "The Terrifying Reaper That Shoots Hellfire from 50,000 Feet").

110. "MQ-9 Reaper," *U.S. Air Force*, August 18, 2010, accessed August 27, 2014, http://www.af.mil/AboutUs/FactSheets/Display/tabid/224/Article/104470/mq-9-reaper.aspx.

111. "MQ-1B Predator," *U.S. Air Force*, July 20, 2010, accessed August 29, 2014, http://www.af.mil/AboutUs/FactSheets/Display/tabid/224/Article/104469/mq-1b-predator.aspx.

112. Josh Levs, "CNN Explains: U.S. Drones," *CNN*, February 8, 2013, accessed August 30, 2014, http://www.cnn.com/2013/02/07/politics/drones-cnn-explains/.

113. Tarantola, "The Terrifying Reaper That Shoots Hellfire from 50,000 Feet."

114. Stephen Trimble, "Sierra Nevada Fields ARGUS-IS Upgrade to Gorgon Stare Pod," *Flightglobal*, July 2, 2014, http://www.flightglobal.com/news/articles/sierra-nevada-fields-argus-is-upgrade-to-gorgon-stare-400978/.

115. Trimble, "Sierra Nevada Fields ARGUS-IS Upgrade."

116. Trimble, "Sierra Nevada Fields ARGUS-IS Upgrade."

117. Everstine, "Report Details Air Force Plans for Future Drones."

118. Kate Brannen, "U.S. Options Limited by Lack of Drones over Syria," *Foreign Policy*, October 7, 2014, accessed March 21, 2015, http://foreignpolicy.com/2014/10/

07/u-s-options-limited-by-lack-of-drones-over-syria/; Jeff Schogol, "Air Force Increases Combat Air Patrols for Reaper Pilots," *Air Force Times*, February 6, 2015, accessed March 21, 2015, http://www.airforcetimes.com/story/military/2015/02/02/more-missions-for-reaper-pilots/22752129/; John Reed, "Predator Drones 'Useless' in Most Wars, Top Air Force General Says," *Foreign Policy*, September 19, 2013, accessed January 19, 2015, http://foreignpolicy.com/2013/09/19/predator-drones-useless-in-most-wars-top-air-force-general-says/.

119. Everstine, "Report Details Air Force Plans."

120. Everstine, "Report Details Air Force Plans."

121. Brannen, "U.S. Options Limited by Lack of Drones"; Schogol, "Air Force Increases Combat Air Patrols."

122. Schogol, "Air Force Increases Combat Air Patrols."

123. Kate Brannen, "Air Force's Lack of Drone Pilots Reaching 'Crisis' Levels," *Foreign Policy*, January 15, 2015, accessed July 28, 2015, http://foreignpolicy.com/2015/01/15/air-forces-lack-of-drone-pilots-reaching-crisis-levels/.

124. "Drone Wars: The Constitutional and Counterterrorism Implications of Targeted Killing: Hearings before the Senate Judiciary Committee's Subcommittee on the Constitution, Civil Rights and Human Rights," 113th Congress, First Session (Prepared Statement of Martha McSally), 2, April 23, 2013, accessed July 23, 2015, http://www.judiciary.senate.gov/imo/media/doc/04-23-13McSallyTest imony.pdf.

125. Luis Martinez, "Air Force Moves to Ease Drone Pilot Shortfall and Heavy Workload," *ABC News*, January 15, 2015, accessed January 19, 2015, http://abcnews.go.com/Politics/air-force-moves-ease-drone-pilot-shortfall-heavy/story?id=282584 52; see also Brannen, "Air Force's Lack of Drone Pilots."

126. Martinez, "Air Force Moves to Ease Drone Pilot Shortfall."

127. Martinez, "Air Force Moves to Ease Drone Pilot Shortfall."

128. Maggie Ybarra, "Drone Pilots Stressed by Long Work Hours Fighting Mideast Terrorists, Air Force Says," *Washington Times*, January 15, 2015, accessed January 19, 2015, http://www.washingtontimes.com/news/2015/jan/15/drone-pilots-stressed-long-work-hours-fighting-mid/.

129. "Air Force Drone Crews Got So Demoralized That They Booed Their Commander," *War Is Boring*, September 29, 2014, accessed July 28, 2015, https://medium.com/war-is-boring/air-force-drone-crews-got-so-demoralized-that-they-booed-their-commander-cfd455fea40f.

130. Ybarra, "Drone Pilots Stressed by Long Work Hours Fighting Mideast Terrorists."

131. Brannen, "Air Force's Lack of Drone Pilots Reaching 'Crisis' Levels."

132. Brannen, "Air Force's Lack of Drone Pilots Reaching 'Crisis' Levels."

133. Ybarra, "Drone Pilots Stressed by Long Work Hours Fighting Mideast Terrorists."

134. Kaag and Kreps, *Drone Warfare*, 24.

135. Mark Weiner, "MQ-9 Reaper Drones among Most Accident-Prone in Air Force," *Syracuse*, November 12, 2013, accessed August 29, 2014, http://www.syracuse.com/news/index.ssf/2013/11/mq-9_reaper_drones_among_most_accident-prone_in_air_force.html.

136. Brendan McGarry, "Drones Most Accident-Prone U.S. Air Force Craft: BGOV Barometer," *Bloomberg*, June 18, 2012, accessed August 29, 2014, http://www

.bloomberg.com/news/2012-06-18/drones-most-accident-prone-u-s-air-force-craft-bgov-barometer.html.

137. Craig Whitlock, "When Drones Fall from the Sky—Part One: War Zones," *Washington Post*, June 20, 2014, accessed October 24, 2014, http://www.washington post.com/sf/investigative/2014/06/20/when-drones-fall-from-the-sky/.

138. Whitlock, "When Drones Fall from the Sky."

139. Whitlock, "When Drones Fall from the Sky"; "Military Drone Crashes Near Pennsylvania Elementary School," *RT*, April 5, 2014, accessed October 24, 2014, http://rt.com/usa/military-drone-crashes-pa-school-501/.

140. Reed, "Predator Drones 'Useless.'"

141. Reed, "Predator Drones 'Useless.'"

142. Reed, "Predator Drones 'Useless.'"

143. Brian Glyn Williams, "Death from the Skies: An Overview of the CIA's Drone Campaign in Pakistan—Part One," *Terrorism Monitor* 7 (2009): 8–10; Greg Miller, "Yemeni Victims of U.S. Military Drone Strike Get More than $1 Million in Compensation," *Washington Post*, August 18, 2014, accessed August 30, 2014, http://www.washingtonpost.com/world/national-security/yemeni-victims-of-us-military-drone-strike-get-more-than-1million-in-compensation/2014/08/18/670926f0-26e4-11e4-8593-da634b334390_story.html; 1st Lt. Tiffany Payette, "Predator Provides Close-Air Support to Embattled Marines in Iraq," *U.S. Air Force*, June 20, 2005, accessed August 30, 2014, http://www.af.mil/News/ArticleDisplay/tabid/223/Article/134151/predator-provides-close-air-support-to-embattled-marines-in-iraq.aspx.

144. "International Security Data Site," *International Security*, accessed April 29, 2015, http://securitydata.newamerica.net/.

145. "Pakistan Strikes," The Long War Journal, accessed April 25, 2015, http://www.longwarjournal.org/pakistan-strikes/.

146. "Covert Drone War," The Bureau of Investigative Journalism, accessed April 25, 2015, https://www.thebureauinvestigates.com/category/projects/drones/.

147. "Targeted Killing Database," Center for the Study of Targeted Killing, accessed April 25, 2015, http://targetedkilling.org/.

148. C. Christine Fair, "Drone Wars," *Foreign Policy*, May 28, 2010, accessed August 31, 2014, http://www.foreignpolicy.com/articles/2010/05/28/drone_wars.

149. Farhat Taj, "Drone Attacks: Challenging Some Fabrications," *Daily Times*, January 2, 2010, accessed November 22, 2014, http://archives.dailytimes.com.pk/editorial/02-Jan-2010/analysis-drone-attacks-challenging-some-fabrications-farhat-taj.

150. Fair, "Drone Wars."

151. Kelly McEvers, "Yemen Airstrikes Punish Militants, and Civilians," NPR, July 6, 2012, accessed March 15, 2015, http://www.npr.org/2012/07/06/156367047/yemen-airstrikes-punish-militants-and-civilians; Robert Booth and Ian Black, "Wiki-Leaks Cables: Yemen offered US 'Open Door' to Attack al-Qaida on Its Soil," December 3, 2010, http://www.theguardian.com/world/2010/dec/03/wikileaks-yemen-us-attack-al-qaida.

152. "Covert US Strikes in Pakistan, Yemen and Somalia—Our Methodology," *The Bureau of Investigative Journalism*, last modified August 10, 2011, accessed July 28, 2015, http://www.thebureauinvestigates.com/2011/08/10/pakistan-drone-strikes-the-methodology2/.

153. "Covert US Strikes in Pakistan, Yemen and Somalia—Our Methodology," *Bureau of Investigative Journalism*, August 10, 2011, accessed July 28, 2015, https://www.thebureauinvestigates.com/2011/08/10/pakistan-drone-strikes-the-methodology2/.

154. When classifying the fatalities from our primary source, CSTK always uses low-end estimates of suspected militants killed and high-end estimates of civilians.

155. "Covert US Strikes in Pakistan, Yemen and Somalia—Our Methodology."

156. Protocol Additional to the Geneva Conventions of 12 August 1949, and relating to the Protection of Victims of International Armed Conflicts (Protocol I), 8 June 1977, Article 77.2., accessed July 5, 2015, https://www.icrc.org/applic/ihl/ihl.nsf/Article.xsp?action = openDocument&documentId = 8F7D6B2DEE119FBAC12563CD0051E0A2; and Protocol Additional to the Geneva Conventions of 12 August 1949, and relating to the Protection of Victims of Non-International Armed Conflicts (Protocol II), 8 June 1977, Article 4.3.c., accessed July 5, 2015, https://www.icrc.org/applic/ihl/ihl.nsf/Article.xsp?action = openDocument&documentId = F9CBD575D47CA6C8C12563CD0051E783.

157. International Human Rights and Conflict Resolution Clinic and Global Justice Clinic, *Living Under Drones: Death, Injury and Trauma to Civilians from US Drone Practices in Pakistan* (New York and Palo Alto: NYU School of Law and Stanford Law School, 2012), 53, accessed July 31, 2015, http://chrgj.org/wp-content/uploads/2012/10/Living-Under-Drones.pdf.

158. Carlotta Gall and Ismail Khan, "American Strike in January Missed Al Qaeda's No. 2 by a Few Hours," *New York Times*, November 10, 2006, accessed August 31, 2014, http://www.nytimes.com/2006/11/10/world/asia/10pakistan.html?ref = abufarajall ibbi&pagewanted = all&_r = 0; "Pakistan School Raid Sparks Anger," BBC, October 30, 2006, http://news.bbc.co.uk/2/hi/south_asia/6099946.stm.

159. Gall and Khan, "American Strike in January Missed Al Qaeda's No. 2 by a Few Hours"; "Tehreek Nifaz-e-Shariat Mohammadi," Mapping Militant Organizations, August 25, 2012, accessed August 2, 2015, http://web.stanford.edu/group/mappingmilitants/cgi-bin/groups/view/411#note14; Bill Roggio, "Aftermath of the Bajaur Airstrike," The Long War Journal, October 31, 2006, http://www.longwarjournal.org/archives/2006/10/aftermath_of_the_baj.php.

160. Rahimullah Yusufzai, "80 Die in Air Attack on Bajaur Seminary," *The News International*, October 31, 2006, accessed August 31, 2014, https://archive.today/Gdzzj#selection-767.0-766.1.

161. Gall and Khan, "American Strike in January Missed Al Qaeda's No. 2."

162. Gall and Khan, "American Strike in January Missed Al Qaeda's No. 2."

163. Anwarullah Khan, "82 Die as Missiles Rain on Bajaur: Pakistan Owns up to Strike; Locals Blame US Drones," *Dawn*, October 31, 2006, accessed June 2, 2015, http://www.dawn.com/news/216918/82-die-as-missiles-rain-on-bajaur-pakistan-owns-up-to-strike-locals-blame-us-drones.

164. Gall and Khan, "American Strike in January Missed Al Qaeda's No. 2."

165. Yusufzai, "80 Die in Air Attack on Bajaur Seminary."

166. Yusufzai, "80 Die in Air Attack on Bajaur Seminary."

167. Yusufzai, "80 Die in Air Attack on Bajaur Seminary."

168. "NBC: On-Scene at Blasted Pakistan Madrassa," *NBC News*, October 31, 2006, http://www.nbcnews.com/id/15486181/ns/world_news-south_and_central_asia/t/nbc-on-scene-blasted-pakistan-madrassa/.

169. Jemima Khan, "Pervez Musharraf: 'If You Are Weak, Anyone Can Come and Kick You,'" *New Statesman*, June 13, 2012, http://www.newstatesman.com/politics/politics/2012/06/pervez-musharraf-if-weak-anyone-kick-you.

170. Chris Woods, "Leaked Pakistani Report Confirms High Civilian Death Toll in CIA Drone Strikes," *The Bureau of Investigative Journalism*, July 23, 2013, http://www.thebureauinvestigates.com/2013/07/22/exclusive-leaked-pakistani-report-confirms-high-civilian-death-toll-in-cia-drone-strikes/.

171. Woods, "Leaked Pakistani Report."

172. Yousaf Ali, "'Most Bajaur Victims Were Under 20,'" *The News International*, November 5, 2006, accessed August 31, 2014, http://www.thenews.com.pk/Todays PrintDetail.aspx?ID = 4043&Cat = 13&dt = 11/5/2006.

173. Ali, "Most Bajaur Victims Were Under 20"; the number thirty is based on the article's summary by age, although the list of names only shows twenty-nine under fifteen years of age.

174. TBIJ, it should be noted, does also report possible and nondrone strikes separately.

175. Bill Roggio, "Senior Al-Qaeda and Taliban Leaders Killed in US Airstrikes in Pakistan, 2004–2015," The Long War Journal, last modified February 27, 2015, http://www.longwarjournal.org/pakistan-strikes-hvts; "Drone Wars Pakistan: Leaders Killed," *International Security*, accessed March 21, 2015, http://securitydata.new america.net/drones/pakistan/leaders-killed.html; "Yemen Leaders Killed," *International Security*, accessed March 22, 2015, http://securitydata.newamerica.net/drones/leaders-killed.html?country = Yemen.

176. Mark Osiel, *The End of Reciprocity* (Cambridge: Cambridge University Press, 2009), 143; Mary Kaldor, *New and Old Wars* (Stanford: Stanford University Press, 2001), 8.

177. Kristine Eck and Lisa Hultman, "One-Sided Violence against Civilians in War: Insights from New Fatality Data," *Journal of Peace Research* 44, no. 2 (2007): 241; and Bethany Lacina and Nils Gleditsch, "Monitoring Trends in Global Combat: A New Dataset of Battle Deaths," *European Journal of Population* 21, no. 2–3 (2005): 145–65.

178. This is not, however, an assessment (of micro-proportionality) that must be done on a case-by-case basis and in light of the anticipated military advantages of specific operations.

179. U.S. Joint Chiefs of Staff, *Joint Targeting*, Joint Publication 3-60, Washington, DC: U.S. Joint Chiefs of Staff, April 13, 2007, https://www.aclu.org/files/dronefoia/dod/drone_dod_jp3_60.pdf.

180. Siobhan Gorman, Adam Entous, and Julian E. Barnes, "U.S. to Shift Drone Command," *Wall Street Journal*, March 20, 2013, accessed November 21, 2014, http://online.wsj.com/articles/SB10001424127887324103504578372703357207828.

181. John T. Bennett, "White House Quietly Shifts Armed Drone Program from CIA to DoD," *Defense News*, May 24, 2013, accessed November 21, 2014, http://www.defensenews.com/article/20130524/DEFREG02/305240010/White-House-Quietly-Shifts-Armed-Drone-Program-from-CIA-DoD.

182. Eric Schmitt, "Congress Restricts Drones Program Shift," *New York Times*, January 16, 2014, accessed November 21, 2014, http://www.nytimes.com/2014/01/17/us/politics/congress-restricts-drones-program-shift.html?_r = 0.

183. Jim Acosta, "Obama to Make New Push to Shift Control of Drones from CIA to Pentagon," *CNN Politics*, April 27, 2015, http://www.cnn.com/2015/04/27/politics/drones-cia-pentagon-white-house/.

184. Micah Zenko and Emma Welch, "Where the Drones Are," *Foreign Policy*, May 29, 2012, accessed August 30, 2014, http://www.foreignpolicy.com/articles/2012/05/29/where_the_drones_are.

185. Bill Roggio, "Abu Sayyaf Operative Thought Killed in US Drone Strike Spotted in Philippines," *Threat Matrix*, June 22, 2014, http://www.longwarjournal.org/archives/2014/06/abu_sayyaf_operative_thought_k.php; Akbar Ahmed and Frankie Martin, "Deadly Drone Strike on Muslims in the Southern Philippines," *Brookings*, March 5, 2012, accessed August 30, 2014, http://www.brookings.edu/research/opinions/2012/03/05-drones-philippines-ahmed.

186. Williams, "Death from the Skies," 8–10.

187. Chris Woods, "CIA's Pakistan Drone Strikes Carried out by Regular US Air Force Personnel," *The Guardian*, April 14, 2014, accessed August 30, 2014, http://www.theguardian.com/world/2014/apr/14/cia-drones-pakistan-us-air-force-documentary.

188. Woods, "CIA's Pakistan Drone Strikes."

189. Woods, "CIA's Pakistan Drone Strikes."

190. Ariel Zirulnick, "Obama Admits 'Worst-Kept Secret': US Flies Drones over Pakistan," *The Christian Science Monitor*, January 31, 2012, accessed August 30, 2014, http://www.csmonitor.com/World/Security-Watch/terrorism-security/2012/0131/Obama-admits-worst-kept-secret-US-flies-drones-over-Pakistan.

191. Sebastian Abbot, "UN Expert Urges US to Reveal Civilian Drone Deaths," *Associated Press*, October 18, 2013, accessed August 30, 2014, http://bigstory.ap.org/article/un-calls-us-reveal-civilian-drone-casualties.

192. Field studies, such as Amnesty International's "'Will I Be Next?': US Drone Strikes in Pakistan" may also provide important insights into casualties resulting from drone strikes, but usually deal only with a small number of cases in a single country, and are often factored into the numbers reported by the databases. See Amnesty International, "'Will I Be Next?': US Drone Strikes in Pakistan," Amnesty International Publications, 2013, 18, accessed February 19, 2015, http://www.amnestyusa.org/sites/default/files/asa330132013en.pdf.

193. Tarantola, "The Terrifying Reaper That Shoots Hellfire from 50,000 Feet."

194. "Combined Forces Air Component Commander 2007–2012 Airpower Statistics," AFCENT Public Affairs, December 31, 2012, http://blogs.defensenews.com/saxotech-access/pdfs/dn-RPA-800.

195. "Obama Announces Afghanistan Troop Withdrawal Plan," *CNN*, June 23, 2011, accessed November 21, 2014, http://www.cnn.com/2011/POLITICS/06/22/afghanistan.troops.drawdown/.

196. "U.S. Air Force Stops Reporting Data on Afghan Drone Strikes," Reuters, March 10, 2013, accessed November 21, 2014, http://www.reuters.com/article/2013/03/10/us-usa-afghanistan-drones-idUSBRE92903520130310.

197. "U.S. Air Force Stops Reporting Data on Afghan Drone Strikes."

198. Rand Paul, "Sen. Rand Paul: My Filibuster Was Just the Beginning," *Washington Post*, March 8, 2013, accessed September 13, 2014, http://www.washingtonpost .com/opinions/sen-rand-paul-my-filibuster-was-just-the-beginning/2013/03/08/63 52d8a8-881b-11e2-9d71-f0feafdd1394_story.html.

199. Alice K. Ross, "Don't Ask Who's Being Killed by Drones in Afghanistan," *Vice News*, July 24, 2014, accessed November 21, 2014, https://news.vice.com/article/ dont-ask-whos-being-killed-by-drones-in-afghanistan.

200. Ross, "Don't Ask Who's Being Killed by Drones in Afghanistan."

201. Ross, "Don't Ask Who's Being Killed by Drones in Afghanistan."

202. Ross, "Don't Ask Who's Being Killed by Drones in Afghanistan."

203. Ross, "Don't Ask Who's Being Killed by Drones in Afghanistan."

204. Julian E. Barnes and Siobhan Gorman, "U.S. Military Pushes for More Disclosure on Drone Strikes," *Wall Street Journal*, May 22, 2014, accessed March 21, 2015, http://www.wsj.com/articles/SB1000142405270230374990457957844310441 9368.

205. Barnes and Gorman, "U.S. Military Pushes for More Disclosure on Drone Strikes."

206. Barnes and Gorman, "U.S. Military Pushes for More Disclosure on Drone Strikes."

207. David Rohde and Mohammed Khan, "Ex-Fighter for Taliban Dies in Strike in Pakistan," *New York Times*, June 19, 2004, accessed December 29, 2014, http:// www.nytimes.com/2004/06/19/international/asia/19STAN.html; Mark Mazzetti, "A Secret Deal on Drones, Sealed in Blood," *New York Times*, April 6, 2013, accessed December 29, 2014, http://www.nytimes.com/2013/04/07/world/asia/origins-of-cias -not-so-secret-drone-war-in-pakistan.html?pagewanted=all&_r=1.

208. Rohde and Khan, "Ex-Fighter for Taliban Dies in Strike in Pakistan."

209. "Get the Data: Drone Wars," *The Bureau of Investigative Journalism*, accessed March 16, 2015, http://www.thebureauinvestigates.com/category/projects/drones/ drones-graphs/.

210. Bill Roggio, "Senior Al Qaeda and Taliban Leaders Killed in US Airstrikes in Pakistan, 2004–Present," The Long War Journal, accessed January 2, 2015, http:// www.longwarjournal.org/pakistan-strikes-hvts.

211. Roggio, "Senior Al Qaeda and Taliban Leaders Killed."

212. Mark Mazzetti, "C.I.A. Drone Is Said to Kill Al Qaeda's No. 2," *New York Times*, August 27, 2011, http://www.nytimes.com/2011/08/28/world/asia/28qaeda .html.

213. Joby Warrick and Greg Miller, "Al-Qaeda's No. 2 Leader Killed in U.S. Airstrike," *Washington Post*, June 5, 2012, https://www.washingtonpost.com/world/ asia_pacific/us-strike-said-to-target-al-qaedas-no-2/2012/06/05/gJQAHTZiFV_story .html.

214. Roggio, "Senior Al Qaeda and Taliban Leaders Killed"; Guy Taylor, "Al Qaeda Terrorists Lurk in Shadows in Afghanistan, Waiting for U.S. Withdraw," *Washington Times*, May 20, 2014, accessed January 3, 2015, http://www.washington times.com/news/2014/may/20/al-qaeda-terrorists-lurk-in-shadows-in-afghanistan/ ?page=all.

215. Roggio, "Senior Al Qaeda and Taliban Leaders Killed."

216. This can be seen by averaging the strike totals on tables 1.2 and 1.3 (which presented data on the U.S. campaign as a whole, including data from Yemen and in some cases Somalia and for manned airstrikes as well), and comparing them to the average drone strike totals reported in table 1.5 (for the Pakistan campaign alone). The strikes presented in table 1.5 comprise more than 77.5 percent (403 of 520 strikes) of the strikes included in tables 1.2 and 1.3.

217. See tables 1.2, 1.3, and 1.5: TBIJ's numbers indicate that 21.68 percent of fatalities in Pakistan were civilians as opposed to 20.48 percent overall; NAF's numbers suggest 9.44 percent civilian casualties in Pakistan and 9.22 percent overall.

218. Average of "unknown" numbers reported by CSTK and NAF (803 and 866).

219. Medea Benjamin, "A Chat with Counterterrorism Chief John Brennan," *Common Dreams*, accessed December 31, 2014, http://www.commondreams.org/views/2012/11/05/chat-counterterrorism-chief-john-brennan.

220. Benjamin, "A Chat with Counterterrorism Chief John Brennan."

221. Benjamin, "A Chat with Counterterrorism Chief John Brennan."

222. Benjamin, "A Chat with Counterterrorism Chief John Brennan."

223. Scott Shane, "C.I.A. Claim of No Civilian Deaths from Drones Is Disputed," *New York Times*, August 11, 2011, accessed January 4, 2015, http://www.nytimes.com/2011/08/12/world/asia/12drones.html?pagewanted=all.

224. Jack Serle and Chris Woods, "Secret US Documents Show Brennan's 'No Civilian Drone Deaths' Claim Was False," *The Bureau of Investigative Journalism*, accessed January 4, 2013, http://www.thebureauinvestigates.com/2013/04/11/secret-us-documents-show-brennans-no-civilian-drone-deaths-claim-was-false/.

225. "Howling at the Moon," *Dawn*, January 9, 2010, accessed December 31, 2014, http://www.dawn.com/news/833723/howling-at-the-moon.

226. Avery Plaw, "Counting the Dead: The Proportionality of Predation," in *Killing by Remote Control*, edited by B. J. Strawser (New York: Oxford University Press, 2013), 152.

227. Daniel Nasaw, "Taliban Suicide Attack Kills CIA Agents at US Outpost in Afghanistan," *The Guardian*, December 31, 2009, accessed January 4, 2015, http://www.theguardian.com/world/2009/dec/31/taliban-cia-agents-killed-afghanistan.

228. Nasaw, "Taliban Suicide Attack Kills CIA Agents."

229. Siobhan Gorman, "Suicide Bombing in Afghanistan Devastates Critical Hub for CIA Activities," *Wall Street Journal*, January 1, 2010, accessed January 4, 2015, http://www.wsj.com/articles/SB126225941186711671.

230. Nasaw, "Taliban Suicide Attack Kills CIA Agents."

231. Joby Warrick, "U.S. Missile Strikes in Pakistan Kill Taliban Militants," *Washington Post*, January 7, 2010, accessed January 5, 2015, http://www.washingtonpost.com/wp-dyn/content/article/2010/01/06/AR2010010604597.html.

232. Jane Perlez, "Questions of Motives in Bombing in Pakistan," *New York Times*, May 13, 2011, accessed January 5, 2015, http://www.nytimes.com/2011/05/14/world/asia/14bomb.html?_r=0 .

233. Perlez, "Questions of Motives in Bombing in Pakistan."

234. "Pakistan Army Rejects US Findings on Border Attack," *The Guardian*, December 23, 2011, accessed January 4, 2015, http://www.theguardian.com/world/2011/dec/23/pakistan-army-rejects-us-findings.

235. "Pakistan Army Rejects US Findings on Border Attack."

236. "Pakistan Army Rejects US Findings on Border Attack."

237. Eric Schmitt, "Clinton's 'Sorry' to Pakistan Ends Barrier to NATO," *New York Times*, July 3, 2012, accessed January 4, 2015, http://www.nytimes.com/2012/07/04/world/asia/pakistan-opens-afghan-routes-to-nato-after-us-apology.html?pagewanted = all.

238. Saeed Shah, "Pakistan Orders US to Leave Airbase in Row over Deadly NATO Assault," *The Guardian*, November 27, 2011, accessed January 4, 2015, http://www.theguardian.com/world/2011/nov/27/pakistan-orders-us-leave-shamsi-airbase.

239. "U.S. Fires First Drone since Errant Airstrikes That Killed Two Dozen Pakistani Troops," *NY Daily News*, January 11, 2012, accessed January 4, 2015, http://www.nydailynews.com/news/world/u-s-fires-drone-pakistan-errant-airstrikes-article-1.1004406.

240. LWJ reports fourteen for the year, but the majority of these emanate from a nondrone air strike.

241. Nasarul Minallah, "US Drone Strike Kills Six in North Waziristan: Officials," *Express Tribune*, January 28, 2015, accessed July 28, 2015, http://tribune.com.pk/story/828986/drone-strike-in-north-waziristan-kills-six/.

2

The Debate over Strategy

Are Drones Helping to Defeat al-Qaeda and Associated Forces?

O N THE NIGHT OF August 5, 2009, an American drone targeted Baitullah
Mehsud, the supreme leader of the Pakistani Taliban and at the time
considered the country's number one enemy. Mehsud, a diabetic, was receiving an intravenous treatment for his kidney illness on the roof of his father-
in-law's house in Zanghara, South Waziristan, when the missile struck. The
explosion killed Mehsud, along with bodyguards and family members.[1] Following the incident, there was virtually no popular protest or condemnations
by government officials or in the media.[2] In fact, many Pakistanis celebrated,
with one blogger from Pakistan writing, "If (his death is) true, it would be
good news and shows the value of drone attacks."[3]

By contrast, on September 2, 2012, a drone strike missed its suspected al-
Qaeda target and hit a Toyota truck packed with fourteen people in the
Yemeni city of Radda in al-Bayda province, killing at least twelve civilians,
including a woman, her seven-year-old daughter, and a twelve-year-old boy.[4]
Following the attack, the two survivors and relatives of six victims expressed
willingness to support or even fight alongside al-Qaeda in the Arabian Peninsula (AQAP). "Our entire village is angry at the government and the Americans," said Sultan Ahmed Mohammed, who was riding on the hood of the
truck when the missiles struck. "If the Americans are responsible, I would
have no choice but to sympathize with al-Qaeda because al-Qaeda is fighting
America."[5] These two cases get at the heart of the drone debate over strategy:
On balance, do drone strikes outside conventional armed conflict hurt or
help the United States' goal of disrupting, dismantling, and defeating al-
Qaeda?

This chapter covers the debate over whether targeted killing operations are strategically wise. We begin by discussing the positive strategic dimensions of the U.S. drone campaigns, such as terrorist leadership decapitation, the neutralization of threats while in the operational phase, and the provocation of internal divisions in terrorist organizations by creating a sense of insecurity among militants. We then address the negative consequences of drone strikes, including increased sympathy and recruitment for terrorist organizations. The chapter culminates with a case study of U.S. drone operations in Yemen. This final section discusses how Yemen's government has wavered between prohibiting and welcoming U.S. drone operations in its territory, and also why these strikes may be especially inclined to generate domestic and international political opposition to the U.S. government. It also looks at the tactical successes of the drone campaign in Yemen as well as the potential for increased terrorist recruitment. In particular, it reviews the debate between Yemen scholars Gregory Johnsen, author of *The Last Refuge: Yemen, al-Qaeda, and America's War in Arabia* (2014), and Christopher Swift, a Fellow at the University of Virginia's Center for National Security Law, over whether drone strikes are leading to the growth of AQAP.

I. Tactics and Strategy

The counterterrorism strategy outlined by the U.S. government identifies a number of strategic goals, which include disrupting, degrading, and ultimately defeating al-Qaeda, but also efforts to deny safe havens and building strategic relationships and counterterrorism capabilities with other countries and local communities.[6] In practice, one part of the strategy puts emphasis on violent measures—aimed at eliminating targets—while the other part encourages a nonviolent approach (like countering al-Qaeda ideology). Throughout this chapter, the arguments tend to be split between these two perspectives. In the pro-drone discourse, advocates tend to emphasize the aggressive component of the strategy, measuring success by the number of enemies killed. Drone critics, however, tend to take a broader perspective, arguing that pursuing an overly aggressive policy ultimately strengthens the enemy while also weakening the host nation's ability to counter them.

The difficulty here is trying to find a balance between near- and long-term considerations, a marriage of tactics and strategy. But before exploring this debate, it will be helpful to clarify this distinction between tactics and strategies. Broadly stated, strategies are based on a longer view into the future, while tactics take a short-term perspective focusing on how to achieve immediate results as part of an overall strategy. "Tactics," as military theorist Carl von Clausewitz put it, "is the art of using troops in battle; strategy is the art of using battles to win the war."[7] Viewed this way, the employment of drones to monitor or eliminate targets on the battlefield is a tactical concern. The key problem is that many accuse drone advocates of substituting tactics for strategy. This concern is highlighted in the following statement by Audrey Kurth Cronin, professor of Public Policy at George Mason University and author of *How Terrorism Ends* (2011): "The problem for Washington today is that its drone program has taken on a life of its own, to the point where tactics are driving strategy rather than the other way around."[8]

In the drone campaigns, there are two importantly distinct tactics of drone targeting outside of conventional battlefields. The first is often called a "personality strike." Here, drones target those whose identities have been firmly established through intelligence, including visual surveillance and electronic and human intelligence. In other words, targets are on a predetermined kill list. These strikes usually occur after long and painstaking surveillance with the parameters of action formulated in advance. In some instances, however, drones away from conventional theaters of armed conflict employ a second tactic, which sits uncomfortably between standard combat and the precision targeting of individual terrorists—that is, "signature strikes." In these cases, intelligence officers and drone operators target individuals based on their patterns of behavior.[9] Here drone attacks target "groups of men who bear certain signatures, or defining characteristics associated with terrorist activity, but whose identities aren't known."[10] These "defining characteristics" have never been made public, but reports suggest that signature strikes can, for example, allow drone operators to strike "convoys of vehicles that bear the characteristics of Qaeda or Taliban leaders on the run."[11] A more detailed examination of signature strikes is provided in the case study in chapter 3.

Drones are not the only available means to conduct counterterrorist strikes, but they are arguably the most preferred choice. According to Micah Zenko, after 9/11 "over 95 percent of all nonbattlefield targeted killings have been conducted by drones—the remaining attacks were JSOC raids and AC-130 gunships and offshore sea or air-launched cruise missiles."[12] Sarah Kreps, a former U.S. Air Force acquisitions officer and now an associate professor at Cornell University, provided an even more specific statistic in April 2014: "Of the estimated 465 non-battlefield targeted killings undertaken by the United States since November 2002, approximately 98 percent were carried out by drones."[13] Moreover, the type of conflict is a key factor in deciding how drones will be used. For instance, drones typically play a supportive role in normal or "conventional" combat zones, like Iraq and Afghanistan. Here they "are frequently 'called in' in the midst of military operations with little supporting intelligence."[14] Outside of conventional armed conflict zones, by contrast, drones are often at the forefront of strategic planning, especially in countries like Pakistan where they operate in permissive airspace (that is, where they are able to operate freely because they are not threatened by antiaircraft fire or a hostile air force).

The United States employs drone strikes in a variety of ways, including for "force protection" or as an alliance tool. For example, drone-launched signature strikes have been used against Pakistani militants trying to cross the Pakistani-Afghan border to protect U.S. and coalition troops operating in Afghanistan;[15] they have also been used to support allied states such as Yemen and Pakistan in their battle against insurgents. Deploying drones as an alliance tool also points to the fact that debates on strategy are not as straightforward as they may at first seem—in some cases the United States may be pursuing additional strategic objectives (such as propping up allies) that it does not care to advertise. Zenko, for instance, has suggested that at times the United States appears to be acting as the "*counterinsurgency* air force of Pakistan, Yemen and Somalia."[16] The criticism is that although U.S. officials have primarily defended drone strikes as a *counterterrorism* tactic—that is, as the only means to reach operational al-Qaeda leaders or people who posed significant and imminent threats to the United States—the fact is that "most of the people who are killed don't have as their objective to strike the U.S. homeland."[17]

Although some critics like Zenko have charged, the United States with engaging in counterinsurgency while claiming to be pursuing a counterterrorism strategy, drawing a line between these strategies can be difficult. As Michael Boyle, an associate professor at La Salle University, has noted, "It has now become commonplace for politicians and military officials alike to mention CT and COIN in the same breath, or to treat them as if they were functionally equivalent."[18] Boyle further pointed out that "the official US government definition now frames counterterrorism in classic 'hearts and minds' counterinsurgency language: 'actions taken directly against terrorist networks and indirectly to influence and render global and regional environments inhospitable to terrorist networks.'"[19] In general, counterinsurgency aims to defeat its enemy by winning over the targeted population. In this case, discussions revolve around designing a strategy to win the "hearts and minds." Counterterrorism, on the other hand, aims to defeat its opponents by killing the enemy and destroying their cadres. The distinction between these is complicated by the fact that the United States aims to achieve both goals. As journalist Fred Kaplan said, "[t]hese are wars against guerrillas, insurgents, terrorists, rogues, fought not only to kill the enemy but to influence the population."[20] Even in the case of al-Qaeda, these lines tend to blur as they are a global terrorist organization that occasionally engages in insurgencies "to bait the US and its allies into exhausting wars of attrition."[21]

Keeping this in mind, U.S. officials tend to emphasize the need to protect U.S. assets and service persons, as well as those of allies, as a means of justifying a broader targeting policy.

II. Counterterror Strikes and Tactical Successes

The overarching goal for the United States is to disrupt operations, degrade the overall strength, and ultimately destroy the command structure of hostile groups. As Christopher Swift put in neatly, "[t]he goal is to achieve a rate of systematic organizational collapse that exceeds the terrorist network's capacity to recover and adapt."[22] The argument in favor of the use of drones to achieve these ends can be grounded on two important claims: that is, (1) drone strikes have been successful at killing senior leaders and foot soldiers; and (2) the use of drones has put pressure on terrorist actors operating on the ground, ultimately hindering their ability to communicate with one another and their capacity to strike. The first point emphasizes the number of terrorists killed while the second point emphasizes the psychological impact of drone strikes. We will consider these two claims in turn.

Leadership Targeting

According to Daniel Byman, professor of security studies at Georgetown University, "The drones have done their job remarkably well: by killing key leaders and denying terrorists sanctuaries in Pakistan, Yemen, and, to a lesser degree, Somalia, drones have devastated al Qaeda and associated anti-American militant groups."[23] His remark captures the general view held by proponents of the use of drones in counterterrorism. The large number of high-value targets from al-Qaeda and the Taliban who have been killed since the implementation of the drone campaigns is frequently emphasized by advocates, including U.S. government officials. For example, at the Woodrow Wilson Center on April 30, 2012, John Brennan identified specific leaders killed in drone attacks when highlighting the effectiveness of Obama's counterterrorism policy:

> In Pakistan, al-Qa'ida's leadership ranks have continued to suffer heavy losses. This includes Ilyas Kashmiri, one of al-Qa'ida's top operational planners, killed a month after bin Laden. It includes Atiyah Abd al-Rahman, killed when he succeeded Ayman al-Zawahiri, al-Qa'ida's deputy leader.[24]

A year later, at the National Defense University, President Obama also emphasized the drones' ability to kill terrorist leaders: "Dozens of highly skilled al-Qaida commanders, trainers, bomb makers and operatives have been taken off the battlefield. Plots have been disrupted."[25] The United States has also carried out a number of strikes against high-level operatives in Somalia, such as Ahmed Godane, the cofounder of al-Shabaab who was killed in a U.S. drone strike on September 1, 2014. U.S. officials described Godane's death as a "major symbolic and operational loss" for the militant group.[26] Somalia analyst Abdi Aynte said that it was difficult to imagine al-Shabaab remaining cohesive without his leadership. According to him, "The death of Ahmed Godane could deal a major blow to al-Shabab and could be the beginning of the end."[27]

Supporters of the drone program also argue that the ongoing drone attacks have been making considerable progress in terms of reaching its strategic goal of defeating al-Qaeda. Former CIA director Michael Hayden has argued that drone strikes in Pakistan made the region "neither safe nor a haven" for al-Qaeda leaders.[28] In a similar vein, former Bush counterterrorism adviser Juan Zarate said, "'Al Qaeda' is on its heels partly because 'so many bigwigs' have been killed by drones."[29] In July 2011, then Secretary of Defense Leon Panetta boldly remarked that the United States was "within reach of strategically defeating Al Qaeda,"[30] and by September of that same year Michael Vickers, the U.S. under secretary for intelligence, estimated that there were about four important al-Qaeda leaders left in Pakistan and ten to twenty leaders overall in Pakistan, Yemen, and Somalia.[31] According to former British intelligence officials, the "removal of operational planners" through drone strikes in FATA and Yemen has significantly reduced the terrorist threat to Britain.[32] In fact, in one message written to bin Laden, Atiyah Abd al-Rahman, al-Qaeda's second in command who was killed by a drone strike in Pakistan in August 2011, complained that al-Qaeda's fighters "were getting killed faster than they could be replaced."[33]

Psychological Impact: Fear and Paranoia

The next argument commonly advanced by drone advocates is that the drone campaigns have been successful in disrupting how militants operate on the ground and their ability to communicate and to train new recruits by provoking fear, paranoia, and distrust among their allies. Even some people opposed to the drone program allow that drone strikes do greatly hamper the efficiency of terrorist cells and militant networks. For example, David Kilcullen (former senior counterinsurgency adviser to General David Petraeus and former secretary of state Condoleezza Rice) and Andrew McDonald Exum (currently deputy assistant secretary of defense for Middle East policy), who have together called for a halt to the drone campaigns, nonetheless do acknowledge their disruptive effects:

The appeal of drone attacks for policy makers is clear. For one thing, their effects are measurable. Military commanders and intelligence officials point out that drone attacks have disrupted terrorist networks in Pakistan, killing key leaders and hampering operations. Drone attacks create a sense of insecurity among militants and constrain their interactions with suspected informers. And, because they kill remotely, drone strikes avoid American casualties.[34]

Moreover, the use of drones not only hampers the ability of militants to operate, it also makes them more fearful and less apt to be out in the open planning attacks. Brian Glyn Williams, professor of Islamic history at the University of Massachusetts and author of *Predators: The CIA's Drone War on Al-Qaeda* (2013), argued that the threat of drone attacks "has forced the Taliban and Al Qaeda to dismantle their training camps in favor of hidden classrooms," and to avoid using cell phones for communication "for fear that they will be tracked by signal and killed as Nek Muhammad was."[35] As Byman summarizes: "Drones have turned al Qaeda's command and training structures into a liability, forcing the group to choose between having no leaders and risking dead leaders."[36] During a phone interview, a senior Pakistani journalist who has extensively covered militancy in FATA told the International Crisis Group that "drones are the only thing militants fear."[37] Similar remarks were made by a Yemini journalist who interviewed commanders in AQAP training camps: "Al-Qaeda hates the drones, they're absolutely terrified of the drones . . . and that is why we need them."[38] David Rohde lends support to this view in the course of his description of his experience of being held hostage by the Taliban:

> I was kidnapped by the Haqqani Network and held captive for seven months, from November 2008 to June 2009, in North and South Waziristan.
> My guards absolutely feared drones.
> They would watch very closely whenever a drone was overhead and tracked how many drones appeared. They thought that when several drones gathered overhead, a strike was about to happen.
> They avoided gathering in groups because they feared drone strikes. We were told to not hang our clothes on the walls to dry because they were afraid that it would appear as if a large number of people were there and this would attract the attention of the drones, which would lead to an attack.[39]

The documents recovered during the raid on bin Laden's Abbottabad compound indicate that bin Laden himself was deeply concerned about U.S. drones, prompting him to offer detailed advice on how operatives could avoid being detected and killed by drones.[40] "They can distinguish between houses frequented by men at a higher rate than usual. Also, the visiting person might be tracked without him knowing," bin Laden wrote in one of the letters cautioning his men of the drones' precision.[41] In a different message written to Atiyah Abd al-Rahman, bin Laden encouraged operatives to flee Pakistan: "I had mentioned in several previous messages . . . the importance of the exit from Waziristan of the brother leaders, especially the ones that have media exposure. I stress this matter to you and that you choose distant locations to which to move them, away from aircraft, photography and bombardment while taking all security precautions."[42]

As illustrated above, the most common claims for the effectiveness of drones are based on the number of militants killed, in particular high-value targets, and their effectiveness at disrupting how militants operate on the ground. In this light, critics accuse drone advocates of stressing tactical gains and leaving little or no room for strategic considerations. After all, counting the dead and disrupting the communication between suspected terrorists are only short-term measurements. Drone critics therefore ask whether such strikes have been empirically proven to be effective over the long term. To address these concerns, the rest of this chapter proceeds as follows: We first summarize the debate on whether the strategy of targeting leaders has effectively reduced the threat their organizations pose in the long run with an emphasis on empirical findings. We then examine arguments over whether drone strikes are highly precise or tend to kill civilians and generate backlash over time.

III. Empirical Evidence on the Long-Term
Effectiveness of Drone Strikes

As leadership decapitation (i.e., killing or capturing leaders of terrorist organizations) plays a central role in the U.S. counterterrorism policy, a number of scholars have systematically assessed its effectiveness, providing mixed results. One side holds that leadership decapitations are ineffective and may in fact generate a negative effect of increasing support for the targeted groups. The other view holds that leadership decapitations are effective at weakening terrorist organizations and decreasing both the intensity and frequency of terrorist attacks. In examining the empirical evidence on decapitation, it is important to note that the studies vary significantly in how data is collected, analyzed, and theoretically supported.

Jenna Jordan, an assistant professor at the Georgia Institute of Technology, has argued on the basis of an extensive study of leadership decapitations around the world that the current decapitation strategy against al-Qaeda is not only "misguided" but will continue to be an "ineffective means of reducing terrorist activity."[43] Examining 298 incidents of leadership targeting from

1945 to 2004, Jordan's study showed that leadership "decapitation does not increase the likelihood of organizational collapse," and that it is more likely to have "counterproductive effects," particularly in religious and separatist organizations, by extending the survival of groups that would have otherwise ended.[44] Based on these findings, Jordan concludes that targeting "groups like al-Qaeda or the Taliban is not likely to result in a group's decline, and could actually increase support for the organizations, which increases its ability to survive targeted attacks."[45] The notion that drone strikes increase sympathy and support for terrorist groups and/or contribute to radicalization will be explored further in section V.

In contrast to the argument that leadership targeting does not work, a number of other quantitative studies suggest that decapitation strategies positively contribute to counterterrorism operations. Bryan C. Price, a lieutenant colonel in the U.S. Army and the current director of the Combating Terrorism Center at the U.S. Military Academy at West Point, argues that leadership decapitation—killing the leader, capturing the leader, or capturing then killing the leader at a later date—significantly increases the mortality rate of terrorist groups.[46] In his study, Price analyzed the effects of leadership decapitation on the mortality rate of 207 terrorist groups, from sixty-five countries, that were active from 1970 to 2008.[47] In a critique of Jordan's assessment, he argues that her standards for evaluating the impact of counterterrorism policies were set "too high," and that a two-year survival test was too crude a measure of when decapitation is having a detrimental impact on a terrorist group.[48] For this reason, Price varied the duration of leadership decapitation's effects to one year and two years after the decapitation occurred, but he also allowed the duration to linger indefinitely.[49] He concluded that regardless of the duration specified, killing or capturing a terrorist leader increased the mortality rate of the group. In other words, terrorist groups that underwent leadership attacks were more likely to end than those that had not experienced decapitation. It is also worth mentioning that both Price and Jordan suggest that the earlier leadership decapitation occurs in a group's life cycle, the greater the effect; and that once a group crosses the twenty-year threshold, decapitation becomes much less effective.[50]

Patrick Johnston, a political scientist at the RAND Corporation, reached conclusions similar to Price's when analyzing 118 decapitation attempts from a sample of ninety counterinsurgency campaigns. In his study, Johnston analyzed cases in which governments attempted—successfully and unsuccessfully—to eliminate key leaders (46 of the 118 attempts [39 percent] resulted in the removal of a top-level insurgent leader).[51] The study makes four conclusions about leadership decapitation: removing key insurgents (1) increases the chances of war termination, (2) raises the probability of government victory, and decreases the (3) intensity and (4) frequency of militant attacks.[52] In addition, Johnston claimed that leadership decapitation is more effective as part of a larger campaign.[53] However, it is important to note, as Jordan pointed out, that Johnston focuses exclusively on insurgencies, which runs the risk of not fully capturing the threat posed by terrorist organizations. As Jordan remarked, "Although some terrorist groups are also insurgents, many insurgent organizations do not employ terrorist tactics."[54] Unlike Jordan and Price's study, Johnston's results also suggest that the impact of removing leaders may be larger in older insurgent groups, which is consistent with his hypothesis that leadership decapitation could "help break the morale of insurgencies that have been engaged in long, often difficult campaigns."[55]

Other research focuses more specifically on the effects of drone strikes in Pakistan on targeted groups, taking the measure of impact as the change in the number and lethality of terrorist attacks carried out by the targeted group. Johnston and Anoop K. Sarbahi, an assistant professor at the University of Minnesota, found a strong correlation between drone strikes and a temporary disruption in a range of measures of terrorist violence in Pakistan.[56] Specifically, the study found that drone strikes were associated with short-term reductions in four key dimensions of terrorist violence, including (1) the rate of terrorist attacks and (2) the number of people killed as a result of terrorist attacks.[57] There was also a correlation between drone strikes and (3) decreases in selective targeting of tribal elders "who are frequently seen by terrorist groups as conniving with the enemy and acting as an impediment to the pursuit of their agenda."[58] The study further revealed that the overall disruption in terrorist violence was not (4) the result of militants leaving unsafe areas and conducting attacks elsewhere in the region.[59] Altogether, Johnston and Sarbahi argued that "drone strikes do affect terrorist activities and claims that drones have aided U.S. counterterrorism efforts in Pakistan should not be summarily dismissed."[60] The study supported the concept of "suppression fire," in which attacks are meant to kill the enemy or keep them pinned down and thus unable to fight.[61] If the strategic objective of drone strikes is to "suppress" enemy forces, then whether or not leadership decapitation can effectively result in "organizational collapse" might not be the crucial factor in strategic planning. In a study along similar lines, David Jaeger and Zahra Siddique at the Institute for the Study of Labor examined drone strikes in relation to the Taliban and al-Qaeda in Afghanistan and Pakistan from January 2007 to December 2010, and found that drone strikes did not appear to impact terrorist violence in Afghanistan but were effective in Pakistan. However, the study suggested that "failed" drone strikes in Pakistan, which miss their intended target, will more likely increase militant violence.[62]

IV. The Precision and Accuracy of Drone Technology

The most widespread use of drones is in Pakistan and, unsurprisingly, the most intense debates regarding civilian casualties tend to be about the drone strikes occurring in that region. The ongoing debate over the number of civilians killed seems to call into question the precision of drones, which has been repeatedly praised by advocates. Arguments for the precision and accuracy of drones can be subdivided into two separate claims: (1) that drones are effective as they succeed in killing terrorists while minimizing civilian casualties, and (2) that in comparison to other options—such as the deployment of ground troops or other weapons of war—drones are the most proportionate. Those opposing the drone campaigns counter these claims by arguing (1) that drones strikes have killed civilians and have negatively impacted civilian populations through more subtle harms; (2) the process by which targets are selected, either in terms of the intelligence guiding the strikes or by how targets are defined, can exacerbate the civilian impact of drone strikes; and (3) that the majority of those targeted are in fact lower-ranked operatives.

U.S. officials have been claiming for several years that the strikes have been very accurate and proportional. On January 30, 2012, President Obama declared: "For the most part, they [i.e., drone strikes] have been very precise, precision strikes against al Qaeda and their affiliates."[63] President Obama reiterated his claim about the precision of drones and their ability to minimize collateral damage at the National Defense University: "By narrowly targeting our action against those who want to kill us, and not the people they hide among, we are choosing the course of action least likely to result in the loss of innocent life."[64] In one case even Pakistani military officials acknowledged that drones have become more precise and discriminating. In March 2011, Pakistani Major General Ghayur Mehmood said, "the number of innocent people being killed is relatively low" and that "most of the targets are hard-core militants."[65]

The defense of the drone program (and its accuracy) by officials has also received support from accomplished scholars and think tanks. C. Christine Fair, for example, has characterized drone strikes as "the product of meticulous planning among lawyers, intelligence officers, and others who scrupulously and independently confirm information about potential enemies, working to establish a rigorous 'pattern of life' to minimize the deaths of innocents."[66] She also argues that the strikes "are usually accomplished with minimal civilian deaths."[67] The 2014 Stimson Center Task Force report on drone policy made a similar point. The report rejected the "erroneous belief" that drones kill a disproportionate number of civilians[68] and insisted that the technology enables "greater precision in targeting than most other common means of warfare."[69]

As indicated, advocates of the drone campaigns also point to the fact that drone strikes are the most proportionate "weapon of choice." Daniel Byman claims that the drone critics "often fail to take into account the fact that the alternatives are either too risky or unrealistic."[70] Byman argues that drones are more discriminate than other types of force and "far less bloody" than the United States asking its allies to hunt down targets on their behalf.[71] In a critical analysis of drone strikes and other military actions by states, Avery Plaw reached a similar conclusion in the case of Pakistan: "All things considered, it [i.e., the use of drone strikes] looks like the proportionate alternative if one is committed to going after dangerous militants operating in the FATA with military force."[72] In Plaw's study, he compares CIA drone strikes in Pakistan to other U.S. military operations in FATA, the Pakistani Army Operations in FATA from 2002 to 2007, Israeli targeted killings from 2000 to 2011, and the estimated world combat average for the 1990s. Of all of these, drone strikes in Pakistan show the lowest proportion of civilian casualties compared to total fatalities. Similar arguments are used to defend the drone campaign in Yemen. According to Clinton Watts, a senior fellow at the Foreign Policy Research Institute and former FBI special agent on a joint terrorism task force, "Drones provide the most effective and least casualty-producing method for engaging AQAP. Any other option that could apply equal military pressure on AQAP would likely inflict far more civilian casualties on the Yemeni population."[73] So a key claim advanced in defense of drones is that of the options available to the United States in advancing this particular campaign, drone strikes are the most proportionate in terms of civilian casualties.

While advocates put great emphasis on the precision of drone strikes, a common objection is that drones are not as precise and discriminate as their enthusiasts claim. After all, they have undeniably killed civilians, and some critics suggest a disproportionately large number of civilians.[74] Jeffrey Addicott, a former senior legal adviser to the U.S. Army Special Forces, told Reuters: "The ratio is getting better [i.e., proportion of civilians killed] but based on my military experience, there's simply no way so few civilians have been killed . . . For one bad guy you kill, you'd expect 1.5 civilian deaths, because no matter how good the technology, killing from that high above, there's always the 'oops' factor."[75] In addition, although drone databases show a very sharp drop in both the absolute and proportional number of civilian casualties in recent years (see chapter 1), critics have made their case by stressing the impact that drones have on local communities beyond civilian death tolls. While the presence of drones has instilled fear among terrorists, disrupting their operations, drones have also spread fear among ordinary civilians, disrupting their normal lives. The 2012 Stanford and New York University study *Living Under Drones* interviewed community members, mental health professionals, and journalists who described "how the constant presence of US overhead drones [i.e., in Pakistan] leads to substantial levels of fear and stress in the civilian communities below."[76] This fear of drones and the significant stress produced by constantly worrying about the next strike has resulted in locals being diagnosed with "anticipatory anxiety," mainly attributable to their belief that "[t]hey could be attacked at any time."[77] Other mental health professionals said that they had seen numerous cases of post-traumatic stress disorder (PTSD) that were also connected to drones.[78] The concern is that the subtle harms caused by drones (property destruction, psychological impact, and social disorder) tend to be overlooked when discussing the civilian impact of drone strikes. It is worth noting that the subtle harms described here are common in all conflict zones and that the Taliban presence in FATA has also caused significant harm to civilians.[79]

The next criticism of the claim of drone accuracy focuses on the process by which targets are selected, and suggests that this can exacerbate the civilian impact of drone strikes. Specifically, this criticism of the precision of drones challenges the reliability of intelligence, either from informants on the ground or the camera on the drone that guides strikes. On the former point concerning the reliability of intelligence, the Stanford and NYU study raised questions about the "technical accuracy" of strikes and its relationship with informants on the ground. After first pointing out that "the accuracy of a drone strike fundamentally hinges on the accuracy of the intelligence on which the targeting is premised," they then charge that such intelligence "has often been questioned."[80] As drone operations tend to rely on local sources for intelligence, the concern here is that these "informants" may actually be providing inaccurate intelligence to satisfy their own objectives. Human rights lawyer Clive Stafford Smith of Reprieve articulated these implications:

Just as with Guantanamo Bay, the CIA is paying bounties to those who will identify "terrorists." Five thousand dollars is an enormous sum for a Waziri informant, translating to perhaps £250,000 in London terms. The informant has a calculation to make: is it safer to place a GPS tag on the car of a truly dangerous terrorist, or to call down death on a Nobody (with the beginnings of a beard), reporting that he is a militant? Too many "militants" are just young men with stubble.[81]

Critics suggest that relying on questionable intelligence in life-and-death decisions may very well lead to executions by drones without direct confirmation of who the targets actually are (i.e., targets who may actually be civilians). Indeed, Imtiaz Gul, a researcher who helped a UN team investigate drone strikes in Pakistan and who runs the Center for Research and Security Studies in Islamabad, said most civilian deaths from drone strikes resulted from bad intelligence.[82] After sending his own researchers into parts of Waziristan between 2008 and 2011, Gul told Voice of America:

> Most of the cases in which innocent people got killed basically resulted from faulty information, but not entirely . . . Nobody really told us, and I would presume a number of people our team spoke to also withheld information because usually people also tend to hide the truth even in such situations.[83]

The overall controversy here is about distinction, and whether the United States gathers enough intelligence to sufficiently distinguish civilians from militants before launching a strike. This problem of distinction is further complicated when considering signature strikes, which have come under intense scrutiny in recent years (and will be discussed in more detail in the case study in chapter 3).

The human-rights group Reprieve has also criticized the accuracy of U.S. intelligence on the grounds that publicly available data indicate that drones have targeted or killed the same high-value target multiple times. Reprieve released a report titled "You Never Die Twice: Multiple Kills in the US Drone Program" in November 2014, revealing that drone strikes in Yemen and Pakistan have killed as many as 1,147 people in failed attempts to kill 41 named individuals.[84] According to the report, 24 men were reported killed or targeted multiple times in Pakistan, resulting in the death of 874 people (including 142 children), while 17 other men were reportedly killed or targeted multiple times in Yemen, which resulted in the death of 273 people.[85] The evidence compiled by Reprieve raised the following question about the accuracy of intelligence guiding the "precise" strikes: "If the US intelligence is so poor that it is repeatedly missing its target, how can it know whether those killed are civilians?"[86]

One controversial aspect of Reprieve's numbers is that they present only high-value targets as legitimate targets, while implying that every other fatality is a civilian. It is also worth mentioning that a large percentage of Reprieve's numbers are not based on cases in which U.S. officials confirmed targeting or killing the same individuals. According to Reprieve, "Military or intelligence officials from the relevant country (Pakistan or Yemen) accounted for 49% of all multiple kills reporting [i.e., 64 out of a total of 130 recorded observations]" while U.S. officials accounted for 26 percent (a total of thirty-four).[87] Taking into account the "source" of the information confirming these deaths is important. Bill Roggio from The Long War Journal has cautioned that reports from Pakistani officials on the deaths of high-value targets should be viewed with great skepticism because, as he put it, "they have a terrible track record."[88] The lack of confirmations of death from U.S. officials in many of the forty-one cases highlighted by Reprieve (and the secrecy of the drone program in general) suggests that it is not entirely clear if the drone program is repeatedly missing its mark. Nonetheless, this data reinforces concerns about "failed" drone strikes (and their counterproductive effects) and the quality of intelligence that underlies them.

Another critique often made against the precision of drones is that most of the attacks in countries such as Pakistan and Yemen have been directed against lower-level operatives and antigovernment insurgents, while only a small percentage of strikes have killed leaders. As Peter Bergen (vice president at New America Foundation) and Megan Braun (JD candidate at Yale Law School and a former Rhodes Scholar) point out in the case of Pakistan, from 2004 to 2012, "49 militant leaders" were killed by drone strikes (accounting for only 2 percent of all drone-related fatalities), while "low-level combatants" represent the majority.[89] This view is consistent with media reports. Reuters published an article in 2010 revealing that CIA drone strikes since the summer of 2008 had "killed around 12 times more low-level fighters than mid-to-high-level al Qaeda and Taliban leaders" based on data provided by U.S. government sources.[90] According to the *Washington Post*, even as the Obama administration escalated the number of drone strikes being carried out, "the number of high-ranking militants being killed as a result has either slipped or barely increased."[91] Furthermore, drone attacks employed against low-level operatives can also fuel the perception that strikes are disproportionate in the number of civilians they kill. It has been suggested at least in the case of Pakistan that there is a marked tendency for Pakistanis to not make distinctions between low-level Taliban and Pakistani civilian casualties, distorting the debate over who is being targeted.[92]

Questions have also been raised about the legitimacy and prudence of the processes by which targets are selected. The *New York Times* published an article in 2012 claiming that the United States "counts all military-age males in a strike zone as combatants . . . unless there is explicit intelligence posthumously proving them innocent."[93] In light of the *New York Times* piece, the Stanford and NYU report stated that "claims that drones have killed hundreds of low-level fighters may well mask the deaths of civilians."[94] It is important to acknowledge that U.S. officials reject the claim that they treat all military-age males as presumed combatants when targeting terrorists. "It's a wild oversimplification that lacks context," an aide to the president said of the *New York Times* article.[95] Nevertheless, there seems to be a fundamental debate over what constitutes a legitimate target, muddling discussions on collateral damage, accuracy, and proportionality.

V. Strategic Costs and Potential Blowback

Many commentators argue that the United States' preoccupation with its tactical success is causing it to lose ground at the strategic level. Bruce Riedel, a former CIA analyst and Obama counterterrorism adviser, noted how reliance on strikes is self-perpetuating, yielding undeniable short-term results but failing to change the underlying strategic situation. "The problem with the drone is it's like your lawn mower," said Riedel. "You've got to mow the lawn all the time. The minute you stop mowing, the grass is going to grow back."[96] Furthermore, the Stimson Center Task Force report concluded that, despite the drone program's tactical gains, al-Qaeda's affiliates "have grown in scope, lethality and influence in the broader area of operations in the Middle East, Africa and South Asia."[97] More to the point, "there is no indication that a US strategy to destroy al-Qaida has curbed the rise of Sunni Islamic extremism, deterred the establishment of Shia Islamic extremist groups or advanced long-term US security interests," added the report.[98] According to Cronin, drone strikes "have not thwarted the group's [i.e., al-Qaeda] ability to replace dead leaders with new ones. Nor have they undermined its propaganda efforts or recruitment."[99] Dennis Blair, the former director of National Intelligence, made a similar argument: "Al-Qaeda officials who are killed by drones will be replaced. The group's structure will survive and it will still be able to inspire, finance and train individuals and teams to kill Americans."[100] In other words, there seems to be a common concern that the drone program is winning tactically but failing strategically.

As mentioned earlier, the U.S. counterterrorism strategy also includes efforts to build the capacity and will of states combating terrorism within their borders in order to "constrict the space available to terrorist networks."[101] However, Boyle and other critics have also argued that drone strikes "have lasting political effects that can weaken existing governments" and "undermine their legitimacy."[102] Boyle stresses that local governments "need to be seen as legitimate by the majority of the population."[103] He fears, however, that drone strikes produce the opposite effect. This concern was articulated eloquently by the Pakistani high commissioner to London, Wajid

Shamsul Hasan, in August 2012: "What has been the whole outcome of these drone attacks is that you have directly or indirectly contributed to destabilising or undermining the democratic government. Because people really make fun of the democratic government—when you pass a resolution against drone attacks in the parliament and nothing happens."[104] The main point is that if the central government is viewed as incapable and illegitimate in the eyes of its citizens, it becomes difficult to drain support for terrorist movements who aim to exploit these weaknesses. As the government loses legitimacy and authority, disaffected citizens are likely to seek change outside of the political system, including by resorting to terrorism, which may in turn reinforce the perception of the government's illegitimacy. Thus, the erosion of state authority may become a vicious circle.

Indeed, drone strikes can create a negative perception far beyond the population of countries in which the strikes occur. Critics also raise concerns that the strikes generate negative perceptions of the United States around the world, which can fuel (1) anti-Americanism and ultimately (2) diminish support for U.S. counterterrorism policies. As Cronin put it, "Whatever the truth is, the United States is losing the war of perceptions, a key part of any counterterrorism campaign."[105] Retired army general Stanley McChrystal, former International Security Assistance Force (ISAF) commander in Afghanistan, seems to agree: "What scares me about drone strikes is how they are perceived around the world," he said during an interview. "The resentment created by American use of unmanned strikes . . . is much greater than the average American appreciates. They are hated on a visceral level, even by people who've never seen one or seen the effects of one." The use of drones, McChrystal says, creates a "perception of American arrogance that says, 'Well we can fly where we want, we can shoot where we want, because we can.'"[106]

The growing hostility generated by drone strikes has arguably fueled anti-Americanism. According to the Stimson Center Task Force report, the perceived violation of sovereignty "sparks bitterness, feelings of nationalism or other forms of identity politics violently hostile to US military operations or Americans" among Pakistani and Yemeni tribesmen.[107] Joshua Foust, writing for the American Security Project, stated: "In Pakistan, opposition to the drone strikes has become an issue of national politics, with an entire political party organized around ending their use. In Yemen, there is a growing body of anecdotal evidence that drone strikes are driving anti-Americanism and opposition to the central government."[108] Nathaniel Fick, then the chief executive officer of the Center for a New American Security, similarly observed: "Drone strikes excite visceral opposition across a broad spectrum of Pakistani opinion. The persistence of these attacks on Pakistani territory offends people's deepest sensibilities, alienates them from their government, and contributes to Pakistan's instability."[109]

The more legitimacy and support the local governments lose, the more terrorist organizations stand to gain. As Jenna Jordan argued, community "support for militant groups targeted by drones could be strengthened if there is a belief that they are indiscriminately killing civilians, violating sovereignty, and not adhering to the rule of law."[110] Popular support can also strengthen terrorist groups in a variety of ways. For example, local support is a powerful recruiting tool, and it also allows terrorists to operate covertly, as local communities are more willing to provide shelter.[111]

So the potential of drone strikes to radicalize the local population and inspire potential recruits is of critical concern. As Kaplan argued, "If the most prominent weapon in this war alienates the people who live under its shadow, in some cases driving them into the arms of the enemy, either for protection or on the principle that the enemy of their enemy is their friend, then it is a lousy weapon."[112] Similarly, Kilcullen testified before Congress in March 2009 that drone strikes arouse "a feeling of anger that coalesces the population around the extremists."[113] In a May 2009 *New York Times* editorial titled "Death from Above, Outrage from Below," Kilcullen and Exum argued that drone strikes stoke "public anger" against a "faceless enemy" that is "blowing up people's houses from the air."[114] As a result of these attacks, they stress that every noncombatant casualty "represents an alienated family, a new desire for revenge, and more recruits for a militant movement that has grown exponentially even as drone strikes have increased."[115] Kilcullen also advances these arguments in his book *The Accidental Guerilla* and in a high-profile report for the Center for New American Security.[116] UN investigations on this issue resulted in similar findings. Ben Emmerson, the UN Special Rapporteur on Counter-Terrorism and Human Rights, conducted a three-day visit to Pakistan in March 2013 and spoke with tribal leaders from North Waziristan who claimed that drone strikes had increased radicalization.[117] In accordance with their ethical code of Pashtunwali, Pashtuns are thought to seek *badal* (revenge) when one of their own is killed by a U.S. drone.[118] Referring to this, tribal leaders told Emmerson that the Pashtunwali code "prescribed revenge for the loss of a life and that this entrenched tribal tradition had given rise to a desire, particularly among young men, to seek revenge for the drone strikes, thus radicalizing a new generation."[119] As Cronin writes, "Drones are killing operatives who aspire to attack the United States today or tomorrow. But they are also increasing the likelihood of attacks over the long term, by embittering locals and cultivating a desire for vengeance."[120] Simply put, the concern is that drone strikes can inadvertently create new adversaries (what Kilcullen calls the accidental guerrilla phenomenon),[121] hindering the United States' goal of defeating their enemy.

A closely related concern is that drone strikes can increase the frequency and intensity of attacks by the very same groups targeted. Advancing this point, Leila Hudson, an associate professor at the University of Arizona and director of the Southwest Initiative for the Study of Middle East Conflicts, and two former graduate students at the same university (Colin Owens and Matt Flannes) argued that in Pakistan "there is a substantive relationship between the increasing number of drone strikes and the increasing number of retaliation attacks."[122] Consistent with this view, Jordan also reports that "while there have been periods of decline in the frequency and lethality of al-Qaeda attacks [from 2001 to 2010], they continue to be operationally functional and lethal, despite attacks on its leadership beginning in 2001."[123] It is worth stressing, however, that this result depends on evaluating the organization as a whole (i.e., AQAP, al-Qaeda core, al-Qaeda in Iraq [AQI], and al-Qaeda in the Islamic Maghreb [AQIM], etc.) and therefore including numbers from al-Qaeda affiliates, most of which did not exist at the time of the 9/11 attacks and some of whom have not been subject to sustained campaigns of drone strikes. Consider the fact that from 2001 to 2011 al-Qaeda as a whole carried out 579 attacks, but 384 of these incidents were carried out by AQIM and AQI[124] (groups that have not been the target of a U.S. "drones-first counterterrorism policy").[125] Meanwhile, during that same time period, AQAP carried out 143 attacks, while al-Qaeda core only carried out 52.[126] Nevertheless, Jordan concludes that targeting al-Qaeda "may embolden some of these [affiliated] groups to increase their level of militancy to achieve greater legitimacy within the extremist community."[127]

Yet evidence for the blowback arguments is far from one-sided. Reports from the tribal areas, for example, suggest a more complicated view of Pakistani reactions to drone strikes. Pashtuns of FATA who have been living in the areas targeted by drones seem to have a greater tolerance for the drone strikes than Pakistanis living in other regions, such as Sindh or Punjab.[128] Farhat Taj, from the northwestern region of Pakistan, conducted in-depth interviews with fifteen students from Waziristan, the region most heavily targeted by CIA drones. The results of Taj's study presented some evidence that the strikes are not as unpopular in FATA as has been widely assumed. "The respondents," Taj writes,

> expressed a strong desire for drones as a means to attack the leadership of local Pashtun Taliban. Half of those who supported drone attacks said that people's daily lives are affected most by the local Taliban and not the Arabs or other al-Qaeda militants who generally mind their own business, or have perhaps

assigned the duty of harassment to the local Taliban. One of the respondents suggested that if only ten people amongst the leadership of the local Taliban were killed, the hierarchy of the organization would collapse like a house of cards.[129]

The *Economist* also interviewed twenty residents of the tribal areas in 2013 and confirmed that many FATA residents are strong proponents of the drones due to their precision and accuracy.[130] They also insisted that the drones do not kill many civilians. "No one dares tell the real picture," said an elder from North Waziristan. "Drone attacks are killing the militants who are killing innocent people."[131] In fact, in December 2009, a coalition of FATA-based political parties and civil organizations opposed to terrorism issued the "Peshawar Declaration," which dealt with the drone attacks in detail:

> The issue of Drone attacks is the most important one. If the people of the war-affected areas are satisfied with any counter-militancy strategy, it is the Drone attacks which they support the most. According to the people of Waziristan, Drones have never killed any civilian. Even some people in Waziristan compare Drones with Ababels (The holy swallows sent by God to avenge Abraham, the intended conqueror of the Khana Kaaba). A component of the Pakistani media, some retired generals, a few journalists/analysts and pro-Taliban political parties never tire in their baseless propaganda against Drone attacks.[132]

Similar to the situation in Pakistan, a number of commentators have argued that local Yeminis support the use of drones.[133] This viewpoint will be discussed in more detail in the case study on Yemen at the end of this chapter.

In response to the argument that drone strikes produce resentment among the local population, which in turn creates more enemies than they kill, Amitai Etzioni, a professor of International Relations at George Washington University, said,

> Such arguments do not take into account the fact that anti-American sentiment in these areas ran high before drone strikes took place and remained so during periods in which strikes were significantly scaled back. Moreover, other developments—such as the release of an anti-Muslim movie trailer by an Egyptian Copt from California or the publication of incendiary cartoons by a Danish newspaper—led to much larger demonstrations. Hence stopping drone strikes—if they are otherwise justified, and especially given that they are a very effective and low-cost way to neutralize terrorist violence on the ground—merely for public relations purposes seems imprudent.[134]

There is also reason to believe that claims of drone strikes having a negative effect on public opinion more generally tend to be overstated. For instance, the *Washington Post* recently published an article indicating that Pakistanis are becoming more tolerant of American drone strikes while anti-Americanism in the region is in decline (for more on this point see chapter 5, section III).[135]

In addition to this, the International Crisis Group asserts that the benefits terrorist organizations gain from ongoing drone attacks in regard to recruitment are at best minimal. To support this view, the organization interviewed a local analyst, who claims that "while anti-drone rhetoric does draw some converts, 'the loss of a Baitullah Mehsud or a Qari Hussain is much more damaging than the recruitment of a few dozen foot soldiers.'"[136] They concluded their assessment by reporting that "the main causes for the spread of militancy in FATA are not drone strikes but domestic factors."[137] A similar argument emerges in the Yemen case study. Even some of the sharpest drone critics have acknowledged the weakness of the evidence of blowback, although they do not necessarily concede the point. For instance, Emmerson admitted his findings on drones radicalizing the FATA population were "largely anecdotal" but nonetheless "supported the conclusion that the strikes were frequently cited as a source of radicalization to violent extremism amongst younger Pashtun males."[138]

Those critical of the drone program also stress that the blowback caused by precision strikes can be avoided if emphasis is placed on alternatives that go beyond the use of military force (like law enforcement, diplomacy, and intelligence cooperation). Cronin has argued that relying on drone strikes also means eliminating the possibility of arresting and interrogating suspects and gathering valuable intelligence on the terrorist groups being targeted.[139] As Cronin remarked, "Drones do not capture hard drives, organizational charts, strategic plans, or secret correspondence, and their tactical effectiveness is entirely dependent on the caliber of human intelligence on the ground."[140] Cronin suggests that a more effective way of defeating al-Qaeda would be to publicly discredit it with a political strategy aimed at dividing its followers.[141]

Other proposed strategies also put more emphasis on law enforcement and intelligence cooperation. For instance, the RAND Corporation published a report in 2008 looking at how terrorist groups between 1968 and 2006 met their demise.[142] Of the 268 terrorist organizations that collapsed during that period, the study shows that the primary factors accounting for their demise were groups deciding to join the political process (43 percent), or local law enforcement agencies arresting or killing key members of the group (40 percent). Military force accounted for the end of terrorist groups in only 7 percent of the cases examined.[143] Based on these findings, the authors suggest that policing and intelligence, rather than military force, should form the backbone of U.S. efforts against al-Qaeda.[144] On the other hand, it may well be argued that policing and politics have not established especially reassuring records in suppressing terrorism and promoting civic life in places like Northwest Pakistan, Yemen, and Somalia, and that these may correspondingly represent the rare types of cases in which the local state and its allies are compelled to resort to military force to preserve their authority and legitimacy.

As this brief overview of debates revolving around the efficacy of drone strikes illustrates, there are forceful arguments on both sides of the question, although perhaps no single knock-down argument. These debates over the tactics and strategy between critics and defenders of drone strikes will likely continue, especially if the United States continues to run its drone program in secrecy. The possibility remains, however, that greater clarity or at least additional insight may be obtained by focusing on particular aspects of the drone campaigns. This chapter ends with a case study of the drone campaign in Yemen, which has served as the subject of many of the debates discussed in this chapter.

Case Study: The Drone War Reaches Yemen

On November 3, 2002, a drone targeted a jeep in Marib province along an isolated highway one hundred miles east of Sana'a, the capital of Yemen. The Predator launched a laser-guided Hellfire missile that struck the target and exploded, leaving only charred remains. American and Yemeni officials claimed that the car's occupants had been six members of al-Qaeda, including Ali Qaed Sunian al-Harithi.[145] The Yemeni government identified the other five as Munir Ahmed Abdullah al-Sauda, Saleh Hussein Ali al-Zono, Aoussan Ahmed al-Tirihi, Adel Nasser al-Sauda, and Kamal Darwish. All were Yemeni citizens, although Darwish also had U.S. citizenship.[146] Arms, traces of explosives, and communications equipment were also found in the destroyed vehicle.[147] Three important aspects of the operation should be emphasized. The strike was (1) coordinated with the Yemeni government; (2) the intended target (al-Harithi) was a prominent al-Qaeda leader; and (3) one of the passengers killed, Kamal Darwish, was an Arab American who grew up near Buffalo and, according to the FBI, had recruited Americans for terrorist training at al-Qaeda camps.[148] Darwish was also the head of an al-Qaeda sleeper cell based in Lackawanna, New York.[149] So not only was the incident the first drone attack outside Afghanistan, it was also the first drone attack to kill a U.S. citizen. Additionally, the success of this operation played an influential role in the decision-making process of using armed drones to kill high-value targets on Pakistani soil.[150]

After the USS *Cole* attack, and learning he was wanted for questioning by U.S. investigators, al-Harithi went into hiding along with his deputy, Mohammed Hamdi al-Ahdal.[151] Before the lethal strike took place, Yemeni officials (responding to a U.S. government request) tried to capture al-Harithi in December 2001.[152] After failed negotiations with local tribesmen, Yemini president Ali Abdullah Saleh sent military units, consisting of tanks, fighter jets, and personnel carriers, to the Marib region of Yemen, where al-Harithi was living with allied tribes, to arrest him. Apparently, President Saleh was hoping that an overwhelming show of military force would convince the villagers to turn al-Harithi over.[153] Not deterred by Yemeni soldiers and bound by the tribal and customary code of law to protect their guest, al-Harithi's tribal allies fought back. Nineteen soldiers were killed, nearly two dozen were injured, and thirty-five more soldiers were captured once the firefight was over. Furthermore, while the Yemini military was trying to negotiate the release of soldiers held captive, al-Harithi managed to sneak out and disappear.[154] In view of this deadly failure, the CIA tried a different approach—that is, using a Predator drone based in the French-garrisoned country of Djibouti as part of Combined Joint Task Force-Horn of Africa.[155] While the CIA tracked down al-Harithi using drone surveillance, the U.S. ambassador in Yemen paid off some local tribesmen to keep track of his movements.[156] When the NSA's Yemen-based Cryptological Support Group tracked down al-Harithi by monitoring his cell phone, they tipped off the CIA, which then sent out a patrolling drone to strike the target.[157]

As al-Harithi built up most of al-Qaeda's infrastructure in Yemen it was virtually destroyed following his death, and it soon became apparent that al-Qaeda in Yemen could not function without him.[158] There was also a political fallout between the American and Yemeni governments due to American officials violating their agreement with President Saleh to keep the U.S. part in the operation secret (for more details see chapter 1). It would be over seven years before the Yemeni government would allow another drone strike to take place, but following that hiatus the United States quickly ramped up its drone war in Yemen again.

Restarting the Drone Campaign

After the killing of al-Harithi and the collapse of his organization, Yemen became a less urgent concern for the U.S. government. However, the Obama administration refocused its attention on Yemen in early 2010 following a number of attacks against Western targets. The reemerging threat emanating from Yemen traces back to February 3, 2006, when twenty-three al-Qaeda inmates escaped from prison.[159] Among those who escaped was Nasir al-Wuhayshi, who became the leader of AQAP (which officially formed in 2009).[160]

Taking a lesson from al-Harithi's example, Nasir al-Wuhayshi built an organization that was less dependent on its leadership. According to Gregory Johnsen, "Wuhayshi has constructed AQAP in a way that is designed to survive the loss of key cell leaders. He learned from the first phase of the war [when a 2002] drone strike . . . basically destroyed Al Qaeda in Yemen."[161] The group slowly built its movement from "the ground up rather than the top down"[162] and underwent a series of operational changes, "moving from local targets to regional ones and finally to international ones."[163] The first international strike launched by AQAP was the Christmas Day bombing attempt. On December 25, 2009, Umar Farouk Abdulmutallab attempted to blow up Northwest Airlines Flight 253 as it flew into Detroit by setting off plastic explosives sewn to his underwear.[164] There were 290 people on board the aircraft, and had the attempt succeeded, it would have been the deadliest terrorist attack on American territory since 9/11. It later emerged that al-Qaeda operatives in Yemen had supplied Abdulmutallab with the bomb and trained him in how to detonate it.[165] The attempt marked a significant escalation in AQAP's activities as it was the first time the group is known to have launched an operation outside the Saudi-Yemen area.[166] According to Peter Bergen and Jennifer Rowland, "This incident may have played a key role in the Obama administration's decision to resurrect the dormant drone campaign in Yemen."[167] AQAP was also behind the attempted "parcel bombings" in October 2010, where authorities in the United Arab Emirates and Britain found two explosives-laden packages hidden in printer cartridges sent from Yemen and addressed to synagogues in Chicago.[168] Furthermore, the organization managed to take advantage of the Arab Spring–inspired uprising against President Saleh's rule that began in Yemen in 2011. Months of mass protests calling for President Saleh's resignation and a June 3 bomb attack that resulted in Saleh leaving the country for emergency surgery in Saudi Arabia gave AQAP the opportunity to seize territory in Abyan and parts of Shabwa.[169] At the same time, however, when Saleh ultimately agreed to legally transfer his powers to the vice president, Abdu Rabbu Mansour Hadi, on November 23, 2011, it also allowed the United States to expand military operations in the country when the new president embraced the use of drones.[170]

By the time President Hadi came to power, the Obama administration had already begun to focus attention and resources on Yemen, taking a more active role in combating AQAP. In the lead-up to the drone campaign, the United States launched targeted killing operations by means of ground raids and cruise missile strikes. On December 17, 2009, JSOC launched a Tomahawk cruise missile from a submarine positioned in the waters off the coast of Yemen, killing fourteen AQAP operatives and forty-one local residents (of whom thirty-five were women and children) in the al-Majalah region.[171] Johnsen observed that this strike, and others like it, serve as "a powerful weapon in the hands of AQAP" to bolster recruitment.[172] According to leaked U.S. embassy cables, even President Saleh lamented the use of U.S. cruise missiles, as they were "not very accurate."[173] The Obama administration evidently came to the same conclusion and "decided to turn to drones when," as Brian Glyn Williams puts it, "Tomahawk cruise missile strikes proved to be too clumsy."[174]

Signature Strikes and the Hunt for Anwar al-Awlaki

The 2002 strike on al-Harithi was the beginning of a narrow drone campaign that focused on limited strikes against high-value targets commonly described as personality strikes. By the time drones reappeared in Yemen in 2010, there was a rapid shift to signature strikes—that is, targeting individuals based on their behavior.[175] Initially, the administration had no intentions of using signature strikes in Yemen. Reports indicate that failures (like the al-Majalah cruise missile strike) reinforced the wisdom of targeting a narrow set of AQAP leaders. Moreover, on May 25, 2010, a U.S. drone attack missed its intended target and killed Jabir Shabwani, the thirty-one-year-old deputy governor of Marib province, while he was on a mediation mission to persuade al-Qaeda elements to hand themselves over to the authorities.[176] Military leaders who oversaw the operation suspected they were fed misleading intelligence by the Yemeni government to eliminate a political rival.[177] Following the incident, procedures were reportedly tightened, and the White House allegedly rejected CIA and JSOC proposals to vastly expand who could be targeted to include lower-level al-Qaeda foot soldiers and other supporters.[178] "Permissions are harder to get," a participant in the discussions said of the process of adding new targets; "Brennan wants to make sure we don't get played again."[179] As Hudson, Owens, and Flannes observed, this resulted in the drone campaign going "into a year-long hiatus."[180] However, by 2011 the Obama administration decided to expand the CIA use of armed drones in Yemen.[181]

On June 14, 2011, it was reported that the CIA had started building a secret air base in the Persian Gulf region to begin conducting a drone campaign over Yemen.[182] Prior to this, since December 2009, U.S. strikes in

Yemen had been carried out by the U.S. military with intelligence support from the CIA. According to the *Wall Street Journal*:

> The U.S. military strikes have been conducted with the permission of the Yemeni government. The CIA operates under different legal restrictions, giving the administration a freer hand to carry out strikes even if Yemeni President Ali Abdullah Saleh . . . reverses his past approval of military strikes or cedes power to a government opposed to them.[183]

On September 1, 2011, reports emerged that the CIA had expanded its capabilities in Yemen and planned to step up targeted killing operations. Reports included the agency assembling a new counterterrorism unit whose job was to find AQAP targets in Yemen.[184] A primary target was Anwar al-Awlaki, a U.S. citizen who the American government believed had transitioned from a propagandist to an "operational" terrorist with his involvement in the Christmas Day bomb plot.[185] According to a Justice Department memo released in 2012, al-Awlaki personally directed the plot to take down a plane over Detroit.[186] As a result, the United States gave high priority to the threat posed by al-Awlaki during the initial stages of the drone campaign.

On December 24, 2009, President Obama signed off on an airstrike targeting al-Awlaki in Shabwa province, which resulted in the death of at least thirty militants.[187] According to the Yemeni Embassy in Washington, he was thought to be at the meeting, as were Nasir al-Wuhayshi and his deputy, Said Ali al-Shihri. However, none of these major figures were among the dead.[188] It is interesting to note that if this account is true it would indicate that the United States targeted al-Awlaki prior to his being connected to the Christmas Day bomb plot, which occurred the following day. The United States would fail to kill al-Awlaki again on May 5, 2011, in what would be the first drone strike since the 2010 attack that unintentionally killed Jabir Shabwani.[189] On this date, there was a coordinated attack involving drones and Harrier jets that targeted al-Awlaki twice during a forty-five-minute period outside the village of Jahwa in Shabwa province.[190] In the first attack, drones fired three missiles at a pickup truck carrying al-Awlaki and his colleagues, but missed its target. After the first attack, two other AQAP operatives rushed to the scene and then switched vehicles with al-Awlaki. The two vehicles then took off in opposite directions. Amid the confusion, a single drone tracked and fired a missile at a pickup truck, still believed to have been carrying al-Alwaki, killing the two AQAP operatives while the intended target escaped in a different vehicle.[191] The second attempt at killing al-Awlaki had ended in failure.

However, on September 30, 2011, the United States managed to successfully target and kill Anwar al-Awlaki, making him the first U.S. citizen to be "deliberately" killed by the CIA in a drone strike. He was killed alongside Samir Khan, a U.S. citizen of Pakistani heritage who was producing English-language propaganda for AQAP.[192] The strike represented the first test of the new CIA-led counterterrorism program in Yemen, which would often rely on close cooperation with Special Operations Forces, blurring the lines between military and intelligence operations.[193] Less than a month later, on October 14, 2011, al-Awlaki's son, sixteen-year-old Abdulrahman al-Awlaki, was also killed in a drone strike.[194] These incidents were highly controversial. In the span of one month the United States had killed three American citizens inside Yemen.

It was not until early 2012 that the Obama administration authorized the use of "signature strikes" in Yemen. The first signs of the drone campaign shifting in this direction appeared in April 2012 when the *Washington Post* released a report stating that the CIA was seeking authority to expand its covert drone campaign in Yemen by securing the right to launch signature strikes.[195] Those supporting the plan said "improvements in U.S. intelligence collection in Yemen have made it possible to expand the drone campaign," and also pointed to the success of signature strikes in Pakistan.[196] According to U.S. officials in the report, no decision had been reached on approving the proposal to permit the CIA to conduct such strikes. This would change a week later when reports emerged that the Obama administration had given both the CIA and JSOC "greater leeway" in targeting suspected militants in Yemen with drones.[197]

Abdu Rabbu Mansour Hadi, Yemen's new president, praised this counterterrorism strategy and the precision of drone strikes. "They pinpoint the target and have zero margin of error, if you know what target you're aiming at," said Hadi on September 28, 2012.[198] The broadened scope of potential targets and the full endorsement by the host state allowed the United States to sharply increase the number of drone strikes. In addition, one of the major differences between the Yemeni and Pakistani campaigns has been the larger role that drones play in supporting the Yemeni army in its ground operations against AQAP.[199] Drones, for example, have been used to destroy AQAP ammunition depots and to hit AQAP's defensive positions to assist Yemeni forces in reclaiming key territories, such as Abyan and Shabwah governorates, which serve as AQAP strongholds.[200] Unsurprisingly, these regions are also where the majority of drone strikes have taken place (see table 2.1).

The shift in Yemeni attitude and U.S. targeted killing policy sharply accelerated the rate of drone operations in Yemen. While the number of drone attacks in Pakistan started to wane after 2010, it rose sharply in Yemen, jumping from one operation in 2002 to as many as twelve in 2011. In 2012,

TABLE 2.1
U.S. Air and Drone Strikes in Yemen by Province, 2002 to 2015 (as of March 18, 2015)[1]

Province	Total Strikes	Province	Total Strikes
Abyan	26	Al Bayda'	18
Shabwah	25	Hadramawt	16
Ma'rib	20	Al Jawf	6

1. "Targeted Killing Database," *Center for the Study of Targeted Killing*, accessed April 25, 2015, http://targetedkilling.org/.

the same year the administration gave both the CIA and JSOC "greater leeway" in targeting suspected militants, the number of strikes rose to as high as forty-four. Reported fatalities resulting from the strikes have correspondingly risen from between sixty-nine to eighty fatalities during the period 2002 to 2011, up to as high as 279 in 2012 alone. Reported fatalities decreased in 2013 with casualties ranging between 99 and 120, but rose again in 2014 (to between 109 and 140 total fatalities). As of March 18, 2015, U.S. drone strikes had killed an estimated 628 people in Yemen, 558 of whom were identified in media reports as suspected militants according to CSTK; TBIJ reported 536 killed (see table 2.2).

As the table above shows, we can reasonably infer at least three things from both databases tracking the drone campaign in Yemen:

1. The databases show that the civilian death toll is between fifty-seven and eighty-two (between 9.08 percent and 15.3 percent in terms of the proportion of total fatalities who were civilians).
2. Despite their differences, both databases show a very sharp increase in drone attacks in 2012 (jumping to forty-four), followed by a gradual decrease in the following years (with the databases showing between three and six strikes so far in 2015).
3. Both databases show that the civilian death toll sharply increased in 2013 but then dropped to its lowest levels in 2014 and 2015.

There have also been a number of successful killings of high-value militant leaders who command, control, and inspire organizations. A recent example of this is the drone strike on June 12, 2015, that killed Nasir al-Wuhayshi.[201] After the death of AQAP's leader, the U.S. government described the strike as "a major blow," bringing them one step "closer to degrading and ultimately defeating" al-Qaeda and its affiliates.[202] In the narrative of drone advocates, al-Wuhayshi's death will likely increase the mortality rate of the group, hinder its capacity to carry out strikes, and could help break the group's morale.

TABLE 2.2

Drone Strikes in Yemen, 2002 to 2015 (as of March 18, 2015)[1]

Source	Years	Total Strikes	Total Killed	Suspected Militants Killed	Civilians Killed	"Unknowns" Killed	Civilian Deaths as Percentage of Total
Center for the Study of Targeted Killing (CSTK)	2002–2011	14	69	52	8	9	11.59%
	2012	44	279	254	24	1	8.6%
	2013	28	120	97	21	2	17.5%
	2014	24	140	136	4	0	2.86%
	2015	6	20	19	0	1	0.00%
	Total 2002–2015	116	628	558	57	13	9.08%
The Bureau of Investigative Journalism (TBIJ)	2002–2011	13	80	—	36	—	45%
	2012	44	236	—	10	—	4.24%
	2013	21	99	—	27	—	27.27%
	2014	18	109	—	7	—	6.42%
	2015	3	12	—	2	—	16.67%
	Total 2002–2015	99	536	—	82	—	15.3%

1. "Targeted Killing Database," Center for the Study of Targeted Killing, accessed April 25, 2015, http://targetedkilling.org/; TBIJ numbers are based on averages within the ranges provided, for TBIJ data see: "Get the Data: Drone Wars," The Bureau of Investigative Journalism, https://www.thebureauinvestigates.com/category/projects/drones/drones-graphs/.

In the narrative pushed by drone critics, removing al-Wuhayshi is unlikely to diminish AQAP's capabilities and effectiveness and may in fact have the opposite effect of increasing its resolve and intensifying its desire to use violence in retaliation. Only time will tell which of these perspectives is correct, and it wouldn't be surprising to find out that the answer is somewhere in between. In any case, there is still an ongoing debate regarding whether or not drones create popular resentment in Yemen. On this point, we will turn to the debate between Yemen scholars Gregory Johnsen and Christopher Swift over whether drone strikes are leading to the growth of AQAP.

The Johnsen and Swift Debate

In an opinion piece for the *New York Times,* late Yemeni youth activist and founder of the Watan party Ibrahim Mothana wrote, "Certainly, there may be short-term military gains from killing militant leaders in these strikes, but they are minuscule compared with the long-term damage the drone program is causing. A new generation of leaders is spontaneously emerging in furious retaliation to attacks on their territories and tribes."[203] This statement hits the core of the argument against the continued drone campaign in Yemen. The belief is that these drone strikes are angering locals to the point of seeking revenge by joining terrorist groups like al-Qaeda.

By consequence, the rise in drone strikes and the killing of key figures could actually be strengthening the organization. A sharp increase in drone strikes occurred in August 2013 after the electronic interception of al-Qaeda leader Ayman al-Zawahiri's message to Nasir al-Wuhayshi saying to "do something."[204] The increase in drone strikes led commentators to question whether the preceding strikes had been effective in weakening AQAP. Furthermore, civilian casualties also continued to fuel a negative reaction, with some people, like Gregory Johnsen, arguing that drone attacks benefit AQAP's recruitment process: "Now, I don't think U.S. drone and airstrikes are the only reason for the rapid growth of AQAP—one also has to consider the collapse of the Yemeni state in 2011—but in my view it is certainly one of the key factors."[205] According to a local whose relatives were killed in a U.S. strike in Yemen, "[t]hese attacks are making people say, 'We believe now that al-Qaeda is on the right side.'"[206] Other commentators like Christopher Swift have questioned in turn whether there is any correlation between drone strikes and AQAP recruitment.

According to Gregory Johnsen, the Obama administration's counterterrorism approach in Yemen is failing due to "[f]aulty assumptions and a mistaken focus paired with a resilient [and] adaptive enemy."[207] Johnsen offers several arguments to support his case. One of the explanations of

AQAP's resiliency against drone strikes is the origin of militants. As Johnsen pointed out, in Afghanistan and Pakistan, al-Qaeda was largely a group of Arabs in non-Arab countries, while in Yemen, al-Qaeda is made up mostly of Yemenis living in Yemen, embedded in local tribes and networks. This also makes the recruitment process more efficient since potential candidates do not need to travel far to receive specialized training.[208] As Johnsen remarked:

> For years, men like Nasir al-Wuhayshi, the head of AQAP and the man believed by U.S. officials to be recently promoted to al Qaeda's global deputy, had to spend time in training camps in Afghanistan to acquire the requisite experience. But since AQAP has developed its own network in Yemen, that is no longer the case. Now young Yemenis who want to join al Qaeda can study with Ibrahim al-Asiri, the group's top bomb-maker, without ever leaving home.[209]

Altogether, "[t]hese multiple and simultaneous identities, along with the ability of Yemeni AQAP members to move throughout their country, make tracking and targeting them a logistical nightmare."[210] Moreover, this makes the "accidental-guerrilla" phenomenon an even greater concern as AQAP is also part of the tribal community. Johnsen argues that the United States overlooks what Yemenis call *thar*, or revenge. The drone campaign in Yemen is killing individuals who are tied to the local society in a way that many of the foreign fighters in countries like Afghanistan never were. "They may be al Qaeda members, but they are also fathers and sons, brothers and cousins, tribesmen and clansmen with friends and relatives," Johnsen said.[211] He continues arguing that the Yemenis often join the organization less out of ideological fervor, but "rather out of a desire to get revenge on the country that killed their fellow tribesman."[212] The argument behind the concept of *thar* is not too different from the argument reviewed earlier in the chapter about the Pashtuns' tendency to seek *badal* when one of their own is killed in a drone strike. The fundamental point is that the rise of AQAP is in part due to the rise of drone strikes in the region, which instigate radicalization and recruitment. As Nabeel Khoury, a Senior Fellow at the Chicago Council on Global Affairs who served as deputy chief of mission in Yemen (2004 to 2007), explained in 2013, "[g]iven Yemen's tribal structure, the U.S. generates roughly forty to sixty new enemies for every AQAP operative killed by drones."[213] The growth of the organization lends support to this view. In 2009 Yemen's foreign minister Abubakr al-Qirbi said there could be up to three hundred al-Qaeda militants in Yemen.[214] By 2012 American officials estimated that AQAP had expanded to "more than 1,000 members."[215]

Others caution that the "accidental-guerrilla" phenomenon is not a systematic and widespread trend in the region. According to Swift, economic factors are the real explanation behind young men getting involved in the insurgency. Swift conducted forty interviews with local tribesmen, and out of the forty men interviewed, only five believed drone strikes were strengthening AQAP more than weakening it.[216] "None of the individuals I interviewed drew a causal relationship between U.S. drone strikes and al Qaeda recruiting," Swift said.[217] He then goes on to argue that AQAP is building complex webs of dependency within Yemen's rural population by targeting poor areas. The terrorist group provides teenagers with weapons and vehicles as well as paying men's salaries. AQAP also invests in the local community for development projects and provides law enforcement.[218] As the leader of one Yemeni tribal confederation personally told Swift, "Al Qaeda attracts those who can't afford to turn away." He further added that Yemenis could "accept [drones] as long as there are no more civilian casualties."[219] This idea of villagers from conflicted areas reluctantly accepting drone strikes as the lesser evil echoes some claims also made in the debate occurring over drone strikes in Pakistan. Some, like C. Christine Fair, have argued that although most Pakistanis outside of FATA strongly oppose drone strikes, a significant minority of locals inside FATA, the targeted region, support drone strikes albeit grudgingly.[220] Other studies on Yemen suggest that structural factors, like failed institutions, porous borders, and a lack of central control by the government, are also contributing to the growth of AQAP.[221] Yemen suffers from corruption, subpar law enforcement, a fragile economy, and social and political fragmentation, all of which can create an environment conducive to recruitment.[222] With Yemen being one of the poorest countries in the Arab world, the result may be that AQAP succeeds in recruiting isolated individuals and gaining popular support quite independently of whether the United States carries out drone strikes. None of this is to say, however, that drone strikes might not also be a factor in al-Qaeda recruitment. Megan Braun summarized the debate on whether AQAP is a product of its environment or a reaction to drone strikes nicely: "While the rapid growth of AQAP is undoubtedly multicausal, the blame attributable to drones is difficult to assess. The same is true of their value."[223]

Interestingly enough, although Gregory Johnsen and Christopher Swift disagree with one another on what factors are leading to the growth of AQAP, they both agree that the United States needs to do a better job of addressing the issue. Swift says there are two lessons policy makers need to take into consideration: "First, as long as drones target legitimate terrorists, Yemenis grudgingly acknowledge their utility. And second, the more Yemenis perceive the United States as a serious partner, the less drones will pique their national pride."[224] Swift also argues that better coordination is needed between the strategic outcomes Americans and Yeminis are expecting because they "are fighting the same war from different premises."[225] The United States is concerned with suppressing radical ideology while Yemen is concerned about poverty. Additionally, although the United States is carrying out missions intended to gain immediate results, what is necessary for Yemen is long-term development.[226] Like Swift, Johnsen takes issue with the United States neglecting long-term strategies. In his view, the "Yemen campaign is primarily concerned with preventing an immediate attack directed at America or its interests in the Middle East . . . This is a short-term goal that eclipses everything else, from long-term strategy to the stability of Yemen itself."[227]

Today there is a great deal of discussion of the use of drones in Yemen, with many raising questions about its strategic effectiveness. Ibrahim Sharqieh, deputy director of the Brookings Doha Center, said that the U.S. use of drones to target terrorists in Yemen "has not succeeded at all. And on the contrary, it actually contributed to the instability that Yemen has been seeing for the past years."[228] The debate has been further complicated by the successful uprising of the Shiite militia known as the Houthis, which forced President Hadi, his prime minister, and his cabinet to resign on January 22, 2015. [229] To make the situation even more complicated, warplanes and ships from a Saudi-led coalition have been bombing the Houthi rebels in order to restore the Yemeni government. As the Saudi-led intervention launches airstrikes against Houthi forces, the United States continues to carry out drone strikes targeting AQAP (but not Houthis). Despite the ongoing crisis and growing instability, President Obama vowed that the United States would not stop its counterterrorism efforts and that it will continue to go after high-value targets inside Yemen, saying, "It is not neat and it is not simple, but it is the best option that we have."[230]

Amid this chaos, Daniel Byman and Jennifer R. Williams described AQAP as a "clear winner" that "is making the most of the reversal of fortune."[231] Defense Secretary Ashton B. Carter said AQAP "has seized the opportunity of the disorder there and the collapse of the central government,"[232] while Adam Schiff, the ranking Democrat on the House Intelligence Committee, warned that "the pressure has been taken off AQAP."[233] Reinforcing these views, in April 2015, the terrorist group conducted a prison break freeing more than three hundred prisoners, including a known AQAP leader named Khaled al-Batarfi,[234] and took control of the port city of Mukalla, a major airport and an oil export terminal in the southern part of the country.[235] In a country as volatile as Yemen, with massive poverty and instability, there is almost certainly no simple solution. The question remains, however, are drones helping or hurting Yemen's chances at a better future?

Notes

1. Pir Zubair, Sabrina Tavernise, and Mark Mazzetti, "Taliban Leader in Pakistan Is Reportedly Killed," *New York Times*, August 7, 2009, accessed March 15, 2015, http://www.nytimes.com/2009/08/08/world/asia/08pstan.html?pagewanted = 1&_r = 4&emc = eta1&.

2. Jane Mayer, "The Predator War,"*New Yorker*, October 26, 2009, accessed March 15, 2015, http://www.newyorker.com/magazine/2009/10/26/the-predator-war.

3. The following example is drawn from Brian Glyn Williams, *Predators: The CIA's Drone War on al Qaeda* (Washington, DC: Potomac Books, 2013), 8–9.

4. Sudarsan Raghavan, "When U.S. Drones Kill Civilians, Yemen's Government Tries to Conceal It," *Washington Post*, December 24, 2012, accessed February 20, 2015, http://www.washingtonpost.com/world/middle_east/when-us-drones-kill-civilians -yemens-government-tries-to-conceal-it/2012/12/24/bd4d7ac2-486d-11e2-8af9-9b5 0cb4605a7_story.html.

5. Raghavan, "When U.S. Drones Kill Civilians."

6. *National Strategy for Counterterrorism* (Washington, DC: White House, 2011), 8–9.

7. Carl von Clausewitz, *On War*, edited and translated by Michael Howard and Peter Paret (Princeton: Princeton University Press, 1976), 127–32.

8. Audrey Kurth Cronin, "Why Drones Fail: When Tactics Drive Strategy," *Foreign Affairs* (2014): 44.

9. Micah Zenko, "Reforming U.S. Drone Strike Policies," *Council on Foreign Relations Special Report* no. 65 (New York: Council on Foreign Relations Press, 2013), 12.

10. Daniel Klaidman, *Kill or Capture: The War on Terror and the Soul of the Obama Presidency* (Boston: Houghton Mifflin Harcourt, 2012), 41.

11. Eric Schmitt and David E. Sanger, "Pakistan Shift Could Curtail Drone Strikes," *New York Times*, February 22, 2008, accessed March 15, 2015, http://www .nytimes.com/2008/02/22/washington/22policy.html.

12. Zenko, "Reforming U.S. Drone Strike Policies," 8.

13. Sarah Kreps, "The Foreign Policy Essay: Preventing the Proliferation of Armed Drones," *Lawfare*, April 13, 2014, accessed March 15, 2015, https://new.law fareblog.com/foreign-policy-essay-preventing-proliferation-armed-drones.

14. Avery Plaw and Matthew Fricker, "Tracking the Predators: Evaluating the US Drone Campaign in Pakistan," *International Studies Perspectives* 13, no. 4 (2012): 5.

15. Williams, *Predators*, 1.

16. Justin Elliot, "Have U.S. Drones Become a 'Counterinsurgency Air Force' for Our Allies?," *ProPublica*, November 27, 2012, italics added, accessed March 15, 2015, http://www.propublica.org/article/have-u.s.-drones-become-a-counterinsurgency -air-force-for-our-allies.

17. Elliot, "Have U.S. Drones Become a 'Counterinsurgency Air Force'?"

18. Michael J. Boyle, "Do Counterterrorism and Counterinsurgency Go Together?," *International Affairs* 86, no. 2 (2010): 335.

19. Boyle, "Do Counterterrorism and Counterinsurgency Go Together?" 335.

20. Fred Kaplan, "The World as Free-Fire Zone," *MIT Technology Review*, June 7, 2013, accessed March 15, 2015, http://www.technologyreview.com/featuredstory/515806/the-world-as-free-fire-zone/.

21. Boyle, "Do Counterterrorism and Counterinsurgency Go Together?," 335.

22. Christopher Swift, "The Boundaries of War? Assessing the Impact of Drone Strikes in Yemen," in *Drone Wars: Transforming Conflict, Law, and Policy*, edited by Peter L. Bergen and Daniel Rothenberg (Cambridge: Cambridge University Press, 2014), 74.

23. Daniel Byman, "Why Drones Work: The Case for Washington's Weapon of Choice," *Brookings Foreign Affairs* (2013): 32.

24. John O. Brennan, "The Efficacy and Ethics of the President's Counterterrorism Strategy," speech, Woodrow Wilson International Center for Scholars, Washington, DC, April 30, 2012, http://www.lawfareblog.com/text-john-brennans-speech-drone-strikes-today-wilson-center.

25. Barack Obama, "Remarks by the President at the National Defense University," speech, National Defense University, Fort McNair, Washington, DC, May 23, 2013, https://www.whitehouse.gov/the-press-office/2013/05/23/remarks-president-national-defense-university.

26. "Al-Shabaab Leader Ahmed Abdi Godane Killed by US Air Strike in Somalia," *The Guardian*, September 5, 2014, accessed March 15, 2015, http://www.theguardian.com/world/2014/sep/05/al-shabaab-leader-godane-killed-us-airstrike-somalia.

27. Farouk Chothia, "Ahmed Abdi Godane: Somalia's Killed al-Shabaab Leader," *BBC News*, September 9, 2014, accessed March 15, 2015, http://www.bbc.com/news/world-africa-29034409.

28. "U.S. Airstrikes in Pakistan Called 'Very Effective,'" *CNN*, May 18, 2009, accessed March 15, 2015, http://edition.cnn.com/2009/POLITICS/05/18/cia.pakistan.airstrikes/.

29. Mayer, "The Predator War."

30. Elisabeth Bumiller, "Panetta, in Kabul, Says Defeat of Al Qaeda Is 'Within Reach,'" *New York Times*, July 9, 2011, accessed January 15, 2015, http://www.nytimes.com/2011/07/10/world/asia/10military.html.

31. Elisabeth Bumiller, "Soldier, Thinker, Hunter, Spy: Drawing a Bead on Al Qaeda," *New York Times*, September 3, 2011, accessed November 14, 2014, http://www.nytimes.com/2011/09/04/world/04vickers.html?pagewanted=all&_r=0.

32. Ravi Somaiya, "Drone Strike Prompts Suit, Raising Fears for U.S. Allies," *New York Times*, January 30, 2013, accessed January 15, 2015, http://www.nytimes.com/2013/01/31/world/drone-strike-lawsuit-raises-concerns-on-intelligence-sharing.html?pagewanted=2&_r=0.

33. Greg Miller and Julie Tate, "Al-Qaeda's No. 2 Leader Is Killed in Pakistan, U.S. Officials Say," *Washington Post*, August 27, 2011, accessed July 4, 2015, https://www.washingtonpost.com/world/national-security/al-qaedas-no-2-leader-is-killed-in-pakistan-us-officials-say/2011/08/27/gIQAUM69iJ_story.html.

34. David Kilcullen and Andrew McDonald Exum, "Death from Above, Outrage Down Below," *New York Times*, May 16, 2009, accessed March 15, 2015, http://www.nytimes.com/2009/05/17/opinion/17exum.html?pagewanted=all.

35. Brian Glyn Williams, "The CIA's Covert Predator Drone War in Pakistan, 2004–2010: The History of an Assassination Campaign," *Studies in Conflict and Terrorism* 33, no. 10 (2010): 877–80.

36. Byman, "Why Drones Work," 33.

37. International Crisis Group, "Drones: Myths and Reality in Pakistan," *Crisis Group Asia Report* no. 247 (Brussels: ICG, 2013), 23.

38. Swift, "The Boundaries of War?" 83.

39. David Rohde, "My Guards Absolutely Feared Drones: Reflections on Being Held Captive for Seven Months by the Taliban," in *Drone Wars: Transforming Conflict, Law, and Policy*, edited by Peter L. Bergen and Daniel Rothenberg (Cambridge: Cambridge University Press, 2014), 9.

40. Pam Benson, "Bin Laden Documents: Fear of Drones," *CNN*, May 3, 2012, accessed March 8, 2015, http://security.blogs.cnn.com/2012/05/03/bin-laden-documents-fear-of-drones/.

41. Benson, "Bin Laden Documents."

42. Benson, "Bin Laden Documents."

43. Jenna Jordan, "When Heads Roll: Assessing the Effectiveness of Leadership Decapitation," *Security Studies* 18, no. 4 (2009): 754.

44. Jordan, "When Heads Roll," 723, 753–54.

45. Jenna Jordan, "Data on Leadership Targeting and Potential Impacts for Communal Support," in *Legitimacy and Drones: Investigating the Legality, Morality and Efficacy of UCAVs*, edited by Steven J. Barela (Burlington: Ashgate Press, 2015), 235.

46. Bryan C. Price, "Targeting Top Terrorists: How Leadership Decapitation Contributes to Counterterrorism," *International Security* 36, no. 4 (2012): 11, 40.

47. Price, "Targeting Top Terrorists," 25.

48. Price, "Targeting Top Terrorists," 13.

49. Price, "Targeting Top Terrorists," 26.

50. Price, "Targeting Top Terrorists," 43; Jordan, "When Heads Roll," 746–47.

51. Patrick B. Johnston, "Does Decapitation Work? Assessing the Effectiveness of Leadership Targeting in Counterinsurgency Campaigns," *International Security* 36, no. 4 (2012): 54.

52. Johnston, "Does Decapitation Work?," 50.

53. Johnston, "Does Decapitation Work?," 50.

54. Jenna Jordan, "Attacking the Leader, Missing the Mark," *International Security* 38, no. 4 (2014): 11.

55. Johnston, "Does Decapitation Work?," 75.

56. Patrick B. Johnston and Anoop K. Sarbahi, "The Impact of U.S. Drone Strikes on Terrorism in Pakistan," *International Studies Quarterly* (forthcoming), http://patrickjohnston.info/materials/drones.pdf.

57. Johnston and Sarbahi, "The Impact of U.S. Drone Strikes on Terrorism in Pakistan," 3.

58. Johnston and Sarbahi, "The Impact of U.S. Drone Strikes on Terrorism in Pakistan," 3.

59. Johnston and Sarbahi, "The Impact of U.S. Drone Strikes on Terrorism in Pakistan," 3.

60. Johnston and Sarbahi, "The Impact of U.S. Drone Strikes on Terrorism in Pakistan," 3.

61. Williams, *Predators*, 170.

62. David A. Jaeger and Zahra Siddique, "Are Drone Strikes Effective in Afghanistan and Pakistan? On the Dynamics of Violence between the United States and the Taliban," *IZA Discussion Paper* no. 6262 (Bonn: IZA, 2011), 11–12.

63. "President Obama Hangs Out with America," *The White House Blog*, January 30, 2012, accessed March 15, 2015, http://www.whitehouse.gov/blog/2012/01/30/president-obama-hangs-out-america.

64. Obama, "Remarks by the President at the National Defense University."

65. Peter L. Bergen and Jennifer Rowland, "Drones Decimating Taliban in Pakistan," *CNN*, July 4, 2012, accessed March 15, 2015, http://edition.cnn.com/2012/07/03/opinion/bergen-drones-taliban-pakistan/index.html.

66. C. Christine Fair, "Drone Wars," *Foreign Policy*, May 28, 2010, accessed March 15, 2015, http://foreignpolicy.com/2010/05/28/drone-wars-2/.

67. Fair, "Drone Wars."

68. Gen. John P. Abizaid and Rosa Brooks, *Recommendations and Report of the Task Force on US Drone Policy* (Washington, DC: Stimson Center, 2014), 21.

69. Abizaid and Brooks, *Recommendations and Report of the Task Force on US Drone Policy*, 25.

70. Byman, "Why Drones Work," 33.

71. Byman, "Why Drones Work," 35.

72. Avery Plaw, "Counting the Dead: The Proportionality of Predation in Pakistan," in *Killing by Remote Control: The Ethics of an Unmanned Military*, edited by Bradley J. Strawser (Oxford: Oxford University Press, 2013), 150.

73. Azmat Khan, "Understanding Yemen's Al Qaeda Threat," PBS *Frontline*, May 29, 2012, accessed March 15, 2015, http://www.pbs.org/wgbh/pages/frontline/foreign-affairs-defense/al-qaeda-in-yemen/understanding-yemens-al-qaeda-threat/#Jmembers.

74. In one example, for instance, the Pakistani daily *The News* published an article by terrorism expert Amir Mir in April 2009 reporting Predator strikes had killed only fourteen high-value al-Qaeda targets but were responsible for 687 civilian fatalities (that is, 98.14 percent of total fatalities). There is reason to believe these claims are exaggerated. See Avery Plaw, Matt Fricker, and Brian Glynn Williams, "Practice Makes Perfect? The Changing Civilian Toll of CIA Drone Strikes in Pakistan," *Perspectives on Terrorism* 5, no. 5–6 (2011): 57–61.

75. Adam Entous, "Special Report: How the White House Learned to Love the Drone," *Reuters*, May 18, 2010, accessed July 7, 2015, http://www.reuters.com/article/2010/05/18/us-pakistan-drones-idUSTRE64H5SL20100518.

76. International Human Rights and Conflict Resolution Clinic and Global Justice Clinic, *Living Under Drones: Death, Injury and Trauma to Civilians from US Drone Practices in Pakistan* (New York and Palo Alto: NYU School of Law and Stanford Law School, 2012), 80–81.

77. International Human Rights and Conflict Resolution Clinic and Global Justice Clinic, *Living Under Drones*, 81.

78. International Human Rights and Conflict Resolution Clinic and Global Justice Clinic, *Living Under Drones*, 85–86.

79. International Human Rights and Conflict Resolution Clinic and Global Justice Clinic, *Living Under Drones*, 73.

80. International Human Rights and Conflict Resolution Clinic and Global Justice Clinic, *Living Under Drones*, 126.

81. Clive Stafford Smith, "We are Sleepwalking into the Drone Age, Unaware of the Consequences," *Guardian*, June 2, 2012, accessed March 15, 2015, http://www.guardian.co.uk/commentisfree/2012/jun/02/drone-age-obama-pakistan.

82. "Researcher: Most Civilian Drone Deaths 'From Faulty Information,'" *VOA News*, March 15, 2013, accessed March 15, 2015, http://www.voanews.com/content/resaercher-mostcivilian-drone-deaths-from-faulty-information/1622442.html.

83. "Researcher: Most Civilian Drone Deaths 'From Faulty Information.'"

84. Reprieve, *You Never Die Twice: Multiple Kills in the US Drone Program* (London: Reprieve, 2014), 2, 6.

85. Reprieve, *You Never Die Twice*, 2, 6–9.

86. Reprieve, *You Never Die Twice*, 5.

87. Reprieve, *You Never Die Twice*, 10–11.

88. Bill Roggio, "Latest Predator Strike Rumor: AQAP's Leader Killed in North Waziristan," The Long War Journal, January 3, 2011, accessed June 5, 2015, http://www.longwarjournal.org/archives/2011/01/aqaps_leader_killed_in_us_pred.php.

89. Peter Bergen and Megan Braun, "Drone Is Obama's Weapon of Choice," CNN, September 6, 2012, accessed March 15, 2015, http://www.cnn.com/2012/09/05/opinion/bergen-obama-drone/index.html.

90. Entous, "Special Report: How the White House Learned to Love the Drone."

91. Greg Miller, "Increased US Drone Strikes in Pakistan Killing Few High-Value Militants," *Washington Post*, February 21, 2011, accessed January 16, 2015, www.washingtonpost.com/wp-dyn/content/article/2011/02/20/AR2011022002975.html.

92. Plaw and Fricker, "Tracking the Predators," 14.

93. Jo Becker and Scott Shane, "Secret 'Kill List' Proves a Test of Obama's Principles and Will," *New York Times*, May 29, 2012, accessed December 15, 2014, http://www.nytimes.com/2012/05/29/world/obamas-leadership-in-war-on-al-qaeda.html?_r=0.

94. International Human Rights and Conflict Resolution Clinic and Global Justice Clinic, *Living Under Drones*, 130.

95. James Rosen, "Obama Aides Defend Claim of Low Civilian Casualties after Drone 'Kill List' Report," *Fox News*, May 30, 2012, accessed March 15, 2015, http://www.foxnews.com/politics/2012/05/30/obama-aides-defend-claim-low-civilian-drone-casualties-after-kill-list-report/.

96. Greg Miller, "Plan for Hunting Terrorists Signals U.S. Intends to Keep Adding Names to Kill Lists," *Washington Post*, October 23, 2012, accessed March 15, 2015, http://www.washingtonpost.com/world/national-security/plan-for-hunting-terrorists-signals-us-intends-to-keep-adding-names-to-kill-lists/2012/10/23/4789b2ae-18b3-11e2-a55c-39408fbe6a4b_story.html.

97. Abizaid and Brooks, *Recommendations and Report of the Task Force on US Drone Policy*, 29.

98. Abizaid and Brooks, *Recommendations and Report of the Task Force on US Drone Policy*, 29.

99. Cronin, "Why Drones Fail," 46.

100. Dennis C. Blair, "Drones Alone Are Not the Answer," *New York Times*, August 14, 2011, accessed March 15, 2015, http://www.nytimes.com/2011/08/15/opinion/drones-alone-are-not-the-answer.html.

101. *National Strategy for Counterterrorism*, 9.

102. Michael J. Boyle, "The Costs and Consequences of Drone Warfare," *International Affairs* 89, no. 1 (2013): 14.

103. Boyle, "The Costs and Consequences of Drone Warfare," 14.

104. Chris Woods, "CIA Drone Strikes Violate Pakistan's Sovereignty, Says Senior Diplomat," *Guardian*, August 3, 2012, accessed April 14, 2015, http://www.theguardian.com/world/2012/aug/03/cia-drone-strikes-violate-pakistan.

105. Cronin, "Why Drones Fail," 47.

106. David Alexander, "Retired General Cautions Against Overuse of 'Hated' Drones," Reuters, January 7, 2013, accessed March 15, 2015, http://www.reuters.com/article/2013/01/07/us-usa-afghanistan-mcchrys-tal-idUSBRE90608O20130107.

107. Abizaid and Brooks, *Recommendations and Report of the Task Force on US Drone Policy*, 30.

108. Joshua Foust, "Understanding the Strategic and Tactical Considerations of Drone Strikes," *American Security Project* (2013): 13.

109. Joshua Kucera, "US Officials Working to Sway Hearts and Minds in Islamabad," *Eurasia Insight*, July 8, 2009, accessed March 15, 2015, http://www.eurasianet.org/departments/insightb/articles/eav070809b.shtml.

110. Jordan, "Data on Leadership Targeting and Potential Impacts for Communal Support," 241.

111. Jordan, "Data on Leadership Targeting and Potential Impacts for Communal Support," 230.

112. Kaplan, "The World as Free-Fire Zone."

113. *Effective Counterinsurgency: The Future of the U.S. Pakistan Military Partnership: Hearing Before the Committee on Armed Services*, House of Representatives, 111th Congress, First Session, April 23, 2009 (statement of Dr. David Kilcullen, partner, Crumpton Group, LLC, Senior Fellow, EastWest Institute, member of Advisory Board, Center for a New American Security), 21.

114. Kilcullen and Exum, "Death from Above, Outrage Down Below."

115. Kilcullen and Exum, "Death from Above, Outrage Down Below."

116. David Kilcullen, *The Accidental Guerilla* (Oxford: Oxford University Press, 2009), 230–32; Andrew Exum, Nathaniel Fick, Ahmed Humayun, and David Kilcullen, *Triage: The Next Twelve Months in Afghanistan and Pakistan* (Washington, DC: CNAS, 2009), 18.

117. United Nations Office of the High Commissioner for Human Rights, "Statement of the Special Rapporteur Following Meetings in Pakistan," March 14, 2013, accessed March 15, 2015, http://www.ohchr.org/EN/NewsEvents/Pages/DisplayNews.aspx?NewsID=13146&LangID=E.

118. For a discussion of the Pashtunwali code, see Brian Glyn Williams, *Afghanistan Declassified: A Guide to America's Longest War* (Philadelphia: University of Pennsylvania Press, 2012), 16–27.

119. United Nations Office of the High Commissioner for Human Rights, "Statement of the Special Rapporteur."

120. Cronin, "Why Drones Fail," 52.

121. Kilcullen, *The Accidental Guerilla*.

122. Leila Hudson, Colin S. Owens, and Matt Flannes, "Drone Warfare: Blowback from the New American Way of War," *Middle East Policy Council* 18, no. 3 (2011): 126.

123. Jordan, "Data on Leadership Targeting and Potential Impacts for Communal Support," 236.

124. Jordan, "Attacking the Leader, Missing the Mark," 33.

125. Michael Boyle uses the phrase *drones-first counterterrorism policy* to describe President Obama's heavy reliance on drone strikes in places like Yemen and Pakistan. See Boyle, "The Costs and Consequences of Drone Warfare."

126. Jordan, "Attacking the Leader, Missing the Mark," 33.

127. Jordan, "Attacking the Leader, Missing the Mark," 38.

128. Williams, "The CIA's Covert Predator Drone War in Pakistan," 883–84.

129. Farhat Taj, "Drone Attacks: Pakistan's Policy and the Tribesmen's Perspective," *Terrorism Monitor* 8, no. 10 (2010): 4.

130. "Drones over Pakistan, Drop the Pilot: A Surprising Number of Pakistanis Are in Favour of Drone Strikes," *Economist*, October 19, 2013, accessed March 20, 2015, http://www.economist.com/news/asia/21588142-surprising-number-pakistanis-are-favour-drone-strikes-drop-pilot.

131. "Drones over Pakistan."

132. Brian Glyn Williams, "Pakistani Responses to the CIA's Predator Drone Campaign against the Taliban and al-Qaeda," *Terrorism Monitor* 8, no. 7 (2010): 4.

133. Christopher Swift, "The Drone Blowback Fallacy," *Foreign Affairs*, July 1, 2012, accessed March 15, 2015, http://www.foreignaffairs.com/articles/137760/christopher-swift/the-drone-blowback-fallacy.

134. Amitai Etzioni, "The Great Drone Debate," *Military Review* (Fort Leavenworth: CAC, 2013), 7.

135. Tim Craig, "After Years of Tension, Anti-American Sentiment Ebbs in Pakistan," *Washington Post*, May 3, 2015, accessed March 20, 2015, http://www.washingtonpost.com/world/asia_pacific/after-years-of-tension-anti-american-sentiment-ebbs-in-pakistan/2015/05/03/6d0eccfe-dd36-11e4-b6d7-b9bc8acf16f7_story.html.

136. International "Drones: Myths and Reality in Pakistan," 23.

137. International Crisis Group, "Drones: Myths and Reality in Pakistan," 24.

138. United Nations Office of the High Commissioner for Human Rights, "Statement of the Special Rapporteur."

139. Cronin, "Why Drones Fail," 53.

140. Cronin, "Why Drones Fail," 53–54.

141. Cronin, "Why Drones Fail," 46.

142. Seth G. Jones, and Martin C. Libicki, *How Terrorist Groups End: Lessons for Countering Al Qa'ida* (Santa Monica: RAND Corporation, 2008), 4.

143. Jones and Libicki, *How Terrorist Groups End*, 18–20.

144. Jones and Libicki, *How Terrorist Groups End*, 18–19.

145. "CIA 'Killed al-Qaeda Suspects' in Yemen," *BBC News*, November 5, 2002, accessed March 15, 2015, http://news.bbc.co.uk/2/hi/2402479.stm.

146. "Yemen Admits Cooperating with US in Missile Attack," *Middle East Online*, November 20, 2002, accessed March 15, 2015, http://www.middle-east-online.com/english/?id = 3328.

147. "CIA 'Killed al-Qaeda Suspects' in Yemen."

148. Avery Plaw, "The Legality of Targeted Killing as an Instrument of War: The Case of Qaed Salim Sinan al-Harethi," in *The Metamorphosis of War*, edited by Avery Plaw (Amsterdam and New York: Rodopi Press, 2010), 57–72.

149. Williams, *Predators*, 43.

150. Williams, "The CIA's Covert Predator Drone War in Pakistan, 2004–2010," 874.

151. "U.S. Kills al-Qaeda Suspects in Yemen," *USA Today*, November 5, 2002, accessed March 15, 2015, http://usatoday30.usatoday.com/news/world/2002-11-04-yemen-explosion_x.htm.

152. Gregory D. Johnsen, *The Last Refuge: Yemen, Al-Qaeda, and America's War in Arabia* (New York: W. W. Norton & Company, 2014), 93.

153. Johnsen, *The Last Refuge*, 95.

154. Johnsen, *The Last Refuge*, 96–97.

155. Williams, *Predators*, 42.

156. Williams, *Predators*, 42.

157. Williams, *Predators*, 42.

158. Johnsen, *The Last Refuge*, 132.

159. Johnsen, *The Last Refuge*, 194.

160. Jane Novak, "Arabian Peninsula al Qaeda Groups Merge," The Long War Journal, January 29, 2009, accessed March 15, 2015, http://www.longwarjournal.org/archives/2009/01/arabian_peninsula_al.php.

161. Khan, "Understanding Yemen's Al Qaeda Threat."

162. Swift, "The Boundaries of War?," 76.

163. Khan, "Understanding Yemen's Al Qaeda Threat."

164. David Ariosto and Deborah Feyerick, "Christmas Day Bomber Sentenced to Life in Prison," *CNN*, February 17, 2012, accessed March 14, 2015, http://www.cnn.com/2012/02/16/justice/michigan-underwear-bomber-sentencing/.

165. "Al-Qaeda Wing Claims Christmas Day US Flight Bomb Plot," *BBC News*, December 28, 2009, accessed March 14, 2015, http://news.bbc.co.uk/2/hi/middle_east/8433151.stm.

166. "Al-Qaeda Wing Claims Christmas Day US Flight Bomb Plot."

167. Peter L. Bergen and Jennifer Rowland, "Decade of the Drone: Analyzing CIA Drone Attacks, Casualties, and Policy," in *Drone Wars: Transforming Conflict, Law, and Policy*, edited by Peter L. Bergen and Daniel Rothenberg (Cambridge: Cambridge University Press, 2014), 25.

168. "Yemen-Based al Qaeda Group Claims Responsibility for Parcel Bomb Plot," *CNN*, November 6, 2010, accessed March 15, 2015, http://www.cnn.com/2010/WORLD/meast/11/05/yemen.security.concern/.

169. Johnsen, *The Last Refuge*, 278.

170. Tom Finn, "Yemen President Quits after Deal in Saudi Arabia," *The Guardian*, November 23, 2011, http://www.theguardian.com/world/2011/nov/23/yemen-president-quits; Williams, *Predator*, 161.

171. Jeremy Scahill, "The Dangerous US Game in Yemen," *The Nation*, March 30, 2011, accessed March 15, 2015, http://www.thenation.com/article/dangerous-us -game-yemen/; Johnsen, *The Last Refuge*, 253.

172. Azmat Khan, "Study Suggests Yemen Strikes Are Radicalizing Population," PBS *Frontline*, May 30, 2012, accessed March 14, 2015, http://www.pbs.org/wgbh/pages /frontline/foreign-affairs-defense/al-qaeda-in-yemen/study-suggests-yemen-strikes -are-radicalizing-population/.

173. Robert Booth and Ian Black, "WikiLeaks Cables: Yemen Offered US 'Open Door' to Attack al-Qaida on Its Soil," *The Guardian*, December 3, 2010, accessed March 14, 2015, http://www.theguardian.com/world/2010/dec/03/wikileaks-yemen -us-attack-al-qaida.

174. Williams, *Predators*, 161.

175. Hudson, Owens, and Flannes, "Drone Warfare: Blowback from the New American Way of War."

176. "Yemen Strike Kills Mediator, Tribesmen Hit Pipeline," *Reuters*, May 25, 2010, http://uk.reuters.com/article/2010/05/25/uk-yemen-idUKTRE64O17W2010 0525; incident was later on described as a drone strike. See "Yemen Tribesmen Prevent Repairs on Blazing Pipeline," *Reuters*, March 15, 2011, accessed December 5, 2014, http://af.reuters.com/article/energyOilNews/idAFLDE72E02S20110315.

177. Adam Entous, Julian E. Barnes, and Margaret Coker, "U.S. Doubts Intelligence That Led to Yemen Strike," *Wall Street Journal*, December 29, 2011, accessed March 15, 2015, http://online.wsj.com/news/articles/SB10001424052970203899504 577126883574284126.

178. Entous, Barnes, and Coker, "U.S. Doubts Intelligence That Led to Yemen Strike."

179. Entous, Barnes, and Coker, "U.S. Doubts Intelligence That Led to Yemen Strike."

180. Leila Hudson, Colin S. Owens, and David J. Callen, "Drone Warfare in Yemen: Fostering Emirates through Counterterrorism?," *Middle East Policy Council* 19, no. 3 (2012), accessed March 15, 2015, http://mepc.org/journal/middle-east-pol icy-archives/drone-warfare-yemen-fostering-emirates-through-counterterrorism.

181. Jeb Boone, "Yemen's Trouble with Drones," *The Christian Science Monitor*, June 17, 2011, accessed March 15, 2015, http://www.csmonitor.com/World/Middle -East/2011/0617/Yemen-s-trouble-with-drones.

182. "Source: Drone Base Set for Persian Gulf Region," *Fox News*, June 15, 2011, accessed March 15, 2015, http://www.foxnews.com/world/2011/06/15/source-drone -base-set-for-persian-gulf-region/; Siobhan Gorman and Adam Entous, "CIA Plans Yemen Drone Strikes," *Wall Street Journal*, June 14, 2011, accessed March 15, 2015, http://online.wsj.com/news/articles/SB10001424052702303848104576384051572679110.

183. Gorman and Entous, "CIA Plans Yemen Drone Strikes."

184. Greg Miller and Julie Tate, "CIA Shifts Focus to Killing Targets," *Washington Post*, September 1, 2011, accessed March 15, 2015, http://www.washingtonpost.com/ world/national-security/cia-shifts-focus-to-killing-targets/2011/08/30/gIQA7MZGvJ _story.html.

185. Peter Finn, "Al-Awlaki Directed Christmas 'Underwear Bomber' Plot, Justice Department Memo Says," *Washington Post*, February 10, 2012, accessed March 15,

2015, http://www.washingtonpost.com/world/national-security/al-awlaki-directed
-christmas-underwear-bomber-plot-justice-department-memo-says/2012/02/10/gIQ
ArDOt4Q_story.html.

186. Finn, "Al-Awlaki Directed Christmas 'Underwear Bomber' Plot."

187. Scahill, "The Dangerous US Game in Yemen."

188. Sudarsan Raghavan and Michael D. Shear, "U.S.-Aided Attack in Yemen Thought to Have Killed Aulaqi, 2 al-Qaeda Leaders," *Washington Post*, December 25, 2009, accessed March 15, 2015, http://www.washingtonpost.com/wp-dyn/content/article/2009/12/24/AR2009122400536.html.

189. Margaret Coker, Adam Entous, and Julian E. Barnes, "Drone Targets Yemeni Cleric," *Wall Street Journal*, May 7, 2011, accessed March 15, 2015, http://online.wsj
.com/news/articles/SB10001424052748703992704576307594129219756.

190. Coker, Entous, and Barnes, "Drone Targets Yemeni Cleric."

191. Coker, Entous, and Barnes, "Drone Targets Yemeni Cleric."

192. Hakim Almasmari, Margaret Coker, and Siobhan Gorman, "Drone Kills Top Al Qaeda Figure," *Wall Street Journal*, October 1, 2011, accessed March 15, 2015, http://online.wsj.com/news/articles/SB10001424052970204138204576602301252340
820?mg = reno64-wsj&url = http%3A%2F%2Fonline.wsj.com%2Farticle%2FSB1000
1424052970204138204576602301252340820.html.

193. Hakim, Coker, and Gorman, "Drone Kills Top Al Qaeda Figure."

194. Jere Van Dyk, "Who Were the 4 U.S. Citizens Killed in Drone Strikes?," *CBS News*, May 23, 2013, accessed March 15, 2015, http://www.cbsnews.com/news/who
-were-the-4-us-citizens-killed-in-drone-strikes/.

195. Greg Miller, "CIA Seeks New Authority to Expand Yemen Drone Campaign," *Washington Post*, April 18, 2012, accessed March 15, 2015, http://www.washingtonpost.com/world/national-security/cia-seeks-new-authority-to-expand-yemen
-drone-campaign/2012/04/18/gIQAsaumRT_story_1. html.

196. Miller, "CIA Seeks New Authority to Expand Yemen Drone Campaign."

197. Adam Entous, Siobhan Gorman, and Julian E. Barnes, "U.S. Relaxes Drone Rules," *Wall Street Journal*, April 26, 2012, accessed March 15, 2015, http://online.wsj
.com/news/articles/SB10001424052702304723304577366251852418174.

198. Scott Shane, "Yemen's Leader Praises U.S. Drone Strikes," *New York Times*, September 29, 2012, accessed March 10, 2015, http://www.nytimes.com/2012/09/29/
world/middleeast/yemens-leader-president-hadi-praises-us-drone-strikes.html?_r = 0.

199. Bill Roggio, "US Airstrikes in Southern Yemen Kill 30 AQAP Fighters: Report," The Long War Journal, September 1, 2011, accessed March 10, 2015, http://
www.longwarjournal.org/archives/2011/09/us_airstrikes_in_sou.php#.

200. Williams, *Predator*, 163.

201. Jethro Mullen, "Al Qaeda's Second in Command Killed in Yemen Strike; Successor Named," *CNN*, June 16, 2015, accessed July 8, 2015, http://www.cnn.com/
2015/06/16/middleeast/yemen-aqap-leader-killed/.

202. Mullen, "Al Qaeda's Second in Command Killed in Yemen Strike."

203. Ibrahim Mothana, "How Drones Help Al Qaeda," *New York Times*, June 13, 2012, accessed March 15, 2015, www.nytimes.com/2012/06/14/opinion/how-drones
-help-al-qaeda.html.

204. Tom Cohen, "U.S., Britain Pull Some Staff from Yemen Due to Terror Threat," *CNN*, August 6, 2013, accessed March 15, 2015, http://www.cnn.com/2013/08/06/politics/terror-threats/.

205. Khan, "Understanding Yemen's Al Qaeda Threat."

206. Sudarsan Raghavan, "In Yemen, U.S. Airstrikes Breed Anger, and Sympathy for al-Qaeda," *Washington Post*, May 29, 2012, accessed July 1, 2015, https://www.washingtonpost.com/world/middle_east/in-yemen-us-airstrikes-breed-anger-and-sympathy-for-al-qaeda/2012/05/29/gJQAUmKI0U_story.html.

207. Gregory Johnsen, "How We Lost Yemen," *Foreign Policy*, August 6, 2013, accessed March 15, 2015, http://www.foreignpolicy.com/articles/2013/08/06/how_we_lost_yemen_al_qaeda.

208. Johnsen, "How We Lost Yemen."

209. Johnsen, "How We Lost Yemen."

210. Johnsen, "How We Lost Yemen."

211. Johnsen, "How We Lost Yemen."

212. Johnsen, "How We Lost Yemen."

213. Nabeel Khoury, "In Yemen, Drones Aren't a Policy," *Cairo Review of Global Affairs*, October 23, 2013, accessed March 15, 2015, http://www.aucegypt.edu/gapp/cairoreview/Pages/articleDetails.aspx?aid=443.

214. "Yemen Says May Harbor up to 300 Qaeda Suspects," *Reuters*, December 29, 2009, accessed December 3, 2014, http://www.reuters.com/article/2009/12/29/us-yemen-qaeda-minister-idUSTRE5BS2NR20091229.

215. Pam Benson, "New Terrorist Plot to Attack Plane Foiled," *CNN*, May 8, 2012, accessed March 15, 2015, http://edition.cnn.com/2012/05/07/world/meast/yemen-qaeda-plot/.

216. Swift, "The Drone Blowback Fallacy."

217. Swift, "The Drone Blowback Fallacy."

218. Swift, "The Drone Blowback Fallacy."

219. Swift, "The Drone Blowback Fallacy."

220. C. Christine Fair, "Drones over Pakistan—Menace or Best Viable Option?," *Huffington Post*, August, 02, 2010, accessed March 15, 2015, http://www.huffingtonpost.com/c-christine-fair/drones-over-pakistan----m_b_666721.html.

221. Foust, "Understanding the Strategic and Tactical Considerations of Drone Strikes," 12.

222. Chantel Carter, "Pre-Incident Indicators of Terrorist Attacks: Weak Economies and Fragile Political Infrastructures Bring Rise to Terrorist Organizations and Global Networks," *Global Security Studies* 3, no. 4 (2012): 72.

223. Megan Braun, "Predator Effect: A Phenomenon Unique to the War on Terror," in *Drone Wars: Transforming Conflict, Law, and Policy*, edited by Peter L. Bergen and Daniel Rothenberg (Cambridge: Cambridge University Press, 2014), 275.

224. Swift, "The Drone Blowback Fallacy."

225. Swift, "The Drone Blowback Fallacy."

226. Swift, "The Drone Blowback Fallacy."

227. Johnsen, "How We Lost Yemen."

228. "Scholar: U.S. Drone Use Has Contributed to Yemen's Instability," *NPR*, January 21, 2015, accessed July 8, 2015, http://www.npr.org/2015/01/21/378905622/scholar-u-s-drone-use-has-contributed-to-yemens-instability.

229. Greg Botelho and Hakim Almasmari, "Official: Houthis Take U.S. Vehicles, Weapons in Yemen," *CNN*, February 12, 2015, accessed March 15, 2015, http://edition.cnn.com/2015/02/11/middleeast/yemen-unrest/.

230. Roberta Rampton, "Obama Defends U.S. Counterterrorism Strategy in Yemen," *Reuters*, January 25, 2015, accessed March 15, 2015, http://uk.reuters.com/article/2015/01/25/uk-yemen-security-obama-idUKKBN0KY0GD20150125.

231. Daniel Byman and Jennifer R. Williams, "The Foreign Policy Essay: AQAP at a Crossroads," *Lawfare*, April 19, 2015, accessed July 1, 2015, http://www.lawfare blog.com/foreign-policy-essay-aqap-crossroads.

232. Helene Cooper and Eric Schmitt, "Al Qaeda Is Capitalizing on Yemen's Disorder, U.S. Warns," *New York Times*, April 8, 2015, accessed July 1, 2015, http://www.nytimes.com/2015/04/09/world/middleeast/ashton-carter-us-defense-secretary-warns-of-al-qaeda-gains-in-yemen.html?_r = 0.

233. Greg Millier, "Al-Qaeda Franchise in Yemen Exploits Chaos to Rebuild, Officials Say," *Washington Post*, April 5, 2015, accessed July 1, 2015, https://www.washingtonpost.com/world/national-security/al-qaeda-franchise-in-yemen-exploits-chaos-to-rebuild-officials-say/2015/04/04/207208da-d88f-11e4-ba28-f2a685dc7f89_story.html.

234. Oren Adaki, "AQAP Storms Yemeni Prison, Frees Jihadist Leader," The Long War Journal, April 2, 2015, accessed July 8, 2015, http://www.longwarjournal.org/archives/2015/04/aqap-storms-yemeni-prison-frees-al-qaeda-leader.php.

235. Saeed Al-Batati and Kareem Fahim, "War in Yemen Is Allowing Qaeda Group to Expand," *New York Times*, April 16, 2015, accessed July 2, 2015, ahttp://www.nytimes.com/2015/04/17/world/middleeast/khaled-bahah-houthi-rebel-yemen-fighting.html?_r = 0.

3

The Debate over Legality

Are Drone Strikes Permissible under U.S. and International Law?

IT WOULD BE HARD to overstate the importance of the question of the legality of U.S. drone strikes away from conventional battlefields. President Obama provided some sense of the stakes in his speech on U.S. counterterrorism Policy at the National Defense University on May 23, 2013. He began by asserting that at least up to the War on Terror "our commitment to constitutional principles has weathered every war." However, he then suggested that more recently, in the period after 9/11, "we compromised our basic values—by using torture to interrogate our enemies, and detaining individuals in a way that ran counter to the rule of law." Finally, he asserted that since his election his administration had "worked to align our policies with the rule of law" even while they "stepped up the war against al Qaeda." In this way he had sought to restore American integrity while also assuring American security. This issue of how Americans pursue national security in the new millennium, "from our use of drones to the detention of terrorist suspects," he argued, "will define the type of nation—and world—that we leave to our children." As he warned in the following paragraph: "We must define the nature and scope of this struggle, or else it will define us."[1]

So in President Obama's account, our security, our integrity, our very identity is implicated in the question of how we conduct counterterrorism today, and in particular with the use of drones and its legality. For if the drone strikes outside of conventional battlefields on which the Obama administration has relied (conducting over four hundred strikes in the last six years, leading to over three thousand deaths[2]) are illegal, then far from restoring our integrity and strengthening our identity, the Obama administration will have failed disastrously in its goal of correcting the errors of the Bush years. It will also have actively eroded our commitment to "constitutional principles" and basic values like "the rule of law," aggravated our collective crisis of identity, and made it impossible to pass along to future generations the kind of nation that Americans currently living have known.

So are the missile strikes carried out by U.S. drones outside of conventional battlefields since 2002, in places like Pakistan, Yemen, and Somalia, legally permissible? A host of critics, including UN officials and leading legal scholars, have charged that the U.S. drone strikes outside of Afghanistan and Iraq violate international law. Mary Ellen O'Connell, the Robert and Marion Short Professor of Law at Notre Dame University, argues, for example,

> [That] for much of the period that the United States has used drones for targeted killing in Pakistan, Yemen and Somalia, the killings occurred either in the absence of hostilities or when the United States was not participating in hostilities. In other words, the United States has targeted and killed persons under the combatant's privilege to kill where it did not possess that privilege.[3]

In other words, the United States has committed mass murder. Perhaps at the scale it has currently reached (over 3,500 killed in total between the Bush and Obama administrations) it would be better described as a crime against humanity. Indeed, Francis Boyle, professor of law at the University of Illinois College of Law, argues that as the "murderous drone campaign is both widespread and systematic it thus qualifies as a crime against humanity that verges on genocide."[4] Even some of those who strongly support the U.S. use of drones, such as Kenneth Anderson, professor of law at the American University, acknowledge that it "rests upon legal grounds regarded as deeply illegal . . . by large and influential parts of the international community."[5] A few critics have also suggested that U.S. drone strikes may also violate U.S. law. For example, William P. Quigley, professor of law and director of the Loyola University Law Clinic, finds "drone killings illegal under US law" since they "violate [the] ban on assassinations," citing in particular Article 2.11 of Executive Order 12333.[6]

Since 2010, however, the Obama administration has publicly and aggressively defended the United States' right to carry out such drone strikes. Consider the following statements by senior Obama administration officials in high-profile speeches:

- Harold Koh, legal adviser to the Department of State, on March 25, 2010: "The United States is in an armed conflict with al-Qaeda, as well as the Taliban and associated forces, in response to the horrific 9/11 attacks, and may use force consistent with its inherent right to self-defense under international law. . . . *U.S. targeting practices, including lethal operations conducted with the use of unmanned aerial vehicles, comply with all applicable law, including the laws of war.*"[7]

- John Brennan, then counterterrorism adviser and now CIA director, April 30, 2012: "As a matter of international law, the United States is in an armed conflict with al-Qaida, the Taliban, and associated forces, in response to the 9/11 attacks, and we may also use force consistent with our inherent right of national self-defense. There is nothing in international law that bans the use of remotely piloted aircraft for this purpose or that prohibits us from using lethal force against our enemies outside of an active battlefield, at least when the country involved consents or is unable or unwilling to take action against the threat." He further asserted that "these targeted strikes are legal."[8]
- Eric Holder, attorney general of the United States, March 5, 2012: "We are at war with a stateless enemy [i.e., 'al Qaeda and its associates']." Moreover, "international law recognizes the inherent right of national self-defense." Therefore, "it is entirely lawful—under both United States law and applicable law of war principles—to target specific senior operational leaders of al Qaeda and associated forces."[9]
- President Obama, speech at the National Defense University, May 23, 2013: "Under domestic law, and international law, the United States is at war with al Qaeda, the Taliban, and their associated forces." He particularly stressed "America's legitimate claim of self-defense," and insisted that "America's actions are legal."[10]

Some international experts have concurred with the legal claims of U.S. officials, although most states, with a few notable exceptions, have reserved their opinions, neither endorsing nor protesting the attacks.[11]

This chapter focuses primarily on the legal opinions and arguments advanced by scholars and U.S. public officials. It begins with an examination of the debate over the application of domestic U.S. law to drone strikes outside conventional battlefields, and then turns to international law.

I. The Permissibility of Drone Strikes under Domestic U.S. Law

A good introduction to the legal case for the use of drones under U.S. law was offered in a *Wall Street Journal* editorial in January 2010:

President Bush approved their use under his Constitutional authority as Commander in Chief, buttressed by Congress's Authorization for the Use of Military Force against al Qaeda and its affiliates after 9/11. Gerald Ford's executive order that forbids American intelligence from assassinating anyone doesn't apply to enemies in wartime.[12]

Of course, this is a simplified account of the legal case for drone strikes offered by the Bush administration, and that case has been significantly reinforced and elaborated under President Obama, but it is worth stressing these components because they remain at the heart of the issue.

Both the Bush and Obama administrations have invoked two overlapping authorities to justify drone strikes outside of conventional battlefields, both of which are featured in the *Wall Street Journal* summary. To begin with, both administrations have asserted that the president has the power as commander in chief under Article II of the U.S. Constitution to order drone strikes without congressional approval in order to protect the United States from attack, or indeed if it is "in the national interest" (as President Obama did in the case of sending drones to participate in the multistate military intervention in Libya in 2011).[13] Moreover, the Obama administration has explicitly argued that it need not seek congressional approval for drone strikes, or indeed any U.S. military strike, unless the scale of forces being deployed is sufficient to trigger the War Powers Resolution.[14] The trigger according to the Obama administration's Office of Legal Counsel would "typically" involve "exposure of U.S. military personnel to significant risk over a substantial period."[15] Since drone strikes do not expose U.S. military personnel to significant risk, the implication appears to be that the president has significant scope to order drone strikes abroad without obtaining approval from Congress.

However, neither the Bush nor Obama administrations had to rely exclusively on the president's Article II authority as commander in chief because on September 14, 2001, Congress passed an Authorization for Use of Military Force (AUMF) stating that "the President is authorized to use all necessary and appropriate force against those nations, organizations, or persons he determines planned, authorized, committed, or aided the terrorist attacks that occurred on September 11, 2001, or harbored such organizations or persons." Indeed, the Obama administration has relied primarily on the AUMF when offering legal justification for the drone strikes discussed in this book.[16] Such legislation is in most respects similar to a declaration of war (especially where armed conflict results), and the 2001 AUMF explicitly states in Article 2(b)(1) that it "is intended to constitute specific statutory authorization within the meaning of section 5(b) of the War Powers Resolution."[17]

Although the AUMF could be read narrowly as only permitting the use of force against al-Qaeda and the Taliban, President Bush immediately gave it a broad reading in his address to Congress on September 20, 2001: "Our war on terror begins with Al Qaeda, but it does not end there. It will not end until every terrorist group of global reach has been found, stopped and defeated."[18] While the Obama administration has dropped the expression "War on Terror" and the claim that the AUMF might extend to all terrorist groups of global reach,[19] it still sees it as authorizing "war with al Qaeda, the Taliban, and their associated forces," as President Obama put it in his May 2013 speech at the National Defense University.[20]

In the context of war with al-Qaeda and associated groups, the president as commander in chief has clear constitutional authority to direct U.S. forces (including air force drone pilots) to kill individual enemy combatants. For example, the U.S. Air Force has been used to carry out hundreds of drone attacks in Afghanistan (see chapter 1, table 1.4) without instigating much debate.[21] When using the U.S. military to target individuals *outside* of conventional battlefields, the Bush and Obama administrations have relied extensively on Special Forces, and have provided special authorization for such operations. For example, a (classified) al-Qaeda Network Executive Order of 2003 is reported to have directed the military's Joint Special Operations Command (JSOC) "to undertake a global campaign against al-Qaeda, subject to a matrix specifying particular types of operations that could be conducted in various countries without need to go to the Secretary of Defense or even the President to obtain specific additional authorization."[22] In essence, the order established a framework for JSOC to carry out a range of operations against al-Qaeda and affiliates, extending from surveillance to targeted killing.[23] According to Eric Schmitt and Mark Mazzetti of the *New York Times*, "[w]here in the past the Pentagon needed to get approval for missions" from the White House, presumably, "on a case-by-case basis, which could take days when there were only hours to act, the new order specified a way for Pentagon planners to get the green light for a mission far more quickly."[24] According to another report, the al-Qaeda Network Executive Order authorized operations in fifteen countries and provided standing authority to employ lethal force against al-Qaeda targets.[25]

There is also a second agency that the president can direct to carry out targeting operations—the CIA. On September 17, 2001, President Bush signed an executive finding that authorized the CIA to "kill or capture al-Qaeda militants around the globe."[26] Such findings remain secret, but according to journalist and historian Bob Woodward, it gave "the CIA the broadest and most lethal authority in its history," specifically to "kill or capture Qaeda militants around the globe." In essence, the CIA was authorized as part of its covert function to conduct "a secret global war on terror."[27]

So at first glance at least, the president seems to have two clear sources of authority to use force against al-Qaeda and the Taliban and their associated forces (his constitutional authority as commander in chief and Congress's AUMF) and two distinct means to take actions (the military and the CIA).

The main criticism that has been leveled against the Obama and Bush administrations is that the particular way that they have employed force (i.e., drone strikes) may have violated a prohibition in U.S. law. Executive Order 12333 states in Section 2.11 that "No person employed by or acting on behalf of the United States Government shall engage in, or conspire to engage in, assassination."[28] The Stanford University Law School/New York University Law School study *Living Under Drones*, for example, points out that "all U.S. presidents have embraced an executive order issued by President Gerald Ford in 1976 prohibiting political assassination," but argues in regard to the U.S. drone campaigns that "individual strikes could constitute acts of illegal extrajudicial assassination."[29] U.S. lawmakers have also suggested that U.S. drone strikes violate Executive Order 12333 in congressional legislation. Representative Dennis Kucinich proposed such a bill in 2010 (HR 6010), cosponsored by six colleagues. The bill, which was aimed at prohibiting drone strikes against U.S. citizens, specifically invoked Executive Order 12333 (in Section 1(8)), suggesting that the executive order would be violated in such strikes (and presumably other strikes as well since nothing in the executive order's prohibition of assassination is limited to U.S. citizens).[30] Even some defenders of drone strikes have worried that they may violate the executive order. For example, in 2006 the editor of *Middle East Quarterly*, Michael Rubin, argued that "it is time to revoke the ban on assassinating our enemies" precisely because it interfered with policies like the use of drone strikes outside of conventional battlefields.[31]

By contrast, a number of other commentators have argued that Executive Order 12333 does not legally prohibit targeting terrorists today. In the first place, as Kristen Eichensehr, visiting assistant professor of law at UCLA, points out, the order is a matter of "US policy—not law."[32] By consequence, just as such orders are signed and given their authority by one president, subsequent presidents may "circumvent or nullify them" without consulting Congress. Circumvention, Eichensehr suggests, was the strategy employed by President Bush. According to a report from Bob Woodward, when President Bush authorized the CIA to "use all necessary means" to eliminate bin Laden and al-Qaeda, including assassination, he did so on the understanding that Executive Order 12333 does not apply during wartime.[33] President Obama appears to have accepted this distinction and continued to order targeted killings on the basis that there is no conflict with Executive Order 12333. The authors of the *Living Under Drones* study also seem to allow that if there has been a subsequent executive order limiting or lifting Executive Order 12333, then there may not be a violation.[34]

In contrast with Eichensehr, other commentators sympathetic to the drone campaigns have argued that this is not a case of circumvention, but that presidents Bush and Obama are correct to think that Executive Order 12333 would not prohibit drone strikes against targets like al-Qaeda anyway. For example, in a seminal memorandum published in *Army Lawyer* in December 1989, William Hays Parks, the special assistant to the judge advocate general of the U.S. Army and one of the preeminent American experts on the application of international law to military affairs, concluded that

> [the] use of military force against legitimate targets in times of war, *or against similar targets in times of peace* where such individuals or groups pose an immediate threat to United States citizens or the national security of the United States, as determined by competent authority, does not constitute assassination or conspiracy to engage in assassination, and would not be prohibited by the proscription in EO 12333 or international law. . . . a decision by the President to employ *clandestine, low visibility or overt military force* would not constitute assassination if the U.S. military forces were employed against the combatant forces of another nation, a guerilla force or a terrorist or other organization whose actions pose a threat to the security of the United States.[35]

This interpretation has been endorsed by a wide range of legal scholars.[36]

A couple of important additional issues are raised in the rare case where an American is the target or is likely to be killed in a drone strike. Nonetheless, as these represent only a tiny subset of cases, they will only be briefly reviewed here. Two issues are of particular importance. The first is that targeting an American may be thought to violate Fifth Amendment due process rights guaranteeing "no person shall . . . be deprived of life, liberty, or property, without due process of law." However, Attorney General Eric Holder has argued that in cases wherein Americans associate themselves with an enemy force seeking to attack U.S. citizens, the due process clause does not require a judicial process, but can be satisfied by a review within the executive branch:

> Let me be clear: an operation using lethal force in a foreign country, targeted against a U.S. citizen who is a senior operational leader of al Qaeda or associated forces, and who is actively engaged in planning to kill Americans, would be lawful at least in the following circumstances: First, the U.S. government has determined, after a thorough review, that the individual poses an imminent threat of violent attack against the United States; second, capture is not feasible;

and third, the operation would be conducted in a manner consistent with applicable laws of war.[37]

Holder's key argument is that "'due process' and 'judicial process' are not one and the same," particularly when it comes to national security: "The Constitution guarantees due process, not judicial process."[38] The attorney general's reasoning here summarizes the more detailed findings provided in both the Office of Legal Counsel memorandum on the "Applicability of Federal Criminal Laws and the Constitution to Contemplated Lethal Operations Against Shaykh Anwar al-Aulaqi" and the Department of Justice white paper on the "Lawfulness of a Lethal Operation Directed Against a U.S. Citizen Who Is a Senior Operational Leader of Al-Qa'ida or an Associated Force."[39] The memorandum and white paper offer similar reasoning regarding the Fourth Amendment guarantee against "unreasonable search and seizure," which might be read as implying a bar against the deprivation of life without demonstrated reason.[40]

The second issue concerns the application of Section 1119 of Title 18 of the U.S. Code. In particular, Section 1119(b) holds that "[a] person who, being a national of the United States, kills or attempts to kill a national of the United States while such national is outside of the United States but within the jurisdiction of another country shall be punished as provided under section 1111, 1112, and 1113."[41] However, the memorandum and white paper offer a case that this provision of the U.S. Code does not present a bar to targeting suspected terrorists. The memorandum, for example, argues that this subsection "must be construed to incorporate a public authority justification"—that is, it was never intended to, and in fact does not, apply to public officials acting to discharge their lawful duty (like a police officer using lethal force to protect himself or a soldier using lethal force against an enemy).[42]

However, a number of critics have taken issue with these assertions by the Obama and Bush administrations and their Departments of Justice. For example, Anthony D. Romero, director of the American Civil Liberties Union, has declared that "we continue to disagree fundamentally with the idea that due process requirements can be satisfied without any form of judicial oversight by regular federal courts."[43] Senator Rand Paul expressed continuing concerns about the alternative "due process" that the Obama administration appears to be using, remarking: "I still have concerns over whether flash cards and PowerPoint presentations represent due process."[44] The *New York Times* Editorial Board also took issue with the "public authorities" justification that the Department of Justice used to justify an exception to U.S. Code 1119:

The main theory that the government says allows it to kill American citizens, if they pose a threat, is the "public authorities justification," a legal concept that permits governments to take actions in emergency situations that would otherwise break the law. It's why fire trucks can break the speed limit and police officers can fire at a threatening gunman. But it's a dangerous concept if expanded because it could be used to justify all kinds of government misdeeds, especially since Congress has never explicitly authorized an exception for official killing in this kind of circumstance, as the memo acknowledges. The sheer power of drone strikes, several of which have killed many innocent bystanders, is in no way comparable to the kind of police shootings that the memo cites as precedent. (And, in most cities, police shootings are carefully investigated afterward, and officers face punishment if they exceed their authority. Has that ever happened with an errant drone strike?)[45]

Many critics press for the government to be clearer about both its authorities and procedures.[46] Much criticism has also focused on the permissibility of drone strikes under international law.

II. International Law

The consistent position of the Obama administration on the permissibility of drone strikes outside of conventional battlefields under international law involves two key claims: (1) the United States is in an armed conflict (or "at war") with al-Qaeda and its affiliates; and (2) the United States can also use military force against them on the basis of its inherent right of self-defense. These justifications are both contested, and some of the objections overlap. But it is important to stress that they are distinct claims, invoking different issues and with significantly different implications for how the United States can legitimately use force. The following discussion begins with the claim of self-defense.

Self-Defense

The right of states to use force in self-defense is embedded in the UN Charter (1945). The first and perhaps central goal set out in the UN Charter is "to save succeeding generations from the scourge of war." Central to that project is Article 2(4) of the Charter, which declares that "all Members shall refrain in their international relations from the threat or use of force against the territorial integrity or political independence of any state, or in any other manner inconsistent with the Purposes of the United Nations." The Charter, however, also allows two exceptions to this general prohibition, specifically in Article 42, under which the UN Security Council can authorize the use of force, and Article 51. Article 51 reads as follows: "Nothing in the present Charter shall impair the inherent right of individual or collective self-defence if an armed attack occurs against a Member of the United Nations, until the Security Council has taken measures necessary to maintain international peace and security."

Article 51 is notoriously controversial, but there is at least one point of common agreement, and that is that at least two criteria are required to trigger it: "necessity" and "proportionality." Yoram Dinstein, professor emeritus at Tel Aviv University, stresses that in a 1996 advisory opinion the International Court of Justice (ICJ) recognized these two conditions as now constituting customary international law.[47] As Christine Gray of Cambridge University notes, these two conditions are the only commonly agreed-upon requirements and can be said to represent a "minimum test" for the use of armed force in self-defense. Indeed, she argues that in general state practice, necessity and proportionality "are often the *only* factors relied upon in deciding the legality of particular actions."[48]

According to Dinstein, "necessity" requires at least two conditions be met even in the wake of an armed terrorist attack: first, "a repetition of the [terrorist] attack must be expected, so that the extra-territorial law enforcement can qualify as defensive and not purely punitive"; second, "[t]he absence of alternative means for putting an end to the operations of the armed bands or terrorists."[49] Proportionality requires that the state's response "is to be directed exclusively against the armed band or terrorists."[50]

U.S. officials suggest that these key criteria of necessity and proportionality have been met in the case of U.S. drone strikes. In regard to the first criteria of necessity (i.e., further expected attacks), al-Qaeda (and some of its allies) have not only a well-established track record of attacking American targets, but make no mystery of their desire and intent to carry out further attacks against the United States. As President Obama remarked in his speech at the National Defense University, al-Qaeda is "an organization that right now would kill as many Americans as they could if we did not stop them first."[51] In regard to the second criteria of necessity (i.e., the absence of alternative means to end enemy operations), President Obama also pointed out that al-Qaeda and its affiliates tend to locate their bases in areas beyond the reach of law enforcement or even of conventional forces (at least without assuming elevated risks both to soldiers and local civilians). In these scenarios, the resort to drones is, in Obama's words, "in last resort."[52] Finally, in regard to the criteria of proportionality and going exclusively after the enemy, Obama stressed that in the Afghan war theater, the United States "will continue to take strikes against high value al Qaeda targets, but also against forces that are massing to support attacks on coalition forces."[53] Outside of the Afghan theater the United States will "only target al Qaeda and its associated forces" and only those individuals "who pose a continuing and imminent threat to the American people, and when there are no other governments capable of effectively addressing the threat."[54] This is the basis of what President Obama described as America's "legitimate claim of self-defense." But these threshold criteria are not the only considerations relevant to assessing a claim of self-defense, and that claim has been contested on a number of grounds.

Is There a Right of Self-Defense against al-Qaeda?

Some legal critics have challenged the claim that the United States has any right of self-defense against al-Qaeda that could justify anything like the drone campaigns. Three objections are packed into the following passage from O'Connell. She contends that the U.S. claim to a right of self-defense against al-Qaeda "has virtually no support in international law":[55]

> [1.] *The right to use force in self-defense applies to inter-state uses of force.* The law of self-defense was designed to allow a state to take necessary action against another state responsible for attacking the defending state. . . . The law of self-defense is not designed for responding to the violent criminal actions of individuals or small groups. . . . From many ICJ decisions, including, the 1949 Corfu Channel case, the 1986 Nicaragua case, the 1996 Nuclear Weapons case, the 2003 Oil Platforms case, the 2004 Wall case, the 2005 Congo case, and the 2007 *Bosnia v. Serbia* case, it is clear that [2.] *force in self-defense may only be carried out on the territory of a state responsible for a significant armed attack ordered by the state or by a state-controlled group that carried it out.* . . . Where a state is responsible for attacks, the ICJ said in *Nicaragua* and *Oil Platforms* that [3.] *low-level attacks or border incidents do not give rise to the right to use force in self-defense* on the territory of the responsible state.[56]

The three objections italicized in this passage can be summarized as follows: (1) the right of self-defense only "applies to interstate force," and since al-Qaeda is not a state or under the "effective control" of any state, there cannot be a right of self-defense against it; (2) the right to use force would at any rate only apply to the territory of a state that carried out an attack or exercised effective control of a terrorist group that carried out an attack, and since there is no state that has attacked the United States or controls al-Qaeda, there is also no U.S. right to use force on the territory of another state; and (3) attacks must reach a certain magnitude before they trigger the right of self-defense, and since al-Qaeda attacks have not reached that magnitude they do not trigger a right of self-defense.

Other legal scholars, however, take issue with O'Connell's analysis. Dinstein, for example, strongly affirms in the fourth edition of his seminal

War, Aggression and Self-Defense (2005) that states possess a right of self-defense against nonstate actors like terrorist groups that may be triggered by an attack regardless of whether the terrorist group is under the effective control of another state. Indeed, he uses as his principle illustration the United States' right of self-defense against al-Qaeda (despite the fact that al-Qaeda is clearly not under the effective control of any state). He writes,

> The simple proposition that forcible action taken against a state may constitute an armed attack, even if the perpetrators are non-state actors [e.g., a terrorist group] operating from a foreign state . . . was categorically upheld in previous editions of the present book. . . . all lingering doubts on this issue have been dispelled as a result of the response of the international community to the shocking events of 11 September 2001.[57]

Dinstein cites three international responses in particular, each of which recognizes an American right of self-defense in response to the September 11 attacks. First and most importantly, he notes UN Security Council Resolutions 1368 and 1373, which both affirm the "inherent right of individual and collective self-defense in accordance with the Charter" in the context of the "horrifying terrorist attacks."[58] Second, Dinstein notes that NATO voted to invoke, for the first time, Article 5 of the North Atlantic Treaty (1949), providing that "an armed attack against one or more of the Allies . . . 'shall be considered an attack against them all.' "[59] He stresses that "armed attack" is employed with specific reference to Article 51 of the UN Charter and the right of self-defense. Finally, Dinstein notes that in September 2001 the members of the Organization of American States similarly declared that "these terrorist attacks against the United States are attacks against all American States," again with specific reference to Article 51 of the UN Charter as well as Article 3 of the Rio Treaty and the right of self-defense.[60] Dinstein's evidence from the immediate aftermath of the September 11 attacks suggests a willingness on the part of states and international organizations to recognize that the September 11 terrorist attacks constituted an armed attack, and hence to recognize a corresponding right to employ armed force in self-defense against al-Qaeda.[61]

Dinstein also contests O'Connell's second claim that the right to take action in self-defense on the territory of another state can only arise when that state is responsible for an "armed attack" (possibly through its effective control of a terrorist group). He offers the following illustrative case (employing his favorite imaginary states, Arcadia and Utopia):

> If the government of Arcadia does not condone the operations of armed bands or terrorists emanating from within its territory against Utopia, but it is too

weak (militarily, politically or otherwise) to prevent these operations, Arcadian responsibility vis-à-vis Utopia (if engaged at all) may be nominal. Nevertheless, it does not follow that Utopia must patiently endure painful blows, only because no sovereign State is to blame for the turn of events. . . . the host government cannot expect to insulate its territory against measures of self-defense. . . . Just as Utopia is entitled to exercise self-defense against an armed attack by Arcadia, it is equally empowered to defend itself against armed bands or terrorists operating from within the Arcadian territory.[62]

The key point here is that in Dinstein's estimate the law of self-defense permits states to respond to an armed attack by a terrorist group with the use of force on the territory of another state where that group is based. Moreover, this use of force is permissible whether or not that other state was actively working with that terrorist group. If accurate, this would contradict O'Connell's second claim.

O'Connell's third objection to a U.S. right of self-defense against al-Qaeda was that the magnitude of the attacks on the United States may not have reached the threshold triggering a right of self-defense. Given the scale of the attack on 9/11 and the widespread international recognition that it constituted an armed attack, this claim seems open to objection. Moreover, the attack on 9/11 was not an isolated incident, but part of a pattern of al-Qaeda attacks that included the 1998 attacks on U.S. embassies in Africa and that on the USS *Cole* in 2000. O'Connell seems to suggest that the legal threshold for self-defense would have to be surpassed in a single attack, but Dinstein argues that "a series of pin-prick assaults might be weighed in its totality and count as an armed attack."[63] Christian Tams, a professor of International Law at the University of Glasgow, suggests that Dinstein's view "has received increased support in recent practice, but has not officially been endorsed."[64]

Issues with Immediacy, Preemption, and Imminence

A second line of criticism of U.S. appeals to self-defense is that they seem less and less well suited to the kind of sustained military campaigns that the United States has conducted in the years following 9/11. One side of this problem is that self-defense is not generally understood as an unlimited right of military response. Indeed, the exercise of self-defense must follow fairly quickly after the armed attack that triggers it. As summarized by Jan Kittrich, associate lecturer on international law at the University of Hradec Králové,

Traditionally, self-defense responses must be an immediate reaction to the previous armed attack: the defensive measures must be exercised within a reasonable time frame after the attack. Should an unreasonable amount of time elapse between the original armed attack and the defensive response, the reaction could be rendered illegal.[65]

Admittedly, the requirement that an armed response be "timely" is vague and therefore invites controversy, and it is particularly difficult to apply in cases of attack by terrorist groups; as Dinstein observes, "since 'the source of [terrorist] attacks may not be immediately obvious,' the process of gathering intelligence data and pinning the blame on a particular non-state group . . . may ineluctably stretch the interval between the armed attack and the forcible response."[66] Still, after more than a dozen years since the last successful al-Qaeda attack on the U.S. mainland, and during which the United States has used sustained military force against al-Qaeda, it is becoming increasingly difficult to make the link between cause and effect in terms of self-defense.

Of course, U.S. officials often point out that drone strikes are not "responsive" or "punitive" but are intended to disrupt and prevent future attacks. Indeed, the president and most of the officials quoted above invoked the criterion of "imminent threat" as a justification for drone strikes—a criterion that is frequently associated with self-defense, most famously in Daniel Webster's Caroline doctrine (which says that to justify preemptive force a threat must be "instant, overwhelming, leaving no choice of means, and no moment for deliberation"). Moreover, the criterion of "imminence" is specifically invoked in the Department of Justice White Paper on Targeted Killing, although it is defined there in strikingly broad terms:

> The condition that an operational leader present an "imminent" threat of violent attack against the United States does not require the United States to have clear and specific knowledge that a specific attack on U.S. persons and interests will take place in the immediate future . . . the threat posed by al-Qa'ida and its associated forces demands a broader concept of imminence . . . imminence must incorporate considerations of the relevant window of opportunity, the possibility of reducing collateral damage to civilians, and the likelihood of heading off future disastrous attacks on Americans.[67]

This broad definition of "imminence" has met a good deal of resistance. For example, Daphne Eviatar, senior counsel at Human Rights First, has replied that "it is impossible to define the 'imminent' threat needed to justify lethal force in self-defense as anything other than a threat of an aggressive action that is 'about to happen.'"[68] Moreover, an important group of scholars hold that the text of Article 51 precludes any right of preemptive self-defense, even if the threat is imminent. As Ian Brownlie influentially put it in his *International Law and the Use of Force by States* (1963), "The view that

Article 51 does not permit anticipatory action is correct and . . . arguments to the contrary are either unconvincing or based on inconclusive pieces of evidence."[69] Many contemporary legal scholars, such as Mary Ellen O'Connell and Michael Glennon, continue to adhere to this view.[70] For them, drone strikes may be at once too late (according to immediacy) and too early (because no anticipation is permissible, self-defense only applies after an armed attack). However, as Tams observes, there seems to be growing convergence among the balance of states and scholars that states must be allowed to respond at least to imminent threats, even if most continue to reject the "Bush Doctrine" of acting to prevent more remote threats from emerging. To illustrate this point, Tams quotes then UN Secretary-General Kofi Annan's report, *In Larger Freedom* (2005), which "made it clear that Article 51 UNC 'covers an imminent attack,' but '[w]here threats are not imminent but latent,'" only the Security Council can act.[71] The challenge then would be to define the legal contours of imminence in relation to a threat from a transnational terrorist network and determine whether unconventional U.S. drone strikes comply with the definition.

The Limitations Imposed on Self-Defense by Human Rights Law

There may also be a further constraint on the use of force permitted by the right of self-defense, at least in situations where a state of armed conflict does not already exist. In essence, there is a legal argument that absent armed conflict, armed force used in self-defense remains subject to international human rights law, and this will have implications for when and how lethal force may be used. Laurie Blank, director of the International Humanitarian Law Clinic at Emory University Law School, argues that

> in many cases in which a state uses force against a non-state actor outside its own territory, it will be in the context of counterterrorism as self-defense, outside of any armed conflict. In the absence of an armed conflict, international human rights law [IHRL] and the principles governing the use of force in law enforcement will govern. . . . The use of lethal force against suspected terrorists outside of armed conflict can therefore only be used when absolutely necessary to protect potential victims of terrorist acts.[72]

Blank argues that "there are two main components to the necessity prong of the self-defense paradigm [under IHRL]—imminence and alternatives."[73] "Imminence" must involve "clear and present danger" to potential victims of a terrorist act. "Alternatives" require that "there must be no alternatives to the use of force as a means to deter or repel the threat."[74] Together these requirements constitute the criteria of "absolute necessity." While Blank goes on to caution that there remains some debate over "precisely what constitutes a situation of 'absolute necessity,'" it seems likely to be considerably narrower than the very flexible account of "imminence" outlined in the Department of Justice white paper.[75]

Blank also emphasizes one final limitation that human rights law imposes on the use of force under a right of self-defense (outside of armed conflict). She argues that it allows no killing of civilians, even as the unintentional by-product of necessary force. As she puts it, "the LOAC [Law of Armed Conflict] also accepts the incidental loss of civilian lives as collateral damage, within the bounds of the principle of proportionality; human rights law contemplates no such casualties."[76]

Some objections, however, have been raised to the claims advanced by Blank concerning the conditions that human rights impose on the exercise of the right of self-defense outside of armed conflict. U.S. officials, for example, defend the broad conception of imminence outlined in the Department of Justice white paper as appropriate to the times and as increasingly accepted by the international community. As John Brennan put it:

> We are finding increasing recognition in the international community that a more flexible understanding of "imminence" may be appropriate when dealing with terrorist groups, in part because threats posed by non-state actors do not present themselves in the ways that evidenced imminence in more traditional conflicts. After all, al-Qa'ida does not follow a traditional command structure, wear uniforms, carry its arms openly, or mass its troops at the borders of the nations it attacks. Nonetheless, it possesses the demonstrated capability to strike with little notice and cause significant civilian or military casualties.[77]

Moreover, some legal scholars also dispute Blank's second argument that the exercise of the right of self-defense outside of armed conflict permits no civilian casualties. For example, Jordan Paust, the Michael and Teresa Baker Law Professor at the University of Houston, argues that in those circumstances, "some 'incidental' loss of civilian life might be foreseeable but still permissible if the requirements of reasonable necessity and proportionality are met."[78]

So there is controversy and debate over each of the limitations Blank thinks human rights law imposes on the exercise of the right of self-defense outside of armed conflict. But some U.S. officials and scholars sympathetic to U.S. drone strikes have taken a much more ambitious approach and argued that the United States is not actually obliged to uphold key human rights conventions (such as the International Covenant and Civil and Political Rights) outside of its own territory at all. This argument applies particularly when the United States uses force covertly.

Covert Action

American drone strikes in Pakistan have generally been covert operations that the U.S. government refuses to specifically acknowledge officially (although the fact that some operations of this type occur has now been recognized). Such covert operations are of course not a new (or unique) phenomenon, and there are domestic and international laws relating to such practices. As Kenneth Anderson notes, "American domestic law—the law codifying the existence of the CIA and defining its functions—has long accepted implicitly at least some uses of force, including targeted killing, as self-defense towards ends of vital national security that do not necessarily fall within the strict terms of an armed conflict in the sense meant by the Geneva Conventions."[79] The legal framework for lethal U.S. covert action has two core foundations. The first is domestic statutory authority under the National Security Act of 1947, which created the CIA and included as one of its functions that "it shall be the duty of the Agency, under the direction of the National Security Council . . . (5) to perform such other functions and duties . . . as the National Security Council may from time to time direct" (Section 102(d)(5)). The language of the article has been amended to read today as "[t]he Director of the Central Intelligence Agency shall . . . perform such other functions and duties related to intelligence affecting the national security as the President or the Director of National Intelligence may direct."[80] But the reallocation of responsibilities has not altered the conventional understanding of this "fifth function" of the agency to include covert action and in some cases lethal action.[81] As noted in the foregoing discussion of domestic law, such covert actions generally require a presidential finding, such as the one signed by President Bush in September 2001 authorizing the CIA "to kill or capture Qaeda militants around the globe."[82]

The second foundation of U.S. lethal covert operations is U.S. insistence that its legal obligations to uphold human rights are limited to its own territory. As Beth van Schaak of the Center on International and Security Cooperation at Stanford University observes, "Starting in 1995, but more consistently during the Bush administration, the United States in its filings before these human rights bodies has advanced a categorical and contrarian position that the obligations contained in the relevant human rights instruments have no extraterritorial application."[83] The implication of this position is that the United States is not, as a legal matter, bound by human rights treaties outside of U.S. territory. This position obviously has important implications for the covert conduct of lethal operations abroad. For example, among the most important of the human rights treaties is the International Covenant on Civil and Political Rights (ICCPR), which the United States ratified in 1992.[84] Article 6(1) of the ICCPR provides that "every human being has the inherent right to life. . . . No one shall be arbitrarily deprived of his life." Article 4(2) provides that there can be "no derogation" (or suspension) of this article even in case of emergency. Therefore, if the United States were to accept that this obligation extended extraterritorially (as many countries do), it would also have to accept that any targeted killing (in the sense that the goal of the operation is to kill a particular person) is illegal whether conducted at home or abroad, at least outside of armed conflict.

The defense of U.S. drone strikes as covert action unconstrained by human rights has attracted strong criticism. For example, it has been observed that it provides the president with extraordinary latitude to employ lethal action with little scrutiny. The concerns that this raises are well summarized by NYU law professor Philip Alston writing as the UN Special Rapporteur for Extrajudicial, Summary or Arbitrary Executions:

> Empowering Governments to identify and kill "known terrorists" places no verifiable obligation upon them to demonstrate in any way that those against whom lethal force is used are indeed terrorists, or to demonstrate that . . . every other alternative had been exhausted. . . . it actually creates the potential for an endless expansion of the relevant category to include any enemies of the state, social misfits, political opponents, or others.[85]

By contrast, Anderson argues that if the United States were to accept the extraterritorial application of the ICCPR, this would effectively close the legal window on lethal preemptive action outside of armed conflict, which would either prevent the United States from disrupting potential attacks or compel it to violate the human rights of suspected terrorists to do so.[86] It is perhaps in some part to avoid these types of complications attending the application of international human rights law that the United States consistently claims to be at war with al-Qaeda.

Armed Conflict

Indeed, the claim of being at war has several important advantages over appeals to self-defense alone. Most importantly, if there is an armed conflict, then (and only then) can the United States legitimately invoke LOAC as the operative legal framework, at least partially displacing other legal standards (including international human rights law). As Robert Kolb and Richard Hyde remark, "the applicability of LOAC depends on the existence of an armed conflict," or, as Richard Murphy and Afsheen Radsan put it, "for [LOAC] to apply, an armed conflict must exist as a matter of fact."[87]

The issue of whether the United States can legitimately act under LOAC is a crucial one because it permits the killing of one's enemy, at least within broad rules on the conduct of combat. As Christopher Greenwood, a judge on the International Court of Justice, notes in *The Handbook of Humanitarian Law in Armed Conflicts* (2000), "humanitarian law accepts that one of the legitimate objects of warfare is to disable enemy combatants (and in many cases this necessarily involves killing)."[88] As Dinstein has put it, in armed conflict "all combatants can be lawfully targeted."[89] To frame the point more broadly, the implication of the "armed conflict" view is that the United States may employ military force aggressively against al-Qaeda with the purpose of destroying it, and not solely to preempt planned attacks.

The U.S. claim to be at war is certainly not without initial plausibility. On the morning of September 12, 2001, a little before noon, President Bush declared war on those who had perpetrated the 9/11 attacks: "The deliberate and deadly attacks that were carried out yesterday against our country were more than acts of terror, they were acts of war."[90] The U.S. Congress seemed to accept a condition of war in its broadly framed AUMF, and the U.S. Supreme Court also appeared to recognize a state of armed conflict with al-Qaeda in its 2006 decision in *Hamdan v. Rumsfeld*. Moreover, President Obama, despite his many differences with President Bush, has maintained the same basic position in regard to al-Qaeda: As Obama declared on January 7, 2010, "We are at war, we are at war against al-Qaeda. . . . We will do whatever it takes to defeat them."[91]

On the other side of the conflict, al-Qaeda leaders have, in bin Laden's words, "declared *jihad* against the US government" repeatedly since 1996.[92] There is also every indication that al-Qaeda continues to plan and support attacks against the United States and its allies, and that the Afghan Taliban continues to protect al-Qaeda and to carry out attacks on ISAF forces and civilians in Afghanistan.[93] In May 2011, for example, after acknowledging bin Laden's death in an Internet statement, al-Qaeda's spokespersons vowed to "continue attacking America and their allies," declaring "soon . . . their blood will be mingled with their tears."[94] It is therefore far from implausible that the United States regards itself as at war with al-Qaeda.

But the issue in question here is not whether the two sides plausibly see themselves at war, but whether the violence meets the legal definition of "armed conflict."[95] There is important controversy around this question. An early but influential criticism of President Bush's declaration of war came from O'Connell, who asserted, "The President's 'war on terror' does not meet the legal definition of war. Moreover, to the extent there is ambiguity, the United States should err on the side of pursuing terrorists within peacetime criminal law, not the law of war."[96] Similarly, Helen Duffy, the legal director of INTERIGHTS, raised doubts about whether the U.S. war on al-Qaeda "can meet the criteria for the contemporary definition of armed conflict."[97] For one thing, she points out that a legal state of armed conflict must involve at least two clearly identifiable parties with recognizable armed forces engaged in the conflict. Duffy, however, doubts that terrorist organizations and their armed forces can be identified with adequate rigor. She asks, for example, "How one can define and identify with sufficient clarity the relationship between disparate individuals and their membership, support, or sympathy for al-Qaeda?"[98] In other words, how is it possible to be certain who does and who does not qualify as an enemy combatant?

By contrast, many legal scholars accepted from the outset that the United States is at war with al-Qaeda. Thus, in the words of Greg Travalio (the Stanley Professor of Law at Ohio State University) and John Altenburg (counsel at Greenberg, Traurig), "There is no doubt that the United States and others are engaged in a 'war' against terrorism no less real than many other wars fought in the past."[99] In the words of Roy Schöndorf of Debevoise and Plimpton in the *NYU Law Review*, "It is the law of armed conflict, and not that of peace, that should be the [general] frame of reference."[100] Indeed, Schöndorf argues that this is now the prevailing view in the legal literature.[101]

Several factors help to explain these opposed views over whether the legal conditions of armed conflict have been met. One source of these divergent views is that the conditions for an armed conflict are not very clearly spelled out in treaty law.

International Armed Conflict versus Armed Conflict Not of an International Character

The ambiguity over the nature of the conflict in question is rooted in part in the Geneva Conventions. The Geneva Conventions describe two forms of recognized armed conflict, neither of which neatly describes the U.S. armed struggle with al-Qaeda and associated forces, but both of which describe aspects of it. In the main, the Geneva Conventions address international armed conflict (IAC) "between two or more of the High Contracting Parties" (Article 2). By contrast, "armed conflict not of an international character" (or non-international armed conflict [NIAC]) is the subject of Common Article 3, which only specifies that it occur "in the territory of one of the High Contracting Parties." The meaning of NIAC is elaborated in the Second Additional Protocol of 1977, which specifies that NIAC "shall apply to all armed conflicts which are not covered" under the First Additional Protocol and "which take place in the territory of a High Contracting Party between its armed forces and dissident armed forces or other organized armed groups which, under responsible command, exercise such control over a part of its territory as to enable them to carry out sustained and concerted military operations and to implement this Protocol" (Article 1(1)).

The U.S. "war" with al-Qaeda and associated forces does not fit entirely into either category of IAC or NIAC. On the one hand, it is clearly not an IAC involving opposed states. On the other hand, while it does feature a confrontation between the armed forces of a state and an "organized armed group" (as in a NIAC), the hostilities are not limited to the territory of a single member state. Among legal scholars who accept the existence of an armed conflict with al-Qaeda, some have seen it as an IAC, but most have seen it as a NIAC.[102] The official U.S. view is that it is a NIAC.[103]

A second important division of legal opinion concerns the scope of the alleged NIAC with al-Qaeda and affiliated groups—in essence, over whether it is limited to Afghanistan or stretches transnationally to other territories like those of Yemen and Somalia. Jennifer Daskal, assistant professor at Washington College of Law, offers a helpful overview of this debate in which she associates the contending views with the United States on one side and its European allies on the other:

> The debate has largely devolved into an either-or dichotomy. . . . the United States, supported by a vocal group of scholars . . . has long asserted that it is at war with al Qaeda and associated groups. Therefore, it can legitimately detain without charge—and kill—al Qaeda members and their associates wherever they are found, subject of course to additional law-of-war, constitutional, and sovereignty constraints. Conversely, European allies, supported by an equally vocal group of scholars . . . assert that the United States is engaged in a conflict with al Qaeda only in specified regions [i.e., Afghanistan], and that the United States' authority to employ law-of-war detention and lethal force extends only to those particular zones. In all other places, al Qaeda and its associates should be subject to law enforcement measures, as governed by international human rights law and the domestic laws of the relevant states.[104]

Part of the difficulty here is that the rules of NIAC are notoriously underdeveloped in comparison with those of IAC and by consequence invite different interpretations.

In the dispute over the scope of the NIAC, much of the divergence of opinion can be boiled down to three sources. The first is whether the definition of NIAC is read as limiting it to a single territory, or as allowing that it could bleed over into the territory of more than one state. The second is whether the law is seen as strictly limited to what is explicitly stated, or whether it is possible to infer from conventions and customary practice, drawing perhaps on other sources of law. The third is over whether the other sources of law that are taken as guides to interpretation are human rights law or the law of international armed conflict.

U.S. officials have tended to favor the second option in regard to each of these three sources of conflict, leading to an understanding of the NIAC with al-Qaeda that is geographically expansive. Consider, for example, the following key passage from the Department of Justice's memorandum on targeting an American, which discusses how a state of armed conflict could extend across international borders:

> [S]ome commentators have suggested that the conflict between the United States and al-Qaida cannot extend to nations outside Afghanistan in which the level of hostilities is less intense or prolonged than in Afghanistan itself. There is little judicial or other authoritative precedent that speaks directly to the question of the geographic scope of a non-international armed conflict in which one of the parties is a transnational, non-state actor and where the principal theater of operations is not within the territory of the nation that is a party to the conflict. Thus, in considering this issue, we must look to principles and statements from analogous contexts. . . .
>
> In looking for such guidance, we have not come across any authority for the proposition that when one of the parties to an armed conflict plans and executes operations from a base in a new nation, an operation to engage the enemy in that location can never be part of the original armed conflict—and thus subject to the laws of war governing that conflict—unless and until the hostilities become sufficiently intensive and protracted within that new location. That does not appear to be the rule, or the historical practice, for instance, in a traditional international conflict. . . . Nor do we see any obvious reason why that more categorical, nation-specific rule [i.e., that armed conflicts are territorially bounded by nations] should govern in analogous circumstances in this sort of non-international armed conflict.[105]

The Department of Justice's memorandum begins with the idea that nothing in the Geneva Conventions clearly limits a NIAC to a single national territory, and then draws explicitly on the law of IAC to infer the rules for NIAC bleeding across borders (favoring the second approach in regard to each of the three sources of conflict described above). It is easy to see, however, how very different conclusions could be drawn if one began from the premises that a NIAC can only exist on the territory of a single state, that the rules of such conflict are limited to what is explicitly provided in treaties and conventions, and where there is any gap it should be filled by reference to human rights law. It is relying on these approaches that O'Connell, for example, is able to conclude: "That the United States is engaged in armed conflict against al Qaeda in Afghanistan does not mean that the United States can rely on the law of armed conflict to engage suspected associates of al Qaeda in other countries. . . . Armed conflict exists in the *territorially limited zone* of intense armed fighting by organized armed groups."[106]

The implications of these two approaches—which Daskal distinguishes as American and European—to the scope of international armed conflict are crucially different, and not only in terms of where military force can be used, but for whether there is today an armed conflict with al-Qaeda and its affiliates at all. To get a full picture of what is at stake, and how critical the issue of the scope of armed conflict is, it will be necessary to tackle the contested question of the threshold of violence that triggers a NIAC. But the most important implication can be at least roughly sketched as follows: On the American model, the threshold of war only has to be surpassed once, and it is possible to draw on evidence globally from everywhere fighting is occurring. On the European model, the armed conflict must be established in each state based only on evidence from within that state, and if the combatants move to a new state then the process must begin again. The American approach supplies support for the idea of a global NIAC with al-Qaeda and associated forces, while the European model suggests an armed conflict in Afghanistan in which al-Qaeda and the Taliban are participants.

So what, then, is the legal threshold for the existence of a non-international armed conflict? The international conventions addressing NIAC do not contain any clear and specific definition of the threshold of armed conflict—that is, what exact criteria must be met in order for there to be an armed conflict—and commentators notoriously take broader and narrower views on this issue. Nonetheless, there is some jurisprudence and some recent studies that can provide at least broad guidance. For example, O'Connell chaired a committee on the "use of force" for the International Law Association (ILA), which was charged with identifying at least minimum conditions for the existence of an armed conflict. The committee identified the following criteria:

1. The existence of organized armed groups,
2. Engaged in fighting of some intensity.[107]

So one useful starting point in exploring whether an armed conflict exists between the United States and al-Qaeda and perhaps other terrorist groups is whether these criteria are met. Before exploring this question, however, it will be useful to make two observations.

First, there remains important disagreement over the minimum conditions that trigger armed conflict. For example, probably the most influential jurisprudence on the question suggests a slightly different criterion of "protracted" violence (rather than focusing on "intensity"). The International

Criminal Tribunal for the former Yugoslavia (ICTY) found, in *Tadic Interlocutory Appeal,*

> that *an armed conflict exists whenever there is* a resort to armed force between States or *protracted armed violence between governmental authorities and organized armed groups* or between such groups within a State. International humanitarian law applies from the initiation of such armed conflict and extends beyond the cessation of hostilities until a general conclusion of peace is reached; or, in the case of internal conflicts, a peaceful settlement is achieved.[108]

The key point for present purposes is that in the case of non-international armed conflict the *Tadic* definition does not mention the need for a certain "intensity" of violence, but instead suggests that there must be "protracted armed violence."

Nonetheless, the ASIL and Tadic accounts do agree broadly on the kinds of things that indicate the presence of a NIAC, including the presence of an organized armed group in violent conflict with the state or other groups, and the nature of the violence, which might be measured in terms of the types of weapons that are being used, the kind of destruction being caused, the number of casualties (both military and civilian) that result, and how long it lasts. A useful point of reference here might be something like the Correlates of War survey, a cooperative project founded at the University of Michigan but now including 740 institutional members and devoted to the "systematic accumulation of scientific knowledge about war."[109] The Correlates of War criterion for the existence of non-international armed conflict is "1,000 battle-related deaths per year among all the qualified war participants."[110] Although originally this assessment included civilian deaths at least in relation to civil wars, in 1997 the methodology was updated with an eye to improving consistency across the data sets to exclude civilian casualties.[111] Of course, those who believe in an armed conflict with al-Qaeda may take issue with the exclusion of civilian casualties since a terrorist group's principal means of conducting war may be seen as killing civilians, and there doesn't seem to be any obvious reason why these lives should count less than those of soldiers. For this among other reasons this standard should be seen as illustrative of one possible threshold rather than as in any way legally decisive. One other important reservation about the Correlates of War standard is that where the *Tadic* judgment suggests that the legal framework of armed conflict "extends beyond the cessation of hostilities until a general conclusion of peace is achieved; or, in the case of internal conflicts, a peaceful settlement is achieved," the Correlates of War survey is only concerned with where combat is actually occurring and so cuts off any time the number of combat-related deaths fall under one thousand per year. Nonetheless, the Correlates of War standard can provide at least an illustrative example of one kind of standard that could be used to assess whether the threshold for armed conflict (at least of a non-international kind) has been met.

If the Correlates of War standard is applied only to the United States and its allies and al-Qaeda casualties, it is not clear that it has ever been met outside Afghanistan, at least unless U.S. allies and al-Qaeda affiliates are interpreted broadly (on the American model). Table 3.1 (below) summarizes the casualties of all core al-Qaeda attacks from 1997 to 2014 as reported by the University of Maryland Global Terrorism Database (GTD). If the focus

TABLE 3.1
Fatalities of al-Qaeda Attacks (Exempting Iraq), 1997 to 2010

Year(s)	University of Maryland's Global Terrorism Database[1]	
	Civilian Fatalities	Military Fatalities
1997	0	0
1998	235	0
1999	0	0
2000	0	19
2001[2]	2,942	55
2002	247	33
2003	47	9
2004	3	33
2005	8	0
2006	20	0
2007	20	43
2008	34	7
2009	0	0
2010	0	0
2011	3	0
2012	0	0
2013	0	0
2014	0	0
Total	**3,559**	**199**

1. University of Maryland Global Terrorism Database (GTD) at http://www.start.umd.edu/gtd/. Military Fatalities uses an advanced search with Perpetrator set to al-Qaeda, Years 1997–2014, all incidents, target: military. Accessed July 20, 2015, http://www.start.umd.edu/gtd/search/Results.aspx?start_yearonly=1997&end_year only=2014&start_year=&start_month=&start_day=&end_year=&end_month=&end_day=&asmSelect 0=&asmSelect1=&perpetrator=20029&target=4&dtp2=all&success=yes&casualties_type=b&casualties _max. Civilian Fatalities follows the same parameters except that target includes all categories except military. Accessed July 20, 2015, http://www.start.umd.edu/gtd/search/Results.aspx?expanded=no&casualties_type =f&casualties_max=&start_yearonly=1997&end_yearonly=2014&dtp2=all&success=yes&perpetrator =20029&target=5%2C6%2C1%2C8%2C9%2C7%2C2%2C10%2C11%2C12%2C13%2C3%2C14%2C15% 2C16%2C17%2C18%2C19%2C20%2C21%2C22&ob=GTDID&od=desc&page=1&count=100.

2. The GTD includes the 189 who died in the crash at the Pentagon on 9/11 as both civilians and military, so for the sake of precision we distinguish the fifty-five uniformed military who were killed from civilians: Andrea Stone, "Military's Aid and Comfort Ease 9/11 Survivors' Burdens," *USA Today*, August 20, 2002, accessed June 28, 2015, http://usatoday30.usatoday.com/news/sept11/2002-08-20-pentagon_x.htm.

is limited to military casualties, then it appears that they have never exceeded fifty-five in any given year.

Of course, one of the points that this data illustrates is that al-Qaeda and its affiliates are not in the business of fighting militaries but of killing civilians, which represent over 94 percent of fatalities on table 3.1. A second point is that the level of violence clearly does not approach the Correlates of War threshold for a NIAC.

The case for armed conflict on the Correlates of War standard becomes somewhat easier to make if one includes data from Afghanistan. The number of U.S. and ISAF casualties reported by iCasualties is provided on table 3.2 (below).

These numbers do not yet include either Afghan Security Forces or Taliban killed in Afghanistan. While only limited information is available on the number of Afghan Security Forces and Taliban who have died in the thirteen years of the conflict, an Afghan government report in 2014 stated that thirteen thousand members of the Afghan security forces had been killed in the period from October 2001 to March 2014,[112] while estimates on the number of Taliban insurgents killed up to March 2014 range from twenty thousand to thirty-five thousand according to Voice of America.[113] While no breakdown of the numbers is available by year, these estimates suggest that the threshold of one thousand combat-related deaths was certainly reached by

TABLE 3.2
Coalition Military Fatalities in Afghanistan by Year[1]

Year	US	UK	Other	Total
2001	12	0	0	12
2002	49	3	18	70
2003	48	0	10	58
2004	52	1	7	60
2005	99	1	31	131
2006	98	39	54	191
2007	117	42	73	232
2008	155	51	89	295
2009	317	108	96	521
2010	499	103	109	711
2011	418	46	102	566
2012	310	44	48	402
2013	127	9	25	161
2014	55	6	14	75
Total	2,356	453	676	3,485

1. iCasualties, "Operation Enduring Freedom," accessed February 15, 2015, http://icasualties.org/oef/.

2009 and 2010, and probably much earlier. Also, according to UNAMA at least fifteen thousand Afghan civilians have also been killed since 2007, when it started its tally, the majority of them (65.41 percent) at the hands of anti-government forces.[114] At any rate, at least most drone critics are prepared to acknowledge a state of armed conflict in Afghanistan that has persisted from the initial invasion, although some like O'Connell insist that armed conflict has evolved from an IAC between the United States and the Taliban government into a NIAC in which the United States is aiding the elected Afghan government to put down a domestic insurgency.[115] Still, it is accepted as legally permissible to conduct drone strikes there under the rules of LOAC. But the real division of opinion begins to emerge once the focus is shifted to Pakistan (and even more so to Yemen and Somalia).

War with al-Qaeda or a Non-International Armed Conflict in Pakistan?

The U.S. drone campaign in Pakistan appears to have begun on June 17, 2004, with the killing of Nek Muhammad (as described in chapter 1), followed by three strikes in 2005 (killing a total of fifteen, including at least five civilians). Were these strikes, like those across the border in Afghanistan, conducted in a circumstance of armed conflict and therefore subject to LOAC? On the "European" view, which insists that each national territory be treated separately, it is not clear that both of the ILA criteria for armed conflict were met. For example, while there was a good deal of violence in the FATA area, including clashes between government security forces and Pashtun tribes, it may certainly be argued that the level of violence had not yet crossed the intensity/protraction threshold in 2004. The numbers on table 3.3, provided by the South Asian Terrorism Portal, indicate 627 fatalities resulting from clashes between militants and security forces (and 132 of these were civilians).

However, table 3.3 also indicates a steady increase in the level of violence since 2002 to 2003. Critics like O'Connell correspondingly recognize that eventually the NIAC threshold was crossed, in her view in 2009 (although the Correlates of War threshold would suggest 2007).[116] So the drone strikes from 2004 to 2008 appear to her to occur outside of armed conflict and therefore to have only self-defense as a possible justification. But there is little evidence to suggest that the kind of threat of imminent attack existed (at least on a conventional understanding of imminence) to warrant the resort to lethal force in self-defense, especially outside of armed conflict. Moreover, even once the NIAC threshold was breached, the United States would only

TABLE 3.3
South Asian Terrorism Portal Reports on Fatalities Resulting from Clashes between Militant and Security Forces in FATA[1]

Year	Civilians	Security Forces	Militants	Total
2014	159	194	2,510	2,863
2013	319	198	1,199	1,716
2012	549	306	2,046	2,901
2011	488	233	2,313	3,034
2010	540	262	4,519	5,321
2009	636	350	4,252	5,238
2008	1,116	242	1,709	3,067
2007	424	243	1,014	1,681
2006	109	144	337	590
2005	92	35	158	285
2004	132	195	300	627
April 2002–2003	2	14	18	34

1. Results for 2006 to 2014 from South Asia Terrorism Portal, FATA Assessment, 2015, http://www.satp.org/satporgtp/countries/pakistan/Waziristan/index.html; data for 2005 is from South Asia Terrorism Portal, Pakistan Assessment, 2008, http://www.satp.org/satporgtp/countries/pakistan/assesment2008.htm; data for 2004 is assembled from South Asian Terrorism Portal, FATA Timeline 2004, accessed May 1, 2015, http://www.satp.org/satporgtp/countries/pakistan/Waziristan/timeline/2004.htm; data for 2002 to 2003 is assembled from South Asia Terrorism Portal, FATA Timeline 2003, http://www.satp.org/satporgtp/countries/pakistan/Waziristan/timeline/2003.htm; and FATA Timeline 2002, accessed June 30, 2015, http://www.satp.org/satporgtp/countries/pakistan/Waziristan/timeline/2002.htm.

have a right to use military force insofar as it acted against insurgents at the invitation of the Pakistani government—a condition of which O'Connell is skeptical.[117]

Similar objections can be raised about drone strikes outside of Pakistan, including, for example, the first strike carried out in Yemen on November 3, 2002, which killed Ali Qaed Sunian al-Harithi and five companions.[118] In the context of a war with al-Qaeda and affiliated organizations, al-Harithi might well be considered a legitimate target. If the premise of an overarching NIAC is rejected, however, it is not obvious how this strike could be legally justified. There is little to indicate that there was a separate NIAC in Yemen at the time, and no evidence suggesting that al-Harithi was imminently threatening the United States, so a claim of self-defense is open to question. In other words, the justification of the al-Harithi strike appears to depend on the (American) overarching NIAC theory. However, it is worth noting that the vast majority of U.S. drone strikes in Yemen have occurred since 2011 (see the case study in chapter 2), when a more plausible case for a NIAC can be made.

Nonetheless, whether one favors the overarching NIAC with al-Qaeda or a separate NIAC within Yemen itself, an additional challenge arises for justifying U.S. drone strikes. The issue is that they are directed against members of al-Qaeda in the Arabian Peninsula (AQAP), a distinct group founded in 2009 that may not be properly included in the U.S. conflict with al-Qaeda (or encompassed within the AUMF, which specifically refers to those who "planned, authorized, committed or aided the terrorist attacks that occurred on September 11, 2001"). In order to justify these strikes within the conflict with al-Qaeda and under the AUMF, U.S. officials must rely on the idea of "associated forces."

Associated Forces

President Obama and his officials consistently assert that the United States is at war with al-Qaeda and "associated forces."[119] While the latter term sounds troublingly vague, officials like Jeh Johnson, who was then the general counsel of the Department of Defense, have attempted to spell out its meaning:

> Nor is the concept of an "associated force" an open-ended one, as some suggest. This concept, too, has been upheld by the courts in the detention context, and it is based on the well-established concept of cobelligerency in the law of war. The concept has become more relevant over time, as al Qaeda has, over the last 10 years, become more decentralized and relies more on associates to carry out its terrorist aims. An "associated force," as we interpret the phrase, has two characteristics to it: (1) an organized, armed group that has entered the fight alongside al Qaeda, and (2) is a cobelligerent with al Qaeda in hostilities against the United States or its coalition partners.[120]

The Obama administration's view is that since these groups have aligned themselves with al-Qaeda, and have sufficient structure and definition to be a party to a NIAC, they can be targeted.[121] Moreover, there are indications that Congress has "expressly embraced" the notion of "associated forces" as the National Defense Authorization Act (enacted in 2012) authorizes detention on this basis.[122]

At the same time, there has been considerable resistance to the claim that groups allied to al-Qaeda (such as AQAP or al-Shabaab) can be treated as effectively akin, including in the U.S. judiciary. For example, the D.C. Circuit Court concluded in *al-Bihani v. Obama* in 2010,

> the laws of co-belligerency . . . have only applied to nation states. . . . The 55th [i.e., the group with which al-Bihani was fighting] clearly was not a state, but

rather an irregular fighting force present within the borders of Afghanistan at the sanction of the Taliban. Any attempt to apply the rules of co-belligerency to such a force would be folly, akin to this court ascribing powers of national sovereignty to a local chapter of the Freemasons.[123]

The court's logic here would also seemingly preclude applying the concept of cobelligerency to larger groups, like al-Shabaab or AQAP, as they also are not states. Some legal scholars have enthusiastically embraced the court's assessment, including Kevin Jon Heller of the School of Oriental and African Studies School of Law, who argues that there is "no justification for the [U.S.] government's attempt . . . to import the concept of co-belligerency into non-international armed conflict."[124] Others, like Jack Goldsmith, the Henry Shattuck Professor of Law at Harvard Law School, defend the practice of drawing on IAC to work out the law applying to a NIAC, which spills across borders, and correspondingly the U.S. government's use of the concept of cobelligerency.[125] A parallel debate, turning on similar grounds, has also emerged over who within these groups can and cannot be legitimately targeted within a NIAC.

The Controversy over Combatants

U.S. officials, supported by the Office of Legal Counsel, have adopted the view that any member of al-Qaeda or an affiliated group can be targeted as a matter of law. In his 2012 remarks at the Wilson Center, for example, John Brennan argued that "the use of force against *members* of al-Qaida is authorized under both international and U.S. law . . . which courts have held extends to those who are part of al-Qaida, the Taliban, and associated forces."[126] Some scholars, however, have objected to this criterion as too broad. Kristina Benson of the UCLA School of Law, for example, has argued that "even in the context of a War on Terror, actors do not become a legitimate target due to official membership status in a terrorist organization, nor through their physical association with members of a terrorist organization."[127] Critics like Benson have forcefully argued that legitimate targets are limited to those who are directly participating in hostilities at the time that they are targeted. Alston in his 2010 report as UN Special Rapporteur for Extrajudicial, Summary or Arbitrary Executions neatly summarized the argument for this view: "[u]nder the [LOAC] applicable to non-international armed conflict, there is no such thing as a 'combatant'—i.e., a non-state actor entitled to the combatant's privilege—[so] it follows that states are permitted to attack only civilians who 'directly participate in hostilities.'"[128]

However, the DOJ Memorandum on Targeted Killing takes direct issue with Alston's interpretation of LOAC and advances a much broader account of who can be targeted. David Barron, then acting assistant attorney general, writes in response to Alston, "We do not think this is the proper understanding of the laws of war in a non-international armed conflict, or of Congress's authorization under the AUMF."[129] Barron points first to the International Committee of the Red Cross's *Interpretive Guidance on the Notion of Direct Participation in Hostilities* (2009), which holds that "a member of a non-state armed group can be subject to targeting by virtue of having assumed a 'continuous combat function' on behalf of that group . . . anywhere and at any time."[130] Barron regards this as sufficient to bring al-Awlaki within the reach of the AUMF, but he also endorses a broader standard by embracing Judge Walton's reasoning in *Gherebi v. Obama*. There Judge Walton writes, "The Court adopts the government's 'substantial support' standard for detention," and by extension for targeting, in preference to "the 'direct participation' model advanced by the petitioners."[131] The former approach, which draws on the rules of IAC,[132] permits the targeting of any person who provides "substantial support" to enemy "armed forces." The point is nicely summarized by Goldsmith and Curtis Bradley (the Van Alstyne Professor of Law at Duke University) when they write: "Terrorist organizations do have leadership and command structures, however diffuse, and persons who receive and execute orders within this command structure are analogous to combatants" in IAC.[133] Still, even if one accepts this logic and the broad understanding of legitimate targets it suggests, there remains a big question over whether the United States has the right to use lethal force against enemy combatants on the territory of states with whom it is not at war (as in the cases of Pakistan, Yemen, and Somalia).

Sovereignty and Consent

Another frequent criticism of U.S. drone strikes in Pakistan, Yemen, and Somalia is that they violate the sovereignty of these countries, with whom the United States is not at war. The most conventional route to legally justify military operations on the territory of another state is through the consent of the state on whose territory the strikes take place (or the territorial state). According to long-standing international custom, military assistance may, as Oppenheim put it in his *International Law*, be "rendered by one state to another at the latter's request and with its consent, which may be given *ad hoc* or in advance by treaty."[134] This customary law finds expression in Article 20 of the International Law Commission's (ILC) Draft Articles on State Responsibility, which provides,

Valid consent by a state to the commission of a given act by another State precludes the wrongfulness of that act in relation to the former State to the extent that the act remains within the limits of that consent.[135]

However, the ILC commentary also specifies that such consent must meet certain conditions that are well summarized by Natalino Ronzitti, the chair of International Law at the Libera Università degli Studi Sociali Guido Carli of Rome:

> Consent must answer the following requisites to operate as a circumstance precluding wrongfulness: i) it must be given prior to the commission of the international wrong; ii) it must be given by an authority which can be said to express the will of the local state; iii) the local State's expression of will must be valid, not vitiated by so-called "vices de volonté"; iv) the action by the infringing state must be kept strictly within the limits of the consent given by the local sovereign authority; v) the infringing state must not violate an *erga omnes* [i.e., owed to all, or general] obligation.[136]

If the United States has received consent from Pakistan, Yemen, and Somalia that fulfills these criteria, that would provide a legal explanation both for why drone strikes do not violate these countries' sovereignty and for why the United States is permitted to attack targets that would be permissible for these states themselves to go after. There are widespread reports that the United States has received consent to conduct drone strikes from the presidents of Yemen, Somalia, and Pakistan that would at least cover most drone strikes. For example, Yemen's president Hadi praised U.S. drone strikes in his country, saying that the United States "helped with their drones because the Yemeni Air Force cannot carry out missions at night."[137] Somali president Mohamoud has also praised U.S. drone strikes in his country and affirmed that they are conducted with his support: "We support it so far, because so far the U.S. drones have killed only foreign fighters in Somalia and we appreciate it. We don't have any sympathy for the foreigners."[138]

The Pakistani case, however, is more complicated, with widespread reports that presidents Musharraf and Zardari privately consented to strikes while they and other senior Pakistani officials publicly condemned them. Still, some critics of drone strikes, such as O'Connell, have argued what is really required is "express consent," by which they seem to mean public, explicit and specific consent.[139] Indeed, in the absence of such public consent from the current Pakistani president (and in view of the fact that the Pakistani Parliament has overwhelmingly condemned drone strikes as a violation of Pakistani sovereignty), UN Human Rights Rapporteur Ben Emmerson concluded that the U.S. drone campaign in Pakistan "involves the use of force on the territory of another state without its consent, and is therefore a violation of Pakistan's sovereignty."[140]

However, even in the absence of consent, U.S. officials including John Brennan have asserted the right to use force on the territory of another state if that state "is unable or unwilling to take action against the [terrorist] threat."[141] Some legal scholars (including some critics of drone strikes[142]) accept this standard for justifying a military intrusion into the territory of another state. Ashley Deeks of the University of Virginia School of Law writes, for example,

> International law traditionally requires the victim state to assess whether the territorial state is "unwilling or unable" to suppress the threat itself. Only if the territorial state is unwilling or unable to do so may the victim state lawfully use force.[143]

Other scholars, however, have insisted there is little in either conventional or customary international law to support such a right. Kevin Jon Heller, for example, writes as follows in direct response to Deeks:

> To be sure, it appears that customary international law is slowly evolving away from the *Nicaragua* standard, especially in the wake of 9/11. But it is far from clear whether that standard has been replaced by the "unwilling or unable" test.[144]

So insofar as the United States must invoke the "unwilling or unable" standard, they are venturing onto at least sharply contested legal grounds.

However, even if one accepts that the U.S. drone strikes respect the sovereignty of local states and indeed are otherwise compliant with the *jus ad bellum* (the right to resort to force), big questions remain over whether the United States complies with LOAC in the actual conduct of its lethal operations.

Compliance with Rules on the Conduct of War

The discussion of international law thus far has been concerned with whether LOAC applies to U.S. drone strikes outside conventional battlefields. If it does, there remains the question of whether U.S. operations comply with LOAC rules on the conduct of war. The next few subsections therefore consider what are broadly taken to be the most basic principles governing the conduct of armed conflict, including humanity, necessity, distinction, and proportionality.

The Principle of Humanity

The overall purpose of LOAC can aptly be summarized as containing and limiting the destructive effects of war, especially on those most vulnerable and least able to defend themselves, without preventing the conduct of war itself. This purpose gives rise to the principle of humanity, which is aptly summarized in the United Kingdom's *Manual of Armed Conflict*, which broadly "forbids the infliction of suffering, injury or destruction not actually necessary for the accomplishment of legitimate military purposes."[145]

Drone defenders argue that the United States is complying with this central governing principle of LOAC because it is pursuing its legitimate military objectives (here neutralizing the threat from al-Qaeda and its affiliates) in the least harmful ways available, particularly with regard to civilians. As Anderson argues, drones are "often the most expedient—and, despite civilian casualties that do occur, most discriminatingly humanitarian—manner to neutralize a terrorist without unduly jeopardizing either civilians or American lives."[146]

By contrast, drone critics disagree. For example, Lord Bingham, one of Britain's most senior judges, argued that unmanned drones are among the weapons that "have been thought to be so cruel as to be beyond the pale of human tolerance" and should be among those weapons that "the international community should decide should not be used."[147]

The Principle of Military Necessity

The principle of necessity derives directly from the principle of humanity, and is formulated as follows in the current *United States Field Manual*: "The law of war . . . requires that belligerent[s] refrain from employing any kind or degree of violence which is not actually necessary for military purposes," and permits only those "which are indispensable for securing the complete submission of the enemy as soon as possible."[148] The principle is now recognized as part of customary international law.[149] Under this principle, drone strikes would only be legitimate if they constitute an indispensable means of attacking legitimate military targets.

U.S. officials, including President Obama and then Secretary of Defense Leon Panetta, have persistently argued that drone strikes are "the only game in town" in regard to reaching enemy militants and training camps. If this is the case, then it may be well be argued that they are "indispensable for the complete submission of the enemy as soon as possible."

While not directly disputing this logic, some commentators have raised concerns that the very nature of drones may also ultimately tempt the U.S.

government into operations that exceed military necessity. As Michael Walzer, emeritus professor at Princeton's Center for Advanced Studies wrote in 2013 in regard to U.S. use of drones: "Here is the difficulty: the technology is so good that the criteria for using it are likely to be steadily relaxed. That's what seems to have happened with the U.S. Army or with the CIA in Pakistan and Yemen."[150]

The Principle of Distinction

The principle of distinction can be seen as an elaboration of the principle of military necessity intended to clarify what is and is not a legitimate military target. It is codified in Article 48 of the First Additional Protocol of the Geneva Conventions: "In order to ensure respect for and protection of the civilian population and civilian objects, the Parties to the conflict shall at all times distinguish between the civilian population and combatants and between civilian objects and military objectives and accordingly shall direct their operations only against military objectives." It is widely recognized as today forming customary law binding on all countries even in non-international armed conflict.[151]

U.S. officials insist that they fully comply with the principle of distinction and target only combatants and military objects.[152] The main criticism of U.S. drone strikes in regard to the compliance with the principle of distinction concerns signature strikes. Many observers of the drone program have challenged the legality and morality of signature strikes on the grounds that they rely on imprecise determinations of combatant status. A case study of arguments over signature strikes is provided at the end of this chapter.

The Principle of Proportionality

The principle of proportionality, which is now recognized as part of customary international law both for IACs and NIACs,[153] is defined as follows in the ICRC's omnibus 2005 codification of *Customary International Humanitarian Law*:

> Launching an attack which may be expected to cause incidental loss of civilian life, injury to civilians, damage to civilian objects, or a combination thereof, which would be excessive in relation to the concrete and direct military advantage anticipated, is prohibited.[154]

The principal focus of the principle of proportionality, then, is the level of "collateral damage" to innocent bystanders that can be reasonably *anticipated* in particular operations and where that level becomes unacceptable—

that is, where it becomes excessive in relation to *anticipated* military advantage.[155]

Critics have charged that the U.S. drone campaigns have violated the principle of proportionality. In O'Connell's words, for example, "we see that U.S. use of drones is failing the relevant tests of the lawful use of force. It is failing . . . under the principle of proportionality."[156] As evidence she cites a report originating in the Pakistani press that U.S. drone strikes killed fifty civilians for each legitimate target they killed, which she calls "a textbook example of a violation of the proportionality principle."[157]

U.S. officials, by contrast, have insisted that U.S. drone strikes uphold the principle of proportionality and in fact result in relatively few noncombatant deaths. Harold Koh, for example, insisted that "the principles of distinction and proportionality . . . are implemented rigorously throughout the planning and execution of lethal operations to ensure that such operations are conducted in accordance with all applicable law."[158] Others outside the administration but familiar with the program, like Senate Select Committee on Intelligence Chair Dianne Feinstein, have stressed "the very low number of civilian casualties that result from such strikes"—in fact, she suggests that the Intelligence Committee's fact checking of reports from the executive have shown that "the number of civilian casualties that have resulted from such strikes each year has typically been in the single digits."[159] John Brennan also asserted that U.S. "targeted strikes conform to the principle of proportionality," and insisted that "it is hard to imagine a tool that can better minimize the risk to civilians than remotely piloted aircraft."[160]

Both sides of this exchange have been charged with tailoring numbers to suit their arguments—Feinstein with underestimating civilian casualties and O'Connell with exaggerating them.[161] The best available numbers from publicly accessible open-source databases have been provided in chapter 1 and the case studies in chapters 1 and 2.

Unfortunately, this type of aggregated data cannot answer the question of whether there have been violations of proportionality. This is for two main reasons. The first is that, as McNeal puts it, "each strike must be assessed on a case-by-case basis."[162] The second is that, in Laurie Blank's words, "Proportionality in the LOAC is a prospective analysis, viewed from the perspective of the commander at the time of the attack."[163] In other words, it turns on the number of civilian deaths that the planner (reasonably) anticipated and the expected military gains in the planner's mind and how they compared. Evidently, these are difficult to know, especially in regard to covert strikes. It is worth bearing in mind, however, that the legal standard for establishing that a violation of proportionality amounts to a war crime is fairly demanding. For example, the 1998 Rome Statute of the International Criminal Court defines the war crime associated with violating proportionality as follows: "*Intentionally launching* an attack in the knowledge that such attack will cause incidental loss of life or injury to civilians or damage to civilian objects . . . which would be clearly excessive in relation to the concrete and direct overall military advantage anticipated" (Article 8(2)(b)(iv); italics added). The key point here is that the accused must have been fully aware that an operation would violate proportionality and have intentionally proceeded nonetheless.

In light of the difficulties in assessing violations of proportionality, it is not surprising that so much critical attention has focused on the question of signature strikes, and whether they represent violations of the (at least slightly less elusive) principle of distinction. The following case study examines this fraught issue in more detail.

Case Study: Signature Strikes

The single aspect of the U.S. drone campaigns that has probably attracted the most critical attention is the use of signature strikes, or what are sometimes called "crowd killings" or "terrorist attack disruption strikes" (TADS).[164] The nature of these strikes and some of the main objections are well summarized by Michael Boyle:

> The increasingly indiscriminate nature of the drone strikes can also be seen in the adoption of so-called "signature strikes," where the targeting criterion is not the combatant status of an individual but rather their "pattern of behavior." In these cases, strikes are authorized without knowledge of the identity of the target, solely on the basis of behaviour—such as gathering at a known al-Qaeda compound, loading a truck with what appears to be bomb-making material or even crossing a border multiple times in a short period—that appears suspicious. The obvious risk is that innocent civilians will be killed on the basis of a misinterpretation of their behavior by drone operators, or that the standards by which a "pattern of life" is identified might be too lax.[165]

The Stanford/NYU *Living Under Drones* study concludes that the legality of so-called signature strikes is "highly suspect."[166] Micah Zenko calls on the U.S. government to "either end the practice of signature strikes or provide a public accounting of how it meets the principles of distinction and proportionality."[167]

However, U.S. officials and some commentators have defended the signature strikes as legal and effective. When asked about signature strikes after his Wilson Center speech on April 30, 2012, John Brennan responded,

Everything we do . . . that is carried out against al-Qaida is carried out consistent with the rule of law, the authorization on the use of military force and domestic law. And we do it with a similar rigor, and there are various ways that we can make sure that we are taking the actions that we need to prevent a terrorist attack. That's the whole purpose of whatever action we use, the tool we use, it's to prevent attack, and to save lives.[168]

An unnamed U.S. official in 2011 reported that the United States killed twice as many "wanted terrorists" through signature strikes as through personality strikes.[169] Daniel Byman has also stressed that signature strikes are "in keeping with traditional military practice; for the most part, U.S. soldiers have been trained to strike enemies at large, such as German soldiers or Vietcong guerillas, and not specific individuals."[170]

Reliance on signature strikes has grown as the drone campaigns have developed. The early U.S. drone strikes under President George W. Bush were generally what are called "personality strikes," intended to hit specific, identified individuals whose names appear on kill lists. In 2008, President Bush authorized the use of signature strikes in Pakistan and expanded the target profile to include "low-level fighters whose identities may not be known."[171] These moves came in response to the rapid destabilization in the FATA region, and were intended to support the war effort in Afghanistan.[172] According to an anonymous U.S. official, as the rapidity of drone strikes reached its height in Pakistan, in 2009 and 2010, as many as half of all kills were classified as signature strikes.[173] In 2010, a Reuters report claimed that of five hundred militants killed by drones between 2008 and 2010, only 8 percent were the sort of "top-tier militant[s]" or even "mid-to-high level organizers" who might plausibly have been on a kill list.[174]

The use of signature strikes again expanded significantly in April 2012 when the Obama administration authorized their limited use in Yemen. According to senior U.S. officials, the Yemen policy authorized "targeting fighters whose names aren't known but who are deemed to be high-value terrorism targets or threats to the U.S."[175] However, "The White House stopped short of authorizing attacks on groups of lower-level foot soldiers who are battling the Yemeni government."[176] One U.S. defense official called the new targeting policy "signature lite."[177] There are also reports that the United States has employed signature strikes in Somalia.[178] Indeed, across Pakistan, Yemen, and Somalia, according to at least one 2013 report, "the vast majority of drone strikes carried out by the CIA have been signature strikes, not 'personality strikes.'"[179]

It is not difficult to imagine why the United States might be attracted to the use of these strikes. They enable the United States to leverage its control of the air and the enormous volume of intelligence it is able to gather. They also take advantage of drones' capability to shift rapidly from intelligence gathering to attack. U.S. officials have also emphasized that the CIA "killed most of their [kill] 'list people' when they didn't know they were there," probably meaning signature strikes.[180] Signature strikes also contribute to disrupting coordination of targeted groups, increasing psychological stress, and preventing the training of new members. Even critics like Cronin have acknowledged that such strikes help to generate a "threat of instant death from above [that] has made recruitment more difficult and kept operatives from establishing close ties with civilians, who fear that they might also be killed."[181] Byman stresses the aggregate disruption of "terrorists' ability to communicate and train new recruits."[182] In essence, these strikes permit the U.S. government to impose a sustained condition of war on those who claim to be waging it on them.

However, it is equally obvious why many people would oppose this tactic. Michael Boyle puts the central objection well: "Killing these people in drone strikes and presuming that they are guilty by association violates the principle of non-combatant immunity that lies at the heart of international humanitarian law."[183] In essence, they violate the legal and ethical principle of distinction (that only those clearly identified as combatants should be targeted). Boyle's point is that it is difficult to believe, especially in the absence of uniforms or visible insignia, that the combat status of a potential target can usually be established beyond reasonable doubt without knowing that person's identity. The NYU/Stanford *Living Under Drones* study reinforces this concern by stressing that the procedures being used to identify targets are unknown and opaque: "It is unclear what, if any, process is in place for decisions regarding the so-called 'signature strikes,' which are particularly problematic and open to abuse and mistake."[184] Indeed, Robert Kolb has argued that "the criteria used for signature strikes are inherently imprecise" due to their reliance on "patterns of life."[185] Kristina Benson reinforces the concern in a more visceral way by arguing that "there is mounting evidence that [the] signature strike protocol does a poor job of distinguishing between combatants and non-combatants, resulting in a disproportionate amount of civilian casualties and the infliction of grave psychological trauma on civilians in a given strike zone."[186] In essence, Benson argues that in addition to violating the principle of distinction, signature strikes also violate the legal and moral principle of proportionality. Finally, Micah Zenko argues that signature strikes tend to undermine the credibility of the drone program more generally, both at home and abroad, and that the U.S. government should therefore reconsider signature strikes if it hopes to "secure the [ongo-ing] ability to conduct drone strikes, and potentially influence how others will use armed drones in future."[187]

So are signature strikes highly suspect legally (and morally), or are they a normal and effective tactic of war? Perhaps the most nuanced and illuminat-ing legal examination of signature strikes to date comes in a 2013 article in the *Journal of International Criminal Justice* by Kevin Jon Heller titled " 'One Hell of a Killing Machine': Signature Strikes and International Law." Heller's conclusion is that some signature strikes are likely legal and some are not, depending on the particular signature on which they rely.

Assessing Signatures

Heller begins by pointing out that "a signature strike must be justified under either international humanitarian law (IHL) or international human rights law (IHRL)," depending on whether or not it occurs in a context of armed conflict. He acknowledges that many signature strikes have occurred in a context of local non-international armed conflicts, but points out that at least a few have not.[188] Under IHL the cardinal rule of conduct is the principle of distinction. In a NIAC, the principle of distinction limits legitimate targets to militants with a continuous combat function or CCF (who can be targeted anytime) and civilians directly participating in hostilities or DPH (who can only be targeted when preparing, conducting, and returning from military operations). The attacking party is expected to have a high level of confidence that anyone targeted fits into one or the other of these two categories, and since civilians who DPH is the more limiting in regard to when they can be targeted, it effectively sets limits on when signature strikes would generally be permissible. Heller then considers a list of signatures that the United States reportedly uses in carrying out signature strikes and arranges them into three categories: those that are "legally adequate," those that are "possibly legally adequate," and those that are clearly "legally inadequate." Heller lists the following five "legally adequate" signatures:

(A1) Planning attacks: the United States reportedly carries out drone strikes against individuals " 'whose identities aren't known' when they 'are plotting against U.S. interests.' "[189] This signature appears to be legally adequate because planning an attack satisfies the three key elements of DPH: "it is 'likely to adversely affect the military operations'; there is a 'direct causal link' between planning an attack and that adverse effect; and planning an attack is 'specifically designed' to have an adverse effect."[190]

(A2) Transporting weapons: the United States is reported to use drone strikes "when surveillance indicates that men are 'transporting weapons.' "[191] These strikes are "legally justified, because both weapons and the means of transporting weapons, such as a truck, are legitimate military objectives."[192]

(A3) Handling explosives: reports indicate that the United States uses drone strikes against individuals "involved in 'bomb-making' or 'unloading explosives.'"[193] These signature strikes would "clearly be legal, because the bombs and explosives would qualify as legitimate military objectives no less than the weapons or weapons transport discussed above."[194]

(A4) Al-Qaeda compound: media reports suggest that the United States is willing to use drones to attack "'known al-Qaeda compounds.'"[195] These signature strikes "are legally unproblematic, assuming that the evidence supports the object's categorization."[196]

(A5) Al-Qaeda training camp: the United States also reportedly employs drones to target al-Qaeda "'training camps.'"[197] These signature strikes "are legal for the same reason that strikes on AQ compounds are legal: training camps make an effective contribution to military action."[198]

Heller also identifies five signatures that he thinks may "possibly be legally adequate"—that is, one would have to assess the specific facts and circumstances to determine whether legal standards were met:

(B1) Groups of armed men travelling towards conflict: many reports suggest that the United States "considers armed men travelling towards a combat zone to be legitimate targets."[199] This signature may be legally adequate if the United States "has evidence that the men are travelling to the combat zone for a specific hostile purpose."[200]

(B2) Operating an AQ training camp: the United States also reportedly "uses drones to attack individuals who 'are operating a training camp' for terrorists."[201] These signature strikes "are unproblematic in so far as the targeted individuals are in geographic proximity to the training camp itself. . . ."[202]

(B3) Training to join al-Qaeda: reports indicate that the United States employs drones against "'fighters training for possible operations in Afghanistan.'"[203] This is generally permissible "with one caveat. . . . that '[t]his case must be distinguished from persons comparable to reservists who, after a period of basic training or active membership, leave the armed group and re-integrate into civilian life.'"[204]

(B4) "Facilitators": some reports have suggested that the United States has targeted persons who merely facilitate terrorist attacks rather than participating in them directly. According to Heller, "it is highly likely that at least some of those signature strikes are unlawful."[205] However, he also notes that at least certain kinds of "facilitation" would make a person liable to targeting, at least while they are being performed, "such as gathering military intelligence in enemy territory, providing ammunition to fighters during hostilities, and acting as a guide."[206]

(B5) Rest areas: according to some reports, the United States "considers 'facilities' where fighters 'rest' to be legitimate targets."[207] However, the legality of signature strikes based on these criteria would depend on how "rest facilities" are defined. If what is meant "are military barracks, they are by nature legitimate military objectives."[208] However, rest facilities are not legitimate military targets if they "are simply civilian houses that occasionally provide lodging to fighters."[209]

Finally, Heller lists a set of criteria that he thinks would be legally inadequate to justify a signature strike:

(C1) Military-age male in area of known terrorist activity: according to multiple media reports, the United States considers all "'military age males in a strike zone as combatants' who can be targeted by a drone, because 'simple logic' indicates that 'people in an area of known terrorist activity . . . are probably up to no good.'"[210] Attacks based on these criteria are "plainly inconsistent with the principle of distinction."[211]

(C2) Consorting with known militants: the United States reportedly uses drone strikes to target persons fraternizing with known militants. According to Heller, "this signature is no more legally justifiable than the 'military-age male' signature" and for similar reasons.[212]

(C3) Armed men travelling in trucks in Al-Qaeda in the Arabian Peninsula–controlled area: According to at least one report, the United States has used drones to target groups of armed men travelling in trucks in areas "'currently under the . . . control' of . . . AQAP."[213] This signature "is similar to the inadequate 'military-age male in an area of known terrorist activity' signature; it simply arms the military-age males."[214]

(C4) "Suspicious" camp in AQ-controlled area: a final reported U.S. practice is the carrying out of drone strikes against suspicious compounds in militant-controlled areas. According to Heller, the State Department has apparently protested against reliance on this signature, "and for good reason as it does not satisfy the principle of distinction."[215]

Moreover, beyond the issue of the adequacy of the signature used to justify a strike, Heller stresses that drone operators also must have convincing evidence that "the target is exhibiting the signature behavior." In cases of doubt, "the attacker must presume that the target is a civilian."[216] While it is difficult to assess the adequacy of the evidence on which the United States relies, given the secrecy surrounding drone strikes, Heller suggests that there are some reasons to be skeptical of whether the standard is always met. In the first place, "it is clear that serious errors have been made concerning target identification."[217] In the second place, it is "an open question whether the United States is capable of accurately distinguishing between members of organized armed groups and civilians who DPH," which has significant implications for when they can be targeted.[218]

In circumstances that are subject to IHRL (in which at least some signature strikes have occurred), the rules would be significantly more restrictive. In essence, IHRL will permit lethal force to be used "only when that suspect himself poses a threat to the lives of others" and only where the suspect cannot be apprehended or deterred through non-lethal means."[219] IHRL also has "zero-tolerance for collateral damage" that "significantly limits the range of permissible signature strikes."[220] Nonetheless, Heller argues that at least three of the foregoing criteria would be sufficient to warrant a signature strike under IHRL, provided that the persons targeted pose an imminent threat and that no civilians would be endangered by the targeting operation. Those criteria are A1: Planning Attacks, A2: Transporting Weapons, and A3: Handling Explosives (which he sees as analogous respectively to planning, preparing, and executing a plan of attack).[221] He regards it as doubtful that all U.S. airstrikes under IHRL have met these conditions.[222]

Double Taps

A final category of signature strike that requires some individual attention is the so-called double tap. These are drone strikes that involve at least two rounds of attack separated by a pause, and where the second volley targets those involved in rescue efforts following the first strike. Critics stress that it seems doubtful that engaging in rescue operations would constitute a sufficiently clear pattern of life to warrant assigning combatant status, at least without some further corroboration. Thus, Christof Heyns has declared that "allegations of repeat strikes coming back after half an hour when medical personnel are on the ground are very worrying. To target civilians would be crimes of war."[223] On the other hand, if pickup trucks filled with armed fighters arrive at the scene, immediately cordon it off and defend the perimeter, and begin burying the dead, that would lend at least some credibility to the view that these may be Taliban militants. If this suspicion were then confirmed by intercepted communications or human intelligence on the ground, or both, then a designation as combatants might be warranted.

However, much of the debate over double taps, which date back to at least 2009 in Pakistan, has focused less on the question of whether the criteria for establishing combatancy are adequate than on the effect of such strikes—in particular, whether they produce disproportionate civilian casualties. For example, a report by Leon Watson in the *Daily Mail* was titled "America's Deadly Double Tap Drone Attacks Are 'Killing 49 People for Every Known Terrorist in Pakistan.'"[224] In February 2012 Scott Shane reported in the *New*

York Times that The Bureau of Investigative Journalism had found at least fifty civilian rescuer deaths in double tap drone strikes.[225] By contrast, Brian Glyn Williams reports in *Perspectives on Terrorism* that there appear to be "few if any" ordinary civilians rescuers in these followup attacks:

> In many, if not most, cases, those who are removing the victims from the rubble are themselves Taliban (there are very few if any EMT paramedics or first responders in this undeveloped area). The first responders are not, as the *Living Under the Drones* report states, "average civilians."
>
> There are many . . . accounts in the Pakistani press which make it clear that the Taliban have a policy of cordoning off drone strikes impact zones as they are moving to assist or retrieve their wounded or dead comrades. It is, by contrast, all but impossible to find reports in the Pakistani press of *average civilians* rushing to the scene of a drone strike on Taliban terrorists/insurgents to help out wounded militants or retrieve their bodies. So well known is the Taliban's propensity to cordon off areas where their comrades have been killed or wounded in a drone strike that a FATA-based Pakistani official even offered the Americans some advice on how to kill more Taliban using drones. According to *Al Jazeera*, "He explained that after a strike, the terrorists seal off the area to collect the bodies; in the first 10–24 hours after an attack, the only people in the area are terrorists. You should hit them again—there are no innocents there at that time."[226]

Williams's analysis suggests both that the strength of the "rescuer" signature may be considerably greater than it initially appears, and that this is reflected in a much lower civilian casualty count than is often reported. He also repeatedly emphasizes that senior Taliban leadership have been killed in these attacks.

Still, even if Williams is correct that the cordoning off of an initial strike site is a standard Taliban practice, and that many (or most) killed in double taps are in fact Taliban, it remains unclear whether this behavior in itself should be considered an adequate signature to determine combatant status given that some who respond, at least initially, may not be Taliban, and if it is not considered adequate, what further corroboration is necessary. Indeed, the debate over "double taps" raises in an especially acute form the inescapable questions that are raised by all signature strikes—what patterns reliably establish combatancy, what evidence of these patterns is required, and what is the impact of conducting such strikes on the ground? Heller offers a considered answer from a legal perspective, Williams from a practical perspective, but they leave the readers with the challenge of balancing and synthesizing what they think may constitute an acceptable overall framework, if indeed any is possible.

Notes

1. Barack Obama, "Remarks by the President at the National Defense University," speech, National Defense University, Fort McNair, Washington, DC, May 23, 2013.

2. See tables 1.2 and 1.3 in chapter 1.

3. Mary Ellen O'Connell, "The Choice of Law against Terrorism," *Journal of National Security Law and Policy* 4 (2010): 362.

4. Sherwood Ross, "Obama Drone Campaign 'Verges on Genocide,' Legal Authority Says," *Global Research*, February 16, 2014, accessed July 29, 2015, http://www.globalresearch.ca/obama-drone-campaign-verges-on-genocide-legal-authority-says/5369027.

5. Kenneth Anderson, "Targeted Killing in U.S. Counterterrorism Strategy and Law," working paper of the Series on Counterterrorism and American Statutory Law (Washington and Palo Alto: Brookings Institution, Georgetown University Law Center, and the Hoover Institution, 2009), 16.

6. William P. Quigley, "Illegality of US Drone Killings," *Pax Christi USA*, 2012, accessed May 1, 2015, https://paxchristiusa1.files.wordpress.com/2012/11/bill-quigleys-presentation-on-drones.pdf.

7. Harold Koh, "The Obama Administration and International Law," speech, American Society for International Law, Washington, DC, March 25, 2010.

8. John O. Brennan, "The Efficacy and Ethics of U.S. Counterterrorism Strategy," speech, Woodrow Wilson International Center for Scholars, Washington, DC, April 30, 2012.

9. Eric Holder, "Attorney General Eric Holder Speaks at Northwestern University School of Law," speech, Northwestern University School of Law, Evanston, Illinois, March 5, 2012.

10. Obama, "Remarks by the President at the National Defense University."

11. Daniel Byman, "Do Targeted Killings Work?" *Foreign Affairs* 85 (2006): 96; Mary Ellen O'Connell, "When Is a War Not a War?" *ILSA Journal of International and Comparative Law* 12, no. 2 (2005), 539; Joshua Bennett, "Exploring the Legal and Moral Bases for Conducting Targeted Strikes Outside of the Defined Combat Zone," *Notre Dame Journal of Law, Ethics and Public Policy* 26, no. 2 (2012): 550.

12. "The Drone Wars: Weapons Like the Predator Kill Far Fewer Civilians," *Wall Street Journal*, January 9, 2010, accessed June 15, 2015, http://www.wsj.com/articles/SB10001424052748704130904574644632368664254.

13. "Authority to Use Military Force in Libya," 35 Op. O.L.C. 2, April 1, 2011, 1, accessed May 1, 2015, http://www.justice.gov/sites/default/files/olc/opinions/2011/04/31/authority-military-use-in-libya.pdf.

14. "Authority to Use Military Force in Libya," 6–8.

15. "Authority to Use Military Force in Libya," 8, and more generally 6–13.

16. Ann Marie Slaughter, "Drones, Detention and the Dilemmas of 21st-Century Foreign Policy," speech, University of Virginia School of Law, April 19, 2013; Koh, "The Obama Administration and International Law"; Obama, "Remarks by the President at the National Defense University."

17. See Curtis A. Bradley and Jack L. Goldsmith, "Congressional Authorization and the War on Terrorism," *Harvard Law Review* 118 (2005): 2047, 2057; the main difference between an authorization of force and declaration of law concerns whether certain standby statutory authorities giving special powers to the president are triggered automatically (in the latter case) or depend on the existence of an armed conflict or national emergency or specific congressional approval. For an illuminating discussion of an authorization to use force and a declaration of war, see Jennifer Elsea and Richard Grimmett, "Declarations of War and Authorizations for the Use of Military Force: Historical Background and Legal Implications," Congressional Research Service Report for Congress, 7-5700, March 17, 2011.

18. George W. Bush, "President Bush Addresses the Nation," speech, to Joint Session of Congress and the Nation, September 20, 2001.

19. See Jennifer Daskal, "The Geography of the Battlefield: A Framework for Detention and Targeting Outside the 'Hot' Conflict Zone," *University of Pennsylvania Law Review* 161, no. 5 (2013): 1177, footnote 27, for a good discussion.

20. Obama, "Remarks by the President at the National Defense University."

21. Even outspoken critics such as Mary Ellen O'Connell allow that the drone is "A Lawful Battlefield Weapon" in conventional armed conflicts such as in Afghanistan—see Mary Ellen O'Connell, "Lawful Use of Combat Drones," testimony to House Subcommittee on National Security and Foreign Affairs, April 10, 2010, 1–2, https://www.fas.org/irp/congress/2010_hr/042810oconnell.pdf.

22. Robert Chesney, "Military-Intelligence Convergence and the Law of the Title 10/Title 50 Debate," *Journal of National Security Law and Policy* 4 (2012): 539, 574.

23. Gregory McNeal, "Targeted Killing and Accountability," *Georgetown Law Journal* 102, no. 3 (2014): 692.

24. Eric Schmitt and Mark Mazzetti, "Secret Order Lets U.S. Raid Al Qaeda," *New York Times*, November 9, 2008, accessed June 15, 2015, http://www.nytimes.com/2008/11/10/washington/10military.html?pagewantedall.

25. Chesney, "Military-Intelligence Convergence," 575; Dana Priest and William Arkin, *Top Secret America: The Rise of the New American Security State* (New York: Little, Brown and Company), 236–37.

26. Chesney, "Military-Intelligence Convergence," 563.

27. Bob Woodward, *Bush at War* (New York: Simon & Schuster, 2002), 68, 76, 78.

28. Executive Order 12333, accessed June 15, 2015, http://www.archives.gov/federal-register/codification/executive-order/12333.html.

29. International Human Rights and Conflict Resolution Clinic and Global Justice Clinic, *Living Under Drones: Death, Injury and Trauma to Civilians from US Drone Practices in Pakistan* (New York and Palo Alto: NYU School of Law and Stanford Law School, 2012), 120, 121.

30. "Text of: To prohibit the extrajudicial killing of United States citizens, and for other purposes," *HR 6010*, accessed May 1, 2015, https://www.govtrack.us/congress/bills/111/hr6010/text.

31. Michael Rubin, "An Arrow in Our Quiver," *National Review*, August 28, 2006, accessed May 1, 2015, http://www.meforum.org/989/an-arrow-in-our-quiver.

32. Kristen Eichensehr, "On the Offensive: Assassination Policy under International Law," *Harvard International Review* 25, no. 3 (2003): 37.

33. Bob Woodward, "CIA Is Told to do 'Whatever Necessary' to Kill Bin Laden," *Washington Post*, October 21, 2001, accessed May 1, 2015, http://www.washington post.com/wp-dyn/content/article/2007/11/18/AR2007111800655.html; Colonel Kathryn Stone, " 'All Necessary Means'—Employing CIA Operatives in a Warfighting Role Alongside Special Operations Forces," USAWC Strategy Research Project, US Army War College, Carlisle Barracks, Pennsylvania, 2003, 2.

34. International Human Rights and Conflict Resolution Clinic and Global Justice Clinic, *Living Under Drones*, 120–21.

35. William Hays Parks, "Memorandum of Law: Executive Order 12333 and Assassination," *Army Lawyer*, December 1989, 4, 8, italics added.

36. For example, William Banks and Peter Raven-Hasen, "Targeted Killing and Assassination: The U.S. Legal Framework," *University of Richmond Law Review* 37 (2003): 745–50; Howard Wachtel, "Targeting Osama Bin Laden: Examining the Legality of Assassination as a Tool of U.S. Foreign Policy," *Duke Law Journal* 55, no. 3 (2005): 678–80; Robert Turner, "It's Not Really 'Assassination': Legal and Moral Implications of Intentionally Targeting Terrorists and Aggressor-State Regime Elites," *University of Richmond Law Review* 37 (2003): 787–89.

37. Holder, "Attorney General Eric Holder Speaks at Northwestern University."

38. Holder, "Attorney General Eric Holder Speaks at Northwestern University."

39. Department of Justice (DOJ), "Memorandum re: Applicability of Federal Criminal Laws and the Constitution to Contemplated Lethal Operations Against Shaykh Anwar al-Aulaqi," http://www.nytimes.com/interactive/2014/06/23/us/23 awlaki-memo.html, 38–41; DOJ, "White Paper: Lawfulness of a Lethal Operation Directed Against a U.S. Citizen Who Is a Senior Operational Leader of Al-Qa'ida or an Associated Force," http://msnbcmedia.msn.com/i/msnbc/sections/news/020413 _DOJ_White_Paper.pdf, 1–2, 5–6.

40. DOJ, Memorandum, 41; DOJ, White Paper, 9.

41. DOJ, White Paper, 10; DOJ, Memorandum, 12–21.

42. DOJ, Memorandum, 12, 13–21; DOJ, White Paper, 10.

43. J. D. Tucille, "ACLU Calls Bullshit on Obama's 'Due Process' Promises," *Reason.Com*, May 24, 2013, accessed May 1, 2015, http://reason.com/blog/2013/05/ 24/aclu-calls-bullshit-on-obamas-drone-spee.

44. Statement on Twitter, accessed May 1, 2015, https://twitter.com/randpaul/ status/337662401132511234.

45. Editorial Board, "A Thin Rationale for Drone Killings," *New York Times*, June 23, 2014, accessed June 15, 2015, http://www.nytimes.com/2014/06/24/opinion/ a-thin-rationale-for-drone-killings.html.

46. Editorial Board, "A Thin Rationale for Drone Killings."

47. International Court of Justice, *Nicaragua v. United States*, 1986, 245, accessed May 1, 2015, http://www.icj-cij.org/docket/files/70/6503.pdf; Yoram Dinstein, *War, Aggression and Self-Defence*, 4th ed. (Cambridge: Cambridge University Press), 208–9.

48. Christine Gray, *International Law and the Use of Force*, 2nd ed. (New York: Oxford University Press, 2004), 124.

49. Dinstein, *War, Aggression and Self-Defence*, 250; Michael Schmitt, "Counter-Terrorism and the Use of Force in International Law," *International Law Studies* 79 (2003): 36.

50. Dinstein, *War, Aggression and Self-Defence*, 250.

51. Obama, "Remarks at the National Defense University."

52. Obama, "Remarks at the National Defense University."

53. Obama, "Remarks at the National Defense University."

54. Obama, "Remarks at the National Defense University."

55. O'Connell, "The Choice of Law Against Terrorism," 358.

56. O'Connell, "The Choice of Law Against Terrorism," 358–59.

57. Dinstein, *War, Aggression and Self-Defence*, 206–7.

58. Dinstein, *War, Aggression and Self-Defence*, 207.

59. Dinstein, *War, Aggression and Self-Defence*, 207–8.

60. Schmitt, "Counter-Terrorism and the Use of Force in International Law," 8–23.

61. Dinstein, *War, Aggression and Self-Defence*, 206–8, 222.

62. Dinstein, *War, Aggression and Self-Defence*, 245.

63. Dinstein, *War, Aggression and Self-Defence*, 202.

64. Christian Tams, "The Use of Force against Terrorists," *European Journal of International Law* 20, no. 2 (2009): 390.

65. Jan Kittrich, "Can Self-Defense Serve as an Appropriate Tool Against International Terrorism?" *Maine Law Review* 61 (2009): 159.

66. Dinstein, *War, Aggression and Self-Defence*, 250.

67. DOJ, "White Paper," 7.

68. Daphne Eviatar, "Drones & the Law: Why We Don't Need A New Legal Framework For Targeted Killing," in *Preventive Force*, edited by Kerstin Fisk and Jennifer Ramos (New York: NYU Press, 2015).

69. Ian Brownlie, *International Law and the Use of Force by States* (Oxford: Oxford University Press, 1963), 278.

70. Mary Ellen O'Connell, "The Myth of Preemptive Self-Defense," *The ASIL Task Force on Terrorism* (2002), 5, accessed May 1, 2015, http://www.asil.org/taskforce/oconnell.pdf, 5; Michael Glennon, "Military Action Against Terrorists Under International Law," *Harvard Journal of Law and Public Policy* 25 (2002): 539, 553.

71. Tams, "The Use of Force against Terrorists," 389.

72. Laurie Blank, "Targeted Strikes: The Consequences of Blurring the Armed Conflict and Self-Defense Justifications," *William Mitchell Law Review* 38, no. 5 (2012): 1667–68; Philip Alston, "The CIA and Targeted Killing Beyond Borders," *Harvard National Security Journal* 2 (2011): 304.

73. Blank, "Targeted Strikes," 1666.

74. Blank, "Targeted Strikes," 1667.

75. Blank, "Targeted Strikes," 1667–68. Absolute Necessity Standard: "[l]aw enforcement officials may use force only when strictly necessary and to the extent required for the performance of their duty." United Nations General Assembly Resolution 34/169.

76. Blank, "Targeted Strikes," 1682.

77. John Brennan, "Strengthening Our Security by Adhering to Our Values and Laws," September 16, 2011, accessed June 15, 2015, http://www.whitehouse.gov/the-press-office/2011/09/16/remarks-john-o-brennan-strengthening-our-security-adhering-our-values-an.

78. Jordan Paust, "Self-Defense Targetings of Non-State Actors and Permissibility of U.S. Drones in Pakistan," *Journal of Transnational Law and Policy* 19, no. 2 (2010): 270–71.

79. Anderson, "Targeted Killing in U.S. Counterterrorism Strategy and Law," 3, 9.

80. 50 USC 3036: Director of the Central Intelligence Agency, accessed July 29, 2015, http://uscode.house.gov/view.xhtml?req = granuleid:USC-prelim-title50-sec tion3036&num = 0&edition = prelim.

81. For example, NSC 5412, accessed May 1, 2015, https://history.state.gov/hist oricaldocuments/frus1950-55Intel/d250; Chesney, "Military-Intelligence Convergence," 553; Steve Coll, *Ghost Wars* (New York: Penguin Books, 2004), 141.

82. Schmitt and Mazzetti, "Secret Order Lets U.S. Raid al-Qaeda."

83. Beth Van Schaak, "The United States' Position on the Extraterritorial Application of Human Rights Obligations," *International Law Studies* 90 (2014): 22–23.

84. Kristina Ash, "US Reservations to the International Covenant on Civil and Political Rights: Credibility Maximization and Global Influence," *Northwestern Journal of International Human Rights* 3, no. 1 (2005), accessed July 3, 2015, http://schol arlycommons.law.northwestern.edu/cgi/viewcontent.cgi?article = 1018&context = njihr.

85. Philip Alston, "Civil and Political Rights, Including the Questions of Disappearances and Summary Executions," E/CN.4/2005/7, December 22, 2004, para. 41, accessed June 30, 2015, http://daccess-dds-ny.un.org/doc/UNDOC/GEN/G05/101/ 34/PDF/G0510134.pdf?OpenElement.

86. Anderson, "Targeted Killing in U.S. Counterterrorism Strategy and Law," 7–9.

87. Robert Kolb and Richard Hyde, *An Introduction to the International Law of Armed Conflict* (Oxford: Hart Publishing, 2008), 74; Richard Murphy and Afsheen Radsan, "Due Process and Targeted Killing of Terrorists," *Cardozo Law Review* 31 (2009): 405, 416.

88. Christopher Greenwood, "Historical Development and Legal Basis," in *The Handbook of Humanitarian Law in Armed Conflicts*, edited by Dieter Fleck (Oxford: Oxford University Press, 2000), 19–20.

89. Dinstein, *War, Aggression and Self-Defence*, 94.

90. G. W. Bush, "Remarks by the President in Photo Opportunity with National Security Team," speech, Cabinet Room, White House, Washington, DC, September 12, 2001.

91. Alex Spillius, "Barack Obama: U.S. Is at War with al-Qaeda," *The Telegraph*, January 8, 2010, accessed May 12, 2015, http://www.telegraph.co.uk/news/world news/barackobama/6950879/Barack-Obama-US-is-at-war-with-al-Qaeda.html.

92. B. Lawrence, ed., *Messages to the World: The Statements of Osama bin Laden* (New York: Verso, 2005), 46–47, 23–30, 41–42, 48, 52, 61, 69–70.

93. Avery Plaw and Carlos Colon, "Correcting the Record," in *Legitimacy and Drones: Investigating the Legality, Morality and Efficacy of UCAVs*, edited by Steven J. Barela (Burlington: Ashgate Press, 2015).

94. Douglas Stanglin, "Al-Qaeda Confirms bin Laden's Death, Threatens New Attacks," *USA Today*, May 6, 2011, accessed June 30, 2015, http://content.usatoday .com/communities/ondeadline/post/2011/05/al-qaeda-confirms-osama-bin-ladens -death-in-internet-statement/1#.UEF1pNZlQvk.

95. Helen Duffy, *The "War on Terror" and the Framework of International Law* (Cambridge: Cambridge University Press, 2005), 218–19.

96. O'Connell, "When Is a War Not a War," 1.

97. Duffy, *The "War on Terror" and the Framework of International Law*, 250–51.

98. Duffy, *The "War on Terror" and the Framework of International Law*, 252.

99. Greg Travalio and John Altenburg, "Terrorism, State Responsibility and the Use of Military Force," *Chicago Journal of International Law* 4 (2003): 100–101.

100. Roy Schöndorf, "Extra-State Armed Conflict: Is There a Need for a New Legal Regime?" *New York University Journal of International Law and Politics* 37, no. 1 (2005): 5.

101. Shöndorf, "Extra-State Armed Conflict," 14.

102. Plaw and Colon, "Correcting the Record."

103. Department of Justice, "Memorandum," 24–25; Department of Justice, "White Paper," 3.

104. Daskal, "The Geography of the Battlefield," 1169–71. Recent statements by U.S. officials suggest a policy of mediating between these two extremes, at least for purposes of targeted killing.

105. DOJ, "Memorandum," 25.

106. *Al-Aulaqi v. Obama*, 727 F. Supp. 2d 1 (D.D.C. 2010) (No. 10-01469), Declaration of Prof. Mary Ellen O'Connell, para. 14, accessed July 3, 2015, https://www.aclu.org/legal-document/al-aulaqi-v-obama-declaration-professor-mary-ellen-oconnell?redirect = national-security/al-aulaqi-v-obama-declaration-professor-mary-ellen-oconnell.

107. Use of Force Committee, "Final Report on the Meaning of Armed Conflict in International Law," *International Law Association*, 2, accessed October 2, 2014, http://www.ila-hq.org/en/committees/index.cfm/cid/1022.

108. *Prosecutor v. Dusko Tadic*, Decision on the Defence Motion for Interlocutory Appeal on Jurisdiction, 1995, para. 70, italics added, accessed June 30, 2015, http://www.icty.org/x/cases/tadic/acdec/en/51002.htm.

109. Correlates of War Project Series at http://www.icpsr.umich.edu/icpsrweb/ICPSR/series/232.

110. Meredith Reid Sarkees, "The COW Typology of War: Defining and Categorizing Wars," 15, accessed October 10, 2014, http://www.correlatesofwar.org/COW2%20Data/WarData_NEW/COW%20Website%20-%20Typology%20of%20war.pdf.

111. Sarkees, "The COW Typology of War," 1.

112. Rod Nordland, "War Deaths Top 13,000 in Afghanistan Security Forces," *New York Times*, March 3, 2014, accessed June 30, 2015, http://www.nytimes.com/2014/03/04/world/asia/afghan-cabinet-releases-data-on-deaths-of-security-personnel.html?partner = rss&emc = rss&smid = ttw-nytimes&_r = 1.

113. Akmal Dawi, "Despite Massive Taliban Death Toll No Drop in Insurgency," *Voice of America*, March 6, 2014, accessed June 3, 2015, http://www.voanews.com/content/despite-massive-taliban-death-toll-no-drop-in-insurgency/1866009.html.

114. UNAMA, "UNAMA Reports on the Protection of Civilians," 2014, 2008, 2007, accessed June 15, 2015, http://www.unama.unmissions.org/Default.aspx?tabid = 13941&language = en-US.

115. Mary Ellen O'Connell, "Drones Under International Law," *International Debate Series* (St. Louis: Whitney R. Harris World Law Institute, 2010), 4, 8.

116. Mary Ellen O'Connell, "Unlawful Killing with Combat Drones: A Case Study of Pakistan, 2004–2009," in *Shooting to Kill: The Law Governing Lethal Force in Context*, Notre Dame Legal Studies Paper No. 09-43, edited by Simon Bronitt (forthcoming), 21, http://ssrn.com/abstract = 1501144.

117. O'Connell, "Unlawful Killing with Combat Drones," 21.

118. William Banks, "Legal Sanctuaries and Predator Strikes in the War on Terror," in *Denial of Sanctuary*, edited by Michael Innes (London: Praeger Security International, 2007), 114–20.

119. DOJ, "Memorandum," 21; and see the quotations in section I of this chapter.

120. Jeh C. Johnson, "National Security Law, Lawyers and Lawyering in the Obama Administration," speech, Yale Law School, New Haven, Connecticut, February 22, 2012.

121. Robert M. Chesney, "Beyond the Battlefield, Beyond Al Qaeda: The Destabilizing Legal Architecture of Counterterrorism," *Michigan Law Review* 112 (2013): 163, 199–200.

122. Chesney, "Beyond the Battlefield, Beyond Al Qaeda," 200.

123. *Ghaleb Nassar Al-Bihani v. Barack Obama*, January 5, 2010, 11, accessed June 30, 2015, https://ccrjustice.org/sites/default/files/assets/2010-01-05Al%20Bihaniv.Obama_CourtofAppealsOpinion.pdf.

124. Kevin Jon Heller, "Goldsmith Responds about 'Co-Belligerency,'" *Opinio Juris*, October 18, 2010, accessed May 1, 2015, http://opiniojuris.org/2010/10/18/goldsmith-responds-about-co-belligerency/.

125. Jack Goldsmith, "The D.C. Circuit Has Not Rejected Co-Belligerency," *Lawfare*, October 18, 2010, accessed July 3, 2015, http://lawfareblog.com/dc-circuit-has-not-rejected-co-belligerency.

126. Brennan, "The Efficacy and Ethics of U.S. Counterterrorism Strategy" (italics added).

127. Kristina Benson, "Kill 'Em and Sort It Out Later: Signature Drone Strikes and International Humanitarian Law," *Pacific McGeorge Global Business and Development Law Journal* 17 (2014): 31.

128. Philip Alston, "Report of the Special Rapporteur on Extrajudicial, Summary or Arbitrary Executions," Fourteenth Session of the UN General Assembly Human Rights Council, May 28, 2010, 19, para. 58, accessed May 15, 2015, http://reliefweb.int/sites/reliefweb.int/files/resources/A38037358F1EF91B492577370006546B-Full_Report.pdf.

129. Department of Justice, "Memorandum," 22 fn28.

130. Nils Melzer, *Interpretive Guidance on the Notion of Direct Participation in Hostilities*, International Committee of the Red Cross, 2009, https://www.icrc.org/eng/assets/files/other/icrc-002-0990.pdf, 34, 37–38.

131. *Gherebi v. Obama*, 609 F. Supp. 2d 43 (2009), 70, accessed June 30, 2015, https://scholar.google.com/scholar_case?case = 12110841923472534802&q = Gherebi + v. + Obama&hl = en&as_sdt = 6,40&as_vis = 1.

132. "As for the criteria used to determine membership in the 'armed forces' of the enemy, the Court agrees with the government that the criteria set forth in Article 4 of the Third Geneva Convention and Article 43 of Additional Protocol I should inform the Court's assessment," *Gherebi v. Obama*, http://www.lawfareblog.com/wp-content/uploads/2013/01/Gherebi-v.-Obama.pdf.

133. Bradley and Goldsmith, "Congressional Authorization and the War on Terrorism," 2114–15.

134. Lassa Oppenheim, *International Law,* 9th ed. (Oxford: Oxford University Press. 1992), 435; see also Dinstein, *War, Aggression and Self-Defence,* 112–13.

135. Draft Articles on State Responsibility for Internationally Wrongful Acts with Commentaries Art. 20 (International Law Commission ed., 2001).

136. Natalino Ronzitti, "Use of Force, Jus Cogens and State Consent," in *The Current Legal Regulation of the Use of Force,* edited by Antonio Cassesse (Dordrecht: Martinus Nijhoff, 1986), 148.

137. Scott Shane, "Yemen's Leader Praises U.S. Drone Strike," *New York Times,* September 29, 2012, accessed May 1, 2015, http://www.nytimes.com/2012/09/29/world/middleeast/yemens-leader-president-hadi-praises-us-drone-strikes.html?_r = 0.

138. Josh Rogin, "Somali President Asks for More American Help," *Foreign Policy,* January 18, 2013, accessed June 20, 2015, http://foreignpolicy.com/2013/01/18/somali-president-asks-for-more-american-help/.

139. O'Connell, "Unlawful Killing with Combat Drones," 18.

140. Alex Rodriguez, "US Drone Strikes Violate Pakistan Sovereignty," *Los Angeles Times,* March 15, 2013, accessed June 20, 2015, https://www.globalpolicy .org/home/163-general/52352-un-investigator-us-drone-strikes-violate-pakistan -sovereignty.html.

141. Brennan, "The Efficacy and Ethics of US Counterterrorism Strategy."

142. International Human Rights and Conflict Resolution Clinic and Global Justice Clinic, *Living Under Drones,* 105.

143. Ashley Deeks, "Unwilling or Unable: Towards a Normative Framework for Extraterritorial Self-Defense," *Virginia Journal of International Law* 52, no. 3 (2012): 483; also see Noam Lubell, *Extraterritorial Use of Force Against Non-State Actors* (New York: Oxford University Press, 2011).

144. Kevin Jon Heller, "Ashley Deeks' Problematic Defense of the 'Unwilling or Unable' Test," *Opinio Juris,* December 15, 2011, accessed June 15, 2015, http://opinio juris.org/2011/12/15/ashley-deeks-failure-to-defend-the-unwilling-or-unable-test/; also see Dawood I. Ahmed, "Defending Weak States against the 'Unwilling or Unable Doctrine,'" *Journal of International Law and International Relations* 9, no. 1 (2013).

145. *United Kingdom Manual of the Law of Armed Conflict* (Oxford: Oxford University Press, 2004), section 2.4.

146. Anderson, "Targeted Killing in U.S. Counterterrorism Strategy and Law," 2.

147. "Joshua Rozenberg's Interview with Lord Bingham on the Rule of Law," 2009, accessed June 1, 2015, http://www.biicl.org/files/4422_bingham_int_transcript .pdf.

148. *United States, United States Field Manual* 27-10 para. 3 (Department of Defense, 1956).

149. Nils Melzer, *Targeted Killing in International Law* (Oxford: Oxford University Press, 2008), 284–86.

150. Michael Walzer, "Targeted Killing and Drone Warfare," *Dissent,* January 11, 2013, accessed May 1, 2015, http://www.dissentmagazine.org/online_articles/tar geted-killing-and-drone-warfare.

151. Jean-Marie Henckaerts and Louise Doswald-Beck, *Customary International Humanitarian Law* (Cambridge: Cambridge University Press, 2005), 3, 5.

152. Brennan, "The Efficacy and Ethics of American Counterterrorism Policy."

153. *Prosecutor v. Zoran Kupreki, et al.*, Judgment of January 14, 2000, para. 524, accessed May 1, 2015, http://www.icty.org/x/cases/kupreskic/tjug/en/kup-tj0001 14e.pdf.

154. Jean-Marie Henckaerts and Louise Doswald-Beck, *Customary International Humanitarian Law, Volume I: Rules* (Cambridge: Cambridge University Press), 46.

155. Melzer, *Targeted Killing*, 358–59; Blank, "Targeted Strikes," 1690.

156. O'Connell, "Drones Under International Law," 8; see also O'Connell, "Lawful Use of Combat Drones."

157. O'Connell, "Unlawful Killing with Combat Drones."

158. Koh, "The Obama Administration and International Law."

159. Lee Ferran, "Intel Chair: Civilian Drone Casualties in 'Single Digits' Year-to-Year," ABC News, February 7, 2013, accessed May 1, 2015, http://abcnews.go.com/blogs/headlines/2013/02/intel-chair-civilian-drone-casualties-in-single-digits-year-to-year/.

160. Brennan, "The Efficacy and Ethics of US Counterterrorism Strategy."

161. Gregory McNeal, "Are Targeted Killings Unlawful? A Case Study in Empirical Claims with Empirical Evidence," in *Targeted Killings: Law and Morality in an Asymmetrical World*, edited by Claire Finkelstein, Jens Ohlin, and Andrew Altman (Oxford: Oxford University Press, 2012), 327–38; Conor Friedersdorf, "Dianne Feinstein's Outrageous Underestimate of Civilian Drone Deaths," *The Atlantic*, February 11, 2013, accessed May 1, 2015, http://www.theatlantic.com/politics/archive/2013/02/dianne-feinsteins-outrageous-underestimate-of-civilian-drone-deaths/2730 35/.

162. McNeal, "Are Targeted Killings Unlawful?," 750.

163. Blank, "Targeted Strikes," 1690.

164. Micah Zenko, "Reforming US Drone Strike Policies," *Council Special Report* 65 (New York: Council on Foreign Relations, 2013), 12, 4.

165. Michael J. Boyle, "The Costs and Consequences of Drone Warfare," *International Affairs* 89, no. 1 (2013): 8–9.

166. International Human Rights and Conflict Resolution Clinic and Global Justice Clinic, *Living Under Drones*, 103.

167. Zenko, "Reforming US Drone Strike Policies," 26.

168. Brennan, "The Efficacy and Ethics of US Counterterrorism Strategy."

169. Sarah Holewinski, "Just Trust Us: The Need to Know More About the Civilian Impact of US Drone Strikes," in *Drone Wars: Transforming Conflict, Law, and Policy*, edited by Peter Bergen and Daniel Rothenberg (Cambridge: Cambridge University Press, 2015), 46.

170. Daniel Byman, "Why Drones Work: The Case for Washington's Weapon of Choice," *Foreign Affairs* (2013): 42.

171. Adam Entous, "CIA Drones Hit Wider Range of Targets in Pakistan," *Reuters*, May 5, 2010, accessed March 15, 2015, http://www.reuters.com/article/2010/05/06/us-pakistan-usa-cia-idUSTRE6450KT20100506; International Human Rights and Conflict Resolution Clinic and Global Justice Clinic, *Living Under Drones*, 11–12.

172. Marek Madej, "Tactical Efficacy: UAVs and UCAVs," in *Legitimacy and Drones: Investigating the Legality, Morality and Efficacy of UCAVs*, edited by Steven J. Barela (Burlington: Ashgate Press, 2015), 254.

173. John Kaag and Sarah Kreps, *Drone Warfare* (Cambridge: Polity Press, 2014), 32.

174. Entous, "CIA Drones Hit Wider Range of Targets in Pakistan"; Adam Entous, "How the White House Learned to Love the Drone," *Reuters*, May 18, 2010, accessed May 1, 2015, http://www.reuters.com/article/2010/05/18/us-pakistan -drones-idUSTRE64H5SL20100518.

175. Adam Entous, Siobhan Gorman, and Julian E. Barnes, "U.S. Relaxes Drone Rules: Obama Gives CIA, Military Greater Leeway in Use Against Militants in Yemen," *Wall Street Journal*, April 26, 2012, accessed March 15, 2015, http://www.wsj .com/articles/SB10001424052702304723304577366251852418174; Greg Miller, "White House Approves Broader Yemen Drone Campaign," *Washington Post*, April 25, 2012, accessed March 15, 2015, http://www.washingtonpost.com/world/national -security/white-house-approves-broader-yemen-drone-campaign/2012/04/25/gIQA 82U6hT_story.html.

176. Entous, Gorman, and Barnes, "U.S. Relaxes Drone Rules."

177. Entous, Gorman, and Barnes, "U.S. Relaxes Drone Rules."

178. Kevin Jon Heller, "'One Hell of a Killing Machine': Signature Strikes and International Law," *Journal of International Criminal Justice* 11 (2013): 112.

179. Heller, "'One Hell of a Killing Machine,'" 90.

180. Greg Miller, "CIA Seeks New Authority to Expand Yemen Drone Campaign," *Washington Post*, April 18, 2012, accessed July 29, 2015, https://www.washing tonpost.com/world/national-security/cia-seeks-new-authority-to-expand-yemen -drone-campaign/2012/04/18/gIQAsaumRT_story.html.

181. Audrey Kurth Cronin, "Why Drones Fail: When Tactics Drive Strategy," *Foreign Affairs* (2014): 46.

182. Byman, "Why Drones Work," 33.

183. Boyle, "The Costs and Consequences of Drone Warfare," 7.

184. International Human Rights and Conflict Resolution Clinic and Global Justice Clinic, *Living Under Drones*, 14.

185. Robert Kolb, "Systemic Efficacy: 'Potentially Shattering Consequences for International Law,'" in *Legitimacy and Drones: Investigating the Legality, Morality and Efficacy of UCAVs*, edited by Steven J. Barela (Burlington: Ashgate Press, 2015), 313.

186. Benson, "Kill 'Em and Sort It Out Later," 18.

187. Zenko, "Reforming Drone Strikes," 25.

188. Heller, "'One Hell of a Killing Machine,'" 92, 111–12.

189. Heller, "'One Hell of a Killing Machine,'" 94.

190. Heller, "'One Hell of a Killing Machine,'" 94.

191. Heller, "'One Hell of a Killing Machine,'" 95.

192. Heller, "'One Hell of a Killing Machine,'" 95.

193. Heller, "'One Hell of a Killing Machine,'" 95–96.

194. Heller, "'One Hell of a Killing Machine,'" 95–96.

195. Heller, "'One Hell of a Killing Machine,'" 96.

196. Heller, "'One Hell of a Killing Machine,'" 96.

197. Heller, "'One Hell of a Killing Machine,'" 96.

198. Heller, "'One Hell of a Killing Machine,'" 96.

199. Heller, "'One Hell of a Killing Machine,'" 100.
200. Heller, "'One Hell of a Killing Machine,'" 100.
201. Heller, "'One Hell of a Killing Machine,'" 101.
202. Heller, "'One Hell of a Killing Machine,'" 101.
203. Heller, "'One Hell of a Killing Machine,'" 102.
204. Heller, "'One Hell of a Killing Machine,'" 102.
205. Heller, "'One Hell of a Killing Machine,'" 102.
206. Heller, "'One Hell of a Killing Machine,'" 102.
207. Heller, "'One Hell of a Killing Machine,'" 103.
208. Heller, "'One Hell of a Killing Machine,'" 103.
209. Heller, "'One Hell of a Killing Machine,'" 103.
210. Heller, "'One Hell of a Killing Machine,'" 97.
211. Heller, "'One Hell of a Killing Machine,'" 97.
212. Heller, "'One Hell of a Killing Machine,'" 97–98.
213. Heller, "'One Hell of a Killing Machine,'" 98.
214. Heller, "'One Hell of a Killing Machine,'" 98–99.
215. Heller, "'One Hell of a Killing Machine,'" 99.
216. Heller, "'One Hell of a Killing Machine,'" 103.
217. Heller, "'One Hell of a Killing Machine,'" 104–5.
218. Heller, "'One Hell of a Killing Machine,'" 104–5.
219. Heller, "'One Hell of a Killing Machine,'" 113.
220. Heller, "'One Hell of a Killing Machine,'" 114.
221. Heller, "'One Hell of a Killing Machine,'" 115.
222. Heller, "'One Hell of a Killing Machine,'" 119.
223. Quoted in Azmat Kahn, "New Study Asserts That Drone Strikes in Pakistan Target Rescuers, Funerals," PBS *Frontline*, February 6, 2012, accessed July 8, 2015, http://www.pbs.org/wgbh/pages/frontline/afghanistan-pakistan/secret-war/new-study-asserts-drone-strikes-in-pakistan-target-rescuers-funerals/.
224. Leon Watson, "America's Deadly Double Tap Drone Attacks Are 'Killing 49 People for Every Known Terrorist in Pakistan,'" *Daily Mail*, September 25, 2012, accessed July 15, 2015, http://www.dailymail.co.uk/news/article-2208307/Americas-deadly-double-tap-drone-attacks-killing-49-people-known-terrorist-Pakistan.html.
225. Scott Shane, "U.S. Said to Target Rescuers at Drone Strike Sites," *New York Times*, February 5, 2012, accessed July 15, 2015, http://www.nytimes.com/2012/02/06/world/asia/us-drone-strikes-are-said-to-target-rescuers.html?_r=0.
226. Brian Glyn Williams, "New Light on CIA 'Double Tap' Drone Strikes on Taliban 'First Responders' in Pakistan's Tribal Areas," *Perspectives on Terrorism* 7, no. 3 (2013): 81.

4

The Ethical Debate

Are Drones Consistent with the Ideals of Just War?

THERE HAS BEEN A LIVELY DEBATE about the morality of drone strikes outside of conventional battlefields from the first U.S. strike in 2002. In many respects, this debate follows the broad outlines of an older debate over targeted killing (TK).[1] However, drone strikes differ from more conventional targeted killings in several important ways—most notably perhaps, they are often seen as military operations, which can't be said of some of the more "treacherous" means of targeted killing, such as having an undercover operative stab a victim with a poison needle.[2] So it is that part of the larger TK debate that deals with military operations that is most directly relevant for drone strikes.

The following chapter summarizes some of the key arguments in the moral and ethical debates over whether drones should be used to carry out lethal operations outside of traditional battlefields.[3] We focus on this question, rather than the use of drones in armed conflict, because there is a fairly widespread acceptance even among many of the most outspoken critics of U.S. drone strikes in Pakistan, Yemen, and Somalia that drones are legitimate weapons within armed conflict.[4] The really interesting debate is over whether drone strikes should ever be used outside of conventional battlefields, and if so, when.[5]

We begin the chapter by summarizing the argument of a 2011 article from the *Journal of Military Ethics*, which made a particularly provocative moral claim. It argues that the choice to use drones rather than other weapons systems is in many contexts not merely justifiable but morally obligatory. The article, by Bradley J. Strawser, an assistant professor of philosophy in the defense analysis department at the U.S. Naval Postgraduate School, is titled

"Moral Predators: The Duty to Employ Uninhabited Aerial Vehicles." It provides a useful starting point for the following discussion, because in addition to advancing an especially careful and systematic case for this view, Strawser tries to respond directly to six of the most important objections to using drones.

I. The Duty to Use Drones

As noted, Strawser contends that "there is an ethical obligation to use UAVs" (that is, unmanned aerial vehicles or drones), at least in some circumstances.[6] His argument rests on the claim that "if an agent is pursuing a morally justified yet inherently risky action, then there is a moral imperative to protect this agent if it [is] possible to do so, unless there exists a countervailing good that outweighs the protection of the agent."[7] This claim rests on what Strawser calls the Principle of Unnecessary Risk (PUR): "If X gives Y an order to accomplish good goal G, then X has an obligation, other things being equal, to cho[o]se a means to accomplish G that does not violate the demands of justice, make the world worse, or expose Y to potentially lethal risk unless incurring such risk aids in the accomplishment of G in some way that cannot be gained via less risky means."[8] In short, in seeking to prevent terrorism, we should try to avoid exposing our troops to risk, all other things being equal.

A number of critics, including Uwe Steinhoff (associate professor of politics and public affairs at the University of Hong Kong) and Stephen Kershnar (professor of philosophy at the State University of New York at Fredonia), have objected that "if persons consent to take certain risks . . . there is no obvious obligation to neutralize those risks if one can."[9] Strawser responds that whether or not this is true of contracts in general, "military members in Western militaries" at least "expect their commanders not to risk their lives unnecessarily."[10] In light of this expectation (in effect, his PUR), Strawser formulates his central contention more carefully as the claim "OP": "For any just action taken by a given military, if it is possible for the military to use UAV platforms in place of inhabited aerial vehicles without a significant loss of capability, then that military has an ethical obligation to do so."[11]

Six Objections to the Morality of Drone Use

Strawser considers a spectrum of six possible objections to his claim OP and dismisses each in turn. The first is the argument that UAVs are impermissible because they will lead to autonomous weapons systems. Medea Benjamin, for example, raises the concern in her *Drone Warfare: Killing by Remote*

Control (2013) that "pretty soon, drones could also end up killing autono-mously."[12] Indeed, she argues that "the path toward autonomy is a slippery slope" down which we are almost bound to slide.[13] Strawser points out, how-ever, that this type of slippery slope argument is inherently weak, for there is no causal necessity to slide from one position that may be fully defensible (for instance, defending the use of UAVs to disrupt terrorist attacks in prog-ress) to another that may not be (such as the use of fully autonomous robots to kill). In other words, nothing about UAVs impels a movement to auton-omy. Indeed, he argues that there clearly is "a plausible middle ground stop-ping point."[14] There is, for example, "the possibility of maintaining the employment of UAVs while at the same time working for the banning of IAWs [Independent Autonomous Weapons]," as he himself does.[15]

A second possible objection is that UAV limitations could lead to *jus in bello* violations (such as breaches of the just war theory [JWT] principles of distinction or proportionality). Megan Braun and Daniel Brunstetter, for instance, point to a "separation factor" that arises with the use of drones. They argue that "the fact that the pilot can be situated thousands of miles away at a computer console rather than in the line of fire can potentially make discriminating between combatants and noncombatants more diffi-cult."[16] It could also make it harder to avoid civilian casualties due to the "soda straw effect." This point is made effectively in Columbia Law School Human Rights Clinic's report on *The Civilian Impact of Drones: Unexamined Costs, Unanswered Questions*:

> During the later stages of targeting, drone operators may be hampered by what is known as the "soda straw" effect. As a weaponized drone zooms in to pin-point the target, it loses a wider picture of the area—like viewing a small amount of liquid through a soda straw, instead of the entire glass. The soda straw effect creates a risk that civilians may move into the vicinity of the strike without being noticed by drone operators, and therefore without having been considered as part of a targeting analysis.[17]

Strawser agrees that if the soda straw effect or the separation factor sig-nificantly impairs drone operators' ability to respect just war principles, then obviously drones shouldn't be used. He points out that this is already pro-vided for in OP's antecedent "if it is possible . . . without a significant loss of capability." In other words, a diminished capacity to uphold the principles of proportionality or distinction would qualify as a significant loss of capabil-ity, and in that case the rest of OP, including the obligation to use drones, would not follow. However, Strawser suggests that there is good reason to think that there is no loss (and possibly even a gain) in capability—that is, that "UAVs are better, not worse, at noncombatant discrimination."[18] As discussed in chapter 2, there is growing evidence and agreement that drones have the capability to be more discriminating than available alternatives, and also some evidence that they have performed comparatively well in the field, particularly in recent years. At any rate, this is an empirical question that needs to be resolved through investigation, not a philosophical one.

A third moral objection to drone strikes is that they produce cognitive dissonance for pilots, harming them and perhaps leading to their being less discriminating. In relation to drone operators being harmed, Peter W. Singer raises the following concern:

> We're seeing higher levels of combat stress among remote units than among some units in Afghanistan. We found significantly increased fatigue, emotional exhaustion and burnout. Drone operators are more likely to suffer impaired domestic relationships, too.[19]

In relation to a desensitization effect on drone operators leading to their acting recklessly and endangering civilians, Philip Alston writes, for example,

> Because operators are based thousands of miles away from the battlefield, and undertake operations entirely through computer screens and remote audio-feed, there is a risk of developing a "Playstation" mentality to killing.[20]

Jeremy Waldron, the Chichele Professor of Social and Political Theory at Oxford University, elaborates on the notion that targeting could have the effect of distancing and ultimately desensitizing targeters to killing: "Such strategems make murderers of our citizens, and . . . being a murderer in this sense is . . . something vicious one has become, a dishonorable character one has taken on, that cannot be sloughed off as soon as the circumstances that call for targeted killing have passed."[21] He raises a concern that people who conduct such operations might be rendered "unfit to be citizens."[22]

Strawser responds with three points suggesting that harm to soldiers is less significant than it may first appear (especially when compared to direct participation in combat), and then by pointing out that drones permit pilots to be more discriminating than alternative weapons and thus avoid some of the moral costs than can sometimes attend combat. First, he argues that there's little evidence of harm to drone warriors (recent reports suggest a lower incidence of PTSD than soldiers in conventional combat[23]). There are also means of mitigating potential psychological harms to drone operators, such as requiring direct approval for strikes through the chain of command, additional training and counseling for pilots and sensor operators, and the provision of more precise rules of engagement. Finally, psychological harms are generally less serious than the harms risked by putting operators into conventional combat. As to drones being less discriminating, as already noted there is some evidence suggesting that civilian casualties resulting from drone strikes have been low, particularly in recent years, in comparison with other types of military operations (see chapter 1).[24] There are also some plausible explanations of why drone pilots *can* be more discriminating, as "the remote pilot can take more time in evaluating a target before firing," and they "do not experience the same level of stress because there is no danger to themselves."[25]

A fourth objection to Strawser's thesis concerns "the use of UAVs for targeted killings," particularly "by the Central Intelligence Agency."[26] The specific complaint is that "assassinations fall outside the bounds of acceptable just-war theory/practice and that UAVs somehow make this practice too easy."[27] Jeremy Waldron complains that "drone warfare is conducted by unlawful combatants—that is, CIA people who are not in the military chain of command, who are not subject to military ethics—and that has been a very, very sore bone of contention in the critique of the practice."[28] Strawser responds that while he shares "ethical concerns over assassinations," the rightness or wrongness of this policy has nothing to do with the platform being employed (he asks if it would be better with B-52s?).[29] A further important point that has come to light since the publication of Strawser's article is that CIA drone strikes in Pakistan (and likely elsewhere) are actually flown by regular air force personnel—the 17th Reconnaissance Squadron, to be precise—and so much of Waldron's complaint about the trigger being pulled by people outside "the chain of command" and not subject to "military ethics" may be misplaced.[30] As to the point about drones making it too easy, Strawser argues that the weapons platform does not seem to make an ethical or legal difference, and if there is arguably some additional psychological appeal to using drones then this is just a variation of the slippery slope argument addressed above. Thus "there is nothing peculiar to UAVs in regard to the ethical concerns over their present use in targeted killings around the globe."[31] In other words, the issue is properly the ethics of targeted killing, not whether drones are used.

A fifth frequent objection concerns situations in which one side has drones and the other does not. The charge is that this imbalance "crosses an asymmetry threshold that makes the combat inherently ignoble."[32] Paul Kahn, the Winner Professor of Law and the Humanities at Yale Law School, argues that the morality of killing in war depends on the "reciprocal imposition of risk" by combatants.[33] By consequence, he holds that a situation of asymmetry in which one side uses unmanned drones and the other side does not and therefore cannot strike back against actual living combatants violates the morality of war: "We cannot appeal to the morality of warfare to justify this mode of combat."[34] Suzy Killmister, an assistant professor at the University of Connecticut, objects to such asymmetry on slightly different grounds: "In such situations remote weaponry has the consequence of rendering just war theory either an ally of the powerful or obsolete."[35]

Strawser argues that the asymmetry objection is flawed (or at least anachronistic) in assuming that war should be a struggle between two even sides, and all the more so if, as OP stipulates, the warrior using the drone is engaged in a just struggle—"then it is good that the just warrior has the advantage and is better protected."[36]

A direct critique of Strawser's argument on the asymmetry issue has been advanced by Jai Galliott, author of *Military Robots: Mapping the Moral Landscape* (2015). Galliott argues that "when the level of asymmetry in war reaches a certain level, a state may be in violation of the *jus ad bellum* convention."[37] In particular, Galliott points to two important JWT principles that may be violated: "last resort" and "proportionality." In regard to last resort, Galliott suggests that in the kinds of scenarios contemplated by Kahn and Killmister, "it seems implausible that war could be considered a last resort" for the state having drones, since it "would presumably have other less lethal options available to it."[38] In regard to proportionality, he argues that "the harm that the technologically superior state hopes to thwart will in many cases be so insignificant that it would present problems for the proportionality calculus."[39]

Of course, U.S. officials dispute the assumptions built into each of these points. In the first place, the threat posed by nonstate actors can be significant, particularly as it is typically aimed at civilians. U.S. officials often cite the 9/11 attack as an example (which resulted in just under three thousand civilian casualties). Other prominent cases include the Boko Haram attack on Maiduguri, Nigeria, in 2009, killing more than seven hundred people, and the Beslan School seizure by Chechen nationalists in September 2004 that resulted in 334 killed, including many children.[40] Similarly, U.S. officials stress with some plausibility that those planning and organizing such attacks are not easily reached by other means, and that insisting on using other means may result in greater danger to local civilians. President Obama made this point in a Google+ Chat: "A lot of these strikes have been in the FATA and going after al-Qaeda suspects who are up in very tough terrain along the border between Afghanistan and Pakistan. For us to be able to go and get them in another way would involve probably a lot more intrusive military actions."[41]

A sixth objection is that having the option to use drones strikes "makes it too easy for the nation employing UAVs to go to war."[42] Medea Benjamin opines, "While drones make it easier to kill some bad guys, they also make it easier to go to war."[43] Mary Dudziak, the Candler Professor of Law at Emory University, notes that "drones are a technological step that further isolates the American people from military action, undermining political checks" on the use of force.[44] In a powerful *New York Times* op-ed titled "Do Drones Undermine Democracy?" Peter Singer worries that "now we possess a technology that removes the last political barriers to war."[45] The consequence, as he puts it sharply in another piece, is that "by appearing to lower the human costs of war [drones] may seduce us into more wars."[46] Steven Levine, a professor of philosophy at the University of Massachusetts Boston, offers a related worry, enthusiastically echoed by John Kaag of the University of Massachusetts Lowell and Sarah Kreps of Cornell University: "Drones do not just make war too tempting, they also make assassinations and secret intelligence operations too tempting," both because of the extraordinary new capabilities that they demonstrate in these areas, but also because "they lower the visibility of the operation and the potential for pushback" both from abroad and from home.[47] Strawser allows that this is "a legitimate concern," but he nonetheless argues that the objection fails here because "the normative force of PUR upon present actions is too strong to [be] overcome [by] such weak predictive calculations of future possibilities."[48]

Strawser's Reservations

Still, whatever one may think of the various critiques of Strawser's position and his replies, this debate cannot settle the matter of whether drone strikes outside of conventional combat are permissible or even obligatory. Strawser himself emphasized the point in a piece in *The Guardian* responding to what he saw as a misrepresentation of his work: "In the contentious debate over drone warfare, it is necessary to separate US government policy from the broader moral question of killing by aerial robots."[49] Indeed, he himself expresses serious concerns about the policy of conducting drone strikes outside of conventional combat both in *The Guardian* and in his original article. His point in *The Guardian* article is that the moral question of whether it is permissible or even obligatory to use drones in contexts where they can perform equally as well as manned aircraft (i.e., the question of whether they are the most defensible platform) is quite distinct from the questions of whether the way that the U.S. government is choosing to use them is right.

This distinction between policy and morality is reflected in a number of qualifiers that Strawser builds into his argument, most explicitly at the level of PUR. These qualifiers help him to abstract from contentious aspects of current U.S. policy. The key phrase is this: "X has an obligation, other things being equal, to cho[o]se a means to accomplish G that does not *violate the demands of justice, make the world worse*, or expose Y to potentially lethal risk *unless incurring such risk aids in the accomplishment of G* in some way that cannot be gained via less risky means."[50] Uwe Steinhoff points out, however, that if these qualifications of PUR translate to the OP principle that derives from it, as logically he thinks that they must, then OP will only apply where the following qualifiers apply: (a) choosing UAVs to obtain a military goal does not violate the demands of justice, (b) it does not make the world worse, and (c) the capabilities it offers are crucial to the operation and are at least of equivalent quality with those of alternative means.[51] Steinhoff allows that these provisos may insulate OP from some controversy, but only at the price of rendering it rather difficult to relate to reality as we know it, for it would be no easy matter to show that any cases meet these criteria.

Strawser himself seems willing to allow that the application of his principle to policy, and particularly current U.S. policy, may be more limited than it first appears. He points, in particular, to two qualifiers. First, he emphasizes the importance of the criterion that the use of drones "not violate the demands of justice," which means that their use must be "part of a fully justified war effort meeting both *jus ad bellum* and *jus in bello* [Just War] criteria."[52] In several places, however, he expresses reservations about whether current U.S. drone employment would meet this standard, including drone strikes outside of conventional combat. In particular, in his paper on the moral obligation to use drones, he notes that "this paper is in the odd position of arguing for the ethical obligation to use UAVs for a putatively just military action in the current context wherein much, if not all, actual UAV employment is part of military actions which are morally questionable or outright impermissible."[53] So to determine whether his claim OP properly applies to drone strikes in Pakistan, Yemen, and Somalia, we will have to consider the criteria of JWT and their application to those cases in the following section.

II. Drones and Just War

The conventional Western framework for evaluating the justness of a resort to war (and also of its conduct) is JWT.[54] Alex Bellamy, professor of international security at Griffith University, aptly describes JWT as "a two-thousand-year-old conversation about the legitimacy of war that has over time crystalized around several core principles and sub-traditions."[55] Describing JWT as a conversation (rather than as a theory) is useful because it highlights the fact that there is a great deal of lively debate among those working within the tradition over how to interpret the "core principles" (including the criteria of justness to be applied both to the initiation and conduct of war). Bellamy, for example, distinguishes three subtraditions that each read the criteria of just war in slightly different ways—the realist school, the positive law school, and the natural law school.[56] The idea of multiple, contending "subtraditions" gives expression to the idea of an ongoing conversation in which there are both some elements of common agreement (for example, over some of the basic criteria under discussion, like just cause) but also disagreements over interpretation (for instance, over exactly what "right intention" is required in order to be acting justly—does one's motivation have to exclusively be to "uphold the law," or can the desire to advance the "common good" or to "right a wrong" be sufficient?).

The conventional JWT criteria for the justness of resorting to military force (*jus ad bellum*) are just cause, right authority, right intention, last resort, proportionality of ends, and, some say, probability of success. For the conduct of war (*jus in bello*), they include distinction and proportionality.[57] Much of the debate over the use of drones outside of conventional battle-fields has been framed in terms of these JWT criteria. For example, President Obama in his May 23, 2013, speech defending the use of drones outside of conventional battlefields appealed to JWT criteria, insisting that "this is a just war—a war waged proportionally, in last resort, and in self-defense."[58]

Just Cause

In order to qualify as a just war, the United States would first and foremost have to have a "just cause" for resorting to armed force. The president cited the attack of September 11, 2001, and the need to act in self-defense as that just cause for war: "We were attacked on 9/11. Within a week, Congress overwhelmingly authorized the use of force. Under domestic law, and international law, the United States is at war with al Qaeda, the Taliban, and their associated forces."[59] Self-defense against an armed attack is the just cause *par excellence*, and a deliberate mass attack on civilians is a particularly immoral form of attack. There is therefore a strong case that the United States had a just cause for resorting to force against al-Qaeda (particularly as 9/11 was in fact the culmination of a pattern of attacks, including the African embassies attack in 1998 and the attack on the USS *Cole* in 2000). For this reason there was widespread international support for Operation Enduring Freedom (i.e., the invasion of Afghanistan), especially after the Taliban failed to comply fully with President Bush's demand to surrender Osama bin Laden into U.S. custody.[60]

Criticism over the U.S. government's claim to have just cause has mainly focused on where and against whom the United States has fought since then.

Serious doubts have been raised, for example, over whether the United States has just cause to attack the Pakistani Taliban or al-Qaeda affiliates, including groups like al-Shabaab, which had not even been formed at the time of the 9/11 attack and may not present a direct threat to the United States.[61] As James DeShaw Rae, an assistant professor of politics at Sacramento State, put it, "As drone attacks have moved beyond core al-Qaeda and toward a [general] preemptive strategy the just cause element has become more debatable."[62] Moreover, Braun and Brunstetter raise concerns about mission creep: "Initially, only top terrorist leaders were targeted; today, lower officials and even drug lords who may not have a terrorist affiliation are also allegedly being targeted."[63] As noted in chapter 2, the United States has expanded drone targeting to include not only the leaders who ordered the 9/11 attacks but also low-level militants of affiliated organizations who may not have committed nor intend any particular harm against the United States.

Right Authority

The problem of properly defining the enemy becomes particularly marked in relation to the second element of JWT, "right authority." Brian Orend, the director of international studies at the University of Waterloo, frames the standard succinctly in his elegant examination of contemporary JWT, *The Morality of War* (2006): "War must be declared publicly by a *proper* authority."[64] However, as Bellamy notes in *Just War: From Cicero to Iraq*, there is some disagreement among the just war subtraditions concerning just what the "proper authority" is—the positive law school leaning to the view that "states under attack and the UN Security Council have this right," while "natural law and 'realist' [schools] hold that individual states and coalitions may legitimately wage war in other instances."[65] As indicated in President Obama's comments above, the U.S. government sees itself as representing a state under attack—that is, as one that has been the victim of successful attacks and that confronts an enemy intent on continuing to attack. If this assessment is accepted, then all of the subtraditions acknowledge the U.S. right to declare war in its own defense. However, it might also be argued that al-Qaeda has not succeeded in carrying out attacks on the U.S. homeland in more than a decade, although it, and its affiliated organizations, have carried out many attacks in other countries. In this light, the U.S. claim to be "under attack" could be contested, and its claim of a right to wage war correspondingly contested, at least within the "positive law" subtradition (which otherwise allocates this right to the UN Security Council). Kenneth Roth, director of Human Rights Watch, offered an argument along these lines in an August 2013 opinion piece in the *Washington Post* titled "The War against al-Qaeda Is Over." In Roth's view,

> There are . . . limits on . . . when war is an appropriate response to a threat. Those limits are rarely discussed, but nearly 12 years after the Sept. 11, 2001, attacks, with U.S. involvement in the traditional civil war in Afghanistan winding down, it is time to apply those limits to the global "war" against al-Qaeda and its armed affiliates.[66]

Roth argues that in light of the diminished threat, President Obama should officially "call an end" to the state of war.[67] And indeed, the president in his May 2013 speech seems to contemplate exactly this, talking about the changing character of the threat from al-Qaeda and its affiliated organizations and his hope of ending the congressional authorization for the use of force:

> So that's the current threat—lethal yet less capable al Qaeda affiliates; threats to diplomatic facilities and businesses abroad; homegrown extremists. This is the future of terrorism. We have to take these threats seriously, and do all that we can to confront them. But as we shape our response, we have to recognize that the scale of this threat closely resembles the types of attacks we faced before 9/11 . . .
>
> The AUMF is now nearly 12 years old. The Afghan war is coming to an end. Core al Qaeda is a shell of its former self. Groups like AQAP must be dealt with, but in the years to come, not every collection of thugs that labels themselves al Qaeda will pose a credible threat to the United States. Unless we discipline our thinking, our definitions, our actions, we may be drawn into more wars we don't need to fight, or continue to grant Presidents unbound powers more suited for traditional armed conflicts between nation states.
>
> So I look forward to engaging Congress and the American people in efforts to refine, and ultimately repeal, the AUMF's mandate. And I will not sign laws designed to expand this mandate further. Our systematic effort to dismantle terrorist organizations must continue. But this war, like all wars, must end. That's what history advises. That's what our democracy demands.[68]

However, until the AUMF is refined and ultimately repealed, the United States continues to claim proper authority to continue the armed conflict with al-Qaeda and its affiliates and to bring that war to a successful conclusion.

Right Intention

The third JWT criterion is "right intention," which means, in Bellamy's neat formulation, that war must be waged "for the common good, not for self-aggrandizement or because of hatred of the enemy."[69] As Orend puts it, "A state must intend to fight the war only for the sake of a just cause," and therefore should not use force for purposes beyond the accomplishment of its just cause.[70] So if U.S. officials frame their just cause as the prevention of further attacks by al-Qaeda, and their employment of military force is focused on al-Qaeda and is intended to eliminate its capacity and/or will to carry out attacks, then they seem relatively unproblematic in regard to this criterion. Indeed, many of the early drone strikes (2004 to 2008) were focused on key al-Qaeda HVTs and could be said to be serving this purpose.

However, as the drone campaigns have expanded beyond al-Qaeda, the issue of "right intention" has become murkier. Two issues stand out in particular. As noted above, critics question whether the United States has just cause to carry out strikes against groups like AQAP and the TTP, which were not directly involved in the 9/11 attacks, and like al-Shabaab that also may not threaten the United States. The fact that the United States has nonetheless targeted them raises the possibility that it is pursuing other goals, including perhaps the goals of allied states. For example, it has been suggested, including by some of the current authors, that some U.S. drone strikes in Pakistan may have been undertaken at the behest of the Pakistani government against enemies that primarily threatened them and not the United States. A number of commentators have made this claim, for instance, about the targeting of TTP chief Baitullah Mehsud.[71] This may have been a price that the United States had to pay to preserve tacit Pakistani cooperation in a number of areas, including allowing the United States to carry out drone strikes against al-Qaeda targets in North and South Waziristan. The general argument is well articulated by Michael J. Boyle:

> Far from concentrating exclusively on al-Qaeda, the US has begun to use drone strikes against Pakistan's enemies, including the TTP, the Mullah Nazir group, the Haqqani network and other smaller Islamist groups. The result is that the US has weakened its principal enemy, Al-Qaeda, but only at the cost of earning a new set of enemies.[72]

A second and related concern is the types of targets the United States has chosen to go after. In essence, as already noted, the United States has gradually expanded the range of targets it is willing to go after from high-level to mid- and low-level members of terrorist organizations who may not pose much direct threat to the United States. For example, Zenko observes:

> Of the estimated three thousand people killed by drones . . . the vast majority were neither al-Qaeda nor Taliban leaders. Instead, most were low-level, anonymous suspected militants who were predominantly engaged in insurgent or

terrorist operations against their governments, rather than in active international terrorist plots.[73]

The key point is that attacking these low-level fighters diverts U.S. efforts away from its own just cause of protecting itself from further terrorist attacks and risks dragging it into other states' domestic conflicts.[74]

There are also accusations that at times U.S. drone operators have deliberately killed persons who are propagandists for terrorist groups. Journalist Jeremy Scahill suggests that this may have been the case with Samir Khan and possibly Anwar al-Awlaki.[75] The United States has also controversially employed signature strikes, which are based on observed patterns of life that suggest militancy rather than on specific knowledge of the target's identity and role in a terrorist organization—as discussed in the case study of chapter 3. The obvious complaint here is that these uses of force do not contribute directly enough to the just cause (of eliminating al-Qaeda's will and capacity to carry out further attacks) to qualify as "rightly intended."

Last Resort

The fourth JWT criterion is last resort. As Michael Walzer remarks in his seminal *Just and Unjust Wars* (1977), "It is obvious that measures short of war are preferable to war itself" and therefore, as Orend neatly summarizes: "There ought to be a strong presumption against the resort to force."[76] On the other hand, as Walzer also acknowledges, "the truth is that there are always other means," so to literally require states to exhaust every possible option (until arriving at absolutely the last resort) would be to condemn them to inaction. So the effective requirement is that there are no less harmful means that are available that have a high probability of success.[77]

The U.S. view on meeting this criterion is well summarized in Leon Panetta's oft-quoted remark that in many cases, drones are "the only game in town."[78] President Obama makes much the same point in his Google + Chat meeting and his May 23, 2013, speech, stressing that al-Qaeda and its affiliates base themselves "in some of the most distant and unforgiving places on Earth," and that other tactics "would pose profound risks to our troops and local civilians."[79]

The criticism on this point is twofold. First, it is sometimes suggested that the United States does not give enough space for other means (like traditional law enforcement with local allied governments) to work. Indeed, Zenko points out that even some "former and current U.S. officials maintain that the United States relies too much on drone strikes at the expense of longer-term strategies to prevent conditions that foster international terrorism."[80] Second, critics have claimed that the use of drones undermines the willingness of allies to cooperate in these nonmilitary measures (by, for instance, sharing intelligence). The Stimson Report on Drones specifically warns that drones strikes may lead to a loss of cooperation from allies:

> Allies may be unwilling to share intelligence data crucial to targeting, for instance, for fear of incurring legal liability in their own courts or for fear of domestic political consequences—or [the loss of assistance] may be indirect—anger at US targeted strikes may translate into lower levels of cooperation with unrelated US diplomatic initiatives.[81]

Probability of Success

The fifth JWT criterion is "probability of success." The basic idea is, as Orend summarizes nicely, "to bar lethal violence known in advance to be futile."[82] Even a just cause does not justify a resort to force if the consequence will only be bloodshed with no prospect of obtaining a just outcome. There is certainly disagreement over how remote the possibility of success has to be before the effort is morally prohibited, and JWT theorists raise concerns that this requirement may place justice beyond the reach of smaller powers (especially in confrontations with great powers),[83] but most just war thinking accepts some such prudential consideration.

To establish that this criterion is met, defenders of U.S. drone strikes can offer two key arguments. First, it is commonly acknowledged that drone strikes are highly effective *tactically*.[84] Second, there is evidence that they have considerably disrupted the efforts of some targeted groups and indeed considerably degraded their capabilities (most notably of al-Qaeda central in Pakistan).[85]

Critics raise at least two key points in response. First, they point out that overreliance on drone strikes as a tactic is likely to be strategically counterproductive in the long term—as former U.S. ambassador to Pakistan Cameron Munter asked, "Do you want to win a few battles and lose the war?"[86] Munter stresses that "the political fallout" can easily eclipse the benefits of drone strikes if they are not used with restraint.[87] As Michael Boyle effectively summarizes, "drone strikes corrode the stability and legitimacy of local governments, deepen anti-American sentiment and create new recruits for Islamist networks aiming to overthrow these governments."[88] Second, even if the United States has had some tactical success in suppressing al-Qaeda in the FATA, targeted groups have grown in numbers in other places, bringing violence and repression with them. Cronin, for example, argues that "such strikes often lead militants simply to go somewhere else."[89] By consequence, the U.S. use of drones "results in violence spreading to neighboring countries or regions," and "partially explains the expanding al Qaeda footprint in the Middle-East and North Africa, not to mention the Caucasus."[90] A combined loss of U.S. credibility, the legitimacy and authority of local states (often U.S. allies), and the spreading and strengthening of targeted groups hardly seems a recipe for long-term success.[91]

(Macro-) Proportionality

The sixth JWT criterion is among the more controversial and contested—the requirement of "proportionality" (sometimes referred to as macroproportionality to distinguish it from the *jus in bello* requirement of proportionality). As Orend nicely summarizes, "It mandates that a state considering a just war must weigh the expected universal (not just selfish national) benefits of [waging war] against the expected universal costs. Only if the projected benefits, in terms of securing the just cause, are at least equal to, and preferably greater than, such costs as casualties may the war action proceed."[92] This standard generates obvious controversy. Michael Walzer, for example, wonders whether it is possible to really do this sort of measurement.[93] Also, some (realist) just war theorists tend to argue that the costs are properly calculated in national rather than universal terms.[94]

U.S. officials and drone advocates make at least a realist case for the (macro-) proportionality of drone strikes when they argue that drone strikes are highly effective. They argue, in effect, that the benefits in terms of disrupting and weakening al-Qaeda and its affiliates to prevent future attacks (their just cause) outweigh the defects of the strikes. These claims are discussed at some length in chapter 2, but it is worth focusing briefly here on John Brennan's April 30, 2012, speech on "The Efficacy and Ethics of U.S. Counterterrorism Strategy," which was devoted in large part to defending drone strikes outside conventional battlefields. Brennan framed the test of effectiveness primarily in terms of national interests—"as a result of our efforts the United States is more secure and the American people safer"—and then focused on the benefits: "al-Qaeda's leadership ranks have continued to suffer heavy losses," "continue to struggle to communicate," and "struggle to attract new recruits."[95] On the other side of the ledger, he stresses that drones "minimize the risk to civilians" and produce less political blowback than any other military option.[96]

Drone critics like Boyle, by contrast, "focus primarily on the strategic costs of the CIA-run drone campaign outside active theatres of war" and argue that "a drones-first counterterrorism policy is a losing proposition over the long term," both for the United States and the world.[97] If, for example, the effect of drone strikes is, as Boyle argues above, to strengthen the targeted groups over the long run, increasing their popularity with local populations while undermining the authority and legitimacy of local governments, and as Cronin argues above, to spread the reach of such groups throughout the region, then the short-term benefits to the United States may quickly be eclipsed by the long-term costs. Moreover, if one additional effect is "the steady undermining of the rule of law," as we will see that Philip Alston argues, then the balance of what Orend calls "universal benefits" to "universal defects" begins to look especially unfavorable.[98]

All of this indicates that U.S. officials can offer a case for compliance on each JWT criteria for the just resort to military force (*jus ad bellum*), but also that critics can offer some forceful objections on each point. Moreover, even if it is assumed for the sake of argument that government officials could defend their claims against these objections, there would remain further requirements for the just use of force that would need to be met in order to legitimize unconventional drone strikes in terms of JWT. At least two criteria are commonly recognized; namely, "distinction" and "proportionality."

Distinction

In Orend's formulation, the criterion of "distinction" requires that "soldiers charged with the deployment of armed force may not do so indiscriminately; rather, they must exert every reasonable effort to discriminate between legitimate and illegitimate targets."[99] By "legitimate targets" Orend means "anyone or anything engaged in harming."[100] At first glance, U.S. officials seem to be in a particularly strong position in regard to establishing that drone strikes meet this criterion. Their public justifications of drone strikes typically explain that they target al-Qaeda leadership, and there seems little serious doubt that al-Qaeda leaders do harm (as illustrated by table 3.1 in chapter 3, which records annual fatalities from al-Qaeda attacks). Similar things may be said of the leadership of the affiliated groups targeted by the United States, such as the TTP (think of the thousands of Pakistanis killed in suicide attacks in the last decade) or al-Shabaab (which, for example, carried out the Westgate Mall attack in Nairobi in 2013, among manifold atrocities). Insofar as U.S. strikes are directed against those carrying out such attacks, they seem to meet the criteria of targeting those who do harm.

Critics may, however, point to two weaknesses in the U.S. justification. In the first place, the United States engages in "signature strikes," which identify targets based on an observed pattern of life rather than knowledge of the individual. It may well be argued that in such cases the degree of effort invested to determine whether a potential target is a combatant and/or doing harm is inadequate—that is, it does not rise to the standard of "exert[ing] every reasonable effort to discriminate between legitimate and illegitimate targets" and hence fails to comply with the criterion of distinction. An overview of the debate over signature strikes is provided in the case study in chapter 3.

The other point sometimes raised by critics is simply that the United States is too aggressive in carrying out strikes, resulting in civilian casualties that could have been avoided had more precautions been taken. For example, in a 2012 report on drone strikes titled "'Will I Be Next?'" Amnesty International described what appears to be the killing of a lone civilian, apparently entirely unconnected with fighting in the country, while she was gathering okra in the family's fields to prepare for their evening meal:[101] "On a sunny afternoon in October 2012, 68-year-old Mamana Bibi was killed in a drone strike that appears to have been aimed directly at her."[102] The report's writers acknowledge that "because the US government refuses to provide even basic information on particular strikes, including the reasons for carrying them out, Amnesty International is unable to reach firm conclusions," particularly regarding their legality.[103] But a striking feature of their investigation of the Mamana Bibi case is the absence of any indicators that she might pose a threat, and consequently the sense that had the United States been using appropriate precautions, they should have easily recognized that she was not an appropriate target. In other words, while the rationale that led to the drone strike remains unknown, the details of the case make it very hard to believe that proper precautions were taken. If one assumes good intention (i.e., that the U.S. drone operators were not deliberately choosing to kill a civilian), the most plausible explanation appears to be that they must have been acting overzealously or overaggressively. But if targeters failed to "exert every reasonable effort to discriminate between legitimate and illegitimate targets," then they are in violation of just war requirements regardless of what can be established as a matter of law.[104] For its part, while it acknowledges that it lacks proof, Amnesty International declared that it is "concerned that these and other strikes have resulted in unlawful killings that may constitute extrajudicial executions or war crimes."[105]

American authorities, for their part, insist that the United States fully complies with the principle of distinction. In his April 2012 speech on "The Efficacy and Ethics of U.S. Counterterrorism Strategy," John Brennan insisted,

> Targeted strikes conform to the principles of distinction, the idea that only military objectives may be intentionally targeted and that civilians are protected from being intentionally targeted. With the unprecedented ability of remotely

piloted aircraft to precisely target a military objective while minimizing collateral damage, one could argue that never before has there been a weapon that allows us to distinguish more effectively between an al-Qaida terrorist and innocent civilians.[106]

Harold Koh offered similar reassurances in his March 2010 speech, focusing more on procedure than capability: "In my experience, the principles of distinction and proportionality that the United States applies are not just recited at meetings."[107] These claims have received some support from scholars who have studied U.S. targeting procedures, such as C. Christine Fair and Gregory McNeal.[108] McNeal's findings will be discussed in some detail in the case study at the end of this chapter.

(Micro-) Proportionality

The final JWT criterion is that of "proportionality" (or micro-proportionality to distinguish it from the *ad bellum* proportionality requirement). As Orend stresses, this is a criterion that applies at the "tactical" level of individual operations, and requires that "the destruction needed to fulfill the goal [of the operation] is proportional to the good of achieving it."[109] This criterion is most notoriously used to determine whether foreseeable civilian harm can be morally justified. A proposed operation would be morally unacceptable if the expected civilian harm was disproportionately high in relation to the value of the military goals the operation is expected to accomplish.

Again, U.S. officials argue strongly that drones comply with the requirements of proportionality. President Obama claimed in his May 2013 speech that the United States upheld especially high standards in regard to proportionality, seemingly beyond what would be required by the law of war:

> Before any strike is taken, there must be near-certainty that no civilians will be killed or injured—the highest standard we can set. . . . Yes, the conflict with al Qaeda, like all armed conflict, invites tragedy. But by narrowly targeting our action against those who want to kill us and not the people they hide among, we are choosing the course of action least likely to result in the loss of innocent life.[110]

John Brennan frames his claim more directly in terms of the JWT principle of proportionality and stresses the degree to which drones enhance the U.S. capacity to maintain compliance:

> Targeted strikes conform to the principle of proportionality, the notion that the anticipated collateral damage of an action cannot be excessive in relation to

the anticipated military advantage. By targeting an individual terrorist or small numbers of terrorists with ordnance that can be adapted to avoid harming others in the immediate vicinity, it is hard to imagine a tool that can better minimize the risk to civilians than remotely piloted aircraft.[111]

These various remarks can be organized into two key claims concerning the proportionality of U.S. drone operations: (1) U.S. targeters uphold the standard of proportionality in each operation (the risk of harm to civilians is not disproportionate to the military objectives targeters reasonably anticipate realizing) and indeed respect significantly more restrictive rules of engagement (i.e., near certainty of no civilian casualties); (2) drones conduce to proportionality because their ability to loiter and await the optimal moment to strike, and the precision and low blast radius of the missiles they carry help to minimize danger to nearby civilians. The relatively low number of civilian casualties in drone strikes compared to other types of military operations provides at least some support for the latter claim.[112]

Critics charge that such claims are misleading—indeed, Braun and Brunstetter complain that aggregating disparate targeting cases together, drawing averages, and comparing across weapons systems constitute a kind of "proportionality relativism."[113] As they accurately note, the proportionality calculation is supposed to be done for each operation individually.[114] Of course, Braun and Brunstetter also aggregate across cases (for example, using the number of strikes that do and do not kill civilians as an indicator of proportionality), and then compare across data sets from different countries (between Pakistani and Afghan drone strikes), even while recognizing that U.S. military strategies in these countries are quite distinct (that is, counterinsurgency in Afghanistan and counterterrorism in Pakistan).[115] Their analysis suggests that CIA drone strikes in Pakistan on the whole do not meet the JWT standard of (micro-) proportionality, in part because they compare unfavorably to U.S. drone strikes in Afghanistan in terms of the harm that they inflict on civilians:

> The data indicate that 23 per cent of CIA strikes [in Pakistan] caused collateral damage, which is a far higher percentage than what the US military tolerates [in Afghanistan]. The observed outcome of collateral damage from CIA drone operations [in Pakistan] is more than twice as high as the US military's accepted threshold [in Afghanistan] of 10 per cent and orders of magnitude higher than the military's actual collateral damage rate of 1 per cent. If based on a comparison with other tactics, this may be seen as reason for optimism; however, we argue that 23 per cent should be considered excessive. While the military's operations are arguably in compliance with the proportionality criterion, the CIA drone program, if held to the same standard, would be disproportionate on the whole.[116]

However, Avery Plaw and Carlos Colon (two of the authors of this book) point out that the Afghan and Pakistani civilian casualty numbers in recent years appear to have drawn about even (both overall and in terms of the proportion of strikes resulting in civilian casualties).[117] In fact, there are some indications that the proportion of civilian casualties in Pakistan has dipped below that in Afghanistan. Indeed, in a November 2014 *New Yorker* piece, Steve Coll (author of *Ghost Wars*) reported that "since Brennan became C.I.A. director, according to the data compiled by the Bureau of Investigative Journalism, there has not been a single documented civilian casualty, child or adult, as a result of a drone strike in Waziristan," where virtually every U.S. drone strike in Pakistan takes place.[118]

Nonetheless the basic fact remains that even if the overall number of civilians being killed by drone strikes has been sharply reduced (along with the proportion of strikes causing civilian casualties), whether in Pakistan or Afghanistan, none of that precludes the possibility that at least some drone strikes may at some point have breached the proportionality criterion, and could even constitute war crimes. Coll also reports the following case:

> On the morning of March 17, 2011, roughly thirty-five maliks, government-approved tribal leaders, had gathered for a *jirga*, a traditional dispute-resolution meeting. The subject was a feud over a chromite mine.
>
> "There were two tribes in the area, Manzarkhel and Maddakhel," the tribal leader Malik Jalal told me. "The dispute was between these two tribes. They were taking chromite out, but there was a question of who owned what." The Pakistani government knew of the *jirga* session. *Khasadars*, or local police, paid by the government, were in attendance, according to court filings.
>
> That morning, Jalal was a little more than two miles away. "I could see the drones in the air, and I actually saw the missiles fly and then heard the explosions," he said. "When I reached the spot, I saw many body parts." The FATA government's contemporaneous ledger of strikes recorded that forty-one people died, and it noted, "The attack was carried out on a *jirga* and it is feared that all the killed were local tribesmen."
>
> Angry protests erupted in Pakistan.[119]

If what the FATA government's report suggests is true—that none of the victims were Taliban, then this attack might well have violated proportionality (and distinction). Of course, one would have to give consideration to the question of the military goal that the planners thought they would achieve, and whether they exercised due precaution in planning and due care in executing the operation, but it is not at all clear that these considerations would establish that the strike was legal.

It becomes even more difficult to make a case for the proportionality of the foregoing case if one accepts the argument advanced by some drone critics that the proportionality standard should be elevated in the case of unconventional drone strikes. In a chapter titled "Disciplining Drone Strikes: Just War in the Context of Counterterrorism," David True, an associate professor of religion at Wilson College, makes a case that as a result of drones enabling greater precision in targeting, we should limit proportionality by not permitting foreseeable harm to civilians in the first place.[120] True argues that the use of drones outside of conventional battlefields should "demonstrate a special respect for non-combatants." In the case of drones being deployed in unconventional conflicts, "the war principle of discrimination should be revised so that foreseen deaths are no longer permitted or excused."[121] True goes on to say that "this change would heighten the military's responsibility, but such change is in keeping with the greater capabilities of the weapon."[122]

III. The Spirit of JWT

Nonetheless, while examination of particular cases under specific criteria like micro-proportionality may be suggestive, they are almost bound to remain inconclusive given the limited information available on what planners knew and what they intended and anticipated. There have, however, been some interesting attempts to argue that drone strikes outside of conventional battlefields at a more general level have been consistent with the spirit of JWT. For example, Daniel Statman, a professor of philosophy at the University of Haifa, has advanced a bold defense of TK in general (and drones in particular) in a chapter in Altman, Finkelstein, and Ohlin's *Targeted Killings: Law and Morality in an Asymmetrical World* (2012), titled "Can Just War Theory Justify Targeted Killing?" Statman concludes that "there is nothing about TK that is inconsistent with the main theories of just warfare."[123]

Statman's argument in support of this conclusion is that all three leading contemporary variants of JWT converge in authorizing the use of targeted killing (including by drones) against militants of terrorist groups like al-Qaeda. He identifies the three leading variants of JWT as (1) individualist (associated with Jeff McMahan), (2) collectivist (associated with Noam Zohar), and (3) contractualist (associated with Yitzhak Benbaji).[124]

Three Variants of JWT

The distinguishing feature of the individualist JWT theorists is that they believe that "the permission to kill human beings in war is continuous with the morality of individual self-defense."[125] By consequence, targeted killing is only justifiable when confronted with an "unjust threat," for which the target is "morally responsible," where "there is no other way of neutralizing the threat," and where the killing is "not disproportionate to the evil prevented."[126]

The collectivists, by contrast, insist that it is not individuals who go to war with each other, but collectives (nations, armies, groups, etc.): "When we kill enemy soldiers, we do not kill them qua individuals, but qua agents of the enemy collective."[127] Some soldiers bear no personal responsibility for the war (e.g., reluctant conscripts), so we need a collective perspective to explain why it is permissible for them to be killed. This consists in two conditions: (1) the individual must be part of the relevant collective (i.e., the army or armed group) and (2) there must be a state of war.[128] It should be noted, however, that in explaining why certain persons who do not bear personal responsibility are liable to be killed, the collectivist perspective does not seek to deny that those who do bear personal responsibility might also be permissible targets.

Finally, contractualists hold that "the most central aspects of *jus in bello* are based on a tacit agreement between states on how war is to be conducted."[129] This agreement is "binding because it is mutually beneficial and fair."[130] So in order to be morally justifiable, TK would have to either be consistent with the terms of the contract, or it would have to be shown that the contract does not pertain.

Why Each Variant of JWT Allows Targeted Killing

Statman argues that each of these variants of JWT will permit TK, albeit under slightly different conditions (but all compatible with conditions that often surround U.S. drone strikes). For individualists, "the crucial condition that must be satisfied to justify killing human beings in self-defense is that they are morally responsible for some grave threat whose neutralization is the end in mind," and there is no other viable means of attaining this end.[131] Whether they are soldiers in the conventional sense makes no difference—the core issue is whether they meet what Statman calls "the Responsibility condition," which means essentially that they knowingly contribute to the grave threat.[132] So as long as al-Qaeda militants meet this condition, and cannot be stopped by other means, they are permissible targets on the individualist variant of JWT. Indeed, Statman argues that "within the individualist view, TK is not just one permissible tactic among others, but the preferred one (unless it happens to be impractical or ineffective). It does a much better job of distributing the self-defensive harm in accordance with moral responsibility."[133]

On the collectivist variant, Statman recognizes that there is an important debate around whether al-Qaeda constitutes a collective in the required sense, and so whether there can be a clash of collectives that triggers the special morality that collectivists associate with war.[134] But he argues that this hardly matters, because the collectivist element of this approach to JWT is framed as a supplement, which resolves anomalies arising from the individualist morality of the first approach. Thus, in the absence of that supplement, collectivists can fall back on "the responsibility condition": "Hence individualist morality would be sufficient to justify the use of TK against [al-Qaeda activists], just like in Individualism."[135]

Finally, on the contractualist model, he argues that contract rules could be binding on both sides insofar as they are mutually beneficial. Under the contractual war convention, targeting is entirely permissible. However, the persistent refusal of terrorist groups to play by the rules violates the reciprocity condition and undermines the interest of states in complying in turn. But if the contractual rules do not apply, then the only remaining question is whether TK is a violation of fundamental moral norms like the prohibition against rape or torture. Here Statman stresses that TK can be (and in his discussion, it is) used against those who meet "the responsibility condition" and hence are deliberately posing a grave threat. He argues that if we accept the morality of killing soldiers who may be conscripted and (possibly) not much of a threat, then there cannot be any natural obstacle to killing those who are deliberately posing a grave threat, especially to civilians. Thus, he writes, "Not only would contractualism license TK, it would recommend it as a preferred tactic."[136]

IV. The Idea of *Jus ad Vim*

Yet not all just war theorists are persuaded that U.S. drones strikes, or at least the great majority of them, are consonant with the spirit of JWT. In a 2013 article titled "From *Jus ad Bellum* to *Jus ad Vim*: Recalibrating our Understanding of the Moral Use of Force," Daniel Brunstetter and Megan Braun follow Michael Walzer in arguing that traditional JWT would benefit today from recognizing a new category of "measures short of war" as distinct from "actual warfare."[137] By "measures short of war," they mean operations that are "limited in scope," like "no fly zones, pinpoint air/missile strikes, CIA operations," which "fall short of the quantum and duration associated with traditional warfare."[138] They point out rightly that states have relied increasingly on such limited measures in the last couple of decades, especially to respond to "the rise of non-state actors such as al-Qaeda and its affiliates, which pose significant threats to international peace and security, but do not have international legal status and operate in the porous or disputed border regions of sovereign states."[139] Yet, as they note, the conflicts with these terrorist groups and the limited measures states employ against them do not fit neatly into the traditional legal and ethical frameworks of "armed conflict" or "law enforcement" that were primarily designed to regulate wars (either between or within states) or criminal behavior (within states) respectively. These nonstate actors are far more dangerous than criminal gangs, and their transnational character often puts them outside the reach of the domestic law of the states they seek to attack—indeed, against whom they are, in their minds, waging war. At the same time, the powers and privileges of belligerency sometimes assumed by states seem excessive and indeed dangerous in relation to the scope of the threat, particularly when they are seen as extending to anywhere and everywhere these nonstate actors operate. But these are the only two options available under the current international legal regime and within the moral framework of JWT that informs it.[140]

The *jus ad vim* is intended to offer a third possibility, at least in cases of last resort. When confronted with terrorist groups operating out of a "host country [that] does not have the will and or capacity to deal with the threat they pose," Braun and Brunstetter concur with Walzer that "international policing actions, in conjunction with actions by local authorities, should be tried first."[141] But if that proves unavailing, then what can be done, and under what rules? In such cases, they argue, we would be better served by "measures short of war" (subject to appropriately restraining principles that preserve human rights as much as possible) than by a wholesale declaration of war and the invocation of all the rights and powers of belligerency. So just as JWT establishes criteria for determining when actual warfare is justly initiated (*jus ad bellum*) and conducted (*jus in bello*), we should similarly develop criteria for determining the justness of "measures short of war," criteria that they refer to as *jus ad vim*.[142]

Jus ad Vim Criteria

In their formulation, *jus ad vim* requirements for the resort to force should include the following:

1. **Just Cause:** "Within the context of *jus ad vim*, a state has just cause to use measures short of war when responding to *injuria* against its interests or citizens. This includes responding to terrorist bombings, attacks on embassies or military installations, and the kidnapping of citizens. . . . Imminent threats of terrorist attacks also provide just cause."[143]

2. **Last Resort:** "Some attempt at nonviolent diplomatic measures must be tried before resorting to force, even if the limited levels of violence of *jus ad vim* mean that this requirement is less exacting than in the case of war. . . . There must be an imminent threat and conditions that rule out policing measures."[144]

3. **(Macro-)Proportionality:** This means "defining what constitutes a successful outcome and determining which actions will enable this outcome," on the basis of a "probability of success criterion."[145] These actions then define "the maximally just level of force . . . not what level to begin with and potentially escalate from."[146]

4. **Right Intention:** "Right intention must therefore be directed toward upholding the rights of the Other. In this sense, right intention for *jus ad vim* means quelling a specific threat, while causing the least amount of damage possible by protecting civilians."[147]

They also suggest an entirely new criterion that does not appear in standard JWT:

5. **Probability of Escalation:** "If engaging in *jus ad vim* actions has a high probability of resulting in war, then one could argue that such actions are not justifiable."[148] As they specify in a 2014 article, "limited force should not run the risk of increased violence."[149]

Finally, in Braun and Brunstetter's formulation, the foregoing criteria should *not* be seen as forming a threshold that only needs to be crossed once to justify an ongoing campaign against nonstate actors. These are rather ongoing requirements that need to be met separately in each resort to force, even against the same target:

Whereas in war, principles such as just cause and last resort need only be satisfied at the outset of a conflict, *jus ad vim* requires that they be continually reassessed in advance of each use of force. Additionally, by moving beyond the persistent and broad nature of a general threat that one assumes in warfare, and examining individual operations geared towards a particular threat, a theory of *jus ad vim* makes it possible to assess whether the response is calibrated to the gravity of that threat. This nuanced approach proves essential when examining the proportionality of drone strikes.[150]

In the case, then, of a state pursuing a series of distinct operations against a nonstate actor, such as a drone campaign, compliance with *jus ad vim* on Braun and Brunstetter's account would require each and every strike be justified in terms of the foregoing criteria (as well as those that follow).

Assuming the foregoing conditions on the resort to force are met, Braun and Brunstetter suggest that the actual use of force under *jus ad vim* should also be regulated by elevated *jus in bello* standards, including human rights considerations:

> *Jus ad vim* demands a stricter relationship between the use of force short of war and the *jus in bello* principles of proportionality and discrimination. In addition, we assert that human rights concerns of civilians not usually considered in the proportionality calculus need to be taken into account. Such ethical constraints severely restrict the scope of proportionality balancing—the conscious decision that anticipated military advantage outweighs collateral damage—that can be employed.[151]

Applying these standards to U.S. drone strikes outside of conventional battlefields in Pakistan, Braun and Brunstetter draw two key conclusions:

1. "When viewed through the lens of *jus ad vim*, the CIA's proportionality balancing in Pakistan . . . is . . . highly problematic."[152] Indeed, they assert that "if we judge the CIA's use of drones in Pakistan according to the standards of *jus ad vim*, then it falters on [two] counts."[153] First, it fails in regard to "the threshold of harm that can be committed against civilians [which] should be lower than in zones of war."[154] Second, it violates the *jus ad vim* principle that "the human rights of civilians living under drones cannot be violated in order to protect the rights of US citizens."[155]
2. However, "This does not mean that drones are never permitted to protect American lives from terrorists operating in these regions, but . . . If strikes are to be justified they will need to conform to a highly restrictive standard of proportionality and exhibit strong respect for human rights."[156]

Criticism of the Case for *Jus ad Vim*

Avery Plaw and Carlos Colon contest these conclusions on three grounds:

1. Braun and Brunstetter's formulation of *jus ad vim* and its requirements is in several respects unrealistic and unhelpful. Plaw and Colon argue that a careful examination of the data and reflection on the virtues and defects of conventional JWT criteria suggest that a rigorous application of the traditional criteria will provide a more appropriate, flexible, and

realistic framework for evaluating drone strikes outside of conventional battlefields.[157]

2. Whatever one thinks about their account of *jus ad vim*, the strikes on which Braun and Brunstetter focus (i.e., in Pakistan), or at least most of them, are not appropriate applications for it. The areas of Pakistan targeted by drones *are* clearly in a state of armed conflict and therefore the appropriate standards are those of armed conflict (i.e., traditional *jus in bello* rather than *jus ad vim*).[158]

3. Finally, even if their *jus ad vim* standards are applied (erroneously) to Pakistan, their case that these drone strikes in general fail standards of proportionality is not convincing. One reason for this is that Braun and Brunstetter include in their count of "civilians" killed the entire category of "unknowns," which their source (the New American Foundation) defines as individuals who "were described in a manner that made it *ambiguous whether they were militants or civilians*."[159] Once the data is disaggregated, the Pakistani drone strikes at least technically meet the minimum standard of proportionality Braun and Brunstetter appear to approve in Afghanistan.[160]

Nonetheless, it might well turn out that a significant number of victims of drone strikes in Pakistan who are currently listed as "unknowns" will turn out to be civilians, and this could tip the balance against the proportionality of drone strikes, at least under Braun and Brunstetter's *jus ad vim* criteria (if it were deemed applicable). Alternately, their claims might identify possible violations of proportionality in other regions or periods where there was no state of armed conflict. These possibilities bring to the fore the deeper question: Which standards are more appropriate to the evaluation of drone strikes outside of conventional battlefields, the more conventional JWT criteria discussed in section II and that inform Statman's analysis in section III, or the new *jus ad vim* standards suggested by Braun and Brunstetter?

V. The Temptation to Violence

Independent of the debate over the compliance of nonbattlefield drone strikes with the requirements of Just War Theory, a separate ethical debate has developed focused on the long-term consequences of drone strikes and whether they are wholly bad. Indeed, it is sometimes argued that they are so bad as to be disqualifying. Two main lines of argument stand out here. The first concerns how other states are likely to behave in light of the precedents established by drone strikes. The worry is that U.S. drone strikes are setting a precedent for other countries that will ultimately lead to more violence and instability in the international system. The second line of argument concerns the incentives that the United States is setting for itself and raises worries about how it is likely to behave in the future. The argument is that this extremely low-cost form of warfare effectively circumvents the usual checks and balances on the resort to force, and by consequence the U.S. government, and the executive branch in particular, is going to be increasingly drawn to this option, so that we may soon find ourselves in a circumstance of perpetual war.[161]

Jeremy Waldron summarizes the first argument neatly: "If we defend norms like N1 [a rule he invents that would allow unconventional drone strikes] we should consider their use in the hands of others (such as our enemies)."[162] Iran, Russia, and China, for example, all have armed drones (as will be detailed in chapter 6), and all are occasionally attacked by terrorist groups based in surrounding countries. The precedent that we are setting could serve to justify Russian drone strikes in Ukraine against groups allegedly plotting terrorist attacks in Russia, which could easily escalate into a wider and more violent conflict (or the Chinese could conduct a drone strike against an East Turkestan Islamic Movement training camp in northwest Pakistan, or the Iranians against a Jundallah training camp in Pakistan).

But it need not be a country that the United States sees as an enemy or a potential enemy that could promote instability by following the U.S. lead in using drones. The broader danger is well encapsulated by Craig Martin, associate professor at Washburn University School of Law, in a chapter examining the impact of the U.S. adoption of targeted killing on the international norms governing the use of force:

> Consider the ramification if India had characterized the Mumbai attack of 2008 as an "armed attack" justifying the use of force in self-defense against Lashkar-e-Taiba, quite independent of whether there was sufficient evidence to establish that its operation could be attributed to Pakistan. The use of force against the group within the territory of Pakistan would have nonetheless been viewed as an act of war by Pakistan, and there would have been a real risk of a full-blown armed conflict between nuclear powers.[163]

The Obama administration has acknowledged these worries about the precedents the United States is setting and the long-term concerns that they raise. As Micah Zenko aptly summarizes, "It is the stated position of the Obama administration that its strategy toward drones will be emulated by other states and nonstate actors. In an interview, President Obama remarked, 'I think creating a legal structure, processes, with oversight checks on how we use unmanned weapons is going to be a challenge for me and for my successors for some time to come—partly because technology may evolve fairly rapidly for other countries as well.' "[164]

Moral Hazard

Indeed, as the second line of consequential argument emphasizes, the U.S. government itself could be seduced by the dangerous precedent that it is setting now into causing more violence and conflict than it otherwise would in the future. Kaag and Kreps put the argument well: "Morally, drones create a moral hazard by shielding U.S. citizens, politicians, and soldiers from the risks associated with targeted killings."[165] Peter W. Singer puts it even more succinctly when he argues that "by appearing to lower the human costs of war [drones] may seduce us into more wars."[166] Braun and Brunstetter offer a slightly different rationale for the same worry: "Because drone strikes are seen as a level of force short of war, their use may also be seen as a measure to which the principle of last resort does not apply."[167] In other words, leaders may be tempted to use them before they really have to (or have a sufficiently compelling case to do so). This point about drone strikes seeming like something less than going to war is especially significant given that the Obama administration did not seek congressional authorization for the use of drones in Libya, on the grounds that it was unnecessary since U.S. personnel were not being endangered. This suggests that drones may allow the executive to circumvent the conventional checks on the U.S. use of force abroad, beginning with the need for congressional authorization. Zenko and Kreps summed up these varied considerations nicely in June 2014:

> For the United States, drones have significantly reduced the political, diplomatic and military risks and costs associated with the use of military force, which has led to a vast expansion of lethal operations that would not have been attempted with other weapons platforms. Aside from airstrikes in traditional conflicts such as Libya, Iraq, and Afghanistan—where one quarter of all International Security Assistance Force (ISAF) airstrikes in 2012 were conducted by drones—the United States has conducted hundreds in non-battlefield settings: Pakistan (approximately 369), Yemen (approximately 87), Somalia (an estimated 16), and the Philippines (at least 1, in 2006). Of the estimated 473 non-battlefield targeted killings undertaken by the United States since November 2002, approximately 98 percent were carried out by drones. . . .
>
> Senior U.S. civilian and military officials, whose careers spans the pre- and post-armed conflict era[,] overwhelmingly agree that the threshold for the authorization of force by civilian officials has been significantly reduced. Former secretary of defense Robert Gates asserted in October 2013, for example, that armed drones allow decision-makers to see war as a "bloodless, painless, and odorless" affair, with technology detaching leaders from the "inevitably

tragic, inefficient, and uncertain" consequences of war. President Barack Obama admitted in May 2013 that the United States has come to see armed drones "as a cure-all for terrorism" because they are low risk and instrumental in "shielding the government" from criticisms "that a troop deployment invites." Such admissions from leaders of a democratic country with a system of checks and balances point to the temptations that leaders with fewer institutional checks will face.[168]

In essence then, the argument is that since drones permit the president to employ force abroad without seeking congressional approval, and without the public scrutiny generated by troop deployments and ultimately without body bags coming home, drones create a situation of "moral hazard."[169] In other words, they allow presidents to act recklessly, employing force around the world, with little or no political cost at home. Kaag and Kreps offer the following predicted result: "Precision guided munitions and drones give you a society with perpetual asymmetric wars."[170]

VI. Promoting Humanitarian Intervention

A forceful rejoinder to the "moral hazard" objection was advanced by Zack Beauchamp (of the Center for American Progress) and Julian Savulescu (who is the Uehiro Chair in Practical Ethics at Oxford) in a chapter titled "Robot Guardians: Teleoperated Combat Vehicles in Humanitarian Military Intervention" in B. J. Strawser's collection *Killing by Remote Control: The Ethics of an Unmanned Military* (2013). While acknowledging that it is possible that in at least some cases the possession of combat drones might lower the threshold for a state to resort to war,

> [they] suggest that lowering the threshold is not, as commonly assumed, necessarily a bad thing. In at least one case, the bug is in fact a feature: drones have the potential to significantly improve the practice of humanitarian interventions, understood here [as] the use of military force to protect foreign citizens from mass violence like genocide or ethnic cleansing.[171]

In essence, their argument is that the main obstacle to many humanitarian interventions that we should undertake (i.e., which are either morally obligatory or supererogatory) is casualty aversion. They offer the example of the Rwandan genocide of 1994, in which five hundred thousand to one million Rwandans, mostly Tutsis, were killed in around three-and-a-half months, while the UN withdrew its peacekeepers under U.S. pressure, motivated (they suggest) by casualty aversion.[172] They also point to the genocide in Darfur between 2003 and 2007, in which no international intervention took place, and suggest that "were there a means by which the risk to intervening forces could be dramatically lowered or even eliminated, it seems likely that in at least some cases states would launch justified interventions in cases that they otherwise might not."[173]

Moreover, Beauchamp and Savulescu argue that even when states do initiate humanitarian interventions, "casualty aversion can still hamper their ability to conduct the fighting in accordance with a central *jus in bello* rule: the necessity of preserving non-combatant life."[174] The argument here is that states typically adopt strategies and tactics that protect their own troops, often with the effect of increasing the danger to local civilians. Beauchamp and Savulescu offer the example of the Kosovo intervention of 1999 in which "NATO committed to a 'zero casualty'" policy in regard to its own forces.[175] One result was the refusal to put boots on the ground, and another was that commanders established a fifteen-thousand-foot floor for bombers so as to protect NATO pilots from ground fire, despite the fact that this "significantly impeded pilot ability to verify their targets."[176] Human Rights Watch estimates that "more than half of civilian casualties of the bombing campaign were caused by hits on 'illegitimate or questionable' targets."[177] In the assessment of respected JWT scholar Jean Elshtain, "Our ends were tainted by our means—means that will surely haunt us in the future."[178] If drones can remove the concern with casualty aversion, they can allow states intervening in order to prevent atrocities to fight better by better protecting local civilians. In sum, then, "drones will both (1) make it more likely that states launch justified humanitarian interventions; and (2) improve the conduct, morally speaking, of such interventions once launched."[179]

Moreover, Beauchamp and Savulescu argue that the types of wars whose initiation and conduct are most likely to be affected by drones are in fact humanitarian interventions. Their argument is that cases like "Somalia, Rwanda, and Kosovo . . . demonstrate that policymakers willing in principle to conduct humanitarian intervention can be uniquely deterred by casualty aversion."[180] By contrast, states may decide against going to war in the national interest for diverse reasons—such as "nuclear deterrence, economic interdependence, or shared democratic institutions"—and there "is little reason to suppose that lowering the casualty threshold would have much of an effect on these other barriers to war."[181] By consequence they argue that "the most likely sort of war to be enabled [by the possession of drones] is humanitarian war."[182]

Of course, it may be objected that even if this latter point turns out to be accurate, it does not preclude the possibility that some "bad" wars might also be enabled by the possession of combat drones, and that the harm

incurred by these wars might outweigh the benefits of humanitarian interventions. Also, it must be allowed that there is something peculiarly unhu-
manitarian about interventions carried out by remotely operated robots.
Finally, Peter W. Singer and Uwe Steinhoff have argued that there is something objectionable about the idea that only a small elite of industrially
advanced countries will enjoy this enhanced capacity to intervene militarily
(even for humanitarian purposes)—that such a country, as Singer puts it,
"alone gets the right to stop bad things . . . only at the time and place of its
choosing, and, most important, only if the costs are low enough."[183] Beauchamp and Savulescu, by contrast, stress the consequential benefits that may
attend increased humanitarian interventions, and point out: "It strains cre-
dulity that any victim of any genocide would care enough about the species
of their savior to make them prefer to be murdered."[184]

VII. The Erosion of Virtue

Leaving aside the important but contested terrain of consequential moral
argument, it is well worth also considering a telling critique of drones from
a different ethical tradition—that is, the idea of virtue ethics (most famously
advocated by Aristotle). The core idea here, eloquently advanced by Robert
Sparrow, an associate professor at Monash University, is that the use of
drones tends to undermine the need to, and perhaps even the possibility of,
cultivating the martial virtues that have generally been seen as defining the
U.S. military, such as courage and honor. As Sparrow puts it,

> By transforming combat into a "desk job" that can be conducted from the
> safety of the home territory of advanced industrial powers without the need for
> physical strength or martial valor, long-range robotic weapons call the relevance
> of such accounts into question.[185]

To creatively paraphrase, the drone is a cowardly weapon that threatens to
make cowards of those who embrace it.

Sparrow's analysis focuses on four virtues—courage, loyalty, honor, and
mercy—all of which he argues are central to a warrior code and are threatened by reliance on drones. Courage involves a "willingness to face fear and
overcome it," but the use of drones clearly calls "into question the need for
courage for those who operate them" because, of course, they remain perfectly safe.[186] To demonstrate loyalty, "soldiers must be willing to place themselves at risk, indeed to sacrifice themselves, for the sake of the larger
objectives," but again drone operators remain perfectly safe and so cannot

demonstrate it, and have "little opportunity to develop and cultivate it."[187] According to Sparrow, honor is "how well one lives up to one's chosen ideals,"[188] and there are at least three reasons to be concerned that drone operators will have insufficient opportunity and/or incentive to cultivate it: First, as they "face fewer challenges to acting ethically [not being themselves under physical threat], they may have less reason to cultivate a sense of honor"; second, distance makes "it more difficult to respect—and to earn respect from those against whom they fight"; and third, they "are alienated from two groups of people who should properly be an important resource for the development and maintenance of a sense of honor: enemy warriors and civilians in the territory where war is being fought."[189] Finally, for Sparrow, mercy is "to refrain, out of compassion, from killing or causing suffering when one is both able and would be justified in doing so."[190] But Sparrow worries that the context in which drone operators work "makes it harder for them to exercise discretion."[191] More importantly, Sparrow argues that mercy must be motivated by "compassion," and that it is "fundamentally a response to the needs of the concrete other," which is obscured by the mediated, distanced relationship between operator and target.[192]

Sparrow's conclusion is that "unmanned operations pose a profound threat to the martial virtues."[193] This conclusion should, he thinks, be troubling because "we should be very cautious about giving up on the warrior virtues."[194] They "function to reduce the horror of war and tame the worst excesses of young men sent out to kill strangers in foreign lands."[195] They have "developed and evolved over many years and through many conflicts," and we should think twice before abandoning them.[196]

VIII. The Dangers of Autonomy

Another major ethical concern involves the direction in which the U.S. military (and others after it) will seek to develop the aerial combat drone. With armed aerial drones particularly in mind, Noel Sharkey, a professor at the University of Sheffield, aptly articulates the main concern as follows: "All roadmaps of the US forces have made clear the desire and intention to develop and use autonomous battlefield robots. Execution of these plans to take the human out of the loop is well underway. The end goal is that robots will operate autonomously to locate their own targets and destroy them without human intervention."[197] For Sharkey then, the air force's evident commitment to develop automated drones necessarily means taking "the human out of the loop," and that raises a host of moral concerns, as will be seen below, especially when it comes to lethal operations.

By contrast, George Lucas, the Class of 1984 Distinguished Chair in Ethics at the Vice Admiral James B. Stockdale Center for Ethical Leadership at the United States Naval Academy, has suggested drawing a distinction between two kinds of autonomous systems. On the one hand, there are semiautonomous drones, capable of completing certain functions like flying and doing surveillance on their own, but which still require human oversight and require human control for carrying out attacks. On the other hand, there are fully autonomous drones capable of running themselves, including selecting and attacking targets.[198] It is difficult to dispute that there has been and likely will continue to be a general movement toward semiautonomy. What is less clear is if there is any inevitable movement toward fully autonomous drones designed to carry out lethal operations.

Nonetheless, much of the critical debate has focused on lethal fully autonomous drones. So do autonomous drones, capable of carrying out lethal operations, present special moral problems? Several commentators have argued that they do, and have advanced specific moral objections to the possible future introduction of autonomous drones. Sharkey, for example, has argued forcefully that weapons are not moral agents and that persons have a right not to be attacked by nonmoral agents.[199] Sparrow argues along parallel lines that the use of autonomous drones would not always allow someone to be held accountable for actions taken, including attacks, and it is wrong to cause a person to be attacked when no one can be held accountable.[200]

Both of these moral objections to autonomous drones have, however, drawn criticism. In a recent chapter arguing that "Autonomous Weapons Pose No Moral Problems" that are not also characteristic of nonautonomous weapons, Stephen Kershnar responds to the first objection (i.e., that persons have a right not to be attacked by nonmoral agents) as follows: "If this were true, then unjust attackers would have a right not to be disabled or killed by land mines, heat-seeking missiles, and smart-bombs."[201] This seems absurd, and the reason for its absurdity, Kershnar suggests, is that while people have rights to things like life and liberty (and hence not to be killed arbitrarily), those rights relate to the circumstances in which they can or cannot be harmed, not to the means employed.

In regard to the second objection to autonomous drones (Sparrow's claim that they violate potential victims' rights that someone be accountable for any harm done to them), Kershnar responds as follows:

> Having someone to hold accountable does not affect the permissibility of defensive violence. To see this, consider the following case. A person who is about to die from cancer may still use lethal force to defend his family or friends from

attack even though his imminent death prevents those whom he attacks from being able to hold someone accountable.[202]

Here Kershnar's point is that the right of self-defense is not limited as to means except that they be proportionate to the threat—that is, one is not limited to accountable means in the necessary defense of oneself, family, or friends. On the other hand, Kershnar argues that the right of self-defense is forfeited when one is attempting to unjustly kill someone else, so that in such cases it cannot be the basis of any claim of rights violation that a murder can only be resisted with accountable weapons. The implication for present purposes is that if the targets of drone strikes are really terrorists involved in attempting to kill others, they can have no rights claim based on self-defense concerning the weapons that are used to frustrate their murderous intent.

Overall, Kershnar's argument is that autonomous weapons systems do not necessarily violate any rights that nonautonomous weapons do not, and therefore that they pose "no moral special problem."[203] In other words, they are liable to be used justly or unjustly as with any other weapon. The core of his view is that "people's rights are justified by autonomy and people's autonomy is not affected by whether the (lethal) attacking object is a moral agent or accountable (that is, can be punished or provide compensation)."[204] This claim is obviously based on a particular account of rights (as grounded in autonomy), but Kershnar thinks that other accounts of rights produce a similar result. However, it's not entirely clear that this is, or must be, the case with absolutely any account of rights (for example, a constructivist account where rights are established by human agreement), or indeed with any form of consequentialist or virtue ethics. A virtue ethicist might ask whether we wish to be the kind of people who would delegate questions of life and death to a machine. Would we see this as admirable behavior? Concluding no, the virtue ethicist might advocate for the establishment of a rule akin to Asimov's first law of robotics—"A robot may not injure a human being or, through inaction, allow a human being to come to harm"[205]—and a corresponding right of human beings against being killed by the decision of autonomous artificial intelligence. Moreover, regardless of whether individual rights would be violated by the possible future use of autonomous drones, they may nonetheless present particular moral difficulties if they are used—for example, as Sharkey points out, they might leave us with nobody we could hold accountable in the instance that they were involved in a war crime.

So even if Kershnar's argument that there is no necessary rights violation is accepted, there may still be moral reasons for resisting possible future reliance on autonomous drones. This could also, in turn, provide a basis to be leery of contemporary drones on the grounds that their current use might produce a slippery slope toward fully autonomous drones. Here it may be useful to refer back to Strawser's response in section I (above), which was that there was nothing inevitable about a shift from remotely piloted to fully autonomous drones, and in fact that there were many reasonable stopping places along the way. Moreover, Lucas has argued that even if drones with fully autonomous capacities were developed, they need not be used for targeting. Current plans, he points out, draw exactly this distinction:

> Policy guidance on future unmanned systems, recently released by the Office of the US Secretary of Defense, now distinguishes carefully between "fully autonomous" unmanned systems and systems that exhibit various degrees of "semiautonomy." DoD policy will likely specify that lethal kinetic force may be integrated only, at most, with semiautonomous platforms, involving set mission scripts with ongoing executive oversight by human operators. Fully autonomous systems, by contrast, will be armed at most with non-lethal weapons and more likely will employ evasive action as their principal form of protection. Fully autonomous systems will not be designed or approved to undertake independent target identification and mission execution.[206]

A possible use of autonomous drones under these guidelines might be the removal of naval mines (where there is little danger of civilian harm). Of course, it should be stressed that here Lucas only establishes contemporary guidance on the development of autonomous systems, and this guidance could change, particularly under the pressure of future combat.

Lucas also raises a second point that provides some assurance regarding the capabilities that autonomous drones would have to achieve before being deployed, but also lends some credence to concerns about future changes in guidelines on their use:

> We would certainly define the engineering design specifications as requiring that our autonomous machines perform as well or better than human combat[ant]s under similar circumstances in complying with the constraints of the law of armed conflict and applicable rules of engagement for a given conflict. If they can, and if they do achieve this benchmark engineering specification, then their use is morally justifiable. If they can't, or if our designers and manufacturers have not taken due care to ensure that they can, then we have no business building or deploying them. It is really just as simple as that.[207]

Here Lucas is reassuring in insisting that "due care" would be demonstrated before any introduction of fully autonomous drones even in limited capacities, such as those discussed above. But at the same time the assurance that drones would be required to demonstrate compliance with LOAC and rules of engagement (ROE) equal to or better than manned counterparts also points to the likely temptation that commanders will experience to deploy them more broadly, possibly including lethal missions. A moral argument like Kershnar's might well represent a complementary influence, encouraging commanders to consider lethal missions for wholly autonomous robots on the grounds that there is no moral prohibition on such missions because they involve no clear rights violation. Still, even in a possible future scenario where (1) there are fully autonomous drones that can meet Lucas's engineering standards of superior LOAC and ROE compliance, and (2) where it is determined that there is no necessary rights violations associated with such missions, and (3) where there is pressure to adopt these measures either on the basis of the need for better results in the field or from competitive pressure from rivals, the ultimate question will remain whether this comes to be viewed as an acceptable way to conduct war, one about which the nation at war can feel, if not proud, at least sanguine. At the moment, neither current patterns in public opinion nor in public discourse seem to portend such a view.

For the moment, then, such future developments remain in the domain of the speculative imagination. What is arguably the most immediate ethical concern is what is actually being done with drones today, especially outside of conventional armed conflict. Yet how can the current use of armed drones, and its compliance with any of the ethical standards discussed above, be ascertained in the absence of clear oversight and accountability in regard to current operations? A frequent complaint of critics is that there has been neither. The case study of this chapter examines a particular debate around these two critical issues.

Case Study: Oversight and Accountability

Two widespread criticisms of the U.S. drone campaigns outside of conventional battlefields are that they fail to meet legally required standards of oversight and accountability. Former UN Special Rapporteur for Extrajudicial, Summary or Arbitrary Executions Philip Alston argues, for example, that "assertions by Obama administration officials, as well as by many scholars, that these operations [i.e., unconventional drone strikes] comply with international standards are undermined by the total absence of any forms of credible transparency or verifiable accountability."[208] In particular, Alston identifies four criteria that he contends are (and should be) legally required even in a state of armed conflict. Specifically, states are required:

- [1] To ensure that forces and agents have access to reliable information to support the targeting decision, including an appropriate command and control structure, as well as safeguards against faulty or unverifiable evidence.
- [2] To ensure adequate intelligence on the "effects of the weapons that are to be used . . . the number of civilians that are likely to be present in the target area at the particular time; and whether they have any possibility to take cover before the attack takes place."
- [3] To assess the proportionality of an attack in relation to each individual strike.
- [4] To ensure that when an error is apparent, those conducting a targeted killing are able to abort or suspend the attack.[209]

While Alston's discussion encompasses all of the unconventional U.S. drone strikes, he focuses in particular on those carried out under the authority of the CIA. Alston's assessment of the CIA program is that while some mechanisms of potential oversight exist, "none of the many existing oversight mechanisms have been even minimally effective in relation to targeted killings, and that the resulting legal 'grey hole' cannot be justified on national security grounds."[210] In particular, in his estimate,

> The CIA's internal control mechanisms, including its Inspector General, have had no discernible impact; executive control mechanisms have either not been activated at all or have ignored the issue; congressional oversight has given a "free pass" to the CIA in this area; judicial review has been effectively precluded; and external oversight has been reduced to media coverage that is all too often dependent on information leaked by the CIA itself. As a result, there is no meaningful domestic accountability for a burgeoning program of international killing. This in turn means that the United States cannot possibly satisfy its obligations under international law to ensure accountability for its use of lethal force, either under IHRL or IHL. The result is the steady undermining of the international rule of law and the setting of legal precedents which will inevitably come back to haunt the United States before long when invoked by other states with highly problematic agendas.[211]

He concludes that in practice, "the CIA's approach is characterized by neither transparency nor accountability[.]"[212]

Alston's conclusions are not, however, without critics, among them Pepperdine University associate professor of law Greg McNeal. In a lengthy 2014 article on "Targeted Killing and Accountability," McNeal claims to "provide the first qualitative empirical accounting of the targeted killing process, beginning with the creation of kill lists and extending through the execution of targeted strikes."[213] After applying "a robust analytical framework for assessing the accountability mechanisms" to the "targeting killing process," he comes to the following conclusion:

> There are multiple overlapping mechanisms of accountability operating to constrain the individuals within the targeted killing process. No single mechanism is effective on its own; however, when taken together, the myriad mechanisms at work create a complex scheme of accountable governance that exerts influence before, during, and after targeting decisions. . . . each complements the others, making for a potentially robust scheme of control.[214]
>
> Critics contend that these bureaucrats and their political superiors are unaccountable. I argue that these critiques are misplaced because they fail to credit the extensive forms of bureaucratic, legal, political, and professional accountability that exist within the targeted killing process.[215]

The problem, according to McNeal, is that scholars have lacked a sufficient understanding of the U.S. government's targeted killing practices.[216] Drawing on diverse quantitative and qualitative data and two years of fieldwork, McNeal attempts to correct the deficiency by reconstructing and evaluating the accountability mechanisms surrounding targeting practices. His findings can in part be presented as answers to Alston's four minimum accountability requirements, showing in each case how they are being met.

Command, Control, and Kill Lists

Alston's first requirement is for "command and control structure, as well as safeguards against faulty or unverifiable evidence." McNeal argues that this requirement is addressed, at least for personality strikes, in the process by which individuals are nominated to the "kill lists." McNeal details each of the steps toward nomination to a "kill list" and offers the following summary, which goes some distance toward establishing the existence of an articulated command-and-control structure, including safeguards against faulty evidence:

> Based on this information, we can sketch a general picture of the kill-list approval process. First, military and intelligence officials from various agencies compile data and make recommendations based on internal vetting and validation standards. Second, those recommendations go through the NCTC [National Counterterrorism Center], which further vets and validates rosters of names and other variables that are further tailored to meet White House standards for lethal targeting. Third, the President's designee (currently the counterterrorism adviser) convenes an NSC [National Security Council] deputies meeting to get input from senior officials, including top lawyers from the appropriate agencies and departments, such as the CIA, FBI, DOD, State Department, and NCTC. . . . In practice, an objection from one of these key

attorneys almost certainly causes the President's designee in the NSC process to hesitate before seeking final approval from the President. Finally, if the NSC gives approval, the President's counterterrorism advisor shapes the product of the NSC's deliberations and seeks final approval from the President. At this stage, targets are evaluated again to ensure that target information is complete and accurate, targets relate to objectives, the selection rationale is clear and detailed, and collateral damage concerns are highlighted.[217]

The final decisions are then left to the president.

As McNeal notes, the government has repeatedly emphasized that its planned target lists are frequently updated and vetted against the most up-to-date intelligence to ensure that the person being targeted remains a member of an organized armed group.[218] He emphasizes that both the military and the CIA follow this process in planning drone strikes.[219]

When it comes to actually executing an operation against a person on the kill list, McNeal reports that a further set of safeguards and checks is triggered. The first and most important step is to positively identify the person being targeted with "reasonable certainty" and to confirm that he or she is a legitimate military target on the kill list.[220] According to McNeal, multiple sources of intelligence will be used to corroborate information about a potential target who will then be subject to finding, fixing, and tracking, including "pattern of life analysis," in order to assure identity before action is taken.[221] He stresses in particular that "a potential target is presumed to be a civilian until proven otherwise—hence the requirement of positive identification in U.S. operations."[222]

Once positive of the target's identity, the process moves to the approval stage. Before an operation can be initiated, military personnel must inform a strike approval authority (often a commanding officer) of any assumptions or uncertainties associated with information informing the operation.[223] McNeal appears to find these procedures for target identification adequate as he does not make recommendations in this area.

Estimating Collateral Effects

Alston's second threshold requirement for targeting operations is to ensure adequate intelligence on the "effects of the weapons that are to be used . . . the number of civilians that are likely to be present in the target area at the particular time; and whether they have any possibility to take cover before the attack takes place." McNeal argues that U.S. procedures for assessing potential harm to civilians and for mitigating this danger are robust, and involve not just strict legal compliance, but policies aimed at keeping danger levels well below legal requirements.[224] In particular, he explains that the military is required, as per the order of the chairman of the Joint Chiefs of Staff, to employ a multistep process known as "Collateral Damage Methodology" (CDM) to evaluate potential unintended strike effects. He reports that the intelligence community follows a similar preexecution procedure, although it involves fewer levels of decision making and a different approval authority. Also, the requirement for higher-level review kicks in at a different threshold of potential harm to civilians.[225]

The CDM process employs scientific evidence derived from research, experiments, history, and battlefield intelligence, and is designed to respond quickly to developing circumstances at the location of attack. CDM data are based on field tests, computerized models, and a history of documented direct combat observations.[226] The "munitions technical data," including the effects radius of weapons, are updated at least every six months based on new tests and battlefield reports, and allow analysts to identify a "collateral hazard area" (CHA).[227] The CDM uses worst-case-scenario variables for the determination of CHA—a larger margin of error than what would normally be used in combat.[228]

Once the CHA is established, the CDM examines whether any possible noncombatants are within it. In addition to direct and detailed observations permitted by drone surveillance, the CDM analysis also draws on regularly updated population density tables, which take account of factors like time of day, regular religious and social events, holidays, and more.[229]

If it is determined that there are any possible noncombatants potentially within the CHA, then the CDM moves to examining the possibilities for mitigation of the danger to these noncombatants, a step that U.S. policy refers to as collateral damage minimization (of CDM).[230] One element is to examine whether it is possible to reduce the danger of collateral harm by using different weapons. Commanders may have a range of weapons systems at their disposal, such as different sized bombs or laser-guided missiles. The weapon they select will determine the effects radius, and the estimate of likely collateral damage.[231] A further level of mitigation involves a process called "weaponeering"—that is, deciding how weapons will be used. This involves, for example, selecting fusing combinations that can diminish the danger to civilians while still killing the target.[232] Other possibilities include changing the direction from which missiles or bombs will be launched (to shift the effects radius away from civilians), warhead burial, proximity fuses, and aim-point offset.[233] At this point, if CDM has not sufficiently reduced the danger to noncombatants, then the operation cannot proceed without a proportionality assessment and decision to approve from a predetermined approval authority.[234] The CDM procedure then moves to a proportionality analysis (Alston's third accountability threshold).

Proportionality Analysis

Alston's third minimal requirement was to "assess the proportionality of an attack in relation to each individual strike." McNeal reports that, when CDM (detailed above) has been exhausted and a high risk of collateral damage remains, a "proportionality assessment" by a predetermined approval authority is required.[235] The relevant authority, and the criteria determining who it is in any given case, will be determined by the agency conducting the operation and the theater of operations. McNeal offers an example based on U.S. military operations in Afghanistan. In this context, if the unavoidable collateral damage is low, proportionality assessment and decision-making authority is assigned to generals. If, however, the expected collateral damage is high, proportionality assessment must be performed and authorization given by the president or the secretary of defense.[236] The threshold for what counts as a high or low count of expected noncombatant casualties is determined by a "Non-Combatant Casualty Cut-Off Value" (NCV): This defines the number of expected civilian deaths that is considered "high" and therefore triggers a process known as Sensitive Target Approval and Review (STAR), which typically requires approval by the president or secretary of defense.[237] For example, the NCV in Afghanistan as of 2009 for preplanned operations was one civilian casualty, so that any operation in which there was a likelihood of one or more persons being killed would require proportionality assessment and approval by the president or secretary of defense regardless of how important the military target. McNeal notes that the CIA and JSOC use similar review processes, though both have their own chains of command and approval authority criteria.[238]

Aborting Operations

The final criterion invoked by Alston is that states are required "to ensure that when an error is apparent, those conducting a targeted killing are able to abort or suspend the attack."[239] According to McNeal, government officials claim that they have in fact diverted missiles off target *after* launching missiles from drones but *before* impact in order to prevent harm to noncombatants.[240] U.S. officials also suggest that they would abort a preplanned mission if a target they were pursuing took affirmative action to change his combat status. For example, if Anwar al-Awlaki had renounced his membership in al-Qaeda before the drone strike that killed him, they suggest that the United States would have discontinued operations targeting him.[241]

The foregoing points support a case that U.S. procedures meet Alston's threshold criteria of accountability. The main thrust of McNeal's analysis, however, is to suggest that the U.S. targeting bureaucracy includes multiple levels of internal and external accountability that go well beyond meeting minimum threshold requirements of accountability. He focuses in particular on four general mechanisms of accountability: (1) legal; (2) bureaucratic; (3) professional; and (4) political. He argues that "taken together, these mechanisms of accountability amount to 'law-like' institutional procedures that can discipline the discretion of bureaucrats involved in the targeted killing process."[242]

Mechanisms of Accountability

In terms of the first category of "legal accountability," McNeal allows that on its own it represents a relatively weak check on targeting decisions. In the United States, he notes, such accountability is assessed in terms of criminal or civil penalties, or injunctive relief. In the case of the military, this accountability is ensured through the court-martial process (with service persons possessing the right to appeal their case to an Article III court).[243] In the case of the CIA, the parallel mechanism of accountability is an inspector general (IG) referral to the Department of Justice for prosecution.[244]

Alston is unimpressed with the legal accountability mechanism of the CIA. Following a review of the IG since the creation of the office in 1952, for example, Alston concludes,

> This brief overview of the role of the CIA Inspector-General reveals an office vested with extensive powers and important protections for its independence, but also one which, as far as can be publicly ascertained, has not succeeded in bringing about significant changes in CIA policy or practice, even in cases that seem to disclose major breaches of the applicable law.[245]

McNeal acknowledges that to date the IG has not sought to prosecute any CIA officer in connection with drone strikes.[246] Nonetheless, he argues that the threat of criminal prosecution through an IG referral to the Department of Justice (or potentially through the criminal courts of other states) helps to promote accountability.[247] Other commentators, such as Murphy and Radsan, have suggested that the role of the IG could be strengthened by "a categorical requirement that all CIA targeted killings be subject to IG review."[248]

A more important source of accountability, according to McNeal, may be bureaucratic oversight: "Bureaucratic accountability exercises a high degree of control over bureaucratic action. It has the potential to seriously constrain how individuals in the targeted killing process behave."[249] In essence, because compliance with rules, norms, and expectations are regularly monitored and evaluated in hierarchies like the CIA or the armed forces, and are central to individuals' prospects for advancement, these internal procedures provide an effective and important framework of accountability. This is especially true where the president is the final authority.[250] Unfortunately, as McNeal notes, the fact that these accountability mechanisms are exercised internally and are therefore opaque to the outside observer encourages ongoing questions about their effectiveness.[251] Alston does not examine bureaucratic oversight.

The third source of accountability cited by McNeal is "professional." His focus here seems to be the individual's professional reputation. The main consideration he mentions is "deference to expertise," and the means of control are "informal reprimands, poor evaluations, shunning," presumably by professional colleagues.[252] He presents these mechanisms as imposing "low levels of control."[253] Professional accountability standards may be established, for example, through training or codes of ethics. As McNeal notes, "Ethical lapses, lapses in judgment, or more serious breaches that do not rise to the level of criminal matters may nevertheless hinder one's career."[254] In essence, his argument appears to be that lapses in ethics and judgments in regard to organizational values can damage an individual's career prospects. In this way, CIA officers and service persons are held to account for failures to adhere both to explicit guidelines and their spirit. Of course, this form of accountability will not only often be opaque to outsiders but is often elusive to many within the organization (who are not aware of the individual's reputation). Again, Alston does not examine this type of accountability.

The fourth and final source of accountability cited by McNeal is "political." In his definition, "Political accountability mechanisms exist where the 'system promotes responsiveness to constituents.' "[255] This produces control that is "external and limited."[256] McNeal considers three sources: congressional oversight, domestic public opinion, and international political constraints.

Congressional Oversight

In regard to congressional oversight, McNeal acknowledges that the degree of oversight may not be readily apparent (as much occurs behind closed doors), but recent evidence has come to light that it is fairly extensive in regard to drone strikes outside of conventional battlefields. The following statement, for example, appears in a February 13, 2013, press release from Senator Dianne Feinstein, the chair of the U.S. Senate Select Committee on Intelligence (SSCI):

> The committee has devoted significant time and attention to targeted killings by drones. The committee receives notifications with key details of each strike

shortly after it occurs, and the committee holds regular briefings and hearings on these operations—reviewing the strikes, examining their effectiveness as a counterterrorism tool, verifying the care taken to avoid deaths to non-combatants and understanding the intelligence collection and analysis that underpins these operations. In addition, the committee staff has held 35 monthly, in-depth oversight meetings with government officials to review strike records (including video footage) and questions every aspect of the program.[257]

This frequency of review does suggest fairly robust oversight, but McNeal himself raises some concerns about the SSCI's ability to effectively oversee drone strikes. In particular, he points to "an expertise problem."[258] In essence, the members of the committee simply know far less about running covert lethal operations than the CIA, and due to the secrecy of operations, the SSCI members cannot access help as easily as members of other committees.[259] He also voices concern that because no major domestic constituency is directly affected by drone strikes, members of the oversight committees may not be strongly motivated to tackle the issue.[260]

Alston is far more critical of congressional oversight of drone strikes and the CIA in general. He remarks, "In general, it is widely acknowledged that the oversight system has suffered from extensive shortcomings and the relationship between the CIA and Congress has been poor for many years."[261] He points in particular to the extensive reforms recommended by the 9/11 Commission that have not been enacted.[262] One particular concern on which Alston focuses is what he calls (borrowing a term from Peter W. Singer) "double-hatting around the law," meaning "morphing the roles of warrior, spy and civilian actors."[263] In essence, when the CIA and the military collaborate on covert military operations, both the rules of engagement and accountability obligations become blurred. CIA covert operations require a presidential finding, carry strict reporting obligations to the Congressional Intelligence Committees in the Senate (SSCI) and House (HPSCI), and are regulated under Title 50 of the United States Code. Military operations do not require presidential findings and do not entail specific reporting requirements (the military reports more flexibly to the Armed Services Committees in Congress under Title 10 of the U.S. Code), but service persons are generally subject to the Uniform Code of Military Justice (UCMJ), which CIA operatives generally are not. Alston argues that double-hatting permits strategic exploitation of these differences to avoid accountability to Congress.[264]

Accountability and Public Opinion

The second aspect of political accountability McNeal considers is popular opinion at home. He argues that there is ample evidence suggesting that presidents care very much about how their actions may be viewed by the public, and given the president's prominent role in approving targets and strikes, this is a program with which the president is closely associated.[265] While targeting abroad is not most voters' highest priority issue, they are sensitive to the matter of civilian casualties, for example. This dynamic effectively renders presidents accountable via public opinion for the incidence of civilian casualties. McNeal adds that when the president nominates officials to positions involved with targeting, the approval process also provides a high-profile mechanism of political accountability, inviting a public discussion of the effectiveness of the president's policy (as with John Brennan's appointment as CIA director).[266]

The last source of political accountability that McNeal emphasizes is "international political constraints." These are of two basic types. The first concerns foreign governments and the "political costs" that they can impose on Washington when U.S. actions provoke their domestic constituencies. He offers as an example a strike that angers domestic public opinion in Pakistan.[267] Pakistan could then reduce cooperation in various ways, or bring complaints about the strikes to various international bodies, all of which would create difficulties for the United States. McNeal also points to states like the United Kingdom, which provide "support to targeting" but could modulate their help if confronted with domestic political pressure. By consequence, strikes likely to affect them "will receive greater scrutiny from more politically accountable actors such as the President."[268] So the sensitivities of other states (and the domestic opposition they face) promote areas of increased accountability.

The second type of international political constraint involves global political opinion, and the need to avoid the isolation and the discrediting of U.S. policy. As McNeal observes, the U.S. government itself has stressed "the importance of international public opinion."[269] For this reason it is sensitive to condemnation in international forums like the UN and to high-profile, widely circulated criticism by NGOs. As this criticism often focuses on civilian casualties, for example, it provides the United States with a powerful reason to minimize such casualties, effectively imposing a form of political accountability.

In discussing external sources of accountability, Alston does not address public opinion and its influence on the political leadership directly, but focuses rather on organizations that help to influence and shape public opinion. His premise is perhaps that to the degree that public opinion is molded by the influence of government and other important stakeholders, it is that much less effective as a check on that power. In particular, he considers civil society organizations and the media, both domestic and international. In both cases he emphasizes the limitations in their abilities to impose effective accountability on the CIA program. In the former case, he acknowledges the importance of the Freedom of Information Act (FOIA), which has been used to force the publication of a range of key government documents connected with the drone campaigns. He cautions, however, that "while the mere fact that FOIA requests can be filed in an effort to obtain information about the CIA's targeted killings policies and programs is impressive, the reality is much less so."[270] He points out that the CIA has been successful in protecting most of its documents from public disclosure.

Alston also acknowledges that "the role of the media in relation to targeted killings has been of major importance," both in terms of exposing the campaigns and mobilizing opposition.[271] However, he points out that the media also often cooperate with the government, even to suppress important information—he gives as an example the *New York Times* declining to publish information on NSA warrantless wiretapping for almost a year. He also points out that by using leaks strategically supplied by the CIA and other government officials, "the media have also played a powerful role in legitimizing the targeted killings program."[272] In essence then, the media are best viewed as a two-edged sword that can be used both to reveal the truth and to shape the narrative in a way that protects government agencies from criticism, confrontation, and exposure.

This case study provides only a very basic overview of some of Alston and McNeal's arguments, and there is much room for debate over each point, but based at least on what has been summarized here it might well be thought that McNeal's case is particularly strong at the level of meeting the basic thresholds of accountability. Alston's critique, by contrast, is especially forceful in both insisting that a lethal program of this scope ought to be held to elevated standards of oversight and accountability and in challenging whether it is. It may be worth pointing out, however, that McNeal and Alston converge in at least some of their recommendations. To begin with, they both argue that the Obama administration needs to do more to explain to the public its targeting criteria (at least in general terms), its overall targeting process, its assessment of the results (in the aggregate), and as McNeal puts it, generally "defend the process."[273] McNeal argues that it is in the administration's interest to do so while Alston argues that it is obliged to do so.[274] Finally, both suggest additional oversight: McNeal recommends the creation of an internal review board within the executive, whereas Alston wants the United States to show greater willingness to subject itself to review by UN agencies and personnel.[275] Here the agreement is on the need for some body separate from the president and his cabinet to act as a check on the targeting process, although their suggestions for the form this body should take are quite different.

Notes

1. Avery Plaw, *Targeting Terrorists: A License to Kill?* (Burlington: Ashgate, 2008).

2. Plaw, *Targeting Terrorists*, 58–59.

3. There is a long-standing debate over the meanings and relationship of "morality" and "ethics." For the purposes of this chapter, we take morality to be concerned with duties or obligations to oneself and/or to others, and ethics as concerned with how to live well within a community or sometimes with performing functions or vocations well.

4. Mary Ellen O'Connell, "Lawful Use of Combat Drones," Testimony to House Subcommittee on National Security and Foreign Affairs, April 28, 2010, 1–2, accessed June 18, 2015, https://fas.org/irp/congress/2010_hr/042810oconnell.pdf.

5. Although, as noted in chapter 3, there is some gray area around the threshold of armed conflict.

6. Bradley J. Strawser, "Moral Predators: The Duty to Employ Uninhabited Aerial Vehicles," *Journal of Military Ethics* 10, no. 16 (2011): 343.

7. Strawser, "Moral Predators," 343.

8. Strawser, "Moral Predators," 344.

9. Uwe Steinhoff, "Killing Them Safely: Extreme Asymmetry and Its Discontents," in *Killing by Remote Control: The Ethics of an Unmanned Military*, edited by Bradley Strawser (Oxford: Oxford University Press, 2013), 199.

10. Strawser, "Moral Predators," 363, note 6.

11. Strawser, "Moral Predators," 346.

12. Medea Benjamin, *Drone Warfare: Killing by Remote Control* (New York: Verso, 2013), 162.

13. Benjamin, *Drone Warfare*, 163.

14. Strawser, "Moral Predators," 350.

15. Strawser, "Moral Predators," 350.

16. Daniel Brunstetter and Megan Braun, "The Implications of Drones on the Just War Tradition," *Ethics and International Affairs* 25, no. 3 (2011): 339–40.

17. Human Rights Clinic and Center for Civilians in Conflict, *The Civilian Impact of Drones: Unexamined Costs, Unanswered Questions* (New York and Washington, DC: Columbia Law School and Center for Civilians in Conflict, 2012), 37.

18. Strawser, "Moral Predators," 351–52.

19. Peter W. Singer quoted in "Interview with Defense Expert P. W. Singer: 'The Soldiers Call It War Porn,'" in *Spiegel Online International*, March 12, 2010, accessed August 5, 2014, http://www.spiegel.de/international/world/interview-with-defense -expert-p-w-singer-the-soldiers-call-it-war-porn-a-682852.html.

20. Philip Alston, "Report of the Special Rapporteur on Extrajudicial, Summary or Arbitrary Executions, Philip Alston, Addendum, Study on Targeted Killings,"

A/HRC/14/24/Add.6, May 28, 2010, para. 84, accessed May 12, 2015, http://www 2.ohchr.org/english/bodies/hrcouncil/docs/14session/A.HRC.14.24.Add6.pdf.

21. Jeremy Waldron, "Justifying Targeted Killing with a Neutral Principle," in *Targeted Killing: Law and Morality in an Asymmetrical World,* edited by Claire Finkelstein, Jens David Ohlin, and Andrew Altman (New York: Oxford University Press, 2012), 125.

22. Waldron, "Justifying Targeted Killing with a Neutral Principle," 124.

23. Azhmat Khan, "As Drone Use Surges, Pilots Report High Stress Levels," PBS *Frontline,* December 19, 2011, accessed August 5, 2014, http://www.pbs.org/wgbh/ pages/frontline/afghanistan-pakistan/kill-capture/as-drone-use-surges-pilots-report -high-stress-levels/.

24. See Matthew Fricker and Avery Plaw, "Tracking the Predators: Evaluating the US Drone Campaign in Pakistan," *International Studies Perspectives* 13, no. 4 (2012). For data suggestive of reduced civilian casualties see the case studies in chapters 1 and 2.

25. Strawser, "Moral Predators," 353, 355.

26. Strawser, "Moral Predators," 353–54.

27. Strawser, "Moral Predators," 354.

28. Jeremy Waldron quoted in "Jeremy Waldron Successfully Argues Against Drone Warfare in Oxford Union Debate," *NYU Law School,* accessed August 6, 2014, http://www.law.nyu.edu/news/Jeremy-Waldron-Oxford-Union-debate.

29. Strawser, "Moral Predators," 354.

30. Chris Woods, "CIA's Pakistan Drone Strikes Carried Out by Regular US Air Force Personnel," *The Guardian,* April 14, 2014, accessed May 23, 2015, http://www.- theguardian.com/world/2014/apr/14/cia-drones-pakistan-us-air-force-docu mentary.

31. Strawser, "Moral Predators," 355.

32. Strawser, "Moral Predators," 335–56.

33. Paul W. Kahn, "The Paradox of Riskless War," *Philosophy and Public Policy Quarterly* 22, no. 3 (2002): 2.

34. Kahn, "The Paradox of Riskless War," 3.

35. Suzy Killmister, "Remote Weaponry: The Ethical Implications," *Journal of Applied Philosophy* 25, no. 2 (2008): 122.

36. Strawser, "Moral Predators," 356.

37. Jai Galliott, "Uninhabited Aerial Vehicles and the Asymmetry Objection: A Response to Strawser," *Journal of Military Ethics* 11, no. 1 (2012): 63.

38. Galliott, "Uninhabited Aerial Vehicles and the Asymmetry Objection," 63.

39. Galliott, "Uninhabited Aerial Vehicles and the Asymmetry Objection," 63.

40. "Nigeria Accused of Ignoring Sect Warnings Before Wave of Killings," *The Guardian,* August 2, 2009, accessed July 29, 2015, http://www.theguardian.com/ world/2009/aug/02/nigeria-boko-haram-islamist-sect; "Beslan School Siege Fast Facts," *CNN News,* August 21, 2014, accessed July 29, 2015, http://www.cnn.com/ 2013/09/09/world/europe/beslan-school-siege-fast-facts/.

41. "President Obama Hangs Out with America," *The White House Blog,* January 30, 2012, accessed March 15, 2015, http://www.whitehouse.gov/blog/2012/01/30/ president-obama-hangs-out-america.

42. Strawser, "Moral Predators," 358.

43. Benjamin, *Drone Warfare*, 150.

44. Mary Dudziak, "To Whom Is a Drone Loyal?," *Balkinization Blog*, September 27, 2009, accessed August 5, 2014, http://balkin.blogspot.com/2009/09/to-whom-is-drone-loyal.html.

45. Peter Singer, "Do Drones Undermine Democracy?," *New York Times*, January 21, 2012, accessed August 6, 2014, http://www.nytimes.com/2012/01/22/opinion/sunday/do-drones-undermine-democracy.html?pagewanted = all&_r = 0.

46. Peter Singer, "Wired for War," *Wilson Quarterly* (2009), quoted in Benjamin, *Drone Warfare*, 152.

47. Steven Levine, "Drones Threaten Democratic Accountability," *Three Quarks Daily*; John Kaag and Sarah Kreps, *Drone Warfare* (Cambridge: Polity Press, 2014), 130–33.

48. Strawser, "Moral Predators," 359.

49. Bradley Strawser, "The Morality of Drone Warfare Revisited," *The Guardian*, August 6, 2012, accessed July 8, 2015, http://www.theguardian.com/commentisfree/2012/aug/06/morality-drone-warfare-revisited.

50. Strawser, "Moral Predators," 344—italics added.

51. Steinhoff, "Killing Them Safely," 198.

52. Strawser, "Moral Predators," 348.

53. Strawser, "Moral Predators," 362.

54. Michael Walzer, *Just and Unjust Wars*, 4th ed. (New York: Basic Books, 2006).

55. Alex Bellamy, *Just War: From Cicero to Iraq* (Cambridge: Polity Press, 2006), 2.

56. Bellamy, *Just War*, 117–21, 127.

57. Brian Orend, *The Morality of War*, 2nd ed. (Peterborough: Broadview Press, 2013), 34–64; Bellamy, *Just War*, 127.

58. Barack Obama, "Remarks by the President at the National Defense University," speech, National Defense University, Fort McNair, Washington, DC, May 23, 2013.

59. Obama, "Remarks by the President at the National Defense University."

60. Alex Bellamy, "Is the War on Terror Just?" *International Relations* 19 (2005): 287, 292.

61. For example, Bronwyn Bruton, "Al-Shabab Mainly a Local Problem in Somalia," *New York Times*, October 1, 2013, accessed Match 15, 2015, http://www.nytimes.com/roomfordebate/2013/09/30/does-al-shabab-pose-a-threat-on-american-soil/al-shabab-mainly-a-local-problem-in-somalia.

62. James DeShaw Rae, *Analyzing the Drone Debates* (New York: Palgrave Macmillan, 2014), 81.

63. Brunstetter and Braun, "The Implications of Drones," 354.

64. Orend, *The Morality of War*, 52—italics added.

65. Bellamy, *Just War*, 124.

66. Kenneth Roth, "The War against al-Qaeda Is Over," *Washington Post*, August 2, 2013, accessed July 13, 2015, http://www.washingtonpost.com/opinions/the-war-against-al-qaeda-is-over/2013/08/02/3887af74-f975-11e2-b018-5b8251f0c56e_story.html.

67. Roth, "The War against al-Qaeda Is Over."

68. Obama, "Remarks by the President at the National Defense University."

69. Bellamy, *Just War*, 122.

70. Brian Orend, *Michael Walzer on War and Justice* (Montreal: McGill-Queens University Press, 2000), 87.

71. Avery Plaw and Matt Fricker, "Tracking the Predators: Evaluating the US Drone Campaign in Pakistan," *International Studies Perspectives* 13 (2012): 355–58.

72. Michael J. Boyle, "The Costs and Consequences of Drone Warfare," *International Affairs* 89, no 1 (2013): 12.

73. Micah Zenko, "Reforming US Drone Strike Policies," *Council Special Report* 65 (New York: Council on Foreign Relations, 2013), 10.

74. Audrey Kurth Cronin, "Why Drones Fail: When Tactics Drive Strategy," *Foreign Affairs* (2014): 48.

75. Jeremy Scahill, *Dirty Wars* (New York: Nation Books, 2013), 360, 376–81, 398–402, 498–506.

76. Walzer, *Just and Unjust Wars*, 85; Orend, *The Morality of War*, 60.

77. Walzer, *Just and Unjust Wars*, 213.

78. "Director's Remarks at the Pacific Council on Foreign Policy," May 18, 2009, *News & Information*, accessed February 15, 2015, https://www.cia.gov/news-information/speeches-testimony/directors-remarks-at-pacific-council.html.

79. Obama, "Remarks of the President at the National Defense University."

80. Zenko, "Reforming US Drone Strike Policies," 10; see also Cronin, "Why Drones Fail."

81. Gen. John P. Abizaid and Rosa Brooks, *Recommendations and Report of the Task Force on US Drone Policy* (Washington, DC: Stimson Center, 2014), 28–29.

82. Orend, *The Morality of War*, 61.

83. Walzer, *Just and Unjust Wars*, 67–73, Orend, *The Morality of War*, 61.

84. Cronin, "Why Drones Fail," 44; Boyle, "The Costs and Consequences of Drone Warfare," 2–3, 11.

85. John O. Brennan, "The Efficacy and Ethics of U.S. Counterterrorism Strategy," speech, Woodrow Wilson International Center for Scholars, Washington, DC, April 30, 2012; Daniel Byman, "Why Drones Work: The Case for Washington's Weapon of Choice," *Foreign Affairs* (2013): 32–35; Patrick Johnston and Anoop Sarbahi, "The Impact of U.S. Drone Strikes on Terrorism in Pakistan," April 21, 2015, 36–39, accessed July 15, 2015, http://patrickjohnston.info/materials/drones.pdf.

86. Tara McKelvey, "A Former Ambassador to Pakistan Speaks Out," *Daily Beast*, November 20, 2012, accessed May 1, 2015, http://www.thedailybeast.com/articles/2012/11/20/a-former-ambassador-to-pakistan-speaks-out.html.

87. McKelvey, "A Former Ambassador to Pakistan Speaks Out."

88. Boyle, "The Costs and Consequences of Drone Warfare," 3; Gregory Johnsen, "Yemen Scholar Says U.S. Drone Strikes May Have Driven al-Qaeda Membership," PBS Newshour, August 6, 2013, accessed July 22, 2015, http://www.pbs.org/newshour/bb/terrorism-july-dec13-yemen2_08-06/.

89. Cronin, "Why Drones Fail," 45; also see Abizaid and Brooks, *Recommendations and Report of the Task Force on US Drone Policy*, 29.

90. Cronin, "Why Drones Fail," 47.

91. Johnsen, "Yemen Scholar Says U.S. Drone Strikes May Have Driven al-Qaeda Membership."

92. Orend, *The Morality of War*, 62.

93. Walzer, *Just and Unjust Wars*, 129.

94. Bellamy, *Just War*, 118.

95. Brennan, "The Efficacy and Ethics of U.S. Counterterrorism Strategy."

96. Brennan, "The Efficacy and Ethics of U.S. Counterterrorism Strategy."

97. Boyle, "The Costs and Consequences of Drone Warfare," 3.

98. Philip Alston, "The CIA and Targeted Killing Beyond Borders," *Harvard National Security Journal* 2 (2011): 446.

99. Orend, *The Morality of War*, 113.

100. Orend, *The Morality of* War, 113.

101. Amnesty International, *"Will I Be Next?" US Drone Strikes in Pakistan* (Amnesty International Publications, 2013), 18.

102. Amnesty International, *"Will I Be Next?" US Drone Strikes in Pakistan*, 7.

103. Amnesty International, *"Will I Be Next?" US Drone Strikes in Pakistan*, 8.

104. Orend, *The Morality of War*, 113.

105. Amnesty International, *"Will I Be Next?" US Drone Strikes in Pakistan*, 8.

106. Brennan, "The Efficacy and Ethics of U.S. Counterterrorism Strategy."

107. Harold Koh, "The Obama Administration and International Law," speech, American Society for International Law, Washington, DC, March 25, 2010.

108. C. Christine Fair, "Drone Wars," *Foreign Policy*, May 28, 2010, accessed July 14, 2015, http://foreignpolicy.com/2010/05/28/drone-wars-2/.

109. Orend, *The Morality of War*, 125.

110. Obama, "Remarks by the President at the National Defense University."

111. Brennan, "The Efficacy and Ethics of U.S. Counterterrorism Strategy."

112. Plaw and Fricker, "Tracking the Predators."

113. Megan Braun and Daniel Brunstetter, "Rethinking the Criterion of Assessing CIA-Targeted Killings: Drones, Proportionality and *Jus Ad Vim*," *Journal of Military Ethics* 12, no. 4 (2013): 304–10.

114. Braun and Brunstetter, "Rethinking the Criterion," 305.

115. Braun and Brunstetter, "Rethinking the Criterion," 311, 315–16, 305.

116. Braun and Brunstetter, "Rethinking the Criterion," 315.

117. Avery Plaw and Carlos Colon, "Correcting the Record: Civilians, Proportionality and *Jus ad Vim*," in *Legitimacy and Drones: Investigating the Legality, Morality and Efficacy of UCAVs*, edited by Steven J. Barela (Burlington: Ashgate Press, 2015), 173–77.

118. Steve Coll, "The Unblinking Stare: The Drone War in Pakistan," *New Yorker*, November 24, 2014, accessed May 12, 2015, http://www.newyorker.com/magazine/2014/11/24/unblinking-stare.

119. Coll, "The Unblinking Stare."

120. David True, "Disciplining Drone Strikes: Just War in the Context of Counterterrorism," in *Drone Wars: Transforming Conflict, Law, and Policy*, edited by Peter L. Bergen and Daniel Rothenberg (Cambridge: Cambridge University Press, 2015), 295.

121. True, "Disciplining Drone Strikes," 295.

122. True, "Disciplining Drone Strikes," 295.

123. Daniel Statman, "Can Just War Theory Justify Targeted Killing? Three Possible Models," in *Targeted Killings: Law and Morality in an Asymmetrical World*, edited by Claire Finkelstein, Jens Ohlin, and Andrew Altman (New York: Oxford University Press, 2012), 111.

124. Statman, "Can Just War Theory Justify Targeted Killing?," 94–97.

125. Statman, "Can Just War Theory Justify Targeted Killing?," 95.

126. Statman, "Can Just War Theory Justify Targeted Killing?," 95–96.

127. Statman, "Can Just War Theory Justify Targeted Killing?," 96.

128. Statman, "Can Just War Theory Justify Targeted Killing?," 96–97.

129. Statman, "Can Just War Theory Justify Targeted Killing?," 97.

130. Statman, "Can Just War Theory Justify Targeted Killing?," 97.

131. Statman, "Can Just War Theory Justify Targeted Killing?," 100.

132. Statman, "Can Just War Theory Justify Targeted Killing?," 98.

133. Statman, "Can Just War Theory Justify Targeted Killing?," 101.

134. Statman, "Can Just War Theory Justify Targeted Killing?," 103.

135. Statman, "Can Just War Theory Justify Targeted Killing?," 104.

136. Statman, "Can Just War Theory Justify Targeted Killing?," 107.

137. Daniel Brunstetter and Megan Braun, "From *Jus ad Bellum* to *Jus ad Vim*: Recalibrating Our Understanding of the Moral Use of Force," *Ethics & International Affairs* 27, no. 1 (2013): 87.

138. Brunstetter and Braun, "From *Jus ad Bellum* to *Jus ad Vim*," 87.

139. Brunstetter and Braun, "From *Jus ad Bellum* to *Jus ad Vim*," 88.

140. Brunstetter and Braun, "From *Jus ad Bellum* to *Jus ad Vim*," 89–91.

141. Brunstetter and Braun, "From *Jus ad Bellum* to *Jus ad Vim*," 89.

142. Brunstetter and Braun, "From *Jus ad Bellum* to *Jus ad Vim*," 87.

143. Brunstetter and Braun, "From *Jus ad Bellum* to *Jus ad Vim*," 95–96.

144. Brunstetter and Braun, "From *Jus ad Bellum* to *Jus ad Vim*," 97.

145. Brunstetter and Braun, "From *Jus ad Bellum* to *Jus ad Vim*," 98.

146. Brunstetter and Braun, "From *Jus ad Bellum* to *Jus ad Vim*," 98.

147. Brunstetter and Braun, "From *Jus ad Bellum* to *Jus ad Vim*," 100.

148. Brunstetter and Braun, "From *Jus ad Bellum* to *Jus ad Vim*," 98.

149. Braun and Brunstetter, "Rethinking the Criterion," at 318.

150. Braun and Brunstetter, "Rethinking the Criterion," at 317.

151. Braun and Brunstetter, "Rethinking the Criterion," 306, 319; Brunstetter and Braun, "From *Jus ad Bellum* to *Jus ad Vim*," 100–101.

152. Braun and Brunstetter, "Rethinking the Criterion," 318.

153. Braun and Brunstetter, "Rethinking the Criterion," 319.

154. Braun and Brunstetter, "Rethinking the Criterion," 318.

155. Braun and Brunstetter, "Rethinking the Criterion," 319.

156. Braun and Brunstetter, "Rethinking the Criterion," 319.

157. Plaw and Colon, "Correcting the Record," 164–65.

158. Plaw and Colon, "Correcting the Record," 165.

159. See New American Foundation, "Drone Wars: Pakistan: Key Findings," accessed July 31, 2015, http://securitydata.newamerica.net/drones/key-findings.html ?country = Pakistan, italics added.

160. Braun and Brunstetter, "Rethinking the Criterion," 315; Plaw and Colon, "Correcting the Record," 173–77.

161. Kaag and Kreps, *Drone Warfare*, 2.

162. Waldron, "Justifying Targeted Killing with a Neutral Principle," 118.

163. Craig Martin, "Targeted Killing, Self-Defense and the *Jus ad Bellum* Regime," in *Targeted Killings: Law and Morality in an Asymmetrical World*, edited by Claire Finkelstein, Jens Ohlin, and Andrew Altman (Oxford: Oxford University Press, 2012), 242.

164. Zenko, "Reforming U.S. Drone Strike Policy," 24.

165. Kaag and Kreps, *Drone Warfare*, 2, 107–13.

166. Peter W. Singer, "Robots at War: The New Battlefield," *Wilson Quarterly*, Winter 2009, accessed July 14, 2015, http://archive.wilsonquarterly.com/essays/ro bots-war-new-battlefield; Benjamin, *Drone Warfare*, 152.

167. Brunstetter and Braun, "The Implications of Drones," 339.

168. Micah Zenko and Sarah Kreps, "Limiting Armed Drone Proliferation," *Council Special Report* no. 69 (New York: Council on Foreign Relations, 2014), 9–10.

169. Kaag and Kreps, *Drone Warfare*, 2, 107–13.

170. John Kaag and Sarah Kreps, "The Moral Hazard of Drones," *New York Times*, July 22, 2012, accessed July 31, 2015, http://opinionator.blogs.nytimes.com/ 2012/07/22/the-moral-hazard-of-drones/.

171. Zack Beauchamp and Julian Savulescu, "Robot Guardians: Teleoperated Combat Vehicles in Humanitarian Interventions," in *Killing by Remote Control: The Ethics of an Unmanned Military*, edited by Bradley Strawser (Oxford: Oxford University Press, 2013), 106.

172. Beauchamp and Savulescu, "Robot Guardians," 109–10.

173. Beauchamp and Savulescu, "Robot Guardians," 110–11.

174. Beauchamp and Savulescu, "Robot Guardians," 111.

175. Beauchamp and Savulescu, "Robot Guardians," 112.

176. Beauchamp and Savulescu, "Robot Guardians," 112–13.

177. Beauchamp and Savulescu, "Robot Guardians," 113.

178. Jean Elshtain quoted in Beauchamp and Savulescu, "Robot Guardians," 113, foonote 16.

179. Beauchamp and Savulescu, "Robot Guardians," 106.

180. Beauchamp and Savulescu, "Robot Guardians," 118.

181. Beauchamp and Savulescu, "Robot Guardians," 118.

182. Beauchamp and Savulescu, "Robot Guardians," 119.

183. Singer, "Robots at War"; and Uwe Steinhoff, "Killing Them Safely," 207.

184. Beauchamp and Savulescu, "Robot Guardians," 125.

185. Robert Sparrow, "War without Virtue?," in *Killing by Remote Control: The Ethics of an Unmanned Military*, edited by Bradley Strawser (Oxford: Oxford University Press, 2013), 86.

186. Sparrow, "War without Virtue?," 89, 93–94.

187. Sparrow, "War without Virtue?," 90, 96.

188. Sparrow, "War without Virtue?," 91.

189. Sparrow, "War without Virtue?," 98.

190. Sparrow, "War without Virtue?," 92.

191. Sparrow, "War without Virtue?," 100.

192. Sparrow, "War without Virtue?," 101.

193. Sparrow, "War without Virtue?," 103.

194. Sparrow, "War without Virtue?," 105.

195. Sparrow, "War without Virtue?," 105.

196. Sparrow, "War without Virtue?," 105.

197. Noel Sharkey, "The Automation and Proliferation of Military Drones and the Protection of Civilians," *Law, Innovation and Technology* 3, no. 2 (2011): 235.

198. George Lucas, "Engineering, Ethics and Industry: The Moral Challenges of Lethal Autonomy," in *Killing by Remote Control: The Ethics of an Unmanned Military*, edited by Bradley Strawser (Oxford: Oxford University Press, 2013), 220–21, 215–16.

199. Noel Sharkey, "Saying 'NO!' to Lethal Autonomous Targeting," *Journal of Military Ethics* 9 (2010): 380.

200. Robert Sparrow, "Killer Robots," *Journal of Applied Philosophy* 24 (2007): 66–67, 73–5.

201. Stephen Kershnar, "Autonomous Weapons Pose No Moral Problems," in *Killing by Remote Control: The Ethics of an Unmanned Military*, edited by Bradley Strawser (Oxford: Oxford University Press, 2013), 236–37.

202. Kershnar, "Autonomous Weapons Pose No Moral Problems," 237.

203. Kershnar, "Autonomous Weapons Pose No Moral Problems," 229.

204. Kershnar, "Autonomous Weapons Pose No Moral Problems," 236.

205. Isaac Asimov, *I, Robot* (New York: Bantam Dell, 1977), 37, 77, 107.

206. Lucas, "Engineering, Ethics and Industry," 221.

207. Lucas, "Engineering, Ethics and Industry," 220.

208. Alston, "The CIA and Targeted Killing Beyond Borders," 283.

209. Alston, "The CIA and Targeted Killing Beyond Borders," 310.

210. Alston, "The CIA and Targeted Killing Beyond Borders," 287.

211. Alston, "The CIA and Targeted Killing Beyond Borders," 283–84.

212. Alston, "The CIA and Targeted Killing Beyond Borders," 294.

213. Gregory S. McNeal, "Targeted Killing and Accountability," *Georgetown Law Review* 102 (2014): 681.

214. McNeal, "Targeted Killing and Accountability," 785.

215. McNeal, "Targeted Killing and Accountability," 758.

216. McNeal, "Targeted Killing and Accountability," 793.

217. McNeal, "Targeted Killing and Accountability," 728–29.

218. McNeal, "Targeted Killing and Accountability," 737.

219. McNeal, "Targeted Killing and Accountability," 703, 731–32 and see footnote 246.

220. McNeal, "Targeted Killing and Accountability," 733.

221. McNeal, "Targeted Killing and Accountability," 734.

222. McNeal, "Targeted Killing and Accountability," 738, 733–34.

223. McNeal, "Targeted Killing and Accountability," 736–37.

224. McNeal, "Targeted Killing and Accountability," 730.

225. McNeal, "Targeted Killing and Accountability," 740–41.

226. McNeal, "Targeted Killing and Accountability," 741.

227. McNeal, "Targeted Killing and Accountability," 743.

228. McNeal, "Targeted Killing and Accountability," 746–47.

229. McNeal, "Targeted Killing and Accountability," 743.

230. McNeal, "Targeted Killing and Accountability," 745.

231. McNeal, "Targeted Killing and Accountability," 739.

232. McNeal, "Targeted Killing and Accountability," 748.

233. McNeal, "Targeted Killing and Accountability," 749.

234. McNeal, "Targeted Killing and Accountability," 750.

235. McNeal, "Targeted Killing and Accountability," 750.

236. McNeal, "Targeted Killing and Accountability," 750–51.

237. McNeal, "Targeted Killing and Accountability," 752.

238. McNeal, "Targeted Killing and Accountability," 753; also see footnote 382.

239. Alston, "The CIA and Targeted Killing Beyond Borders," 310.

240. McNeal, "Targeted Killing and Accountability," 737.

241. McNeal, "Targeted Killing and Accountability," 737.

242. McNeal, "Targeted Killing and Accountability," 758–59.

243. McNeal, "Targeted Killing and Accountability," 760.

244. McNeal, "Targeted Killing and Accountability," 760.

245. Alston, "The CIA and Targeted Killing Beyond Borders," 379.

246. McNeal, "Targeted Killing and Accountability," 770.

247. McNeal, "Targeted Killing and Accountability," 770–71.

248. Richard Murphy and Afsheen John Radsan, "Due Process and Targeted Killing of Terrorists," *Cardozo Law Review* 31 (2009): 405–8, 422–28.

249. McNeal, "Targeted Killing and Accountability," 780.

250. McNeal, "Targeted Killing and Accountability," 782.

251. McNeal, "Targeted Killing and Accountability," 780.

252. McNeal, "Targeted Killing and Accountability," 759, 783.

253. McNeal, "Targeted Killing and Accountability," 334.

254. McNeal, "Targeted Killing and Accountability," 783.

255. McNeal, "Targeted Killing and Accountability," 771.

256. McNeal, "Targeted Killing and Accountability," 771–72.

257. Dianne Feinstein, press release, February 13, 2013, accessed June 15, 2014, http://www.feinstein.senate.gov/public/index.cfm/press-releases?ID = 5b8dbe0c-07b6-4714-b663-b01c7c9b99b8.

258. McNeal, "Targeted Killing and Accountability," 774.

259. McNeal, "Targeted Killing and Accountability," 774.

260. McNeal, "Targeted Killing and Accountability," 775.

261. Alston, "The CIA and Targeted Killing Beyond Borders," 386.

262. Alston, "The CIA and Targeted Killing Beyond Borders," 386, 387–88.

263. Alston, "The CIA and Targeted Killing Beyond Borders," 356–57.

264. Alston, "The CIA and Targeted Killing Beyond Borders," 357.

265. McNeal, "Targeted Killing and Accountability," 776.

266. McNeal, "Targeted Killing and Accountability," 776–77.

267. McNeal, "Targeted Killing and Accountability," 779.

268. McNeal, "Targeted Killing and Accountability," 779.

269. McNeal, "Targeted Killing and Accountability," 780.

270. Alston, "The CIA and Targeted Killing Beyond Borders," 402–3.

271. McNeal, "Targeted Killing and Accountability," 404.

272. Alston, "The CIA and Targeted Killing Beyond Borders," 404.

273. McNeal, "Targeted Killing and Accountability," 785, 784–89.

274. Alston, "The CIA and Targeted Killing Beyond Borders," 432–37, 445.

275. McNeal, "Targeted Killing and Accountability," 789–92; Alston, "The CIA and Targeted Killing Beyond Borders," 432–37.

5

The Politics of Drone Strikes

What Political Considerations Shape the U.S. Drone Policy?

WHATEVER THE LEGALITY AND ETHICS of using drones outside of conventional battlefields, political leaders will be the ones to decide whether and how to use them, and their decisions are likely to be shaped by political considerations. This will mean considering at least some of the following factors: popular opinion (and especially the preferences of their own political bases), the criticism they confront from other leaders (especially those in other branches of government), and their calculation of national and personal interest, including considerations such as personal legacy (the way they will be judged by history, including by the global community). By examining these factors, it may be possible to gain some insight into the political calculus that has shaped the drone policy to date and will help to determine its future.

Before turning to these political considerations, however, it is worth briefly reiterating several features of the American drone program that were touched on in section V of the last chapter which are likely to make drones seem attractive to U.S. political leaders. Indeed, the general ethical concern articulated in section V of that chapter was that drones might be *too attractive for leaders to resist or use responsibly*. So what made critics worry that U.S. political leaders might be too easily seduced by drones?

One politically alluring feature of using drone strikes to combat terrorism was, as Micah Zenko and Sarah Kreps summarized nicely, that they "have significantly reduced the political, diplomatic, and military risks and costs associated with the use of military force."[1] Prominent drone critic Audrey Kurth Cronin made an analogous observation in comparing drones to other counterterrorism tactics. In her words, drones have "all the advantages of lower cost and reduced political risk."[2] Specifically, drones are politically "low cost" and "low risk" both because they are relatively affordable and because they do not put U.S. service persons at risk, and indeed permit many of them to work from within the United States. They thus shield leaders from the traditional political costs of using conventional forces abroad, especially once body bags begin to come home.

Moreover, as also noted in chapter 4, a drone strike policy has the advantage of allowing the executive to act with a relatively high degree of independence from the other branches of government. For example, the president does not require specific congressional approval under the War Powers Resolution to deploy drones abroad, at least in the Obama administration's view, because drones do not put U.S. service persons at risk.[3] Indeed, John Kaag and Sarah Kreps have argued that neither Congress nor the judiciary "has exercised meaningful oversight of drone policy."[4] Drones are thus an instrument the executive can deploy unilaterally, manage with little interference, and for which it can generally take credit.

At the same time, and perhaps most importantly, an active drone policy permits the administration to show that it is taking decisive action to fulfill its primary obligation to secure the safety of the American people, and indeed to quantify its achievements in terms of terrorist leaders and militants killed, bases destroyed, and plots disrupted. In short then, drone strikes permit the administration to demonstrate its strength and efficacy on defense, acting largely on its own, at relatively little political cost or risk.

Yet none of these apparent advantages would count for much if the American people disapproved of drone strikes and those embracing them. Being able to take credit, for example, is only advantageous where there is credit to take. In other words, most of the comparative advantages of drones listed above are premised on the assumption that U.S. citizens approve of the strikes. The following section examines whether the available evidence supports that assumption. Section II examines the main lines of domestic criticism that have been directed against U.S. drone policy. Section III explores in what respect the administration's interest may be thought to align or diverge from the national interest in regard to its drone policy, and how considerations of the administration's legacy may influence this relationship.

I. U.S. Domestic Opinion of Drone Strikes

The most important expression of public opinion in a democracy is an election, and no election in the United States is treated as seriously as the election of a president. Presidential elections persistently show, for example, a substantially higher rate of participation than midterm elections—the average difference between presidential and mid-term elections from 2000 to 2012 was approximately 18.17 percent.[5]

The Mandate to Employ Drones

President Obama can certainly argue that he has earned an electoral mandate to carry out drone strikes outside of conventional battlefields. He won election and reelection while making no mystery of his intention to aggressively target the leadership of al-Qaeda and its affiliates even outside of established armed conflicts. Kenneth Anderson aptly described Obama's 2008 campaign for president as follows:

> It is a slight exaggeration to say that Barack Obama is the first president in American history to have run in part on a political platform of targeted killings—but not much of one. During the campaign, he openly sought to one-up the Republican nominee, Sen. John McCain, in his enthusiasm for the use of targeted strikes in Pakistan against al Qaeda figures. "You know," he said in his speech at the Democratic National Convention, "John McCain likes to say that he'll follow [Osama] Bin Laden to the Gates of Hell, but he won't even go to the cave where he lives." That he would, as president, follow bin Laden to his cave, with or without the cooperation of the Pakistani government, he made perfectly clear. "If we have actionable intelligence about high-value terrorist targets and President [Pervez] Musharraf won't act, we will," he said in another speech. Indeed, while he criticized President Bush for being too aggressive in many aspects of counterterrorism, with respect to targeted killings, his criticism was the polar opposite: "The Bush administration has not acted aggressively enough to go after al Qaeda's leadership," he said. "I would be clear that if Pakistan cannot or will not take out al Qaeda leadership when we have actionable intelligence about their whereabouts, we will act to protect the American people. There can be no safe haven for al Qaeda terrorists who killed thousands of Americans and threaten our homeland today."[6]

Obama went on to decisively win the 2008 election, obtaining 365 votes in the Electoral College and a majority of the votes cast. In 2012 he was running on an established and fairly well-publicized record of greatly intensifying the U.S. targeted killing policy by means of drones, and he did not shy away from this record during the campaign. For example, when criticized by GOP candidates for not being aggressive enough in combating terrorism, Obama responded, "Ask Osama bin Laden and the 22 out of 30 top Al-Qaeda leaders who've been taken off the field whether I engage in appeasement . . . or whoever's left out there."[7] The twenty-two al-Qaeda leaders were killed in drone strikes. Yet Obama won reelection handily, obtaining a majority of all votes cast and 332 Electoral College votes.

The Consensus among Leaders

Of course, President Obama is hardly unique among American political leaders in embracing the targeting of suspected terrorists with drones. Indeed, even Obama's Republican opponent in 2012 gave a "full throated" endorsement of his drone policy. When asked about it, Governor Mitt Romney declared, "I support that entirely and think the president was right to use that technology."[8] Senator John McCain, Obama's 2008 opponent, is of course also a long-standing drone enthusiast (although one who has stressed the importance of coordinating strikes with local governments).[9] It is also worth stressing that President Obama inherited the policy from his Republican predecessor, President George W. Bush. Moreover, Bush's last Democratic electoral opponent, Senator John Kerry (the current secretary of state) also declared that he would "hunt and kill the terrorists wherever they are."[10] In short, the idea of using drones to target suspected terrorists has been widely endorsed among American presidential nominees from both main parties.

Public Support for Drones

The consensus among presidential contenders on this point is not especially surprising, because American public opinion has remained supportive of the targeted killing of terrorists overseas, even when such targeting is specifically by means of drones. This point is illustrated in table 5.1 (below), which provides an overview of polling on U.S. attitudes to drone strikes on "terrorist suspects" or "extremists" overseas from September 2011 to May 2015.

At least two key observations can be made on the basis of the survey data presented in table 5.1. First, most Americans do consistently express support for drone strikes overseas. Since September 2011 support has never fallen below 52 percent and has ranged as high as 83 percent, while opposition has never exceeded 41 percent and has polled as low as 9 percent. Positive responses averaged 66 percent, negative responses 22 percent, and other responses 12 percent.

Second, there is some evidence of erosion in popular support for drone strikes overseas over time, albeit partially offset by a slight uptick in support in some of the most recent polls. Micah Zenko dramatically described falling public support for drone strikes in January 2013:

> Indeed, a negative trend in U.S public opinion on drones is already apparent. Between February and June 2012, U.S. support for drone strikes against suspected terrorists fell from 83 percent to 62 percent—which represents less U.S. support than enhanced interrogations techniques maintained in the mid-2000s.[11]

TABLE 5.1
U.S. Public Opinion on Drone Strikes, September 2011 to May 2015[1]

Date	Agency	Positive	Negative	Other	Sample Size
September 2011	Washington Post/ABC News[2]	76%	22%	2%	1,001
November 2011	CBS News[3]	65%	22%	13%	1,182
February 2012	Washington Post/ABC News[4]	83%	11%	6%	1,000
February 2012	Rasmussen[5]	76%	9%	15%	1,000
June 2012	Pew Research[6]	62%	28%	10%	1,011
July 2012	Pew Research[7]	55%	34%	11%	N/A
February 2013 (Military)	Fairleigh Dickinson Public-Mind[8]	75%	13%	12%	814
February 2013 (CIA)	Fairleigh Dickinson Public-Mind[9]	65%	21%	13%	814
February 2013	Pew Research[10]	56%	26%	18%	1,004
February 2013	New York Times/CBS[11]	71%	20%	9%	N/A
February 2013	NBC News/Wall Street Journal[12]	64%	12%	24%	1,000
March 2013	Fox News[13]	74%	22%	4%	1,010
March 2013	YouTube/Huffington Post[14]	53%	22%	25%	1,000
March 2013	Gallup[15]	65%	28%	8%	502
April 2013	New York Times/CBS[16]	70%	20%	10%	965
May 2013	Rasmussen[17]	69%	14%	17%	1,000
June 2013	New York Times/CBS[18]	72%	22%	6%	1,022
July 2013	Pew Research[19]	61%	30%	9%	1,002
July 2014	Pew Research[20]	52%	41%	7%	1,002
December 2014	Rasmussen[21]	71%	12%	17%	1,000
May 2015	Pew Research[22]	58%	35%	7%	2,002

1. This set of poll results excludes some polls that include various "depends" answers, which complicates the expression of opinions, and polls with exceptionally high "Don't know" and or "Did not answer" results (over 25 percent), or which emphasize the use of drones in "Iraq" or Afghanistan, which is not our primary interest here.

2. Washington Post-ABC News Poll, *Washington Post*, accessed December 18, 2014, http://www.washingtonpost.com/wp-srv/politics/polls/postabcpoll_090111.html.

3. Brian Montopoli, "Poll: Americans' Views on Foreign Policy," *CBS News*, November 12, 2011, accessed December 18, 2014, http://www.cbsnews.com/news/poll-americans-views-on-foreign-policy/.

TABLE 5.1 (Continued)

4. Washington Post-ABC News Poll, *Washington Post*, accessed December 19, 2014, http://www.washingtonpost.com/wp-srv/politics/polls/postabcpoll_020412.html.

5. "Voters Are Gung-Ho for Use of Drones But Not Over the United States," *Rasmussen Reports*, February 13, 2012, accessed February 3, 2015, http://www.rasmussenreports.com/public/politics/current_events/afghanistan/voters_are_gung_ho_for_use_of_drones_but_not_over_the_united_states.

6. "Global Opinion of Obama Slips, International Policies Faulted," *Pew Research Center*, June 13, 2012, accessed February 3, 2015, http://www.pewglobal.org/2012/06/13/chapter-1-views-of-the-u-s-and-american-foreign-policy-4/.

7. "Continued Support for U.S. Drone Strikes," *Pew Research Center*, February 11, 2013, accessed February 3, 2015, http://www.people-press.org/2013/02/11/continued-support-for-u-s-drone-strikes/.

8. PublicMind, *Public Says It's Illegal to Target Americans Abroad as Some Question CIA Drone Attacks* (Madison: Fairleigh Dickinson University, 2013), http://publicmind.fdu.edu/2013/drone/final.pdf.

9. PublicMind, *Public Says It's Illegal to Target Americans Abroad.*

10. "Continued Support for U.S. Drone Strikes."

11. The New York Times CBS News Poll, *New York Times/CBS News*, April 24–28, 2013, accessed February 3, 2015, http://www.nytimes.com/packages/pdf/world/2013/april13b.trn-early-forpol.pdf.

12. NBC News/Wall Street Journal Survey, *NBC News/Wall Street Journal*, February 21–24, 2013, accessed February 3, 2015, http://msnbcmedia.msn.com/i/MSNBC/Sections/A_Politics/_Today_Stories_Teases/13061-FEBRUARY-NBC-WSJ.pdf.

13. Anderson Robbins Research and Shaw & Company Research, "Fox News Poll: Majority Supports Use of Drones," *Fox News*, March 4, 2013, accessed February 3, 2015, http://www.foxnews.com/politics/interactive/2013/03/04/fox-news-poll-majority-supports-use-drones/.

14. Omnibus Poll, *YouGov*, March 6–7, 2013, accessed February 3, 2015, http://big.assets.huffingtonpost.com/toplinesb_drones308.pdf.

15. Alyssa Brown and Frank Newport, "In U.S., 65% Support Drone Attacks on Terrorists Abroad," *Gallup*, March 25, 2013, accessed February 3, 2015, http://www.gallup.com/poll/161474/support-drone-attacks-terrorist s-abroad.aspx.

16. The New York Times CBS News Poll.

17. "36% Favor Use of Drones to Stop Terrorists in the United States," *Rasmussen Reports*, May 28, 2013, accessed February 2, 2015, http://www.rasmussenreports.com/public_content/politics/general_politics/may_2013/36_favor_use_of_drones_to_stop_terrorists_in_the_united_states.

18. "Americans' Views on the Issues," *New York Times*, June 6, 2013, accessed February 2, 2015, http://www.nytimes.com/interactive/2013/06/06/us/new-york-times-cbs-news-poll-june-2013.html?_r=0.

19. "America's Global Image Remains More Positive Than China's," *Pew Research Center*, July 18, 2013, accessed February 2, 2015, http://www.pewglobal.org/2013/07/18/chapter-1-attitudes-toward-the-united-states/.

20. "Global Opposition to U.S. Surveillance and Drones, But Limited Harm to America's Image," *Pew Research Center*, July 14, 2014, accessed September 15, 2014, http://www.pewglobal.org/2014/07/14/chapter-1-the-american-brand/.

21. "Voters Want More Drone Strikes on Terrorists Overseas," *Rasmussen Reports*, December 15, 2014, accessed February 2, 2015, http://www.rasmussenreports.com/public_content/politics/general_politics/december_2014/voters_want_more_drone_strikes_on_terrorists_overseas.

22. "Public Continues to Back U.S. Drone Attacks: Afghanistan Update: Most Say U.S. Has Failed to Achieve Goals," *Pew Research Center*, May 28, 2015, accessed June 14, 2015, http://www.people-press.org/2015/05/28/public-continues-to-back-u-s-drone-atta cks/.

Zenko's suggestion[8] is clearly that U.S. public opinion on drone strikes may be approaching the same type of reversal that occurred in regard to enhanced interrogation.

However, more recent polls indicate some reversal in the trend Zenko identified, particularly when comparisons are made between polls carried out by the same agencies. The most recent Pew poll (reported in May 2015) showed a 58 percent positive opinion of drone strikes, which marks a 6 percent increase from the prior Pew poll from July 2014. Moreover, this uptick finds at least a small measure of corroboration in the other most recent poll from Rasmussen (from December 2014), which at 71 percent positive response marked a 2 percent increase from the previous Rasmussen poll in May 2013. However, it is also important to note that both the recent Pew and Rasmussen results still registered considerably below their high-water marks of public support from 2012, when in February Rasmussen reported a 76 percent positive response and in June Pew reported 62 percent approval. So overall positive response in the most recent polls from Rasmussen and Pew Research come in 5 percent and 4 percent below their high-water mark, respectively.

There is then some evidence of moderate erosion of U.S. support for drone strikes overseas if the results of particular pollsters are tracked over time. However, the decline does not appear nearly as dramatic as Zenko suggested in 2013. Part of the reason for this may be that Zenko compares two different polling agencies asking slightly different questions. In fact, the result he uses for the high end of his comparison is the highest positive result in this set of poll results (i.e., the February 2012 Washington Post/ABC News poll at 83 percent positive response), and the result he chooses for the low end of the comparison is from Pew Research, which consistently reports lower positive response than other polls. For example, in table 5.1 (above), which covers the major polls reported between September 2011 and May 2015, the average positive response on the six Pew polls is 57 percent, while those on all other polls is 70 percent. Specific examples showing this pattern include the February 2013 Pew data, which shows that 56 percent support while a New York Times/CBS poll in the same month reported 71 percent approval.

At least one explanation for variations in these polling results is the slightly different questions that respondents were asked. For example, the Washington Post/ABC News poll asked, "Changing topics, thinking about the following decisions of the Obama administration, please tell me whether you strongly approve, somewhat approve, somewhat disapprove, or strongly disapprove. . . . The use of unmanned, 'drone' aircraft against terrorist suspects overseas."[12] Pew Research asked: "On a different subject, do you approve or disapprove of the United States conducting missile strikes from pilotless aircraft called drones to target extremists in countries such as Pakistan, Yemen and Somalia?"[13]

An important distinction here is that while the Washington Post/ABC News poll was concerned with all uses of the unmanned aircraft, the Pew Research poll explicitly refers to missile strikes launched by drones. Similarly, while Pew Research's question asked about using the drones to target "extremists," the poll conducted by the Washington Post/ABC News used the more visceral term *terrorist suspects*. While such differences in the phrasing of questions cannot be singled out as the lone cause of the different results, they help to illustrate the difficulties of comparing across the pollsters.

Regardless of the nuances of the questions asked, the central political fact remains that a majority of Americans continue to support drone strikes overseas. A further politically salient fact is that this support extends across party lines. While public opinion polling has generally shown higher approval ratings among the Republican voters than Democratic voters, both sides have been shown to generally support the policy.[14] The number of polls that have broken down support for drone strikes outside of conventional battlefields by party affiliation has been relatively few and far between, but their message has been consistent. Gallup,[15] Fairleigh Dickinson University's PublicMind,[16] and Pew Research published the three most prominent polls that report on this question.

The February 2013 poll by Fairleigh Dickinson University's PublicMind showed a substantial difference between the opinions of Democrats and Republicans regarding their approval of drone strikes.[17] When asked if they approved of the U.S. military using drones to target those abroad, Republicans had an 84:7 approval to disapproval ratio.[18] This means for every person opposed there were twelve who supported the policy. Support among Democrats was a little less overwhelming, but still extremely strong.[19] Democrats supported the policy at a 66:19 ratio.[20] In other words, for every person opposed to the policy, there were more than three who supported it. The PublicMind poll also demonstrated that members of both parties were somewhat less supportive when asked whether they approved of drone operations being launched by the CIA. Republicans responded positively by a 76:14 (or over five to one) ratio compared to the Democrats' 57:26 (or a little better than two to one) approval to disapproval ratio.[21]

A March 2013 Gallup poll showed similar overall results. While 79 percent of Republicans supported the use of drones by the U.S. government to target suspected terrorists in foreign countries, a smaller majority of 55 percent of Democrats shared that sentiment.[22] The latest Pew Research poll, conducted from May 12 to 15, 2015, reported similar albeit slightly lower results, with 74 percent of Republicans and 52 percent of Democrats supporting U.S. drone strikes "to target extremists."[23]

If these polls do accurately capture Americans' attitudes to drone strikes, then the policy is not only a popular one, but also one in regard of which both parties might expect some political cover. That is, because a majority in the other party support the policy, they are likely to be less aggressive and unified in their criticism than on issues where there is a clearer partisan divide. So the Obama administration, for example, is in a position to pursue a generally popular policy, which seems to provide Americans with some sense of security, while not offending its own political base and possibly being insulated from Republican criticism (given that a strong majority of Republicans support the policy). This is not to say that there has been no Republican criticism of the president's drone policy—as will be shown below, there has been some important criticism—but only to suggest that it has probably been less intense, unified, and sustained than it has been over some more divisive issues, such as the Affordable Care Act, and to suggest that one reason for this may be that a majority of Republicans actually support the use of drones to target extremists abroad.

II. Domestic Political Criticism of Drone Strikes

Nonetheless, some important caveats must be added to the simple claim that "the American Public Loves Drones" (as one *Washington Post* headline put it).[24] While the U.S. drone program continues to enjoy support that "is not only wide but also bipartisan,"[25] there are also sizable minorities on both sides of the political spectrum that are opposed, and often strongly opposed, to the country's drone policy, particularly in regard to six key issues: (1) the legality of the drone campaigns, (2) signature strikes, (3) the targeting of Americans, (4) civilian deaths, (5) the lack of oversight, and (6) the charge that the administration may prefer killing to capture. Moreover, while the drone program has many supporters in Congress, that has not prevented much of the highest-profile criticism of President Obama's drone policy from emanating from Congress (or at least manifesting at congressional events), including from outspoken Democrats in Congress.

The Legality of the Drone Campaigns

Perhaps the most fundamental criticism that has been leveled against U.S. drone policy is that the entire enterprise is illegal, either under U.S. law or international law or both. These charges have emanated not only from human rights organizations, the UN, other states, and diverse legal scholars but also from within the U.S. government itself, including from Democrats. As noted in chapter 3, for example, Democratic representative Dennis Kucinich proposed a bill in 2010 (HR 6010), cosponsored by six colleagues, that suggested that drone strikes violate Executive Order 12333.[26] Kucinich also asserted that the United States was "violating international law" by attacking "another nation which has not attacked the United States."[27] Leading scholars of international law, such as Mary Ellen O'Connell, concurred with Kucinich's conclusions in congressional testimony. Some leaders of other Western states have also condemned U.S. drone strikes. Swedish Minister of Foreign Affairs Anna Lindh, for example, described one strike as "a summary execution that violates human rights."[28] Many human rights organizations have also suggested that U.S. drone strikes in Pakistan and Yemen violate international law, as have some senior UN officials.

The Obama administration has responded by making the question of the legality of strikes a centerpiece of a high-profile effort to inform and reassure the public about U.S. drone operations overseas. Indeed, the campaign could be said to have started in earnest with State Department legal adviser Harold Koh's speech to the American Society for International Law in March 2010, which laid out the U.S. government's initial legal brief. Speeches by Attorney General Eric Holder (March 5, 2012) and Department of Defense General Counsel and now Secretary of Homeland Security Jeh Johnson (February 22, 2012, and March 18, 2013), among others, elaborated and detailed the rationale.[29] Of course, the U.S. media effort was not limited to legal issues, and John Brennan's Wilson Center speech in April 2012, for example, focused on issues of "the efficacy and ethics" of drone strikes.[30] The climax of this public defense was of course President Obama's speech at the National Defense University on May 23, 2013, devoted substantially to defending the drone program by addressing, among other things, the legal issues.[31] At the same time, the administration also advanced its case in less formal venues, including President Obama's participation in a Google + forum and various talk shows, and Eric Holder's letters to various members of government, along with, no doubt, many unofficial comments and leaks by administration officials. The Obama administration also released a redacted version of an Office of Legal Counsel Memo on Targeting an American (in response to a Second Circuit Court of Appeal Ruling) on June 23, 2014.[32] A white paper summarizing the legal reasoning had previously been leaked to NBC in February 2013.[33]

In addressing the issue of legality, the Obama administration has pursued at least three simultaneous strategies. First, the administration officials sent to defend the program have appealed to laws governing the use of armed force, and particularly governing the conduct of war. In particular, they have based their arguments largely on the fact that the United States has the right to target enemy combatants because it is at war with al-Qaeda and associated forces. Furthermore, the United States can launch such attacks in another state as long as the state gives its consent or is unwilling or unable to act on its own behalf. U.S. officials have also appealed to the right of self-defense as permitting the strikes.[34] Second, the Obama administration has announced standards for the use of drone strikes that seem compliant with domestic and international law (such as only targeting "terrorists who pose a continuing and imminent threat to the American people, and when there are no other governments capable of effectively addressing the threat").[35] Third, it has communicated the intent to carry out reforms in the future that promise to enhance the program's appearance of legal propriety, such as its March 2013 project to shift "lead responsibility for its controversial armed drone program from the CIA to the Defense Department."[36]

There is little evidence that the Obama administration's efforts, particularly pronounced between 2010 and 2013, have met with great success in persuading the American public of the legal justification of its drone program. For example, a poll conducted by Fairleigh Dickinson PublicMind asked Americans in February 2013 whether strikes targeting U.S. citizens were legal. The poll found that 24 percent of respondents felt that such killings were "Legal," 48 percent "Illegal," and 28 percent were "Unsure."[37] In the latest Pew Research survey taken from May 12 to 18, 2015, 64 percent of respondents indicated that they were "very" or "somewhat" concerned about the legality of drone strikes, while only 33 percent indicated that they were "not too" or "not at all" concerned.[38]

Some of the difficulty in persuading the U.S. public of the program's legality may have been due to the fact that the effort to shift drone strikes to the Pentagon stalled,[39] and the seemingly restrictive "continuing and imminent threat" criteria turned out to be far more flexible than it initially sounded once readers examined the leaked white paper on killing Americans (as will be discussed in section III below).[40] Nonetheless, if the Obama administration's defense of its drone program has done little to persuade the American people of its legality, skepticism on this point does not seem to have reversed popular approval of the policy.

Signature Strikes

Another major focus of domestic criticism has been the practice of signature strikes. It was reported in June 2012, for example, that twenty-six members of the U.S. House of Representatives signed a letter addressed to President Obama.[41] The letter, which was signed by twenty-four Democrats, including Dennis Kucinich, and two Republicans, including Ron Paul, demanded a legal justification for the use of signature strikes.[42] In May 2012 and December 2012, three ranking Democrats on the House Judiciary Committee sent letters to Attorney General Holder demanding information on the criteria and justification of signature strikes, and in February 2013 they were joined in a further letter by Republican colleagues.[43] As noted in the case study of the last chapter, there has also been widespread and intense criticism of signature strikes both in domestic discussion and in international forums like the United Nations.

The Obama administration has responded to criticism of signature strikes in three main ways. First, senior officials have defended the legality of the program. Second, the president's May 23, 2013, speech at the National Defense University suggested that the United States would cease, or at least greatly limit, the use of signature strikes outside of the Afghanistan-Pakistan theater. Third, the Obama administration appears to have significantly "curtailed" the use of signature strikes even within Afghanistan and Pakistan, although they still appear to be employed on occasion (for example, in the January 15, 2015, strike on an al-Qaeda compound in the Shawal Valley that unintentionally killed two Western hostages).[44] The degree to which these moves will effectively blunt criticism remains to be seen.

Targeting Americans

Probably the most outspoken and effective congressional critic of the drone campaigns has been the Republican senator Rand Paul. Much of Paul's public opposition has been focused on the targeting of Americans. As he put it, "Our Constitution is precious and no American should be killed by a drone without first being charged with a crime."[45]

On Wednesday, March 6, 2013, Rand Paul held a talking filibuster in opposition to the confirmation of John Brennan as the director of the CIA.[46] Paul decided to take this action after receiving a letter from Attorney General Eric Holder in which Holder refused to rule out drone strikes on American soil in "extraordinary circumstances."[47] During the over twelve hours of Paul's 2013 filibuster, he said:

> When I asked the president, "Can you kill an American on American soil," it should have been an easy answer. It's an easy question. It should have been a resounding and unequivocal, "No." The president's response? He hasn't killed anyone yet. We're supposed to be comforted by that. The president says, "I haven't killed anyone yet." He goes on to say, "And I have no intention of killing Americans. But I might." Is that enough? Are we satisfied by that?[48]

Writing in the *Washington Post* two days after yielding the floor, Paul stated that the Senate has the ability to restrain executive power and that his "filibuster was the beginning of the fight to restore a healthy balance of powers."[49] Paul went on to say that Obama still needs to state that the United States will not kill noncombatant U.S. citizens, adding that the Fifth Amendment applies to all citizens without exclusion.[50] Paul finished his article by saying that the support that he received after his filibuster demonstrated that Americans want someone to "fight for them," a task that he was willing to accept.[51]

There is some evidence that Senator Paul's filibuster had a significant impact on public opinion. For example, an article in *Business Insider* attributed a 19 percent drop in public support for the targeting of Americans to Senator Paul's performance.[52] This claim, as with Micah Zenko's contention about eroding general support, is based on comparing results reported by two different polling agencies. A Fox News poll released just weeks before Senator Paul's filibuster found that 60 percent of individuals approved of drone strikes against U.S. citizens in foreign countries who were *suspected terrorists*, while just 36 percent disapproved.[53] In comparison, a Gallup poll released less than a month later found that 41 percent of total respondents favored these attacks against U.S. citizens in foreign countries who were *suspected terrorists*.[54] Again, some of this variation may be explained by language (i.e., approved versus favored) or polling methods. Moreover, the attribution of causation to Senator Paul's speech is complicated by some polls indicating widespread resistance to targeting Americans before the filibuster (for example, the February 2013 Fairleigh Dickinson poll showing only 24 percent positive response and 48 percent negative reaction). However, other polling reinforces the impression that Senator Paul's speech at least articulated and accelerated a trend in public opinion. For example, a Gallup poll taken on March 20 and 21 found that an impressive 79 percent of respondents "supported Paul's position that drone strikes should not be used on American soil against Americans suspected of terrorism. Just 13 percent say it would be okay."[55]

Not everyone believed that Paul's filibuster was necessary, however, including John McCain, the Republican senior senator from Arizona. McCain argued, "We've done, I think, a disservice to a lot of Americans by making them believe that somehow they're in danger from their government."[56] McCain went on to state that the danger Americans face comes from al-Qaeda, not the government. Experts echoed these views. For example, Steve Vladeck, a professor of law and associate dean at American University, argued on NPR that the Obama administration has been clear that they would only use a drone to attack an American on American soil in an "extreme emergency situation, the likes of which are not that hard to figure out," likely referring to another September 11 or Pearl Harbor.[57] In fact, the Obama administration moved quickly after Senator Paul's filibuster to confirm that in addition to circumstances of extraordinary threat, the potential American target would also have to actually be engaged in combat (i.e., carrying out an attack) on U.S. soil. Specifically, on March 7, after he finished his thirteen-hour filibuster, Senator Paul received a second letter from Attorney General Holder responding directly to his query: "Does the president

TABLE 5.2
Public Opinion on Targeting of U.S. Citizens

Date	Agency	Positive	Negative	Other	Sample Size
November 2011	CBS News[1]	53%	35%	12%	1,182
February 2012[2]	Washington Post/ABC News	79%	17%	4%	1,000
February 2013	Fairleigh Dickinson Public-Mind[3]	24%	48%	28%	814
February 2013	CBS News[4]	49%	38%	13%	N/A
February 2013	Reason-Rupe Public Opinion Survey[5]	31%	57%	12%	1,002
March 2013	Fox News[6]	60%	36%	5%[7]	1,010
March 2013	YouTube/Huffington Post[8]	42%	30%	29%	1,000
March 2013	Gallup[9]	41%	52%	7%	502

1. Montopoli, "Poll: Americans' Views on Foreign Policy."
2. These results were derived from a subset of people who supported drone strikes against terrorists overseas. See Washington Post-ABC News Poll.
3. PublicMind, *Public Says It's Illegal to Target Americans Abroad.*
4. Micah Zenko, "U.S. Public Opinion on Drone Strikes," Council on Foreign Relations, March 18, 2013, accessed July 16, 2015, http://blogs.cfr.org/zenko/2013/03/18/u-s-public-opinion-on-drone-strikes/.
5. Reason-Rupe Poll, *Public Opinion Survey: February 2013 Topline Results* (Los Angeles: Reason Foundation, 2013), 4, http://reason.com/assets/db/13620384648046.pdf.
6. Anderson Robbins Research and Shaw & Company Research, Fox News Poll.
7. The numbers here add up to 101 percent as reported by the source, likely due to rounding.
8. Omnibus Poll.
9. These numbers are for "against US citizens living abroad who are suspected terrorists." See Brown and Newport, "In U.S., 65% Support Drone Attacks on Terrorists Abroad."

have the authority to use a weaponized drone to kill an American not engaged in combat on U.S. soil? The answer to that is no."[58]

A few weeks after his initial drone filibuster, in an apparent deviation from his previous stance that drones should never being used to kill U.S. citizens, Senator Paul appeared on Fox Business Network and stated that his problem is not with whether drones are used in criminal apprehension, but in the monitoring of the everyday activities of Americans. Paul remarked, "If someone comes out of a liquor store with a weapon and $50 in cash, I don't care if a drone kills him or a policeman kills him."[59] After a disgruntled reaction from some in his Libertarian base, Paul released a statement, asserting that his position on drones had not changed:

Let me be clear: it has not. Armed drones should not be used in normal crime situations. They may only be considered in extraordinary, lethal situations where there is an ongoing, imminent threat. I described that scenario previously during my Senate filibuster.

Additionally, surveillance drones should only be used with warrants and specific targets.

Fighting terrorism and capturing terrorists must be done while preserving our constitutional protections. This was demonstrated last week in Boston. As we all seek to prevent future tragedies, we must continue to bear this in mind.[60]

On this latter view, however, it is not entirely clear where Senator Paul's view differs from the Obama administration's.

On Wednesday, May 21, 2014, Senator Paul led another filibuster, this time in opposition to David Barron being appointed to the U.S. Court of Appeals. Paul's opposition rested in Barron's authorship of a drone memo, which gave legal justification for the killing of U.S. citizens by drone attack.[61] Paul stated during this filibuster:

> I rise today to oppose the nomination of anyone who would argue that the President has the power to kill American citizens not involved in combat. I rise today to say that there is no legal precedent for killing American citizens not directly involved in combat and that any nominee who rubber stamps and grants such power to a President is not worthy of being placed one step away from the Supreme Court.[62]

What is odd about this statement is that Barron's drone memo, which has now been released at least in a redacted form, does not contend that the president has the power to attack anyone who is not a combatant, whether American or not. It rather argues that the American government has the right to kill an American who has become a leader of al-Qaeda or the Taliban and in so doing has joined a war against the United States precisely because that person can be treated as a combatant.[63]

Still, it seems clear that Paul's initial filibuster at least tapped into a deep-seated concern that many Americans share about the targeting of other Americans. Further, some polls (such as the March 2013 Gallup poll) seem to suggest that this concern is not entirely assuaged by the designation of combatant.

Civilian Casualties

Just weeks before Paul's initial filibuster, on February 7, 2013, CODEPINK also protested confirmation hearings of John Brennan for the director of the CIA due to his central role in the drone campaigns.[64] With Senator Dianne Feinstein presiding over the hearing, Brennan was interrupted at least four times while trying to deliver his opening line. After the fourth interruption,

Feinstein stopped the hearing, removed Brennan from the room, and had the remainder of the protesters removed.[65] One protester held a sign that said "Brennan = Drone Killing,"[66] while another yelled, "Think about the mothers."[67] Fifteen activists were arrested in total, including CODEPINK coordinator Alli McCracken. Of those fifteen people who were arrested, three went to court and were sentenced to one hundred hours of community service for disrupting Congress.[68]

While Brennan's confirmation did eventually proceed and he became the director of the CIA, there is some recent evidence that the CODEPINK protest tapped into a concern of the general public. For example, in the most recent (May 2015) Pew Research Poll, 48 percent of Americans surveyed reported that they were "very concerned that U.S. Drone attacks endanger the lives of innocent civilians," while 32 percent were "somewhat" concerned.[69] Other recent polls offer some corroboration of this concern (see table 5.3).[70]

Moreover, the Obama administration appears to have recognized and sought to assuage this concern. For example, President Obama and other senior officials such as CIA Director John Brennan have repeatedly sought to reassure the public that civilian casualties are rare. President Obama also asserted in his May 23, 2013, speech at the National Defense University that his administration would only carry out strikes where there was "near certainty that no civilians would be killed or injured." Finally, as noted in chapter 1 (as well as the case studies of both chapters 1 and 2), all of the databases tracking U.S. drone strikes have recorded sharp declines in civilian casualties, particularly over the last three years.

A Preference for Killing?

Another important concern about the drone program that has been raised domestically is the suspicion that rather than limiting the resort to drones to

TABLE 5.3
Americans Concerned with Civilian Casualties

	Source	Concerned	Not Concerned	Don't Know	Sample Size
February 2013	Pew Research[1]	81	15	4	1,004
June 2013	New York Times/CBS[2]	84	14	2	1,022
May 2015	Pew Research[3]	80	19	1	2,002

1. "Continued Support for U.S. Drone Strikes."
2. "Americans' Views on the Issues."
3. Pew Research Center, "Public Continues to Back U.S. Drone Attacks," accessed July 18, 2015, http://www.people-press.org/files/2015/05/5-28-15-Foreign-Policy-release.pdf.

cases of last resort, the Obama administration may actually employ it as the preferred means of dealing with threatening terrorists. In May 2012, for example, the ranking Republican Senate Intelligence Committee member, Saxby Chambliss, stated that the Obama administration's "policy is to take out high-value targets, versus capturing high-value targets,"[71] intimating that Obama would prefer to kill terrorist leaders rather than deal with the legal issues associated with taking prisoners. In May 2012, a *New York Times* article posited,

> The administration's very success at killing terrorism suspects has been shadowed by a suspicion: that Mr. Obama has avoided the complications of detention by deciding, in effect, to take no prisoners alive. While scores of suspects have been killed under Mr. Obama, only one has been taken into American custody, and the president has balked at adding new prisoners to Guantánamo.[72]

This suspicion raised by the *New York Times* finds further reinforcement in a *Human Rights Watch* report that argues that certain individuals in Yemen could have been captured rather than killed.[73] The report argues that the fact that they were executed by drone strikes contradicts President Obama's own guidelines and supports the view that he favors killing over capture. The authors of the report summarized their findings in this way: "Even if some of the attacks described in this report do not violate the laws of war, they appear to fall short of the thresholds set by the Obama administration for carrying out targeted killings. Attacks that do not meet the US policy guidelines would contravene law enforcement standards under international human rights law."[74]

Some legal scholars have not only accepted this accusation that the Obama administration favors killing over capture but have even accepted some personal responsibility for it. Noah Feldman, the Felix Frankfurter Professor of Law at Harvard Law School, wrote in October 2013 that liberals who bemoaned President Bush's use of torture against detainees might have made killing more attractive than capturing.[75] Feldman noted that Obama promised to close the prison in Guantanamo Bay, so he "could hardly add detainees there."[76] While he believed that most of the blame for the drone campaigns would justifiably land on the civilian and military policy makers, Feldman wrote:

> There will be plenty of blame to go around, yet I can't escape the gnawing feeling that people like me—legal critics of the George W. Bush administration's detention policy—bear some moral responsibility for creating incentives for the Obama administration to kill rather than capture.[77]

Moreover, Kenneth Anderson has added the suggestion that killing from a distance (as drones do) can be politically preferable, "because it removes potentially messy questions of surrender."[78]

The impression that the Obama administration would prefer to kill than capture terrorist suspects has generated some heated criticism from both sides of the political spectrum, and perhaps most interestingly from defenders of the Bush administration's counterterrorism policies. Prominent among them was John Yoo, a member of Bush's Justice Department.[79] Yoo was responsible for writing a number of the controversial "Memos on Torture" for the Bush administration.[80] In February 2013 Yoo wrote as follows in the *Wall Street Journal* in response to the drone memo leaked to NBC:

> Rather than capture terrorists—which produces the most valuable intelligence on al Qaeda—Mr. Obama has relied almost exclusively on drone attacks, and he has thereby been able to dodge difficult questions over detention. But those deaths from the sky violate personal liberty far more than the waterboarding of three al Qaeda leaders ever did.[81]

What Yoo was trying to relate is that the Obama administration has been able to avoid the many challenges regarding interrogation and imprisonment because he has instead favored lethal operations. In Yoo's view, these lethal operations are much worse than waterboarding. Yoo believes that waterboarding does not constitute torture and that the technique helped to prevent the recurrence of terrorism in the United States after 9/11.[82]

Yoo was not the only individual to write a critical response regarding the drone memo. Journalist and lawyer Glenn Greenwald also compared Obama's drone memo with Bush's memos on torture, but in a tone more critical of both.[83] Greenwald wrote of the drone memo in *The Guardian*:

> It claims its conclusion is "reached with recognition of the extraordinary seriousness of a lethal operation by the United States against a US citizen." Yet it is every bit as chilling as the Bush OLC torture memos in how its clinical, legalistic tone completely sanitizes the radical and dangerous power it purports to authorize.[84]

Greenwald generally expressed irritation at what he perceived as language that euphemizes the powers that are claimed in the memo and downplays the risks that they entail.

Some comparisons between the Department of Justice documents on targeted killing (the redacted opinion by David Barron and the white paper leaked to NBC in 2013) and the torture memos ended up sounding less like criticism and more like diatribe.[85] In a more overt attack against the Obama administration, Andrew C. McCarthy of *National Review* stated:

Holder and Obama used to sneer that Bush/Cheney counterterrorism posed a "false choice" between our security and "our values." Now, they've decided not only that the commander-in-chief's war powers extend beyond "hot battle-fields" to anyplace on the planet the president chooses, but also that the last thing we need is judicial oversight. After all, the white paper declaims, "matters intimately related to foreign policy and national security are rarely proper subjects for judicial intervention" and "turn on standards that defy judicial application."[86]

So one line of political criticism against Obama's drone policy is that it is no better, or is in fact worse, than what President Bush did in the name of the "War on Terror," including enhanced interrogation (or torture).

Other critics have focused on the charge that President Obama has attracted less outcry than would President Bush or another Republican in the same situation. Tina Brown of *Newsweek* said of Obama in 2013: "He'd be impeached by now for drones, if he was George W. Bush."[87] Along the same lines, Joe Scarborough, former U.S. congressman, said on his television show *Morning Joe* on MSNBC that "if George Bush had done this, it would have been stopped."[88] In *Newsmax*, editor of *National Review* Rich Lowry wrote an article titled "Bush Bashers Give Obama Pass on Drones," which stated:

> The left is still furious that the Bush administration waterboarded three captured terrorists after Sept. 11, 2001. Yet, with a few exceptions, it has blithely accepted the Obama administration's extrajudicial assassination policy that has killed about 1,000 times as many people.[89]

While these concerns may certainly have merit, a poll conducted by Pulse Opinion Research on February 7, 2013, and published by *The Hill*, suggested that the general public was not necessarily giving Obama a pass. The survey, which was based on a national survey of one thousand likely voters, found that the majority (52 percent) believed that Obama was "about the same" or worse than Bush in regard to "balancing national security with the protection of civil liberties."[90] Interestingly, while the poll found that Democrats were slightly more favorable to Obama, the party-loyalty effect was relatively muted.[91]

These accounts of the Obama administration preferring killing to capture may not show the entire picture, however, as there is some evidence that the United States under Obama does sometimes elect for detention rather than killing, at least where there is a possibility of acquiring valuable intelligence. In 2009, for example, the leader of al-Qaeda in Somalia, Saleh Ali Nabhan, was a person that the Obama administration placed on a kill list.[92] An anonymous U.S. official stated that the United States gave Kenyan officials intelligence that led to the July capture of Ahmed Abdullahi Hassan, a close associate of Nabhan, rather than targeting him with a drone.[93] Jeremy Scahill reported that Hassan was then captured and transported to a secret prison in Mogadishu, Somalia, where both Somalians and Americans interrogated him.[94] Two months after capturing Hassan, the United States launched a helicopter raid that resulted in the death of Saleh Ali Nabhan.[95] While the CIA may have ceased operating detention facilities and black sites, it apparently did not bar the U.S. intelligence community from visiting secret prisons being run independently of the agency.[96] Moreover, while this is impossible to confirm, it is quite possible that by doing so they obtained intelligence that facilitated the targeting of Nabhan.

Of course, in this last case of the capture (rather than killing) of Hassan, the United States did not have to assume custody of the prisoner, so the political problem of detainment did not arise. But in at least a few other cases, the United States has seized terrorist suspects abroad *and* detained them, including Ahmed Abdulkadir Warsame (an al-Shabaab military commander who also acted as a liason with AQAP), who was picked up off the Somalia coast in April 2011; Nazih Abdul-Hamed Nabih al-Ruqai'i (better known as Abu Anas al-Libi and accused of involvement in the 1998 bombing of U.S. embassies in Africa), who was captured in Tripoli in October 2013; and Ahmed Abu Khattala (a suspected ringleader of the 2012 Benghazi attack), who was taken in a commando raid in Benghazi in June 2014.[97] In each of these cases, the U.S. government eventually moved to prosecute the detainees in federal court, where it has amassed an impressive conviction rate.[98] These cases lend credence to Attorney General Eric Holder's statement that targeted killing operations are "not a function of not trying to take people to Guantanamo."[99] The United States has other means of handling captives. But each of the captives were also interrogated at sea before entering the judicial system, in Warsame's case for two months,[100] and this tends to reinforce the notion that capture is more seriously considered if the suspect is believed to have valuable information (although location was also likely a significant factor, at least in the al-Ruqai'i and Khattala cases). In the words of one former counterterrorism operator, "I am a firm believer in targeted assassinations when they are people who are no longer of value to your [intelligence] collection processes."[101] Dr. Evelyn Farkas, who participated in the oversight for Special Operations Command (SOCOM) from 2001 to 2008 as a staff member of the Senate Armed Services Committee, stated that in this regard, she did not believe the Obama administration's policies were distinct from those in place during the Bush administration.[102]

President Obama appears to agree that kill operations are sometimes the better choice, but at least publicly he offers a very different rationale. He points to the importance of minimizing risk to civilians and U.S. troops. For example, in his May 2013 speech at the National Defense University, Obama stated,

> It's also not possible for America to simply deploy a team of Special Forces to capture every terrorist. Even when such an approach may be possible, there are places where it would pose profound risks to our troops and local civilians— where a terrorist compound cannot be breached without triggering a firefight with surrounding tribal communities, for example, that pose no threat to us; times when putting U.S. boots on the ground may trigger a major international crisis.[103]

Thus, the prospect of pulling bystanders into the conflict, or incurring U.S. casualties, are risks that are often seen to outweigh the value of capturing a suspected militant.

Obama's preference to reduce the risks to U.S. troops and civilian bystanders appears to be similar in larger conflict areas as well. In the more than six months that the United States has participated in conflict against ISIL without a congressional authorization to use military force,[104] Obama made it abundantly clear that no U.S. ground troops would participate. Since at least June 2014, the United States has flown drones, including the Global Hawk and Predator, as well as manned aircraft, such as the U-2 and P-3, over Iraq and Syria.[105] While the Obama administration had committed not to send combat troops into the fray, hundreds of pilots, sensor operators, and analysts are at work behind the scenes.[106] In September 2014, President Obama reiterated his pledge to not use ground troops in the war against the Islamic State, saying, "After a decade of massive ground deployments, it is more effective to use our unique capabilities in support of partners on the ground so they can secure their own countries."[107] However, former secretary of defense Robert Gates disagreed that the United States could defeat the Islamic State with air power alone.[108] Gates stated:

> So there will be boots on the ground if there's to be any hope of success in the strategy. And I think that by continuing to repeat that [he won't send in ground troops], Obama in effect traps himself.[109]

The majority of Americans also felt in September 2014 that Obama was not being tough enough against the Islamic State.[110] Some 57 percent of Americans, including 83 percent of Republicans and 40 percent of Democrats, felt that the president needed to harden his response.[111] While only 12 percent of Republicans felt Obama was "about right" in his toughness, half of all Democrats shared that sentiment in a poll that was released less than two months prior to the midterm elections.[112] While drones and other airstrikes can be used in unpopular conflicts with relatively little domestic political backlash, at least relative to the use of U.S. combat troops, it appears that such tactics may also be viewed as too passive. The administration has accordingly sought to dramatize the impacts of the air campaign on the ground. For example, toward the end of January 2015, Secretary of State John Kerry noted that half of the Islamic State's commanders and thousands of its fighters had been killed in the coalition's efforts, which included over two thousand airstrikes.[113]

Do Drone Strikes Require Additional Oversight?

Increasing the oversight of the drone campaigns has also been an issue of debate for those on both sides of the aisle. Former secretary of defense Robert Gates, who served for both Republican George W. Bush and Democrat Barack Obama, stated in February 2013 that he believed that the rules that the Obama administration was following were rigorous, but expressed the need for oversight to safeguard any abuses by unknown future administrations.[114] Gates mentioned in particular that drone strikes that target American citizens should be devolved from the president to instead be decided by judicial or congressional processes.[115] Gates said that such a transition of decision-making power "would give the American people confidence that there was, in fact, a compelling case."[116]

Some polling suggests that Americans tend to share Secretary Gates's concern that the program should have more oversight. For example, a CBS News/New York Times poll in June 2013 found that 64 percent of Americans were concerned that drone strikes should receive more oversight (while 30 percent were unconcerned).[117] In a somewhat narrower context, a Huffpost/YouGov poll reported in February 2013 that 46 percent of Americans wanted Congress and the president to work together in setting rules for drone strikes, at least against American targets, while another 16 percent felt that Congress should set the rules alone (in other words, 62 percent favored more congressional oversight of the executive).[118]

Agreement on increased oversight, and the form it could take, has proved elusive, however. Chair of the Senate Intelligence Committee Dianne Feinstein stated that she would consider potential measures for oversight of the drone program, in particular by introducing something similar to the Foreign Intelligence Surveillance Act (FISA) Court. Democratic senator Dick

Durbin also endorsed stronger oversight, stating, "We have to strike a new constitutional balance with the challenges we face today."[119]

Republicans, though divided on the issue, appeared generally more resistant to oversight plans. Senator John McCain rejected the need for additional oversight and posited that the program merely needed to be transitioned from the CIA to the Department of Defense.[120] Senator Lindsey Graham went considerably further and stated that a court-based oversight program would be "the biggest intrusion . . . in the history of the country" in regard to executive power.[121] The chairman of the House of Representatives Intelligence Committee, Mike Rogers, a Republican, rejected such oversight by saying that "there is plenty of oversight here," as the committee goes to the CIA every month to review strikes on terrorist leaders, and that he reviews every airstrike as the committee's chairman.[122] Republican Senator Rand Paul, by contrast, questioned the targeting policy at its foundation, regardless of what oversight might be introduced, stating that "the president, a politician, Republican or Democrat, should never get to decide someone's death by flipping through some flashcards."[123]

Although most Republicans were generally opposed to more oversight, in November 2013, the Senate Intelligence Committee reportedly approved a bill that authorized intelligence activities with language added to increase drone strike oversight.[124] The drone-related clauses in the bill included a provision that spy agencies release casualty statistics on the number of people killed in drone attacks,[125] as well as a clause designed to increase the scrutiny of attacks that target U.S. citizens on foreign soil. Thirteen of the fifteen members of the committee voted to approve the bill, with both opponents belonging to the Republican Party.[126] In April 2014, however, the language was removed from the bill at the request of the director of National Intelligence, James Clapper, who disclosed that the Obama administration was voluntarily exploring ways to disclose more information about the drone strikes.[127]

A further attempt at oversight was made by Senator Carl Levin a couple of months before this language was removed from the Intelligence Committee bill. In February 2014, Levin, the chair of the Senate Armed Services Committee, held a joint hearing with the Senate Intelligence Committee, inviting both the CIA and military counterterrorism representatives.[128] However, the White House reportedly did not allow the CIA to attend, effectively keeping the circle of lawmakers briefed on the covert actions at a minimum.[129] This action may provide evidence for a rule of contemporary U.S. politics suggested by Michael Cohen, Fellow at the Century Foundation:

"The executive branch stonewalls or uses legal justification to avoid oversight, and Congress does precious little to demand that its constitutional prerogatives are respected."[130]

Moreover, Congress's weak efforts to institutionalize increased oversight may not be limited to the domain of drone strikes. Kenneth A. Schultz, professor of political science at Stanford University, has argued that Congress tends to shy away from oversight regarding national security more generally due to there being more risk than reward involved.[131] Part of this risk is that there could be another terrorist attack on an American target, in which case those who had sought to reign in the American use of force to preempt such attacks might receive a share of blame. But a broader and more immediate calculation might simply be that it is dangerous to criticize a program that remains consistently popular among Americans, and has been firmly endorsed by the current political leadership as well as the last few presidential nominees from both parties.

III. National Interests and Political Interests

Of course, the same risks associated with security policy that apply to Congress also apply to presidents, except that as commanders in chief, presidents cannot so easily shy away from responsibility, and they will inevitably bear blame for any successful terrorist attacks (especially on the U.S. mainland) during their tenure in office. Moreover, the blame will be worse if they are unable to show that they took adequate preventive measures. There is then a natural incentive for presidents to lean toward extraordinary security measures, especially those that clearly demonstrate their commitment to the safety of the American people while costing and inconveniencing those people as little as possible. From this perspective, the attractions of the drone program seem obvious. As even prominent drone policy critic Audrey Kurth Cronin grudgingly acknowledges, "Drone strikes offer the ideal, poll-tested counterterrorism policy: cheap, apparently effective, and far away."[132] As Kaag and Kreps put it, "The use of drones provides a win-win proposition for the President, who could appear strong on defense without responsibility for body bags coming home, a development that would likely send his political fortunes tumbling."[133]

Moreover, the drone program at the moment appears to have some of the glitter of success, at least where it counts most. The Obama counterterrorism strategy with its strong reliance on drones appears to have effectively protected the American people (as indeed did the Bush strategy after 9/11 that also relied on drones). As Cronin notes, "Since 2001, the number of fatalities from terrorist attacks on American soil has been lower than at any time since 1968."[134] Evidently, luck has also played a part in this (for example, in the failures of the underwear and Times Square bombing plots), but it seems reasonable to think that drone strikes have also contributed.

It is easy, then, to see why President Obama might embrace, and later defend, drone strikes as a key component of his counterterrorism strategy. They seem to align with his political interests. But it may also be that the president's interests here are closely aligned with the national interest. After all, the safety and welfare of the people are one of the essential purposes of government—and indeed some of the great political theorists of government like Thomas Hobbes and John Locke suggest that it is *the primary purpose* of government.[135] The political importance of the public safety is also well reflected, for example, in the preamble to the American Constitution, which enumerates the basic purposes of government, including to "ensure domestic tranquility," "provide for the common defense," and "promote the general welfare."[136] If drone strikes do promote the safety of the public and ensure domestic tranquility, and thereby contribute to the general welfare, and do so at comparatively little cost or inconvenience, then it is difficult to see how they, and by extension President Obama's defense of them, fail to contribute these essential purposes of American government.

Moreover, it is also correspondingly easy to understand why President Obama might, in seeking to address some public qualms about the drone program, also seek to preserve flexibility and a good deal of secrecy around the program. Among other things, maintaining secrecy prevents the targeted groups from exploiting the rules of the drone program to their advantage, and maintaining room to maneuver permits the program to adapt to changing enemy tactics and to pursue greater efficiencies. It may also be that preserving secrecy and flexibility helps to mute criticism of some of the more troublesome aspects of drone strikes (such as civilian casualties, signature strikes, and a possible preference for killing in some circumstances) and to prevent them from further eroding the popularity of the program.

It is not surprising, then, that when some of the Obama administration's responses to criticism are examined, they often can be found to contain subtle equivocations or promises for future reform that are as yet unrealized, or at best partially realized. For example, in his May 2013 speech at the National Defense University, President Obama asserted that in general, drone strikes would only be employed "against terrorists who pose a continuing and imminent threat to the American people, and when there are no other governments capable of effectively addressing the threat."[137] This helped to show that American drone strikes met the core criteria for actions of self-defense (which President Obama also invoked), that the threat is imminent and the actions necessary (as discussed in chapter 3). To many listeners, this sounded reassuring, at least until they read how the Obama administration interpreted imminence in the Office of Legal Counsel White Paper leaked in February 2013:

> By its nature . . . the threat posed by al-Qa'ida and its associated forces demands a broader concept of imminence in judging when a person continually planning terror attacks presents an imminent threat, making the use of force appropriate. In this context, imminence must incorporate considerations of the relevant window of opportunity, the possibility of reducing collateral damage to civilians, and the likelihood of heading off future disastrous attacks on Americans. Thus, a decision maker . . . must take into account . . . that the U.S. government may not be aware of all al Qa'ida plots as they are developing and thus cannot be confident that none is about to occur; and that, in light of these predicates, the nation may have a limited window of opportunity within which to strike in a manner that both has a high likelihood of success and reduces the probability of American casualties.[138]

The American Civil Liberties Union describes the effect of this broadened definition of "imminence" as follows (while also raising questions about President Obama's purported preference for capture):

> The paper initially suggests . . . that the government's authority to use lethal force is limited to people who present "imminent" threats, but it then proceeds to redefine the word imminence in a way that deprives the word of its ordinary meaning. The paper does something similar with the phrase "capture is infeasible." It initially sounds like a real limitation but by page 8 it seems to mean only that the government won't use lethal force if capture is more convenient. It's the language of limits—but without any real restrictions.[139]

Similarly, as noted in chapter 3, Daphne Eviatar roundly rejects the white paper's interpretation of the imminence requirement on the following grounds: "It is impossible to define the 'imminent' threat needed to justify lethal force in self-defense as anything other than a threat of an aggressive action that is 'about to happen.'"[140] At any rate, whether one accepts or rejects the broadened definition of imminence, one thing that seems clear is that while the Obama administration has sought to reassure the public of the legality of its drone program, it has also subtly sought to retain flexibility in the way it employs drone strikes.

Something similar can be said for what many took to be President Obama's commitment to end signature strikes. Again, when he said "we act against terrorists who pose a continuing and imminent threat to the American people," he seemed to indicate that U.S. authorities would have to know a good deal about the specific individual being targeted, meaning that they would be limited to personality strikes, and signature strikes would in future be disallowed.[141] Many listeners heard this as a clear commitment. For example, former counterterrorism czar Richard Clarke responded to the news of the January 15, 2015, signature strike in Pakistan as follows, "President Obama said he was going to stop them [i.e., signature strikes], and clearly he didn't."[142] However, a careful review of President Obama's remarks reveals that he explicitly carved out an exception for the Afghan theater (which likely includes northwest Pakistan): "In the Afghan war theater we must—and will—continue to support our troops until the transition is complete at the end of 2014. And that means we will continue to take strikes against high value al Qaeda targets, but also against forces that are massing to support attacks on coalition forces."[143] And indeed, as reported in the *Washington Post* on April 26, 2015, "Obama Kept Looser Rules for Drones in Pakistan," including permitting signature strikes, albeit on a more limited basis.[144] Having examined government statements on the new rules governing drone strikes, Politifact concluded as follows:

> Obama has never said himself that he would stop signature drone strikes, which killed two western civilian hostages. An unnamed administration official implied that signature strikes would eventually be phased out, though without any details. In any case, the drone program in Pakistan, which killed the hostages, was generally exempt from these rules.[145]

In short, the Obama administration managed to reassure the public, and seems to have curtailed their signature strike policy somewhat in the light of criticism, but at the same time retained flexibility to employ signature strikes when deemed necessary.

Similar observations can also be made in regard to other areas of domestic criticism. In response to concerns about civilian casualties, for example, President Obama appeared to set a very exacting standard: "Before any strike is taken, there must be near-certainty that no civilians will be killed or injured—the highest standard we can set."[146] But it is not entirely clear what "near" certainty entails, and it is clear that civilian casualties have continued in significant numbers (especially in Yemen, including at least twenty-one in 2013 and at least four in 2014—see the chapter 2 case study). This is not to deny or diminish the significant reduction in civilian casualties in recent years, but only to observe that the administration carefully preserved flexibility in its management of the program.

Similarly, while Attorney General Holder gave Senator Paul the answer that he wanted after his first talking filibuster—that is, that the U.S. government would not target a noncombatant American—it appears that this answer only confirmed a U.S. policy already in place since 2010 (according to the Office of Legal Counsel memo on killing an American). Moreover, the constraint is less restrictive than it might first appear, since the executive branch retains the right to determine who is a combatant, at least for purposes of conducting a drone operation.

Again, the president declared in 2013 that "America does not take strikes when we have the ability to capture individual terrorists; our preference is always to detain, interrogate and prosecute."[147] This commitment obviously goes some way to assuage the concerns of those who worry that the Obama administration prefers targeting to capture. But as the president went on to explain, the capture option depends on feasibility, and there are many issues at stake here (like risk to U.S. service personnel, risk to local civilians, sensitivities of the states in which operations would occur), and it is he and his administration who retain the right to determine feasibility.

Finally, in relation to oversight, in his May 2013 speech the president made the following announcement: "Going forward, I've asked my administration to review proposals to extend oversight of lethal actions outside of warzones that go beyond our reporting to Congress. Each option has virtues in theory, but poses difficulties in practice."[148] He mentioned in particular the possibility of establishing an independent drone court, or possibly an independent oversight board within the executive branch. He finished by saying, "I look forward to actively engaging Congress to explore these and other options for increased oversight."[149] He also talked about repealing the AUMF and shifting away from a military response to terrorism. All of this was clearly calculated to reassure those who worried that the drone strikes were permitting the administration to conduct a war without any of the traditional democratic checks and balances. But like the planned shift of drone strikes from the CIA to the Pentagon discussed in March 2013, no actual progress appears to have been made.

In relation to each of the six major points of domestic criticism, the Obama administration's consistent response has been to address the concern, to provide some reassurance, and in several cases some adjustment to the program, all while retaining flexibility and revealing relatively little. In this way, the Obama administration has preserved public support for a program that is relatively low cost and low risk, and permits the administration to seem relatively active and aggressive in protecting the American people. In one sense, these reservations and deferrals are obviously in the president's interest, because they allow him more control of the program, with less intrusive oversight. However, it might at least in principle also contribute to the national interest if the impact is to improve the efficacy of the program, and thus better protect the American people.

As shown in chapter 2, however, many critics are skeptical of the long-term efficacy of the U.S. drone policy, at least in the way that President Obama has run it. In effect, they suggest that there may be a tendency for the president to favor his own short-term political interests and to ignore long-term costs (that will only manifest once he has left office). In effect, there is at least a potential divergence between the interests of the political leadership, which will tend to focus on relatively short-term security issues ("that the country be kept completely untouched on [his] watch",[150]) and the national interests of the American people in improved security over the long term. Cronin, for example, argues that over the long term, by attacking

> an amorphous and geographically dispersed foe, one with an increasingly marginal connection to the original 9/11 plotters. . . . The United States risks multiplying its enemies and heightening their incentives to attack the country.[151]

In addition to generating a future security threat, the authors of the *Living Under Drones* report argue that the United States is diminishing its standing in the world and undermining its relationships with allies:

> As with other unpopular American foreign policy engagements, including the invasion of Iraq and the practice of torture at Abu Ghraib and elsewhere, drone strikes weaken the standing of the US in the world, straining its relationships with allies, and making it more difficult for it to build multilateral alliances to tackle pressing global challenges.[152]

Moreover, the excessive current reliance on drones may also create serious difficulties for future U.S. foreign policy and global stability:

> With the boundaries for drone strikes in Pakistan, Somalia, and Yemen still unclear, the United States risks encouraging competitors such as China, Iran, and Russia to label their own enemies as terrorists and go after them across borders.[153]

Laurie Blank worries that if other countries follow the precedent that America is setting today, then "the established framework for the protection of the right to life would begin to unravel."[154] Yet these longer-term concerns need not be of paramount political interest to a political leader primarily focused on assuring American security during his term of office.

Legacy Issues

Fortunately, there are at least some reasons for thinking that the Obama administration may become more receptive, as its members reach the end of their time in office, to the kinds of long-term security considerations Cronin and other critics emphasize. After all, it is widely reported that President Obama's decision to establish a rule book constraining (even loosely) the use of drone strikes was driven by a simple truth: "It was an election year. And Mr. Obama might lose."[155] In the words of the *New York Times*'s Peter Baker, "For nearly four years, the president had waged a relentless war from the skies against Al Qaeda and its allies, and he trusted that he had found what he considered a reasonable balance even if his critics did not see it that way. But now, he told his aides, he wanted to institutionalize what in effect had been an ad hoc war, effectively shaping the parameters for years to come 'whether he was re-elected or somebody else became President.' "[156]

President Obama apparently did not want his legacy to include an ad hoc killing program that some future president might abuse. The prospect of retirement arguably diminished his self-interest in the secrecy and flexibility of the program (as his watch over Americans' safety was coming to an end), and increased his sensitivity to what others in the future might think of his policy and whether it genuinely contributed to long-term security. President Obama did of course win reelection in 2012, and did still move forward with codifying his presidential policy guidance on the use of drones and signing it on May 22, 2013.[157] However, the more than three years that then remained on his mandate may help to explain the caveats and temporary carve-outs that appeared, as well as the seemingly slow implementation of reform. Nonetheless, as he approaches the end of his second term, he may again have an eye on history, the future trajectory of the drone program, and popular perceptions of it both at home and also abroad.

At home, while public support has eroded slightly, as noted above, it nevertheless remains fairly robust. However, President Obama's announcement on April 23, 2015, that a drone strike had killed two Western hostages of al-Qaeda, and the simultaneous announcement that two more Americans had been unintentionally killed in drone strikes, provoked new rounds of criticism and debate over the program. These announcements also precipitated a commitment from the president to a full review to identify any changes necessary to prevent a repetition of similar errors: "We will do our utmost," he promised, "to ensure it is not repeated."[158] This presents a propitious opportunity to tighten the guidelines and rules governing the program and to follow up these announcements, and the accompanying apology, with more transparency and accountability.

Global Public Opinion on Drones

President Obama, however, appears to face a challenging prospect in regard to burnishing his legacy in countries around the globe, at least when it comes to drones. Drone strikes are generally unpopular outside of the United States with a few isolated exceptions, and they are deeply unpopular in many places—see table 5.4. Nevertheless, recent analysis has raised the possibility that the global opinion of drones may be considerably more nuanced than initially suggested by these polls.[159]

The most prominent international polls concerning drone strikes to date were completed by Pew Research's Global Attitudes Project. Pew's Spring 2014 report showed only three of forty-four countries surveyed had a majority of respondents who approved of the U.S. drone strike policy. Of these three countries, Israel had the highest favorability with 65 percent approving of the program, followed by Kenya with 53 percent, and the United States with 52 percent. The report also showed a plurality favoring drone strikes in Nigeria (with 42 percent approving and 39 percent disapproving). However, in thirty-seven of the forty-four countries surveyed, the majority of respondents disapproved of the drone strikes, with Venezuela and Jordan leading the way with 90 percent disapproval or more.[160] Based on these numbers alone, it would appear that only some U.S. allies with recent experience of terrorism showed popular support for the current U.S. use of drones.

However, some commentators have argued that it is a mistake to read too much into these global polls. For example, in January 2013, C. Christine Fair, Karl C. Kaltenthaler, and William J. Miller wrote an article in *The Atlantic* that questioned how well informed of the drone campaigns the respondents to these polls were.[161] A close look at the 2010 survey data, for example, showed that only 35 percent of Pakistanis surveyed answered that they knew "a lot" or "a little" about the drone strikes, compared to 43 percent who stated that they possessed no knowledge of the campaigns (and 21 percent who refused to answer). Follow-up questions about attitudes to drone strikes were asked only of the 35 percent professing to know "a lot" or "a little" about the drone strikes, although "most of the drone-critical commentary based upon these 2010 data does not acknowledge that conclusions are being drawn from a *minority* of all respondents."[162] While the 2012 Pew data showed an increase in Pakistanis who stated that they knew about the drone campaigns, it was clear that this knowledge was not highly developed, as 41 percent of those who said they were informed believed that the strikes in their country were being carried out without their government's permission.[163]

TABLE 5.4
Global Public Attitudes to U.S. Drone Strikes by Country in Spring 2014[1]

Countries	*Approve*	*Disapprove*
Argentina	5	87
Bangladesh	22	70
Brazil	7	87
Chile	15	68
China	35	52
Colombia	9	86
Egypt	4	87
El Salvador	11	73
France	27	72
Germany	30	67
Ghana	29	47
Greece	8	89
India	28	36
Indonesia	10	74
Israel	65	27
Italy	18	74
Japan	12	82
Jordan	5	90
Kenya	53	38
Lebanon	23	71
Malaysia	6	80
Mexico	14	80
Nicaragua	9	88
Nigeria	42	39
Pakistan	3	66
Palestine Territory	7	84
Peru	10	81
Philippines	24	67
Poland	32	54
Russia	7	78
Senegal	11	86
South Africa	27	46
South Korea	23	75
Spain	12	86
Tanzania	27	67
Thailand	12	79
Tunisia	17	77
Turkey	7	83
Uganda	36	56
United Kingdom	33	59
Ukraine	11	66
United States	52	41
Venezuela	4	92
Vietnam	12	78

1. "Global Opposition to U.S. Surveillance and Drones, But Limited Harm to America's Image."

Antidrone Demonstrations

Still, whatever the limits of the aforementioned Pew data, demonstrations in Pakistan have shown that antidrone sentiment is large enough to cause problems for the United States. The most widely known antidrone protest in Pakistan was launched on Saturday, November 23, 2013.[164] The protest was led by Imran Khan and consisted of over ten thousand demonstrators who gathered to stop NATO trucks moving through the city of Peshawar.[165] During the first day of the protest, Khan said, "There can be no peace unless drones are stopped."[166] Fueled by the killing of Pakistani Taliban leader Hakimullah Mehsud weeks before, Khan and others argued that Mehsud's killing threatened peace negotiations between the Pakistani Taliban and the Pakistani government.[167] On Sunday, November 24, 2013, protesters, some of whom were wielding "wooden batons," stopped trucks and "roughed up" NATO drivers.[168] While Pakistani police were present on Sunday, they were reported to have begun intervening only on Monday to stop protesters from obstructing the supply route.[169] Even with police intervention, many transportation companies did not resume normal business.[170] On Tuesday, February 25, 2014, the Peshawar High Court ordered an end to the truck "inspections," stating that they were against the law.[171]

Protests of drone strikes also sprang up in conflict-ridden Yemen in late 2013, following a wave of U.S. drone attacks. The protests began in August 2013 and spanned multiple Yemeni cities, including its capital, Sana'a.[172] In November 2013, a Yemeni street artist, Murad Subay, spray-painted "antidrone poetry" in Sana'a.[173] Subay stated, "Graffiti in Yemen, or street art, is a new device to communicate with the people." According to *Time*, one of his images was of a drone with the words "Why did you kill my family?" in both Arabic and English underneath it.[174] Further protests against U.S. strikes in Yemen occurred after a December drone strike in the province of Bayda that targeted a wedding ceremony, killing mostly civilians.[175] Those protesting after this attack stopped traffic on main roads and demanded that the United States end drone attacks in the country.[176]

Protests of drone strikes have not been limited to the countries where strikes have occurred, however. There have also been multiple protests against drone strikes in the United Kingdom (where the 2014 Pew Global Attitudes Survey recorded 59 percent disapproval of U.S. drone strikes to 33 percent approval).[177] On Saturday, April 27, 2013, around four hundred protesters marched toward RAF Waddington to protest drone pilots flying missions within Britain.[178] RAF Waddington houses the control center for the UK's international drone missions.[179] In early June 2013, a few weeks after the protest, six individuals were arrested at RAF Waddington for allegedly committing criminal damage.[180] At their trial in October 2013, the six people, including two priests, pleaded not guilty, reasoning that they were preventing worse crimes in Afghanistan. The individuals were found guilty and were sentenced to six months of probation and a fine.[181] Many observers were critical of the sentence, arguing that the judge presiding over the case was too lenient, citing in particular the judge pronouncing that he was delivering his ruling "with a very heavy heart."[182]

Later in the year, in September 2013, over one hundred protesters demonstrated against a drone testing site in Aberporth, Wales. John Cox, the chairman of the group leading the protest, Campaign for Nuclear Disarmament Cymru (Welsh for Wales), stated, "We're trying to raise awareness that Wales is part of the war machine."[183] These protests have continued. In early January 2015, four more people were arrested at RAF Waddington after they entered the base by cutting through a portion of the fence.[184] The protesters called their makeshift entrance a "New Year gateway for peace."[185] It is unclear, however, how responsive governments are to either popular opposition or protests against drones, and it is ultimately governments that form national policy on drones.

Opinions of Foreign Governments and UN Officials

The opinions of foreign governments seem to be spread across a wide spectrum, with some, such as Iraq, requesting drones to patrol their skies[186] and others, like Venezuela, denouncing U.S. unmanned operations.[187] The Pakistani government itself has simultaneously represented two opposed views. It has publicly condemned[188] the drone strikes on its territory while secretly consenting to them.[189] In September 2012, President Hadi of Yemen extolled the U.S. use of drones, as described in chapter 2.[190] In January 2015, however, Hadi and the rest of his government abruptly resigned from their positions amid growing strength of the Iranian-backed Houthi uprising, which managed to capture the capital.[191] The United States nonetheless resumed its drone campaign in Yemen before the end of January 2015, with U.S. officials claiming that the Houthis were turning a blind eye to the attacks.[192]

Some Western governments are also thought to have quietly cooperated with the U.S. drone program. Germany, for example, is reported to have supplied intelligence and general support to the United States, but appears to be coming under increasing pressure to end cooperation. In 2013, it was reported that the German intelligence agency, the BND, was sending large amounts of metadata to the NSA each month.[193] In August of that year, it was suggested that the data given to the NSA may have led to a 2010 drone strike in Pakistan that killed a German citizen.[194] The BND denied that the phone data sent to the NSA could have been used in drone strikes, however, as it did not provide precise locations.[195] This has not convinced everyone though, with German politician Steffen Bockhahn stating, "You can't control [other intelligence agencies] if they take the information and use it with their own intelligence . . . and then use drones."[196] Drones can be equipped with IMSI catchers, which can intercept phone signals.[197] Michael Hayden has reportedly stated, "We kill people based on metadata," lending credence to the idea that the phone data could be facilitating attacks.[198]

In addition to providing data to U.S. intelligence agencies, Germany has come under fire from both the European Parliament and a private individual for allowing infrastructure for the drone campaigns to operate in its territory. In October 2014, it was reported that a Yemeni man was suing Germany for being complicit in a drone strike that killed two of his relatives.[199] He argues that Germany's Ramstein airbase is an integral part of the drone campaign in his country.[200] The airbase is the point where drone imagery is received by satellites and transformed into data carried by fiber optic cables to the pilots in the United States.[201] This exposure is embarrassing for the German government because drones appear to be unpopular at home (Pew reported 67 percent disapproval in 2014) in the European public and in the EU governing body itself. In February 2014, the European Parliament voted 534 to 49 to support a resolution calling for European Union Member States to "not perpetrate unlawful targeted killings or facilitate such killings by other states."[202] This measure seemed aimed in particular at Germany and the UK, who are believed to have supported the U.S. program, but have cited national security to justify remaining tight-lipped about their involvement.[203]

United Nations officials have also entered the global drone debate, calling for more transparency, while stating that drone operations are not necessarily illegal.[204] The UN's discussion around drones has been generally negative, but not usually outright condemnatory. Christof Heyns delivered a report to the UN in October 2013 that was critical of drone strikes.[205] Later in the month, Heyns used this report as the basis for the opinions he articulated to a plenary meeting of the UN General Assembly.[206] Heyns argued that drones, while not intrinsically illegal, would be an issue for the international community largely because they can be sent across international borders covertly.[207] Ben Emmerson also addressed the forum. Emmerson discussed an ongoing investigation that had placed the spotlight on thirty-three drone strikes that are believed to have caused civilian casualties.[208] Emmerson went on to state that the lack of transparency was the biggest roadblock to the evaluation of civilian deaths.[209] The United State defended its use of drones as "necessary, legal and just" at the plenary meeting, but a group of nations, including China, Brazil, and Venezuela, were critical, with Venezuela taking the most acerbic tone.[210]

Hopeful Signs for Obama?

Evidently, most indications of global political attitudes sampled above show wide disapproval of U.S. drone strikes. All of this is bound to be discouraging to President Obama and his senior officials in regard to vindicating this aspect of their policy to a global audience. There are, however, two recent countervailing data points that may provide a modicum of encouragement in regard to winning some support.

The first and more important of these two points involves a recent study of public attitudes in Pakistan, where the great majority of American drone strikes have occurred. A May 3, 2015, article in the *Washington Post* describes a kind of sea change in popular Pakistani opinion about the United States driven by a reported reassessment of drone strikes:

> A Pew Research Center poll released in August showed a significant decline in the percentage of Pakistanis who held negative views of the United States—still a majority at 59 percent, but down from 80 percent two years earlier.[211]

Moreover, these changing views are reportedly being driven by a reevaluation of U.S. drone strikes:

> Observers say the change is being driven by a Pakistani middle class that is now more supportive of American drone strikes—which have declined precipitously in recent years—particularly since a school massacre by the Taliban that killed about 150 students and teachers in December. And as conflict spreads in the Middle East, there is a growing recognition in Pakistan that sectarian violence in Muslim countries isn't all driven by the United States. The Obama administration's efforts to quietly rebuild relationships here are starting to have an effect, analysts say.[212]

As noted in chapter 2, there has long been evidence of a substantial constituency in favor of drone strikes in the FATA, where U.S. strikes have generally taken place, in spite of the obvious dangers of expressing such views. Now that attitude seems to be taking root in other parts of the country. At any rate, if the reports are accurate, they suggest the possibility at least of shifting common views about U.S. drones in one of the most politically sensitive populations around the globe.

One final factor that may impact attitudes to U.S. drone strikes abroad is the widespread approval of U.S. airstrikes against ISIL, which of course include drone strikes. The Pew Research Spring 2015 Global Attitudes Survey based on data from thirty-nine countries showed 62 percent support for U.S. military action against ISIL, with only 24 percent opposed.[213] Moreover, this support came in spite of reports of the Obama administration loosening its targeting rules in Syria and Iraq. As investigative journalist Michael Isikoff reported on *Yahoo News* on September 30, 2014:

> The White House has acknowledged for the first time that strict standards President Obama imposed last year to prevent civilian deaths from U.S. drone strikes will not apply to U.S. military operations in Syria and Iraq. . . .
>
> [National Security Council Spokesperson Caitlin] Hayden said that a much-publicized White House policy that President Obama announced last year barring U.S. drone strikes unless there is a "near certainty" there will be no civilian casualties—"the highest standard we can meet," he said at the time—does not cover the current U.S. airstrikes in Syria and Iraq.
>
> The "near certainty" standard was intended to apply "only when we take direct action 'outside areas of active hostilities,' as we noted at the time," Hayden said in an email. "That description—outside areas of active hostilities—simply does not fit what we are seeing on the ground in Iraq and Syria right now."[214]

The impact of attitudes to striking ISIL has yet to clearly manifest in regard to drone strikes elsewhere, but it is at least possible that supporting drone strikes against ISIL will incline some to be more tolerant of strikes against al-Qaeda, AQAP, the TTP, and/or al-Shabaab.

Whether President Obama and his administration will be motivated by the impending end of his presidency, and the possible opportunities described above, to try to reform U.S. drone policy to consolidate domestic support and to try to build greater political support abroad remains to be seen. Reports of renewed administration efforts to shift the authority to oversee drone strikes from the CIA to the military are suggestive of a reform agenda, but such efforts have proven short-lived in the past.[215] One thing that is clear is that international criticism of the program has grown sharply since 2008, and critics have become increasingly outspoken in some international forums. As yet, many states remain reserved, or even quietly cooperative with the U.S. program, but if opposition continues to grow as it has over the last seven years, it could present an increasingly significant challenge to U.S. drone policy.

Conclusion

This chapter has explored some of the political interests and calculations that may be shaping the character and evolution of the U.S. drone program. The first and most basic finding is that there is a fairly firm political foundation for the program: It retains the support of a majority of Americans (and on most polls a large majority), including members of both major parties. There was also a consensus among presidential contenders in the last three campaigns, and most (although not all) political leaders appear to agree. There is also a strong incentive for political leaders to present themselves as strong on defense, especially where that presents little risk to U.S. service persons and can be achieved at relatively low cost, and drones offer a means of reconciling these considerations. Americans are not, however, without some serious concerns about drones. The chapter explored six major areas of criticism and showed that, in each case, the Obama administration has sought to address the concern and reassure the public, albeit while seeking to maintain secrecy and flexibility around the program. Finally, this chapter has suggested that legacy considerations have helped to prompt the Obama administration toward reform of the drone program, and could potentially do so again as the president reaches the end of his second term. Finally, it notes that while most of the world remains hostile, and in many cases very hostile, to the U.S. drone campaigns, some space for reevaluation has reportedly opened up among some politically sensitive populations.

Case Study: Additional Polls on Attitudes to Drones

A number of polls on attitudes to drones have been discussed in the main body of this chapter, primarily concerning general domestic attitudes to drone strikes and some specific areas of criticism and concern about the program. Toward the end of the chapter, some polls breaking out public attitudes to U.S. drone strikes by country were also introduced. This case study is devoted to briefly introducing and discussing several other polls that have reported interesting or illuminating findings regarding attitudes toward drones, including whether the location of a strike, or the gender of the

TABLE 5.5
Drone Strikes in the United States against Non-U.S. citizens

Date	Agency	Positive	Negative	Other	Sample Size
March 2013	Fox News[1]	56%	40%	4%	1,010
March 2013	YouTube/Huffington Post[2]	33%	47%	20%	1,000
March 2013	Gallup[3]	25%	66%	9%	518

1. Anderson Robbins Research and Shaw & Company Research, Fox News Poll.
2. Omnibus Poll.
3. Brown and Newport, "In U.S., 65% Support Drone Attacks on Terrorists Abroad."

respondent, or the respondent's level of knowledge about the drone campaigns seem to correlate with favorable or unfavorable opinions.

The Importance of Location

Whether a drone strike occurs inside or outside of U.S. borders appears to play an important role in Americans' attitudes to it. A *Fox News* poll released in March 2013 asked whether respondents approved or disapproved of a series of scenarios related to killing U.S. citizens with drones. When asked about killing an American who was a suspected terrorist and in a foreign country, 60 percent of respondents approved and 36 percent disapproved (see table 5.2).[216] These numbers suggest that a moderate majority of Americans, at least at that time, appeared to support cases such as the drone strike that killed American citizen Anwar al-Awlaki of AQAP in Yemen in September 2011.

Support for drone strikes waned, however, when the location shifted from foreign lands to the United States and strikes were described as directed against non-Americans. As indicated in table 5.5, a majority of polls in March 2013 found Americans generally opposed to such drone strikes, with the *Fox News* poll standing out as the sole exception (although the 56 percent who expressed approval already reflected a 4 percent drop from those supporting strikes against Americans overseas).

Yet even respondents to the *Fox News* poll turned mostly negative when asked about killing a U.S. citizen suspected of being a terrorist while on U.S. soil (see table 5.6), with 50 percent disapproving and only 45 percent approving.[217] This indicates that a quarter of those who supported strikes against Americans overseas (i.e., 60 percent of respondents on the same poll) feel differently when the suspected American terrorist was on U.S. soil.[218] While the reasons behind this drop were not provided in the poll, it may have to do with the perceived rule of law in the United States, or reluctance to see the United States as part of the territory of armed conflict (although if the United States is in fact in an armed conflict with al-Qaeda it is hard to see how U.S. territory could be exempted from the conflict), or a feeling that drone strikes in the United States are simply too close to home. As table 5.6 shows, the Gallup poll the same month as the *Fox News* poll reported even less support for killing an American on American soil, with 79 percent negative responses as compared to only 13 percent positive.[219]

Gender, Age, and Race Differences on Drone Strikes

Some polls have also suggested that certain types of respondents tend to exhibit more or less favorable attitudes to drone strikes. For example, several

TABLE 5.6
Drone Strikes in U.S. against U.S. Citizens

Date	Agency	Positive	Negative	Other	Sample Size
March 2013	Fox News[1]	45%	50%	5%	1,010
March 2013	Gallup[2]	13%	79%	7%	518

1. Anderson Robbins Research and Shaw & Company Research, Fox News Poll.
2. Brown and Newport, "In U.S., 65% Support Drone Attacks on Terrorists Abroad."

polls have indicated that women tend to be less favorable toward U.S. drone strikes than men. One such poll, conducted by Pew Research Center in July 2013, demonstrated that in each of twelve countries surveyed, women were less approving of the drone campaigns than men (see table 5.7). While a difference between the sexes in attitudes to the use of military force has long been observed, Pew reported that the statistics on drone strikes showed an "unusually large" difference in opinion between genders.[220]

Japan was noted as the country with the largest gender gap, with 41 percent of men and just 10 percent of women approving of drone strikes.[221] A

TABLE 5.7
Gender Gap In Approval of Drone Strikes (Pew Research Center, July 2013)[1]

	Total Approval	Male	Female
Japan	25%	41%	10%
Czech Republic	32%	47%	17%
Canada	43%	57%	28%
Australia	44%	58%	30%
Germany	45%	58%	33%
Spain	21%	34%	9%
Britain	39%	51%	27%
Poland	35%	45%	26%
United States	61%	70%	53%
France	45%	52%	38%
South Korea	31%	38%	24%
Uganda	43%	49%	36%

1. Stokes, "Big Gender Gap in Global Public Opinion about Use of Drones."

smaller albeit still substantial gap was also reported in the United States, with 70 percent of men and 53 percent of women approving of the attacks.[222] The survey also showed double-digit gender gaps in six of the eight European Union countries that were surveyed.[223] On average, across the twelve countries surveyed, the gender gap was 22 percent, with 28 percent of women approving U.S. drone strikes and 50 percent of men.[224]

A striking result of this gender breakdown is that even in countries where more respondents disapprove than approve of U.S. drone strikes, a clear majority of men are often in favor. For example, in Canada, Australia, and Germany, 57 or 58 percent of men approve the strikes, although the overall percentage approving is at 45 percent or below (the explanation being that 33 percent or less of women approve of the strikes).

In May 2015, a poll by Pew showed a similar seventeen-percentage point gap in the United States, with 67 percent of men and 50 percent of women approving of the use of drone strikes.[225] The same poll also found that among Americans the age cohort from eighteen to twenty-nine was the least likely to approve U.S. drone strikes. Indeed, a plurality of respondents in this cohort (50 percent) disapproved, while 48 percent approved and the remainder didn't know. Levels of approval rose sharply (to 58 percent) in the thirty to forty-nine cohort (versus 34 percent disapproval), and peaked in the fifty to sixty-four cohort (at 67 percent approval to 28 percent disapproval). The approval remained relatively high for those over sixty-five (at 60 percent approval to 28 percent disapproval).[226] So this poll at least strongly suggests that the young (eighteen to twenty-four years of age) are, like women, less likely to approve U.S. drone strikes.

The May 2015 Pew poll also broke out American attitudes on "U.S. drone strikes to target extremists" by racial and ethnic group. Specifically, it reported that "white" respondents were the most supportive (with 66 percent approving to 28 percent disapproving), followed by "black" respondents (at 46 percent approval and 41 percent disapproval). Hispanics, by contrast, actually tended on balance to disapprove of the policy (with 39 percent approval to 54 percent disapproval).[227]

Those with More Education or Who Are Following the Campaigns Are More Supportive

Two other characteristics of respondents that have been reported as correlating with approval of U.S. drone strikes are level of education and the degree to which respondents report that they are following the drone campaigns. For example, the May 2015 Pew poll reports that college graduates supported the strikes by a wide margin of 39 percent (66 percent approving, 27 percent disapproving).[228] Those with some college exhibited slightly less support, with only a 32 percent margin favoring drone strikes (64 percent approval to 32 percent disapproval).[229] Finally, those with only a high school education or less supported drone strikes by a significantly narrower margin of 7 percent (49 percent approval to 42 percent disapproval).[230]

There is also some evidence that levels of support for U.S. drone strikes vary along with the level of attention that respondents are devoting to the campaigns. The Gallup poll published in March 2013, for example, showed that individuals who followed the U.S. use of drones very/somewhat closely supported their use more than those who claimed less knowledge. When asked about whether the United States should launch drone strikes against suspected terrorists in foreign countries, 74 percent of those who claimed to follow the campaigns closely and 58 percent of those who did not follow it closely or at all approved of the statement.[231] Similarly, when asked whether the United States should target U.S. citizens who are suspected terrorists while in the United States, 16 percent of those who claimed knowledge about the campaigns and 11 percent of those who did not follow it closely or at all approved of this statement.[232]

After Terrorist Attacks

Dr. Jennifer Merolla, associate professor at Claremont Graduate University's Department of Politics and Policy, along with Kirstin Fisk, Jennifer Ramos, and Elizabeth Zechmeister conducted research to discover whether the threat of a terrorist attack impacted the American public's approval rating of drone strikes. This study was conducted by giving respondents a news story to read before taking a poll on their feelings about drone strikes. At random, respondents were either given a news article on a terrorist threat or on the economy. The results of the research presented a "modest" but statistically significant difference between the two groups, with those reading about the terrorist threat approving of drone strikes more than the group who read about the economy.[233]

Observations on the Polls

A couple of general observations are possible in light of the foregoing data. First and most generally, the poll data presented in this case study (and indeed in the entire chapter) demonstrates that claims of both advocates and detractors of the drone campaigns are often exaggerated or oversimplified. While the data indeed suggests that drone strikes are more popular in the United States than internationally, this and other commonly recited points are more nuanced than is commonly suggested. For example, support in the United States is not as robust as its advocates claim, and certainly not among women, the young, and minorities, and the attitudes abroad are not as uniformly condemnatory as often suggested by critics, especially among men. Also, levels of support for drone strikes, especially in the United States, depend very much on the context in which the strike occurs and the details of the target. Americans do not, for example, appear to support targeting in the United States, and particularly not against American citizens. Finally, while there appears to have been a downward trend in U.S. support of drone strikes, the drop in approval was probably much less intense than popularly held.

Second, it is possible to combine the results reported in the case study (assuming that all are accurate and stable) to sketch a picture of the Americans most likely to approve of U.S. drone strikes. They are older white men (fifty to sixty-four years of age) who have graduated from a university and are following the campaigns closely, especially when there have been recent reports of terrorist threats. They are especially likely to support drone strikes outside of the United States and against non-Americans.

Finally, the survey results reported here provide some interesting possible insight into why Congress has not been more resistant to the drone program. In short, most congressmen have much in common with the profile of the drone supporter. In the first place, most members of Congress are men (433 men to 108 women).[234] Also, most members of Congress are white (439 whites, 48 blacks, 38 Hispanics),[235] and the vast majority of members of Congress hold university degrees. Nobody in Congress is under thirty, and a great many are in the fifty-to-sixty-four age group (or the only slightly less supportive group of those sixty-five and over).[236] It also seems likely that the average member of Congress is better informed about the drone program than the average citizen, and more aware of terrorist threats against the United States. In every category discussed above, then, the membership of Congress mirrors the groups who tend to be more favorable to drone strikes.

Notes

1. Micah Zenko and Sarah Kreps, "Limiting Armed Drone Proliferation," *Council on Foreign Relations Special Report* no. 69 (New York: Council on Foreign Relations, 2014), 9, http://i.cfr.org/content/publications/attachments/Limiting_Armed_Drone_Proliferation_CSR69.pdf.

2. Audrey Kurth Cronin, "Is This How to Win the 'War on Terrorism?'" *Lawfare*, September 14, 2014, accessed June 15, 2015, http://www.lawfareblog.com/foreign-policy-essay-how-win-war-terrorism.

3. John Kaag and Sarah Kreps, *Drone Warfare* (Cambridge: Polity Press, 2014), 66–68.

4. Kaag and Kreps, *Drone Warfare*, 66.

5. "Voter Turnout," *Fair Vote*, accessed January 18, 2015, http://www.fairvote .org/research-and-analysis/voter-turnout/.

6. Kenneth Anderson, *Targeted Killing in U.S. Counterterrorism Strategy and Law* (Washington and Palo Alto: Brookings Institution, Georgetown University Law Center, and the Hoover Institution, 2009), 2, http://www.brookings.edu/~/media/ research/files/papers/2009/5/11%20counterterrorism%20anderson/0511_counter terrorism_anderson.pdf.

7. Mary Bruce, "Obama Fires Back at GOP Appeasement Charge: 'Ask Osama Bin Laden,'" *ABC News*, December 8, 2011, accessed June 18, 2014, http://abcnews .go.com/blogs/politics/2011/12/obama-fires-back-at-gop-appeasement-charge-ask -osama-bin-laden/.

8. Craig Whitlock, "Romney Endorses Obama on Drones," *Washington Post*, November 22, 2012, accessed June 18, 2014, http://www.washingtonpost.com/blogs/ election-2012/wp/2012/10/22/romney-endorses-obama-on-drones/.

9. Steve Coll, "The Unblinking Stare: The Drone War in Pakistan," *New Yorker*, November 24, 2014, accessed August 24, 2015, http://www.newyorker.com/maga zine/2014/11/24/unblinking-stare; "Transcript of the First Presidential Debate," October 14, 2008, accessed August 24, 2015, http://www.cnn.com/2008/POLITICS/ 09/26/debate.mississippi.transcript/.

10. Ward Thomas, "The New Age of Assassination," *SAIS Review* 25, no. 1 (2005): 35.

11. Micah Zenko, "Reforming US Drone Strike Policies," *Council on Foreign Relations Special Report* 65 (New York: Council on Foreign Relations, 2013), 23.

12. Washington Post-ABC News Poll.

13. Pew Research Center, "Continued Support for U.S. Drone Strikes."

14. PublicMind, *Public Says It's Illegal to Target Americans Abroad as Some Question CIA Drone Attacks*; Alyssa Brown and Frank Newport, Gallup poll, "In U.S., 65% Support Drone Attacks on Terrorists Abroad."

15. Brown and Newport, "In U.S., 65% Support Drone Attacks on Terrorists Abroad."

16. PublicMind, *Public Says It's Illegal to Target Americans Abroad*.

17. PublicMind, *Public Says It's Illegal to Target Americans Abroad*.

18. PublicMind, *Public Says It's Illegal to Target Americans Abroad*.

19. PublicMind, *Public Says It's Illegal to Target Americans Abroad*.

20. PublicMind, *Public Says It's Illegal to Target Americans Abroad*.

21. PublicMind, *Public Says It's Illegal to Target Americans Abroad*.

22. Brown and Newport, "In U.S., 65% Support Drone Attacks on Terrorists Abroad."

23. Pew Research Center, "Public Continues to Back U.S. Drone Attacks."

24. Chris Cillizza, "The American Public Loves Drones," *Washington Post*, February 6, 2013, accessed June 14, 2015, http://www.washingtonpost.com/blogs/the-fix/ wp/2013/02/06/the-american-public-loves-drones/.

25. Cillizza, "The American Public Loves Drones."

26. "Text of: To prohibit the extrajudicial killing of United States citizens, and for other purposes," HR 6010, 111th Cong., Second Session, 2010, https://www.govtrack.us/congress/bills/111/hr6010/text.

27. "US Warned about Sending Troops to Pakistan," *Dawn*, September 14, 2008, accessed July 16, 2015, http://www.dawn.com/news/321160/us-warned-against-sending-troops-to-pakistan-congressman-terms-bush.

28. Brendan Gogarty and Meredith Hagger, "The Law of Man over Vehicles Unmanned: The Legal Response to Robotic Revolution on Sea, Land and Air," *Journal of Law, Information and Science* 19 (2008): 95.

29. Jeh C. Johnson, "National Security Law, Lawyers and Lawyering in the Obama Administration," speech, Yale Law School, New Haven, Connecticut, February 22, 2012, http://www.cfr.org/defense-and-security/jeh-johnsons-speech-national-security-law-lawyers-lawyering-obama-administration/p27448; Jeh C. Johnson, "A 'Drone Court': Some Pros and Cons," speech, Fordham Law School, New York, March 18, 2013, http://centeronnationalsecurity.org/sites/default/files/Jeh%20Johnson%20Speech%20at%20Fordham%20LS.pdf.

30. John O. Brennan, "The Efficacy and Ethics of U.S. Counterterrorism Strategy," speech, Woodrow Wilson International Center for Scholars, Washington, DC, April 30, 2012, http://www.wilsoncenter.org/event/the-efficacy-and-ethics-us-counterterrorism-strategy.

31. Barack Obama, "Remarks by the President at the National Defense University," speech, National Defense University, Fort McNair, Washington, DC, May 23, 2013, https://www.whitehouse.gov/the-press-office/2013/05/23/remarks-president-national-defense-university.

32. Charlie Savage, "Justice Department Memo Approving Targeted Killing of Anwar Al-Awlaki," *New York Times*, June 23, 2014, accessed July 27, 2015, http://www.nytimes.com/interactive/2014/06/23/us/23awlaki-memo.html?_r=0.

33. "Department of Justice White Paper," *MSNBC*, accessed July 27, 2015, http://msnbcmedia.msn.com/i/msnbc/sections/news/020413_DOJ_White_Paper.pdf.

34. Obama, "Remarks by the President at the National Defense University."

35. Obama, "Remarks by the President at the National Defense University."

36. John Bennett, "White House Quietly Shifts Armed Drone Program from CIA to DoD," *Defense News*, May 24, 2013, accessed July 27, 2015, http://archive.defensenews.com/article/20130524/DEFREG02/305240010/White-House-Quietly-Shifts-Armed-Drone-Program-from-CIA-DoD.

37. PublicMind, *Public Says It's Illegal to Target Americans Abroad.*

38. Pew Research Center, "Public Continues to Back U.S. Drone Attacks."

39. Mark Mazzetti and Matt Apuzzo, "Deep Support in Washington for C.I.A.'s Drone Missions," *New York Times*, April 25, 2015, accessed July 27, 2015, http://www.nytimes.com/2015/04/26/us/politics/deep-support-in-washington-for-cias-drone-missions.html?_r=0.

40. Obama, "Remarks by the President at the National Defense University."

41. Huma Imtiaz, "Letter Demands Obama Explain Legal Justification for Drone Strikes," *Express Tribune*, June 13, 2012, accessed January 20, 2015, http://tribune.com.pk/story/393165/letter-demands-obama-explain-legal-justification-for-drone-strikes/.

42. Imtiaz, "Letter Demands Obama Explain Legal Justification for Drone Strikes."

43. Texts of letters can be found here: http://www.propublica.org/documents/item/605032-conyers-nadler-scott121204; and here: http://www.propublica.org/documents/item/606750-letter-to-potus-requesting-doj-memos.

44. Associated Press, "Experts Say U.S. Drone Strikes in Bounds of US Law," *New York Times*, April 23, 2015, accessed January 20, 2015, http://www.nytimes.com/aponline/2015/04/23/us/politics/ap-us-united-states-al-qaida-legal-.html.

45. Jake Miller, "Rand Paul after Filibuster: Drone Debate 'Isn't Over,'" *CBS News*, May 8, 2013, accessed February 18, 2015, http://www.cbsnews.com/news/rand-paul-after-filibuster-drone-debate-isnt-over/.

46. Jim Michaels, "Rand Paul Ends Epic Filibuster over Brennan," *USA Today*, March 7, 2013, accessed September 13, 2014, http://www.usatoday.com/story/news/politics/2013/03/07/rand-paul-brennan-filibuster/1969869/.

47. Scott Shane, "John Brennan, C.I.A. Nominee, Clears Committee Vote," *New York Times*, March 5, 2013, accessed September 13, 2014, http://www.nytimes.com/2013/03/06/us/politics/brennan-vote-by-senate-intelligence-panel.html.

48. Luke Johnson, "Rand Paul Filibusters John Brennan Nomination," *Huffington Post*, March 6, 2013, accessed September 13, 2014, http://www.huffingtonpost.com/2013/03/06/rand-paul-filibuster_n _2819740.html.

49. Rand Paul, "Sen. Rand Paul: My Filibuster Was Just the Beginning," *Washington Post*, March 8, 2013, accessed September 13, 2014, http://www.washingtonpost.com/opinions/sen-rand-paul-my-filibuster-was-just-the-beginning/2013/03/08/6352d8a8-881b-11e2-9d71-f0feafdd1394_story.html.

50. Paul, "Sen. Rand Paul: My Filibuster Was Just the Beginning."

51. Paul, "Sen. Rand Paul: My Filibuster Was Just the Beginning."

52. Brett LoGiurato, "Since Rand Paul's Historic Filibuster, There Has Been a Dramatic Shift in Public Opinion on Drone Strikes," *Business Insider*, April 11, 2013, accessed July 16, 2015, http://www.businessinsider.com/rand-paul-filibuster-drone-polling-polls-2013-4.

53. Anderson Robbins Research and Shaw & Company Research, Fox News poll.

54. Brown and Newport, "In U.S., 65% Support Drone Attacks on Terrorists Abroad."

55. Aaron Blake, "Poll Shows Huge Support for Rand Paul's Filibuster Stance on Drone Strikes," *Washington Post*, March 25, 2013, accessed July 16, 2015, http://www.washingtonpost.com/blogs/post-politics/wp/2013/03/25/poll-shows-huge-support-for-rand-pauls-filibuster-stance-on-drone-attacks/.

56. Carrie Johnson, "When Rand Paul Ended Filibuster, He Left Drones on National Stage," *NPR*, March 8, 2013, accessed September 15, 2014, http://www.npr.org/2013/03/10/173864536/when-rand-paul-ended-filibuster-he-left-drones-on-national-stage.

57. Johnson, "When Rand Paul Ended Filibuster, He Left Drones on National Stage."

58. Eric Holder, letter to Rand Paul, March 7, 2013, http://www.washingtonpost.com/blogs/post-politics/files/2013/03/Senator-Rand-Paul-Letter.pdf.

59. S. V. Dáte, "Rand Paul Elaborates: Armed Drones Not OK for 'Normal Crime'?: It's All Politics," *NPR*, April 24, 2013, accessed September 15, 2014, http://

www.npr.org/blogs/itsallpolitics/2013/04/24/178842706/rand-paul-elaboraes-armed
-drones-not-ok-for-normal-crime.

60. "Sen. Paul Statement on Domestic Drone Use," *Rand Paul: United States Senator*, accessed September 15, 2014, http://www.paul.senate.gov/?p = press_release &id = 779.

61. Jennifer Bendery, "Senate Confirms David Barron, Drone Memo Author, as Federal Judge," *Huffington Post*, May 22, 2014, accessed September 15, 2014, http://www.huffingtonpost.com/2014/05/22/david-barron-drone-memo_n_5373015.html; Andrew Kirell, "Rand Paul Filibusters Another Obama Appointee over Drone Memos," *Mediaite*, May 21, 2014, accessed September 15, 2014, http://www.mediaite.com/tv/watch-rand-paul-filibusters-another-obama-appointee-over-drone-memos/.

62. Adam Chandler, "Author of Drone Memos Passes Senate Despite Writing Drone Memos," *The Wire*, May 21, 2014, September 15, 2014, http://www.thewire.com/national/2014/05/author-of-drone-memos-passes-senate-despite-writing-drone-memos/371384/.

63. Savage, "Justice Department Memo Approving Targeted Killing of Anwar Al-Awlaki."

64. Chris Good and Jason Ryan, "Brennan Interrupted by Protesters, Defends Drone Strikes at Hearing," *ABC News*, February 7, 2013, accessed September 15, 2014, http://abcnews.go.com/Politics/OTUS/brennan-interrupted-protesters-defends-drone-strikes-hearing/story?id = 18433017.

65. Shaun Waterman and Stephen Dinan, "Senate Intelligence Hearing on Brennan's CIA Nomination Halted by Protesters," *Washington Times*, February 7, 2013, accessed September 15, 2014, http://www.washingtontimes.com/news/2013/feb/7/senate-intelligence-hearing-halted-protesters/.

66. Felicia Sonmez, "Code Pink Protests Bring Brennan Hearing to Halt," *Washington Post*, February 7, 2013, accessed September 15, 2014, http://www.washingtonpost.com/blogs/post-politics/wp/2013/02/07/brennan-hearing-comes-to-halt-amid-code-pink-protests/.

67. Waterman and Dinan, "Senate Intelligence Hearing on Brennan's CIA Nomination Halted by Protesters."

68. Steven Nelson, "3 Brennan Confirmation Hearing Protesters Sentenced to 100 Hours of Community Service—US News," *U.S. News & World Report*, August 20, 2013, accessed September 15, 2014, http://www.usnews.com/news/blogs/washington-whispers/2013/08/20/3-brennan-confirmation-protesters-sentenced-to-100-hours-of-community-service.

69. Pew Research Center, "Public Continues to Back U.S. Drone Attacks."

70. Although few polls relating to drone strikes address the possibility of civilian casualties, a poll conducted by the Associated Press and GfK Group in the wake of the unintentional killings of Western hostages Giovanni Lo Porto and Warren Weinstein did ask whether Americans would support drone strikes if there was a danger of American civilian deaths. While 60 percent thought drone strikes against terrorists were generally acceptable, only 47 percent would "approve" strikes if there is a risk of innocent Americans being killed, 36 percent thought such strikes would "favor" such strikes. Ryan Goodman, "New Poll: American Support for Drone

Strikes Plummets When Innocent US Civilians Killed," *Just Security*, May 7, 2015, accessed June 15, 2015, http://justsecurity.org/22795/poll-american-support-drone-strikes-plummets-civilians-killed.

71. Jo Becker and Scott Shane, "Secret 'Kill List' Tests Obama's Principles," *New York Times*, May 29, 2012, accessed July 18, 2015, http://www.nytimes.com/2012/05/29/world/obamas-leadership-in-war-on-al-qaeda.html?pagewanted = all&_r = 0.

72. Becker and Shane, "Secret 'Kill List' Tests Obama's Principles."

73. Human Rights Watch, *"Between a Drone and Al-Qaeda": The Civilian Cost of US Targeted Killings in Yemen* (New York: Human Rights Watch, 2013), 4–5, 7, http://www.hrw.org/sites/default/files/reports/yemen1013_ForUpload.pdf.

74. Human Rights Watch, *"Between a Drone and Al-Qaeda,"* 7.

75. Noah Feldman, "Blame Liberals for Obama's Illegal Drone War," *Bloomberg View*, October 23, 2013, accessed January 22, 2015, http://www.bloombergview.com/articles/2013-10-23/blame-liberals-for-obama-s-illegal-drone-war.

76. Feldman, "Blame Liberals for Obama's Illegal Drone War."

77. Feldman, "Blame Liberals for Obama's Illegal Drone War."

78. Anderson, *Targeted Killing in U.S. Counterterrorism Strategy and Law.*

79. John Yoo, "The Real Problem with Obama's Drone Memo," *Wall Street Journal*, February 7, 2013, accessed July 16, 2015, http://www.wsj.com/articles/SB10001424127887323951904578288380180346300.

80. "A Guide to the Memos on Torture," *New York Times*, accessed September 30, 2014, http://www.nytimes.com/ref/international/24MEMO-GUIDE.html?_r = 0.

81. Yoo, "The Real Problem with Obama's Drone Memo."

82. Rob Mank, "Ten Years after 9/11, John Yoo Defends His Legacy, Legality of Waterboarding," *CBS News*, September 9, 2011, accessed September 30, 2014, http://www.cbsnews.com/news/ten-years-after-9-11-john-yoo-defends-his-legacy-legality-of-waterboarding/.

83. Glenn Greenwald, "Chilling Legal Memo from Obama DOJ Justifies Assassination of US Citizens," *The Guardian*, February 5, 2013, accessed April 11, 2015, http://www.theguardian.com/commentisfree/2013/feb/05/obama-kill-list-doj-memo.

84. Greenwald, "Chilling Legal Memo from Obama DOJ Justifies Assassination of US Citizens."

85. Andrew C. McCarthy, "The Problems of the White Paper," *National Review Online*, February 9, 2013, accessed September 15, 2014, http://www.nationalreview.com/article/340225/problems-white-paper-andrew-c-mccarthy.

86. McCarthy, "The Problems of the White Paper."

87. "Tina Brown: Obama Would 'Be Impeached by Now for Drones, If He Was George W. Bush,'" *Real Clear Politics*, February 8, 2013, accessed September 15, 2014, http://www.realclearpolitics.com/video/2013/02/08/tina_brown_obama_would_be_impeached_by_now_for_drones_if_he_was_george_w_bush.html.

88. Brett Logiurato, "Joe Scarborough Blasts 'Terrifying' Drone Memo," *Business Insider*, February 5, 2013, accessed September 15, 2014, http://www.businessinsider.com/drone-memo-doj-joe-scarborough-obama-department-of-justice-legal-killing-americans-2013-2#ixzz34AxsaQUX.

89. Rich Lowry, "Cheney and Bush Bashers Give Obama Pass on Drones," *News Max*, February 8, 2013, accessed September 15, 2014, http://www.newsmax.com/

RichLowry/Bush-Obama-Drones-Cheney/2013/02/08/id/489535/#ixzz34AzvB9Jx%
20;%20%20;%20.

90. Lara Seligman, "Hill Poll: Voters: Obama No Better Than Bush on Security
vs Civil Liberties," *The Hill*, February 11, 2013, accessed September 15, 2014, http://
thehill.com/polls/282147-hill-poll-voters-obama-no-better-than-bush-on-security
-vs-civil-liberties.

91. Seligman, "Hill Poll: Voters: Obama No Better Than Bush on Security vs
Civil Liberties."

92. Jeremy Scahill, *Dirty Wars: The World Is a Battlefield* (New York: Nation
Books, 2013), 119, 294.

93. Scahill, *Dirty Wars*, 295.

94. Scahill, *Dirty Wars*, 294–95.

95. Scahill, *Dirty Wars*, 205.

96. Scahill, *Dirty Wars*, 205.

97. Karen DeYoung, Adam Goldman, and Julie Tate, "U.S. Captured Benghazi
Suspect in Secret Raid," *Washington Post*, June 17, 2014, accessed July 27, 2015,
https://www.washingtonpost.com/world/national-security/us-captured-benghazi
-suspect-in-secret-raid/2014/06/17/7ef8746e-f5cf-11e3-a3a5-42be35962a52_story
.html; Benjamin Weiser, "Terrorist Has Cooperated with U.S. Since Secret Plea in
2011, Papers Show," *New York Times*, March 25, 2013, accessed July 27, 2015, http://
www.nytimes.com/2013/03/26/nyregion/since-2011-guilty-plea-somali-terrorist-has
-cooperated-with-authorities.html?_r = 0.

98. "Terrorist Trial Report Card: September 11, 2001–September 11, 2011,"
Center on Law and Security, New York University Law School, 2011, accessed April
15, 2015, http://www.lawandsecurity.org/Portals/0/Documents/TTRC%20Ten%20Y
ear%20Issue.pdf.

99. Pete Yost, "AG: Won't Prosecute Reporters for Doing Their Jobs," *Associated
Press*, June 6, 2013, accessed January 22, 2015, http://bigstory.ap.org/article/ag-wont
-prosecute-reporters-doing-their-jobs.

100. Weiser, "Terrorist Has Cooperated"; DeYoung, Goldman, and Tate, "U.S.
Captured Benghazi Suspect."

101. Scahill, *Dirty Wars*, 206.

102. Scahill, *Dirty Wars*, 206.

103. Barack Obama, "Remarks by the President at the National Defense University."

104. Patricia Zengerle, "Obama Asks Congress to Authorize U.S. War on Islamic
State," *Reuters*, February 11, 2015, accessed February 18, 2015, http://www.reuters
.com/article/2015/02/11/us-mideast-crisis-congress-authorization-idUSKBN0LF1K
P20150211.

105. Paul D. Shinkman, "ISIS War Claims Heavy Toll on Drone, Intelligence
Operators at Home," *U.S. News & World Report*, November 18, 2014, accessed January 21, 2015, http://www.usnews.com/news/articles/2014/11/18/isis-war-claims-heavy
-toll-on-drone-intelligence-operators-at-home.

106. Shinkman, "ISIS War Claims Heavy Toll on Drone, Intelligence Operators at
Home."

107. Jim Acosta, Kevin Liptak, and Josh Levs, "Obama, Kerry: No U.S. Troops Will Be Sent into Combat against ISIS in Iraq, Syria," *CNN*, September 17, 2014, accessed January 21, 2015, http://www.cnn.com/2014/09/17/politics/obama-isis/.

108. Dylan Stableford, "Robert Gates: U.S. Can't Beat Islamic State Militants without 'Boots on the Ground,'" *Yahoo! News*, September 17, 2014, accessed January 21, 2015, http://news.yahoo.com/isis-obama-robert-gates-poll-131151869.html.

109. Stableford, "Robert Gates: U.S. Can't Beat Islamic State Militants without 'Boots on the Ground.'"

110. Sarah Dutton et al., "Is Obama Tough Enough in Dealing with ISIS?" *CBS News*, September 17, 2014, accessed January 21, 2015, http://www.cbsnews.com/news/is-obama-tough-enough-in-dealing-with-isis/?utm_source = feedburner&utm_medium = feed&utm_campaign = Feed%3A + cbsnews%2Ffeed + %28CBSNews.com%29.

111. Dutton et al., "Is Obama Tough Enough in Dealing with ISIS?"

112. Dutton et al., "Is Obama Tough Enough in Dealing with ISIS?"

113. "John Kerry: Half of ISIS Leaders Killed by Iraq and Allies," *CBS News*, January 22, 2015, accessed January 22, 2015, http://www.cbsnews.com/news/john-kerry-half-of-isis-leaders-killed-by-iraq-and-allies/.

114. "Lawmakers in Both Parties Urge Oversight of US Drone Program," *Fox News*, February 10, 2013, accessed July 31, 2014, http://www.foxnews.com/politics/2013/02/10/lawmakers-urge-oversight-us-drone-program/.

115. Michael Riley, "Gates Backs Independent Review of Drone Strikes on Americans," *Bloomberg Business*, February 11, 2013, accessed July 30, 2014, http://www.bloomberg.com/news/2013-02-11/gates-backs-independent-review-of-drone-strikes-on-americans.html.

116. Riley, "Gates Backs Independent Review of Drone Strikes on Americans."

117. New York Times/CBS News Poll, "Americans' Views on the Issues."

118. Emily Swanson, "Drone Poll Finds Support for Strikes," *Huffington Post*, February 8, 2013, accessed July 30, 2014, http://www.huffingtonpost.com/2013/02/08/drone-support-poll_n_2647051.html.

119. "Lawmakers in Both Parties Urge Oversight of US Drone Program."

120. Cheryl K. Chumley, "Senate Republicans Shoot Down New Court to Oversee Drone Strikes," *Washington Times*, February 13, 2013, accessed July 30, 2014, http://www.washingtontimes.com/news/2013/feb/13/senate-republicans-shoot-down-new-court-oversee-dr/.

121. Chumley, "Senate Republicans Shoot Down New Court to Oversee Drone Strikes."

122. "Lawmakers in Both Parties Urge Oversight of US Drone Program"; Riley, "Gates Backs Independent Review of Drone Strikes on Americans."

123. Riley, "Gates Backs Independent Review of Drone Strikes on Americans."

124. Mark Hosenball, "Senate Panel Approves Beefed-Up Oversight of Drone Attacks," *Reuters*, November 8, 2013, accessed February 18, 2015, http://www.reuters.com/article/2013/11/08/us-usa-drones-idUSBRE9A713G20131108.

125. Hosenball, "Senate Panel Approves Beefed-Up Oversight of Drone Attacks."

126. Hosenball, "Senate Panel Approves Beefed-Up Oversight of Drone Attacks."

127. Spencer Ackerman, "US Senators Remove Requirement for Disclosure over Drone Strike Victims," *The Guardian*, April 28, 2014, accessed February 28, 2014,

http://www.theguardian.com/world/2014/apr/28/drone-civilian-casualties-senate
-bill-feinstein-clapper.

128. Ken Dilanian, "Sen. Levin's Bid to Boost Drone Oversight Falters in Congress," *Los Angeles Times*, February 12, 2014, accessed February 18, 2015, http://
articles.latimes.com/2014/feb/12/world/la-fg-wn-levin-drone-oversight-20140212.

129. Dilanian, "Sen. Levin's Bid to Boost Drone Oversight Falters in Congress."

130. Michael A. Cohen, "The Imperial Presidency: Drone Power and Congressional Oversight," *World Politics Review*, July 24, 2012, accessed January 22, 2015,
http://www.worldpoliticsreview.com/articles/12194/the-imperial-presidency-drone
-power-and-congressional-oversight.

131. Kenneth A. Schultz, "Tying Hands and Washing Hands: The U.S. Congress
and Multilateral Humanitarian Intervention," in *Locating the Proper Authorities: The
Interaction of International and Domestic Institutions*, edited by Daniel Drezner (Ann
Arbor: University of Michigan Press, 2003), 105–42.

132. Audrey Kurth Cronin, "Why Drones Fail: When Tactics Drive Strategy,"
Foreign Affairs (2013): 52.

133. Kaag and Kreps, *Drone Warfare*, 65.

134. Audrey Kurth Cronin, "Is This How to Win the 'War on Terrorism?'" *Lawfare*, September 14, 2014, https://www.lawfareblog.com/foreign-policy-essay-how
-win-war-terrorism.

135. Thomas Hobbes, *Leviathan: With Selected Variants from Latin Edition of 1668*,
edited by Edwin Curley (Hackett Publishing Company, 1994), 106–9, chap. 17; John
Locke, *Second Treatise of Government*, edited by C. B. Macpherson (Indianapolis, IN:
Hackett Publishing, 1980), 46–47, para. 87 and 88.

136. United States Constitution, preamble, http://www.gpo.gov/fdsys/pkg/CDOC
-110hdoc50/pdf/CDOC-110hdoc50.pdf.

137. Obama, "Remarks by the President at the National Defense University."

138. "Department of Justice White Paper," 7–8.

139. Jameel Jaffer, "The Justice Department's White Paper on Targeted Killing,"
American Civil Liberties Union, February 4, 2013, accessed July 16, 2015, https://
www.aclu.org/blog/justice-departments-white-paper-targeted-killing.

140. Daphne Eviatar, "Drones & the Law: Why We Don't Need a New Legal
Framework for Targeted Killing," in *Preventive Force: Targeted Killing and Technology*,
edited by Kirstin Fisk and Jennifer Ramos (New York: NYU Press, forthcoming).

141. Obama, "Remarks by the President at the National Defense University."

142. Lauren Carroll, "Did Obama Pledge to Stop Using 'Signature Strikes'?,"
Tampa Bay Times, April 28, 2015, accessed July 25, 2015, http://www.politifact.com/
punditfact/statements/2015/apr/28/richard-clarke/did-obama-pledge-stop-using
-signature-strikes/.

143. Obama, "Remarks by the President at the National Defense University."

144. Adam Entous, "Obama Kept Looser Rules for Drones in Pakistan," *Wall
Street Journal*, April 26, 2015, accessed July 25, 2015, http://www.wsj.com/articles/
obama-kept-looser-rules-for-drones-in-pakistan-1430092626; see also Micah Zenko,
"Obama's Drone Strikes Reforms Don't Apply to 46 Percent," *Council on Foreign
Relations*, April 27, 2015, accessed July 25, 2015, http://blogs.cfr.org/zenko/2015/04/
27/obama-drone-strikes-reforms-do-not-apply-to-46-percent/.

145. Carroll, "Did Obama Pledge to Stop Using 'Signature Strikes'?"

146. Obama, "Remarks by the President at the National Defense University."

147. Obama, "Remarks by the President at the National Defense University."

148. Obama, "Remarks by the President at the National Defense University."

149. Obama, "Remarks by the President at the National Defense University."

150. Cronin, "Is This How to Win the 'War on Terrorism'?"

151. Cronin, "Why Drones Fail," 48, 52.

152. International Human Rights and Conflict Resolution Clinic and Global Justice Clinic, *Living Under Drones: Death, Injury and Trauma to Civilians from US Drone Practices in Pakistan* (New York and Palo Alto: NYU School of Law and Stanford Law School, 2012), 140.

153. Cronin, "Why Drones Fail," 54.

154. Laurie Blank, "Targeted Strikes: The Consequences of Blurring the Armed Conflict and Self-Defense Justifications," *William and Mitchell Law Review* 38, no. 5 (2012): 1688, http://web.wmitchell.edu/law-review/wp-content/uploads/Volume38/documents/11.BlankFINAL.pdf.

155. Peter Baker, "In Terror Shift, Obama Took a Long Path," *New York Times*, May 27, 2013, accessed July 27, 2015, http://www.nytimes.com/2013/05/28/us/politics/in-terror-shift-obama-took-a-long-path.html?_r = 0.

156. Baker, "In Terror Shift, Obama Took a Long Path."

157. "U.S. Policy Standards and Procedures for the Use of Force in Counterterrorism Operations Outside the United States and Areas of Active Hostilities," *White House*, May 23, 2013, accessed July 27, 2015, https://www.whitehouse.gov/sites/default/files/uploads/2013.05.23_fact_sheet_on_ppg.pdf.

158. Peter Baker, "Obama Apologizes after Drone Kills American and Italian Held by al Qaeda," *New York Times*, April 23, 2015, accessed July 27, 2015, http://www.nytimes.com/2015/04/24/world/asia/2-qaeda-hostages-were-accidentally-killed-in-us-raid-white-house-says.html.

159. C. Christine Fair, Karl C. Kaltenthaler, and William J. Miller, "You Say Pakistanis All Hate the Drone War? Prove It," *The Atlantic*, January 23, 2013, accessed August 2, 2014, http://www.theatlantic.com/international/archive/2013/01/you-say-pakistanis-all-hate-the-drone-war-prove-it/267447/.

160. Pew Research, "Global Opposition to U.S. Surveillance and Drones, but Limited Harm to America's Image."

161. Fair, Kaltenthaler, and Miller, "You Say Pakistanis All Hate the Drone War? Prove It."

162. Fair, Kaltenthaler, and Miller, "You Say Pakistanis All Hate the Drone War? Prove It."

163. Fair, Kaltenthaler, and Miller, "You Say Pakistanis All Hate the Drone War? Prove It."

164. Salman Masood and Ihsanullah Tipu Mehsud, "Thousands in Pakistan Protest American Drone Strikes," *New York Times*, November 23, 2013, accessed September 13, 2014, http://www.nytimes.com/2013/11/24/world/asia/in-pakistan-rally-protests-drone-strikes.html?_r = 0.

165. Masood and Mehsud, "Thousands in Pakistan Protest American Drone Strikes"; Eyder Peralta, "In Pakistan, Thousands Protest Against U.S. Drone Strikes,"

NPR, November 23, 2013, accessed September 13, 2014, http://www.npr.org/blogs/thetwo-way/2013/11/23/246887028/in-pakistan-thousands-protest-against-u-s-drone-strikes.

166. Masood and Mehsud, "Thousands in Pakistan Protest American Drone Strikes."

167. Masood and Mehsud, "Thousands in Pakistan Protest American Drone Strikes."

168. Associated Press, "Pakistan's Police Stop NATO Supply Truck Blockade," *Fox News*, November 25, 2013, accessed September 13, 2014, http://www.foxnews.com/world/2013/11/25/pakistan-police-stop-nato-supply-truck-blockade/.

169. "Pakistan's Police Stop NATO Supply Truck Blockade."

170. Associated Press, "NATO Supply Trucks Stuck in Pakistan amid Concerns over Protesters Blocking Path," *Fox News*, November 26, 2013, accessed September 13, 2014, http://www.foxnews.com/world/2013/11/26/nato-supply-trucks-stuck-in-pakistan-amid-concerns-over-protesters-blocking/.

171. Zulfiqar Ali and Shashank Bengali, "Pakistan Court Orders End to Blockade on NATO Supply Route," *Los Angeles Times*, February 25, 2014, accessed September 14, 2014, http://articles.latimes.com/2014/feb/25/world/la-fg-wn-pakistan-blockade-nato-afghanistan-supply-route-20140225.

172. "Stepped-Up US Drone Strikes in Yemen Spark Massive Protests," *RT*, August 19, 2013, accessed September 13, 2014, http://rt.com/news/us-drone-strikes-yemen-protests-669/; "Yemenis Protest against US Drone Attacks in Sa'ada," *Press TV*, August 17, 2013, accessed September 13, 2014, http://www.presstv.com/detail/2013/08/17/319179/yemenis-protest-at-us-drone-attacks/.

173. Tik Root, "Yemen's New Ways of Protesting Drone Strikes: Graffiti and Poetry," *Time*, November 30, 2013, accessed September 13, 2014, http://world.time.com/2013/11/30/yemens-new-ways-of-protesting-drone-strikes-graffiti-and-poetry/.

174. Root, "Yemen's New Ways of Protesting Drone Strikes: Graffiti and Poetry."

175. "Yemenis Demand US Apologize for Deadly Wedding Strike," *Al-Akbar English*, December 14, 2013, accessed September 13, 2014, http://english.al-akhbar.com/node/17903.

176. "Yemenis Protest after US Drone Strike Kills 17 in Wedding Convoy," *Ma'an News Agency*, December 14, 2013, accessed September 13, 2014, http://www.maannews.net/eng/ViewDetails.aspx?ID=657091.

177. Pew Research, "Global Opposition to U.S. Surveillance and Drones, But Limited Harm to America's Image."

178. "Hundreds of Anti-Drone Protesters March against UK Flight-Control Centre," *The Guardian*, April 27, 2013, accessed September 13, 2014, http://www.theguardian.com/world/2013/apr/27/anti-drone-protestors-march-uk.

179. "Peace Activists Protest 'Brutal UK Drone Warfare' at RAF Base, 4 Arrests," *RT*, January 5, 2015, accessed January 21, 2015, http://rt.com/uk/219991-anti-drone-activists-arrested/.

180. "Six in Court after Drones Protest at RAF Waddington," *BBC News*, June 5, 2013, accessed September 13, 2014, http://www.bbc.com/news/uk-england-lincolnshire-22765385.

181. "RAF Waddington Drone Protesters Guilty of Fence Damage," *BBC News*, October 7, 2013, accessed September 13, 2014, http://www.bbc.com/news/uk -england-lincolnshire-24434487.

182. Harriet Williamson, "Anti-Drones Protesters' Lenient Sentence Is 'Invitation' to Activists," *The Guardian*, October 11, 2013, accessed September 13, 2014, http:// www.theguardian.com/uk-news/the-northerner/2013/oct/11/anti-drones-protesters -raf-waddington.

183. "UAV Protest Outside Drone Testing Base in Aberporth," *BBC News*, September 9, 2013, accessed September 13, 2014, http://www.bbc.com/news/uk-wales -24018746.

184. "Peace Activists Protest 'Brutal UK Drone Warfare' at RAF Base, 4 Arrests."

185. "Peace Activists Protest 'Brutal UK Drone Warfare' at RAF Base, 4 Arrests."

186. Ghazwan Hassan and Phil Stewart, "Iraq Calls on U.S. to Launch Air Strikes Against Militants," *Huffington Post*, June 18, 2014, accessed September 24, 2014, http://www.huffingtonpost.com/2014/06/18/iraq-us-air-strikes_n_5507719.html.

187. Ed Pilkington and Ryan Devereaux, "US Defends Drone Strikes as 'Necessary and Just' in Face of UN Criticism," *The Guardian*, October 25, 2013, accessed July 30, 2014, http://www.theguardian.com/world/2013/oct/25/un-drones-us-policy-debate.

188. Qasim Nauman, "Pakistan Condemns U.S. Drone Strikes," *Reuters*, June 4, 2012, accessed September 24, 2014, http://www.reuters.com/article/2012/06/04/us -pakistan-usa-drones-idUSBRE8530MS20120604.

189. Steve Almasy, "Report: U.S., Pakistan Had Secret Agreement on Dozens of Drone Strikes," *CNN*, October 25, 2013, accessed September 24, 2014, http://www .cnn.com/2013/10/24/politics/u-s-drones-pakistan-report/.

190. Scott Shane, "Yemen's Leader Praises U.S. Drone Strikes," *New York Times*, September 29, 2012, accessed January 22, 2015, http://www.nytimes.com/2012/09/ 29/world/middleeast/yemens-leader-president-hadi-praises-us-drone-strikes.html?_ r=0.

191. Shuaib Almosawa and Rod Nordland, "U.S. Fears Chaos as Government of Yemen Falls," *New York Times*, January 22, 2015, accessed January 22, 2015, http:// www.nytimes.com/2015/01/23/world/middleeast/yemen-houthi-crisis-sana.html.

192. Zaid Al-Alayaa and Paul Richter, "U.S. Resumes Drone Strikes in Yemen as Houthis Tighten Control," *Los Angeles Times*, February 6, 2015, accessed June 6, 2015, http://www.latimes.com/world/middleeast/la-fg-yemen-houthis-20150206-story .html.

193. Louise Osborne, "Germany Denies Phone Data Sent to NSA Used in Drone Attacks," *The Guardian*, August 12, 2013, accessed June 6, 2015, http://www.the guardian.com/world/2013/aug/12/germany-phone-data-nsa-drone.

194. Osborne, "Germany Denies Phone Data Sent to NSA Used in Drone Attacks."

195. Osborne, "Germany Denies Phone Data Sent to NSA Used in Drone Attacks."

196. Osborne, "Germany Denies Phone Data Sent to NSA Used in Drone Attacks."

197. "Spying Together: German Aid for US Drone Attacks?," *Spiegel Online International*, June 18, 2014, accessed February 19, 2015, http://www.spiegel.de/inter

national/germany/the-german-bnd-and-american-nsa-cooperate-more-closely-than
-thought-a-975445-2.html.

198. "Spying Together: German Aid for US Drone Attacks?"

199. "Yemeni Sues Germany over US Drone Strikes," *The Local*, October 16, 2014, accessed February 19, 2015, http://www.thelocal.de/20141016/yemeni-sues-germany
-to-stop-us-drone-strikes.

200. "Yemeni Sues Germany over US Drone Strikes."

201. "Yemeni Sues Germany over US Drone Strikes."

202. Jessica Elgot, "'Illegal' Drone Strikes Condemned in Landslide Vote by European Politicians," *Huffington Post: United Kingdom*, February 27, 2014, accessed February 19, 2015, http://www.huffingtonpost.co.uk/2014/02/27/europe-meps-vote
-against-drone-strikes_n_4866217.html.

203. Elgot, "'Illegal' Drone Strikes Condemned in Landslide Vote by European Politicians."

204. Pilkington and Devereaux, "US Defends Drone Strikes."

205. Owen Bowcott, "UN Rapporteur Christof Heyns Condemns Use of Drone Strikes," *The Guardian*, October 17, 2013, accessed September 16, 2014, http://www
.theguardian.com/world/2013/oct/17/un-rapporteur-heyns-drone-strikes-yemen
-pakistan.

206. Pilkington and Devereaux, "US Defends Drone Strikes."

207. Pilkington and Devereaux, "US Defends Drone Strikes."

208. Pilkington and Devereaux, "US Defends Drone Strikes."

209. Pilkington and Devereaux, "US Defends Drone Strikes."

210. Pilkington and Devereaux, "US Defends Drone Strikes."

211. Tim Craig, "After Years of Tension Anti-American Sentiment Ebbs in Pakistan," *Washington Post*, May 3, 2015, accessed June 16, 2015, http://www.washington
post.com/world/asia_pacific/after-years-of-tension-anti-american-sentiment-ebbs
-in-pakistan/2015/05/03/6d0eccfe-dd36-11e4-b6d7-b9bc8acf16f7_story.html.

212. Craig, "After Years of Tension."

213. Richard Wike, Bruce Stokes, and Jacob Poushter, "Global Publics Back U.S. on Fighting ISIS But Are Critical of Post-9/11 Torture," *Pew Research Center*, June 23, 2015, accessed July 16, 2015, http://www.pewglobal.org/2015/06/23/global-publics
-back-u-s-on-fighting-isis-but-are-critical-of-post-911-torture/.

214. Michael Isikoff, "White House Exempts Syria Airstrikes from Tight Standards on Civilian Deaths," *Yahoo News*, September 30, 2014, accessed July 16, 2015, http://news.yahoo.com/white-house-exempts-syria-airstrikes-from-tight-standards
-on-civilian-deaths-183724795.html.

215. Jim Acosta, "Obama to Make New Push to Shift Control of Drones from CIA to Pentagon," *CNN Politics*, Monday, April 27, 2015, accessed August 25, 2015, http://www.cnn.com/2015/04/27/politics/drones-cia-pentagon-white-house/.

216. Anderson Robbins Research and Shaw & Company Research, Fox News Poll.

217. Anderson Robbins Research and Shaw & Company Research, Fox News Poll.

218. Assuming the rarity of someone only approving strikes against Americans in the United States.

219. Brown and Newport, "In U.S., 65% Support Drone Attacks on Terrorists Abroad."

220. Bruce Stokes, "Big Gender Gap in Global Public Opinion about Use of Drones," *Pew Research Center*, July 25, 2013, accessed July 25, 2015, http://www.pewresearch.org/fact-tank/2013/07/25/big-gender-gap-in-global-public-opinion-about-use-of-drones/.

221. Stokes, "Big Gender Gap in Global Public Opinion about Use of Drones."

222. Stokes, "Big Gender Gap in Global Public Opinion about Use of Drones."

223. Stokes, "Big Gender Gap in Global Public Opinion about Use of Drones."

224. Stokes, "Big Gender Gap in Global Public Opinion about Use of Drones."

225. Pew Research Center, "Public Continues to Back U.S. Drone Attacks."

226. Pew Research Center, "Public Continues to Back U.S. Drone Attacks."

227. Pew Research Center, "Public Continues to Back U.S. Drone Attacks."

228. Pew Research Center, "Public Continues to Back U.S. Drone Attacks."

229. Pew Research Center, "Public Continues to Back U.S. Drone Attacks."

230. Pew Research Center, "Public Continues to Back U.S. Drone Attacks."

231. Brown and Newport, "In U.S., 65% Support Drone Attacks on Terrorists Abroad."

232. Brown and Newport, "In U.S., 65% Support Drone Attacks on Terrorists Abroad."

233. Jennifer Merolla, "Terrorism Threat Elevates Public Support for Drones," *Huffington Post*, May 28, 2013, accessed July 25, 2015, http://www.huffingtonpost.com/jennifer-merolla-phd/public-opinion-drones_b_3340280.html.

234. Jennifer E. Manning, "Membership of the 114th Congress: A Profile," Congressional Research Report 7-5700, 7.

235. Manning, "Membership of the 114th Congress," 7–8.

236. Annie Lowrey, "Meet the New Yorker Who Is Now Congress' Youngest Member," *New York Magazine*, January 6, 2015, accessed July 19, 2015, http://nymag.com/daily/intelligencer/2014/11/meet-congress-youngest-member.html.

6

Emerging Issues

Will Armed Drones Proliferate Rapidly, and What Impact Will They Have on International Security?

O N September 21, 2014, Hezbollah claimed to have launched a missile from a drone that hit an al-Nusra Front target in Syria, killing at least twenty-three fighters.[1] If the unconfirmed report is accurate, it would be the first time that an organization other than a state has carried out a successful drone strike.[2] Whether or not this report is correct, many observers have begun to envision a future in which the state loses its monopoly on military technology like armed drones. In writing about game changers, Shawn Brimley, Ben FitzGerald, and Kelley Sayler from the Center for a New American Security (CNAS) argue that the "rapid globalization and diffusion of technology has lowered the barriers for smaller states, and even non-state actors, to acquire and field advanced military capabilities or inexpensive but highly effective asymmetric capabilities."[3] Following this line of thought, T. X. Hammes, a retired U.S. Marine colonel and author of *The Sling and the Stone: On War in the 21st Century* (2006), argued that with "the low cost and wide dissemination of the knowledge, software, and hardware, we have to assume both state and non-state actors will use [drones] against us."[4] In short, there are concerns that military technology, and for our purposes drone technology, will widely proliferate and fall into the hands of hostile states and nonstate actors, with destabilizing consequences. These concerns are often reinforced by claims that the United States' global dominance in drone technology is already starting to crumble, with other countries quickly closing the technological gap.

This chapter will cover drone proliferation and the question of whether or not the United States' use of drones is accelerating worrisome trends in the global sphere. First, we will briefly discuss the number of countries developing or aspiring to acquire drone technology. Next, we will review the debate on drone proliferation with a particular emphasis on how quickly states will be able to successfully obtain the technology. The chapter then considers the dangers of proliferation, and whether the use of drones by the United States is setting a dangerous precedent that could be mimicked by other states once their drone capabilities mature, and what might be done to mitigate such concerns. The chapter will end with a case study examining drone strikes launched, or at least contemplated, by other states, with a focus on two emerging drone powers, Israel and China.

I. The Race for Drones

The United States is currently the world's most prolific procurer and user of drones, deploying nearly eleven thousand military drones of many different types and capabilities.[5] This marks a dramatic increase from fewer than two hundred military drones in 2002.[6] According to a report by the Center for Strategic and International Studies (CSIS), of the nearly eleven thousand drones in its possession "only a small number (fewer than 450) are physically capable of carrying armaments in known configurations, and among that group a much smaller number actually carry weapons and are operational at any given time (perhaps 70 to 80 that could be operational at the highest state of readiness)."[7] The vast majority of UAVs fielded by the United States are mini (or micro) drones, such as the Raven and Wasp, which make up 89 percent of the military's drone inventory (9,765 drones in total).[8] Predators and Reapers represent only a small minority of available drones, making up less than 4 percent altogether (fewer than 349 drones in total).[9] To date, Israel and the United Kingdom are the only other countries known to use armed drones in conflict. In a series of test flights conducted between May and July of 2013, the U.S. Navy's X-47B became the first drone in history to take off and land aboard a moving aircraft carrier.[10] According to Michael C. Horowitz (associate professor at the University of Pennsylvania) and Matthew Fuhrmann (associate professor at Texas A&M University), "[t]hat a UAV is now capable of conducting even primitive carrier operations, one of the hardest military tasks in the world, suggests that a new era of UAVs could be around the corner."[11]

Another major player at the forefront of drone innovation is Israel, which has been described as "the first nation to prove the utility of unmanned aircraft."[12] Israel is currently the world's largest exporter of drones, with sales to more than forty-two countries, the majority being in Europe, Asia, and

Latin America.[13] The Israeli Ministry of Defense also cleared the Heron drone for export to some African nations in 2012, and Israeli manufacturers have already sold drones to Angola, Kenya, Ivory Coast, Nigeria, Ethiopia, and Tanzania.[14] According to the Stockholm International Peace Research Institute, Israel was responsible for 41 percent of all drone exports between 2001 and 2011.[15]

Other countries are rapidly following the lead of states like the United States, Israel, and the United Kingdom, and are seeking to acquire their own drone capabilities. Between 2005 and 2013, the number of countries that had acquired drones a little more than doubled from about forty to as many as eighty-two, according to the data compiled by the New America Foundation.[16] More recent estimates put the count higher, reporting that over ninety nations and nonstate groups are known to operate drones.[17] In addition to this, at least twenty-three countries have developed or are developing armed drones, according to a 2014 report from the RAND Corporation.[18] Already, according to *National Defense Magazine*, about "4,000 different unmanned aircraft platforms [are] in circulation on the global market."[19]

Flagging Hegemon?

Surprisingly, while other countries have shown growing interest in obtaining drone technology, especially armed drones, there are some indications that the U.S. military's focus on drone technology may be diminishing. The U.S. military plans to spend $2.4 billion on drones in 2015, which is down sharply from the $5.7 billion that the military requested in the 2013 budget[20] (although both estimates are considerably larger than what the military spent on drones in 2002—around $550 million).[21] The total U.S. expenditure on drone development is not projected to increase significantly over time and is expected to remain relatively flat from 2018 through 2022.[22] Other countries, by contrast, have been gradually increasing their spending on drone procurement and R&D. Still, even at its reduced level of expenditure, the United States will remain the single biggest player in drone development in the foreseeable future.

Growing Competition

Nevertheless, the United States will face an increasingly crowded market of drone suppliers as well as buyers. In general, the drone industry (for both military and civilian purposes) is expected to continue to grow rapidly as global demand increases and new competitors seize opportunities and establish niches in this lucrative market. According to the Teal Group, a defense consulting firm in Virginia, global spending on drone research and procurement will nearly double over the next decade, from current worldwide drone expenditures of $6.4 billion annually to $11.5 billion, and totaling almost $91 billion in the next ten years.[23] The Teal Group study predicts that the United States will account for 65 percent of total worldwide research, development, testing, and evaluation (RDT&E) spending on drone technology over the next decade, and about 41 percent of the procurement.[24] Both the United States and Israel have a significant lead in military drone systems, but Europe, China, and Japan are also expected to press ahead rapidly.[25] According to Global Industry Analysts, "Spending on military robotics in Asia will increase 67 percent, to almost $2.4 billion a year, by 2018, making it the fastest-growing segment of that market."[26] As Mahendran Arjunraja, the lead researcher for a report by international business consulting firm Frost & Sullivan, recently observed: "Asia-Pacific countries clearly understand the advantages offered by UAVs. They have seen the benefits from recent (American) operations and are investing."[27] Officials of the 2013 International Defense Exposition (IDEX) in Abu Dhabi estimated the Middle East drones market to be worth $1 billion through 2021.[28]

In February 2012, the North Atlantic Treaty Organization (NATO) agreed to acquire its first fleet of unarmed drones after seeing how useful the American drones were in the air war against Qaddafi's forces in Libya.[29] Thirteen NATO countries planned to procure five Global Hawks and a ground command-and-control system, while all twenty-eight alliance members agreed to cover future operating costs.[30] France, Greece, Italy, Spain, Sweden, and Switzerland are also codeveloping nEUROn, an advanced armed drone prototype led by the French company Dassault Aviation.[31] In April 2012 the Obama administration also sent a confidential "prenotification" to Congress detailing its plans to sell kits to Italy to arm up to six Reaper drones.[32]

The high stakes of competing successfully in the rapidly growing world drone market was highlighted in a 2012 European Commission report expressing concern about the potential consequences of lagging progress on an indigenous European drone: "If Europe's ambition is maintained at current levels, the United States together with Israel will remain, in the foreseeable future, the dominant players in a growing [drones] market. This is why it is imperative for the EU to take action now."[33] The UK has apparently taken this warning to heart and is already developing some cutting-edge drone technology. In particular, the UK is developing the Taranis, named after the Celtic god of thunder, which has been described as the "most advanced aircraft ever built by British engineers."[34] According to reports, the

Taranis will be capable of using "on-board computers to perform airborne manoeuvres, avoid threats and identify targets" and "[g]round crews will only be consulted to gain authorisation for an attack."[35] British military officials also told *The Guardian* in 2011 that "it is possible that almost one third of the RAF [i.e., Royal Air Force] could be made up of remotely controlled aircraft within 20 years."[36] The RAF has already been successfully flying Reaper drones in Afghanistan since October 2007.[37] The development of drones is not limited to U.S., Israel, and European countries, however. For example, as Micah Zenko and Sarah Kreps have noted: "Russia, China, Iran, South Korea, and Taiwan . . . have begun to develop increasingly sophisticated indigenous drone capabilities. Other countries, including Pakistan, Turkey, Saudi Arabia, and the UAE, have [also] publicized their intent to purchase them."[38]

The drone capabilities of some of these countries are already fairly robust. In surveying China's drone program, for instance, Ian Easton and L. C. Russell Hsiao, from the Asia-focused think tank Project 2049 Institute, remarked that China has already "developed an extensive and organizationally complex UAV infrastructure over the past decade."[39] China is also one of the few countries developing larger and more advanced systems, such as drones specially designed for combat.[40] A report by the Taiwan Defense Ministry estimated that the Chinese Air Force alone had more than 280 drones in 2011.[41] Other branches of China's military reportedly have thousands of drones, making China's drone fleet count second only to the United States.[42] According to the Defense Science Board, a committee of civilian experts appointed to advise the U.S. Department of Defense, "every major manufacturer for the Chinese military has a research center devoted to unmanned systems."[43]

Russia is also investing heavily in a rapidly growing drone program. On May 20, 2014, Russia's Defense Ministry said that the government would spend upward of $9.2 billion on drones through 2020.[44] A little over a week later, on May 29, Deputy Defense Minister Yuri Borisov told reporters that Russia would begin research and development on combat drones with plans to begin testing them in 2017. "We are ready to consider starting a development work this year with plans to complete it and move on to the official tests or experimental military use of future devices in 2017," Borisov said.[45] Russia's state news agency reported on November 13, 2014, that its government also plans to build a drone base for military reconnaissance around the Russian town of Anadyr, just 420 miles off the Alaskan coast.[46] According to Rob O'Gorman and Chris Abbott, analysts at NGO *Open Briefing*, Russia has at least fifty-four types of drones in use or in development, five of which have been identified as combat drones.[47]

Other major countries are quickly following suit. Turkish officials said Turkey's first domestically produced drone, which it plans to arm,[48] is expected to be completed by 2016, while other drone systems are anticipated to be ready in 2018.[49] According to Gorman and Abbott, Turkey has at least twenty-four types of drones in use or in development, four of which have been identified as combat drones.[50] On August 27, 2013, Avinash Chander, the scientific adviser to India's defense minister, announced that the country's Defense Research and Development Organization will soon begin equipping its drones with precision-guided munitions.[51] Three months later, Pakistan's military unveiled two domestically built drones, called Burraq and Shahpar, which are intended to be used only for surveillance.[52] However, on March 13, 2015, Pakistan's military claimed to have successfully armed and tested the Burraq and that it would soon deploy them against terrorists.[53] Saad Muhammad, a retired brigadier general in the Pakistani army, said that the availability of drones will greatly help the Pakistani army with its fight against the Pakistani Taliban.[54]

Iran unveiled its first domestically built drone in 2010 called Karrar, also described as the "ambassador of death," which has a range of one thousand kilometers.[55] In September 2012 Iran introduced the Shahed 129, a drone reportedly capable of carrying out reconnaissance and combat missions with twice the range of the Karrar (2,000 km).[56] In April 2013, Iran unveiled the H-110 Sarir, a long-range drone that Iranian officials purport to be capable of air-to-air combat.[57] Iran claimed to have made technological improvements in its development of drones by reverse engineering the U.S. RQ-170 Sentinel, which Iran allegedly downed in December 2011 with some reports indicating they were in the process of building a copy of the drone.[58] It was also reported in 2012 that Iran had supplied the Assad regime with drones to conduct surveillance on the opposition in efforts to suppress antigovernment protests.[59]

Africa, too, has its leaders in the development of UAVs including armed drones. The South African firm Denel Dynamics, a government-owned arms manufacturer, has begun testing armed versions of the Seeker 400, with hopes of being among the first suppliers of armed drones to market if tests are successful.[60] A company spokesperson for Denel Dynamics said, "It would limit sales only to governments that would be 'accountable and responsible' and agree to 'opportunistic' use of the weapons on justified targets." The company spokesperson added that the "justified" target "could be a pirate, or could be a terrorist."[61]

As the foregoing cases suggest, the rapid development of drones in diverse forms, including armed ones, is a global phenomenon. As the researchers who conducted the *Living Under Drones* study aptly commented, "[w]e are in the midst of a significant period of drone proliferation, pushed forward on the one hand by governments and militaries, and on the other, by manufacturers seeking to expand markets and profit."[62] But how serious will challenges to U.S. predominance in the development and deployment of drones be, and exactly how rapidly and widely will drones, and especially armed drones, proliferate? To begin answering these questions, we will first turn to the debate on proliferation.

II. Debates on the Diffusion of Drones

The interest of a broad range of states in obtaining drones, particularly by developing domestic programs, reinforces worries about drone proliferation. There is a strong belief shared by many commentators that rapid globalization and diffusion of technology will lower the barriers preventing smaller states, and even nonstate actors, from acquiring drone technologies. The problem here is that, as the Defense Science Board has put it, "the barrier to entry for using unmanned, autonomous systems is [already] very low."[63]

The availability of commercial technology is also significantly contributing to the advancement of drone programs around the world, according to the Government Accountability Office (GAO).[64] Indeed, a number of scholars and officials have noted the important role commercial markets are playing in the diffusion of drone technology by promoting and accelerating technological innovations. Horowitz drew attention to this point in the following statement:

> At the moment . . . the future of military technology seems much more likely to be influenced by developments in the commercial world than by technologies designed exclusively for the battlefield . . . nearly three-quarters of [the 400 defense experts polled by CNAS] think the technological influence of commercial companies on the defense sector will grow significantly by 2030.[65]

Robert Work (former chief executive officer at CNAS now serving as the U.S. deputy secretary of defense) and Shawn Brimley made similar observations.[66] Work and Brimley also claimed that "these commercial drivers" will reduce the cost for states attempting to procure and integrate military innovations, which in turn "will likely increase the speed of adoption, potentially increasing the threat that the United States will be surprised by an adversary's ability to field advanced military capabilities."[67] This applies in particular to drone technology. As Daniel Byman observed, "[c]ontrolling the spread of drone technology will prove impossible [as drones] are highly capable weapons that are easy to produce."[68] Byman also added that "[a]rmed drones are more difficult to produce and deploy, but they, too, will likely spread rapidly."[69] In a *New York Times* article titled "Coming Soon: The Drone Arms Race," Peter W. Singer also warns of rapid dissemination: "I think of where the airplane was at the start of World War I: at first it was unarmed and limited to a handful of countries . . . Then it was armed and everywhere. That is the path we're on."[70] In a *Foreign Policy* article, Singer goes on to say that the brief U.S. monopoly on drone technology ended several years ago, as "we already have a [drone] market that is global in both its customers, from Australia to Turkey, and in its manufacturers, from American firms like General Atomics and Lockheed to ASN Technology, one of the major makers in China, and ADE of India."[71] Brimley, FitzGerald, and Ely Ratner from CNAS stress that the rapid diffusion of advanced military technology, including drones, is "not a future trend . . . [as these] capabilities are being fielded—right now."[72]

A number of commentators went as far as to make predictions on when access to the technology will become pervasive. Noel Sharkey has argued that every country will have armed drones within ten years (that is, by 2024). "Once countries like China start exporting these, they're going to be everywhere really quickly," he told *Defense One*.[73] Samuel J. Brannen, a senior fellow at CSIS, goes even further, predicting that "within five years . . . every country could have access to the equivalent of an armed UAV, like General Atomics' Predator, which fires Hellfire missiles."[74] Dennis M. Gormley, a senior lecturer in military affairs at the University of Pittsburgh's Graduate School of Public and International Affairs, encapsulates the view of many experts in the following statement: "Virtually all analysts believe that the global spread of both unarmed and armed UAVs will only expand exponentially in the years to come."[75]

Other scholars, by contrast, have argued that fears of proliferation have been greatly exaggerated. In a *Foreign Policy* article, Zenko and Kreps stated:

> The problem with this now commonly stated assumption—that the world is fully equipped with drones—is that while these news articles hyping a drones arms race are exciting, they are also misleading . . . Contrary to these sensationalist accounts, the international market for armed drones—the most potentially threatening and destabilizing type—is quite small. Actually, it's minuscule.[76]

Those who share this view have three arguments against the widely held expectation of a rapid diffusion of drone technology that focus respectively on: (1) technical limitations, (2) lack of operational experience and organizational support, and (3) strategic considerations. They argue that these considerations together will slow down the rate and speed of proliferation of strategic (long-range, armed) drones, resulting in only a few countries—the wealthiest and most technologically advanced—having access to them in the near future.

The first and probably the most important argument is the technical one. The technology behind highly capable and complex (i.e., medium-to-long-range strategic armed) drones is expensive to produce, and is unaffordable as well as inaccessible to most countries.[77] Previous work conducted by the GAO also stated that the production of advanced armed drone technology will be limited at least "in the near term" to countries with advanced technical know-how: "It is likely that only established UAV developers will be able to produce these systems, given the technical expertise required to successfully integrate weapons onto a UAV."[78]

Andrea Gilli, a postdoctoral Fellow at Metropolitan University Prague, and Mauro Gilli, a PhD candidate at Northwestern University, advanced similar points when investigating the proliferation of three types of drones—loitering attack munitions (LAMs), intelligence, surveillance, and reconnaissance (ISR) drones, and unmanned combat aerial vehicles (UCAVs).[79] In investigating the diffusion of these technologies, they illustrate how wealthy and technologically advanced countries have struggled, and in some cases even failed, to develop "combat effective-drones"[80] and to fully exploit their capabilities. This, in turn, suggests that "poorer and less developed countries are unlikely to fare any better . . . and likely are going to experience even more daunting problems."[81] For instance, looking at countries that are more likely to keep the pace with new technologies, they pointed out how "Germany and the US cancelled their indigenous LAMs; Germany, France and other European countries failed to produce advanced long-range ISR drones; [and] finally, the development of UCAVs has proved demanding also for the US and the UK."[82]

The second argument against the rapid proliferation of drones is, as already indicated, concerned with operational experience and the fact that drones are support intensive. On this point, Gilli and Gilli emphasize the experiential and organizational challenges in operating advanced drone technology. For example, in order to operate drones and exploit their capabilities, extensive training and operational experience is needed for both the pilots and personnel. As the authors noted, "The employment of a single high-end ISR drone (like the MQ-9 *Reaper* or the RQ-[4] *Global Hawk*) calls for 300 to 600 hundred ground-based highly skilled personnel in communications, computers and software."[83] Given that countries like the United States, France, Great Britain, and Germany have struggled to recruit this personnel, Gilli and Gilli argued that "less developed nations will necessarily experience even more acute difficulties."[84] To emphasize the importance of training, they remind their readers that even for the United States, 40 percent of drone crashes are still due to human errors.[85] Further highlighting the personnel and training challenges the United States faces when deploying drones is a report from the Defense Science Board, stating that "the increase in data collected by the Predator led to a 30% increase in the number of analysts needed to sort through its data, yet only 5% of the data collected by the Predator makes it to the dismounted soldier."[86] Gilli and Gilli also argue that Israel, which has been using drones since the 1970s, "truly devised how to fully exploit their [drones] only after their poor performance against Hezbollah in 2006."[87] All of these findings lead to their overarching claim: "While different types of drones will continue to spread, our analysis suggests that only the most advanced and wealthiest countries will be able to field and exploit combat-effective platforms that can affect the global distribution of military power."[88]

The third and final argument is a strategic one—not all emerging drone powers want to project the technology in the same way as the United States. From a strategic perspective, countries are simply not interested in investing resources for the development and advancement of drone technology capable of conducting drone strikes halfway around the world. For instance, as Zenko pointed out, there are a number of countries that pose threats to cross-border adversaries and that could in the future potentially employ armed drones to make good on those threats (i.e., Russia into Georgia or Azerbaijan; Turkey into Iraq; and Saudi Arabia into Yemen). In these cases, "[w]hen compared to distant U.S. drone strikes, these contingencies do not require system-wide infrastructure and host-state support," said Zenko.[89]

A further point is that the diffusion of drone technology is hindered by the fact that there are cheaper and more effective alternatives that already exist. According to the RAND Corporation, for example, high-end drone technology, such as the Predator and Reaper, are easy to counter (by either shooting them down or jamming them). These obstacles will persist into the future and may even intensify as states further develop countermeasures against drones. Moreover, many other alternatives exist that can perform many, if not most, functions of armed drones, including conventional fighters and bombers, helicopters, and cruise missiles.[90] After weighing all possible strategic considerations, countries may simply opt to develop or purchase a less advanced drone system, or some helicopters.

In summary, then, complex drones are costly and difficult to employ. Furthermore, even if countries bought drones from another state to avoid the process of developing them, they would still cost a fortune to maintain. Moreover, as Gilli and Gilli illustrated, even should states acquire drone technology they would still face major obstacles in operating and exploiting drones' capabilities for military operations. In addition, countermeasures against drones could neutralize efforts to deploy them, especially if done inexpertly. As a result, though many agree that drones will proliferate, evidence seems to indicate these factors make it more likely that mini and tactical drones will spread, while advanced, long-range systems will remain limited to a few rich and technologically advanced countries.

However, Singer makes a different kind of argument about drones and the extent to which they pose a risk in terms of their proliferation. "We are no longer in a world where only the United States has the technology, and we are not moving toward a future in which the technology is used only in the same way we use it now." As he then cautions, "This means . . . that the frequent counter arguments to proliferation concerns have to catch up."[91]

Singer's argument is that the question of whether or not states will be able to overcome the technological challenges in obtaining and operating advanced long-range drones is beside the point. The real concern is that the spread of drones, particularly in this case short-range or low-tech drone technology, is opening the door for new kinds of threats that were not previously factored into international rules and conventions relating to the use of force. In other words, even if many states (and nonstate actors) do not obtain access to complex systems, they may still be able to pose a destabilizing threat with less advanced drone technology. This raises the issue that is the focus of the next section, which reviews the debates and concerns surrounding the dangers created by the proliferation of armed drones.

III. Consequences of Proliferation

The risks of proliferation have generated substantial attention and debate. At the forefront of most discussions is the idea that the way in which the United States uses drones and defends them under international and domestic law has made drone technology an attractive option for many states, especially those feeling threatened by nonstate actors. Among the most commonly stated arguments concerning the potential consequences of drone proliferation is an increase in the frequency and intensity of conflict by either (a) lowering the threshold for the resort to force or (b) increasing the kinds of threats nation face (including the likelihood of drones being used by lone wolves and terrorist organizations). These threats will be considered in order below.

One often-repeated argument is that drone proliferation will increase the likelihood of resorting to armed force. This is because drone proliferation not only diminishes some of the risks that the use of force has traditionally entailed but also because it significantly increases the number of ways force

can be used. In particular, sending drones poses no risk to pilots and consequently reduces the danger of combat casualties. Moreover, certain types of
drones are able to hover for long periods over a target and react quickly to
carry out strikes, and therefore they effectively increase the military opportunities states can exploit.[92] Due to these "unique abilities," Zenko and Kreps
argue that drones will potentially increase the frequency of force deployment.[93] Boyle also noted that states may take greater risks and deploy drones
in order to "test the resolve of their rivals, or engage in 'salami tactics' to see
what kind of drone-led incursion, if any, will motivate a response."[94]

Of further concern is the notion that, due to the uncertainty of how states
will respond to drone incursions, and, on the other side, how states deploying
drones will respond to counterdrone tactics, drones "create the potential for
miscalculation and subsequent escalation."[95] These concerns complement
one another. The combined logic is that the inherent advantages drones possess, along with doubts about whether the other side will respond aggressively
to unmanned incursions, can encourage states to take greater risks than they
otherwise would. Simultaneously, the state considering counterdrone measures (such as shooting down the aircraft) may also perceive that it can do
so with low risk, as the other side is unlikely to retaliate, given that the drone
is unmanned and is in its national airspace. As Zenko and Kreps insist, "The
mix of low-risk and ambiguous rules of engagement is a recipe for escalation."[96]

This possibility became a serious concern following an incident in which
a Chinese military drone flew over the disputed Senkaku Islands in the East
China Sea. On September 9, 2013, the Japanese Air Self-Defence Force
scrambled an F-15 fighter jet in response to the unexpected appearance of a
Chinese surveillance drone flying over the contested islands.[97] Japanese officials were furious at the intrusion, but the Chinese government was unapolo-
getic. In a brief statement acknowledging that "the planes" belonged to the
Chinese military, the country's Ministry of National Defense claimed, "China
enjoys freedom of overflight in relevant waters . . . The Chinese military will
organize similar routine activities in the future."[98] A little over a month later,
on October 20, Japan released new rules of engagement for drones that
included plans to shoot down any unauthorized drones that intrude into
Japan's airspace if warnings to leave are ignored.[99] In response to this, the
spokesperson for the Chinese Ministry of Defense warned that if Japan
shoots down a Chinese drone over the Senkaku Islands, it will be considered
"an act of war" that would prompt retaliation.[100] Following China's drone
overflight, Brimley, FitzGerald, and Ratner observed that "[t]he introduction
of indigenous drones into Asia's strategic environment—now made official
by China's maiden unmanned provocation—will bring with it additional

sources of instability and escalation to the fiercely contested South and East China Seas."[101]

Many commentators have also voiced concerns that drones will be deployed more frequently because other nations will emulate the precedents set by the United States. Writing in the *New York Times*, Scott Shane suggests that the United States is creating an international norm on how to employ drones. This "new" norm may be used as justification in the future by other countries like China, Russia, or India when deploying advanced drone technologies against similar enemies. Shane suggests that this norm may create both long-term and short-term problems:

> Eventually, the United States will face a military adversary or terrorist group armed with drones, military analysts say. But what the short-run hazard experts foresee is not an attack on the United States, which faces no enemies with significant combat drone capabilities, but the political and legal challenges posed when another country follows the American example. The Bush administration, and even more aggressively the Obama administration, embraced an extraordinary principle: that the United States can send this robotic weapon over borders to kill perceived enemies, even American citizens, who are viewed as a threat.
>
> "Is this the world we want to live in?" asks Micah Zenko, a fellow at the Council on Foreign Relations. "Because we're creating it."[102]

As Philip Alston has argued, the "expansive and open-ended interpretation" of the United States' right to self-defense, along with its lack of transparent accountability, "threatens to destroy the prohibition on the use of armed force contained in the UN Charter, which is essential to the international rule of law."[103] The immediate concern is that other countries, especially those "less scrupulous than ourselves," as Jeremy Waldron put it,[104] may adopt the controversial rulebook that the United States has created. As Zenko observed, "[h]istory shows that how states adopt and use new military capabilities is often influenced by how other states have—or have not—used them in the past."[105] Additionally, the more loosely justified drone strikes become, the more broadly others can apply the precedent to more situations. The widespread use of drones becomes worrisome as countries like Israel, China, and soon possibly others continue to aggressively develop and market drones.

In short, as the RAND Corporation argued, "U.S. demonstration of the value and military effectiveness of armed UAVs in counterinsurgency and counterterrorism operations clearly adds to how others could view their need for these weapons. As a result, the United States will find it difficult to argue that others could not find the same value," especially if they mimic the same tactics.[106] Leaving aside the question of whether drones "create an escalation risk insofar as they may lower the bar to enter a conflict,"[107] the next concern is to what extent drones pose a threat to global stability. In particular, what kind of emerging threats, enabled by drone technology, will states soon face?

Regardless of whether drones in general undermine natural restraints on the use of force, the GAO warns that "[t]he United States likely faces increasing risks as additional countries of concern and terrorist organizations acquire UAV technology."[108] One of the main reasons, according to the report, is "because some types of UAVs are relatively inexpensive and have short development cycles, [and therefore] they offer even less wealthy countries a cost-effective way of obtaining new or improved military capabilities that can pose risks to the United States and its allies."[109] Furthermore, even these smaller drones with a limited range and firepower can be destabilizing. As Singer put it:

> Yes, only the United States has a global basing and strike architecture (for now), but that is also irrelevant to most of the issues the proliferation presents. No, Turkey cannot strike Mexico with its unmanned aircraft, but it really doesn't want to. It can, however, reach into Northern Iraq and then cite U.S. precedent in Pakistan that would make for a sticky diplomatic situation. No, Hezbollah can't fly its drones outside the Middle East. It has, however, demonstrated enhanced reach in the region with its own unmanned version of a mini-air force that has spooked Israel.[110]

Thus, there is a concern that the technology will not only fall into the hands of hostile states but also become more accessible to nonstate actors, such as terrorist organizations and lone wolves. This point was well made by Michael Horowitz in a May 2014 *Foreign Policy* article: "Small militaries and even nonstate actors will be able to exploit robotics for military ends."[111] Recent events attest to this, especially in the case of Hezbollah, which has been deploying Iranian-designed drones.[112] Hezbollah presents a special case in this regard, as the organization has a history of sending drones over the borders of other states, although primarily for surveillance purposes. On October 6, 2012, Hezbollah flew a reconnaissance drone "tens of kilometers" over sensitive areas like gas and oil facilities in Israel undetected until being shot down near the Dimona nuclear reactor.[113] Hezbollah not only claimed responsibility for this provocative flight but also said that it was their natural right, naming the reconnaissance drone Ayoub, in honor of a deceased Hezbollah party member who helped pioneer their drone technology.[114] In December 2010, an Israeli warplane shot down an unmanned balloon that flew over the Dimona nuclear reactor, while numerous drones were shot down during the 2006 war with Hezbollah.[115] Similarly, Hamas claimed to have acquired several drones, including armed drones,[116] and on July 14, 2014, it was reported that Israel shot down one of them with a Patriot missile.[117] According to *ABC News* military consultant Steve Ganyard, as Patriot missiles come with a price tag of well over $1 million each, "using a Patriot to shoot down a UAV is like using a shotgun to kill a fly."[118] The Syrian rebels fighting the Assad regime have also employed drones.[119]

Lone wolves have also entered the fray, using short-range, low-technology drones that use a basic radio remote control widely available at hobby shops. For instance, in April 2014, FBI agents stopped a Moroccan citizen in the United States who allegedly plotted to turn a radio-controlled model airplane into a drone-like flying bomb and to crash it into a school and a Connecticut federal building.[120] In addition, in July 2012 a physics graduate of Northeastern University, Rezwan Ferdaus, a U.S. citizen, pled guilty to attempting to provide material support to al-Qaeda and planning to blow up the Pentagon and the U.S. Capitol using remote-controlled planes laden with C-4 explosives.[121] Zenko described the threat these kinds of incidents pose more broadly by stating that "primitive drones like those [Rezwan] Ferdaus sought to build could become more prevalent in domestic terror attacks and against U.S. bases or diplomatic outposts abroad."[122] In 2015 the *Wall Street Journal* reported that "authorities in the U.S., Germany, Spain and Egypt have foiled at least six potential terrorist attacks with drones since 2011."[123]

These terrorist plots also have the potential to become even more dangerous if states or nonstate actors are able to arm drones with WMDs. Zenko and Kreps argue that "[d]rones are, in many ways, the perfect vehicle for delivering biological and chemical agents."[124] Similarly, the GAO reported in 2004 that drones are "ideally suited for the delivery of chemical and biological weapons given their ability to disseminate aerosols in appropriate locations at appropriate altitudes" and noted that, "although the primary concern has been that nation-states would use UAVs to launch WMD attacks, there is potential for terrorist groups to produce or acquire small UAVs and use them for chemical or biological weapons delivery."[125] According to Gormley, "[t]he virtue of most U.A.V.s is that they have long wings and you can strap anything to them."[126] However, there have been few examples of terrorists using WMDs and, more importantly, many agree that terrorists equipping drones with WMDs to hit a target is an unlikely circumstance. According to the RAND report, the probability of nonstate actors using drones for WMD attacks could be even lower when considering the other alternatives terrorist groups have at their disposal. "The reason is simple," said the report. "Conventional technologies such as nail bombs and explosives are easier, cheaper, and can even be more lethal."[127] If a terrorist group were to pursue drones for delivering WMDs, "the threat is primarily psychological," according to the report.[128]

Rather than WMDs, Singer suggests that the emerging threat arising out of drone proliferation is many small weapons. The kind of proliferation Singer envisions, as articulated in a *Foreign Policy* article titled "The Global Swarm," is the spread of smaller and smarter drones that will increasingly carry smaller and smaller munitions.[129] Philip Finnegan, director of corporate analysis for the Teal Group, elaborated on this view: "There is the development of smaller and smaller weapons, some of them specifically for UAVs . . . so they'll be able to use smaller platforms."[130] This presents a problem because, as a number of security analysts and scholars have observed, small drones are particularly hard to shoot down and therefore difficult to defend against. The RAND Corporation reported that the United States is not yet prepared to deal with small, short-range systems: "Current U.S. doctrine for short-range air defense is primarily concerned with defeating attacking helicopters with missiles. The United States may have to develop new defensive systems as the threat from small UAVs emerges."[131] According to a June 2015 CNAS report by Sayler, "[i]f used in large numbers, these systems could potentially enable states, non-state groups, and individuals to achieve overmatch against a significantly more capable adversary."[132] The potential danger small drones present was illustrated in a recent incident in which a two-foot-wide recreational quadcopter that weighed about two pounds passed over the White House fence and struck a tree. "The drone was too small and flying too low to be detected by radar . . . because of its size, it could easily have been confused for a large bird," law enforcement officials said.[133] A military official added that the Defense Department "typically scrambles fighter aircraft for aerial threats over Washington, but when it gets to a toy, that's not something the military typically addresses."[134] In responding to the drone landing at the White House, President Obama said it was a drone "you buy in Radio Shack."[135] Although the quadcopter posed no threat and the incident itself was not a terrorist attack (the operator was drinking with his friends and accidently crashed the drone), it does raise questions about the ability of states to defend sensitive facilities against even the most basic drones.

This is a matter of particular concern because the drones employed so far by nonstate actors have been very basic.[136] According to analysis by the GAO, "[f]or the most part, [terrorist] organizations are currently limited to using smaller, more rudimentary UAVs, such as radio-controlled aircraft that are available worldwide from hobby shops or through the Internet."[137] The report went on to note that "there are likely advantages to using UAVs in terrorist attacks, but also factors that may limit the near-term risk."[138] The report illustrates that in certain situations, small drones could potentially be more precise than other weapons, such as mortars or rockets, but as they are unable to carry large explosives, the impact of such attacks might be moderate. The saving grace here is that the capacity of commercial drones to carry payload is limited, but these limits could be transcended if small drones were used in a group or swarm, especially if the group could be effectively coordinated.

The security dilemmas posed by smaller and less complex drones also support the view discussed in section III that short-range systems (mini to tactical drones) are more likely to spread widely. By contrast, long-range drones used during combat, especially those as sophisticated as the Predators and Reapers, are only effective in permissive airspace, as they are relatively easy to shoot down. Moreover, short-range drones are likely to become widely available in the near future because, as the RAND study stressed, they have important commercial applications:

> Many companies in the United States and elsewhere have developed [short-range systems] for assorted uses, such as law enforcement or commercial aerial photography. The low cost of these systems makes it likely that they will soon be widely used.[139]

According to Sayler, "Low-cost drones may lead to a paradigm shift in ground warfare for the United States, ending more than a half-century of air dominance in which U.S. ground forces have not had to fear attacks from the air."[140]

At the same time, drone proliferation doesn't have to be all bad. For instance, the cutting-edge intelligence, surveillance, and reconnaissance capabilities drones provide allows countries to conduct real-time, 24/7 monitoring in tension-prone areas. As Horowitz and Fuhrmann pointed out, "[t]his could solve information problems and reduce uncertainty, which could otherwise lead countries into conflict when they fear that by not acting, their neighbors may gain an edge."[141] Drone proliferation, the authors continue, "could provide a means for monitoring and confidence building, making it less likely that disputes will escalate, and providing a way for countries to engage in disputes without putting their people at risk of death, decreasing public pressure for war if an incident does occur."[142] Furthermore, as drones do not place the operating military personnel at risk, they have the potential to significantly improve the practice of humanitarian interventions (for this discussion see chapter 4).

While drones have clear attractions for states contemplating their acquisition, particularly in terms of giving states more military options, it is still too early to accurately predict how drones will proliferate, and it is even more difficult to determine the impact that they will have on the international system. At any rate, even if it is the case that the United States created a "new" norm, permitting targeted killings against terrorists abroad, at this point there is likely nothing that the United States can do to stop some countries from acquiring armed drones and using them. Against this background, it may be more prudent to focus on how such circumstances can be limited and contained rather than on trying to rule out such practices entirely. As Plaw and João Reis, researcher at CEDIS (Centro de Investigação e Desenvolvimento sobre Direito e Sociedade), proposed, "a more realistic strategy for managing the inevitable proliferation of combat drones and the likelihood of their use by other countries is to try to link the US use of drones to deeply embedded existing norms of armed conflict."[143] To put it another way, maybe "Learning to Live with Drones" (as Plaw and Reis titled their article) is the best strategy going forward. Then again, perhaps this represents a premature capitulation, and the responsible course of action is still to explore how international conventions might be strengthened to prevent the proliferation, at least of combat drones. Much of the discussion over the best course to pursue has centered on the international bodies that regulate the export of drones. These are examined in more detail in the next section.

IV. Drone Exports and Multilateral Regimes

The two principal multilateral regimes that shape and constrain drone exports are the Missile Technology Control Regime (MTCR) and to a lesser extent the Wassenaar Arrangement. Both regimes are consensus based, requiring that all members agree to any proposed changes in regime documents or activities in order to restrict exports of sensitive technologies by placing them on commonly agreed-to lists.[144] Both also seek to coordinate national export licensing efforts aimed at preventing proliferation of specific items. The MTCR is an informal and voluntary association that was established in 1987 to "prevent the proliferation of missiles and unmanned aerial vehicles capable of delivering nuclear weapons."[145] The regime further extended its mandate in 1992 to limit the "proliferation of missile delivery systems for all weapons of mass destruction: chemical and biological weapons as well as nuclear weapons."[146] Since its creation, the number of MTCR partners has increased to a total of thirty-four countries.

The MTCR regulates drones and related technologies used in their production through a set of guidelines contained in an Annex that divides items into two categories (Category 1 and Category II). Under these guidelines, complete drone systems can be controlled as either a Category I or a Category II system, depending on their missile performance (range and payload capacity). Category I includes drones that have the capability to deliver a payload of at least five hundred kilograms (about 1,100 pounds) to a range exceeding three hundred kilometers (approximately 186 miles) and production facilities for such systems.[147] The remainder of the Annex is regarded as Category II, which comprises drones capable of a flight range equal to or greater than three hundred kilometers regardless of payload, and other components, equipment, material, and technology that would be usable in the production of drones not covered in Category I.

So the main distinction between Category I and Category II comes down to whether the drone is capable of delivering a payload that exceeds five hundred kilograms. MTCR member states are further instructed to apply a "strong presumption of denial" standard when considering transfers of items in Category I regardless of purpose. During an interview, Vann Van Diepen, the deputy assistant secretary of state, clarified this point. "The whole thrust of the guidelines for these Category I systems [is that] the first answer is no and then there has to be a really good reason to be able, on what you can justify as a rare occasion, to overcome that strong presumption of denial."[148] MTCR restrictions for Category II exports are less severe due to the civilian applications many of the items also have.[149] This also points to the difficulties in restricting dual-use technology—that is, technologies that have both military and civilian purposes—which presents an obstacle for multilateral regimes regulating their exports. For instance, according to the GAO report, "many countries chose tactical UAVs for their development program" as they "can easily incorporate available dual-use technology."[150] In addition to this, Category II items are not subject to the MTCR "strong presumption of denial," except for exports judged by the exporting country to be intended for use in delivering WMD. As a result, it is easier for countries to export Category II drones.

While the purpose of the MTCR is clearly to prevent the proliferation of delivery systems capable of carrying WMD, the Wassenaar Arrangement was established in 1996 as a voluntary association consisting of forty-one countries that share the goal of limiting the spread of certain conventional weapons and sensitive dual-use items having both civilian and military applications.[151] The purpose of the organization is to "contribute to regional and international security" by "promoting transparency and greater responsibility with regard to transfers of conventional arms and dual-use goods and technologies, thus preventing destabilizing accumulations."[152] The Wassenaar Agreement requires participants to share information on deliveries, especially of dual-use technology. More importantly, the Wassenaar Arrangement is not targeted at any region or group of states, but rather at "states of concern" to members.[153]

A number of issues that can undermine the agreements' effectiveness in regulating the transfer of drone technologies have been raised in relation to the MTCR and to a lesser extent the Wassenaar Arrangement. For one thing, the guidelines of these agreements are not in any way legally binding, and there is no international organization to verify or enforce compliance. Member states interpret the rules and implement them at their discretion.[154] Moreover, as the RAND study reported, "the language in the guidelines of both regimes has been crafted in ways to provide enormous latitude."[155] As a result, translating the requirements into actual practice has become controversial. Although the "strong presumption of denial" clause suggests that member states should not export Category I items, the United States has exported such technologies to close allies.[156]

There is also some reason for concern over the range of technologies to which the MTCR and Wassenaar Arrangement regulations apply. On the good side, the GAO, citing officials from the Department of State, reported that from 2005 to 2011, MTCR members have adopted a total of twenty-two drone-related technical changes, such as restriction on turboprop systems used in Category I drones and inertial navigation systems used in Category II UAVs. However, according to the report, "only 7 percent of [drone] systems are subject to MTCR's strictest controls."[157] In regard to the Wassenaar Arrangement, although the regime controls the export of some key dual-use drone components, it does not apply to all dual-use-enabling technologies that are critical to the development of drone programs.[158] Moreover, according to the GAO analysis, it is very difficult to add certain drone-related dual-use technologies to the Wassenaar control list because they have other commercial applications.[159]

The central issue, however, is that a number of countries either producing or aspiring to acquire drones are not members of both the MTCR and the Wassenaar Arrangement, raising concerns about the potential for nonmembers to undermine the regimes' ability to limit drone proliferation. For instance, the RAND Corporation studied eight countries reportedly developing Category I systems (China, India, Iran, Russia, Taiwan, Turkey, the UAE, and the United States) and three countries reportedly developing only Category II systems (Israel, Pakistan, and South Africa). Of the eight countries developing Category I systems, five are not MTCR members (China, India, Iran, Taiwan, and the UAE). As the RAND Corporation noted, "More countries developing Category I systems—those systems of greatest concern from a proliferation standpoint—fall outside of MTCR" than are within.[160] It should be noted that other sources indicated that Israel, which is also not a member of the MTCR, is also among those producing Category I systems.[161] The Wassenaar Arrangement faces a similar issue, as major arms exporters, such as Belarus, China, and Israel, are not members.

In terms of drone sales, the gap between MTCR members and nonmembers is also evident. As demand for drones continues to grow, a number of drone-producing states aim to take advantage of U.S. export control restrictions on armed systems, especially those not bound to the MTCR guidelines. As Zhang Qiaoliang, a Chinese aerospace spokesman whose statement is often cited, remarked: "The United States doesn't export many attack drones, so we're taking advantage of that hole in the market."[162] As already noted, Israel has in fact already managed to overtake the United States and become the world's largest exporter of drones, according to a major study by the Frost & Sullivan international business consulting firm.[163] Additionally, from 2005 to 2012, Israel earned at least $4.6 billion in sales (this tally includes exports of the drones themselves and operating and communications systems and payloads), while U.S. companies are estimated to have exported less than $3 billion worth of similar products during that same time period.[164] This difference, Kaag and Kreps noted, exposes an important gap in the nonproliferation regime.[165] Still, while Israel is not a member of the MTCR, it has stated that it will unilaterally adhere to it. Nonetheless, with less severe export restrictions it was able to develop a massive drone market.

China has voluntarily pledged in the past to abide by the MTCR guidelines, but its future commitment is uncertain. Mahendran Arjunraja expects China to begin exporting drones in greater numbers once it manages to create high-altitude, long-endurance (HALE) technology. "We expect most of [China's] growth to happen after 2015. That's when China is expected to have HALE . . . technology, and after that they can export to countries like Pakistan and Iran."[166] China has already reportedly sold two of its armed drones, the Yi Long, to the United Arab Emirates, and the CH-3 to Pakistan.[167] Given these concerns, many commentators have proposed ways international regimes could better govern drone sales and usage in the future.

The debates surrounding the future of armed drone exports are mostly contested and unresolved. For example, in the case of U.S. policy there is an ongoing discussion about finding the right balance between supporting legitimate U.S. exports and curbing the spread of drone technologies to dangerous groups or countries. Drone manufacturers and the military have been pressuring the United States to relax transfer restrictions for wider exports. The drone producers argue that if they do not satisfy the growing demands for drones, other states will develop their own or will turn to other drone developers.[168] Therefore, this line of argument maintains that greater flexibility on international exports will provide industrial benefits while decreasing the likelihood of losing potential clients to other producers, like Israel.[169] As a 2012 Congressional Research Service report put it: "Much new business is likely to be generated in the [drone] market, and if U.S. companies fail to capture this market share, European, Russian, Israeli, Chinese or South African companies will."[170] The military makes a similar case, but argues that selected transfers of drone technology to key allies can further national security objectives. For instance, it could enhance security cooperation activities (as allied countries develop their drone capabilities), easing the burden on the United States in present and future conflicts.[171]

At the same time, those observing the growth and spread of armed drones fear that easing restrictions could result in states hostile to the United States acquiring worrying drone capabilities. At the most extreme there are those calling for tougher export controls, arguing that U.S. policy should be aimed at limiting the sale of armed drones, even to its own allies.[172] On this view, Gormley argues that setting the precedent of arming other states "is likely to make it easier for other states to argue the merits of doing the same. Spreading armed drones at a time when norms of international behavior are virtually nonexistent makes no sense."[173]

Others have taken a more flexible approach, proposing a solution that will allow for "more permissive armed drone exports to close allies and partners" but at the same time limit exports to countries of concern.[174] According to Zenko and Kreps, "[g]overning the use of armed drones will not require new treaties or international laws, because adequate legal instruments already exist, such as the MTCR, though it requires clarification."[175] The authors then wrote that the United States has "the unique opportunity to determine which countries acquire these systems" and should take advantage of it by limiting its exports to countries committed to principles such as the following: peacefully resolving all outstanding border or maritime disputes, peacefully brokering domestic political disputes, protecting civilians from harm caused by other weapons platforms, and protecting human rights.[176]

Given the difficulty of reaching consensus support for modifying preexisting frameworks, another suggestion is to create a drone-specific regime to regulate the proliferation of drone technologies. In a later publication, Kaag and Kreps proposed a strategy that would "control and regulate the proliferation of drones through the judicious use of international law to establish arms control regulations on drones."[177] A major difference from previous proposals is that Kaag and Kreps also suggested creating a "drone-specific international institution . . . that would be organized to regulate drone manufacture and distribution."[178] Furthermore, this proposed drone-specific international institution would be "made-up of drone manufacturers around the world, [which] would work closely with countries on the verge of acquiring drone technologies to ensure that they adopt the best practices."[179]

Pressure on the U.S. government to adopt a more flexible stance on export controls appears to have already had some effect. The State Department has recently released a new policy on military drone exports in February 2015 that will allow U.S. drone manufacturers to sell armed drones to its allies but not permit buyers to conduct "unlawful" operations.[180] According to the State Department, this new export policy is "part of a broader United States [drone] policy review which includes plans to work with other countries to shape international standards for the sale, transfer, and subsequent use of military [drones]."[181] However, the belief that this new export policy will better limit the adverse effects of unwanted proliferation may be overly optimistic, because as Singer has observed, "[w]hether it's an F-16, an armed drone or a billy club, once you sell it to another country, you lose control over how it's used."[182]

Others like Gilli and Gilli argue that creating new legal frameworks or updating preexisting ones will be both insufficient and unnecessary.[183] According to them, improving existing policies or creating new ones will be insufficient due to the fact that countries have violated the treaty's provisions, despite their clarity, "when their commercial interests were at stake."[184] Their belief that modifying existing norms will also be unnecessary is connected to their argument that the technological challenges in producing high-end drones and the infrastructural support required to maintain them will severely limit the proliferation of armed drones. As they put it, "[t]he adoption challenges . . . [intrinsic to drones] will represent the biggest constraint to the proliferation of drone warfare,"[185] and such constraints are likely going to grow further as antidrone systems are developed and fielded. The only real solution, Gilli and Gilli argue, is for the United States to continue—and even to increase—its investments in unmanned technologies and in potential countersystems "in order to preserve its technological lead over friends and foes."[186]

Finding the right answer to resolve these disagreements may prove to be difficult. As Richard Haass, president of the Council on Foreign Relations (CFR), said in a report, "There is the reality that drones are proliferating but, as is often the case with new technologies, the international legal and regulatory framework is lagging behind."[187] Many also see the United States as playing a significant role in shaping the "drone doctrines" going forward, especially for those interested in procuring American-made drones.[188] Nonetheless, debates about making amendments to preexisting frameworks or creating new ones, and whether this is necessary in the first place, raises two questions (as initially framed by the RAND study): Do the dangers created by the proliferation of armed drones require restraint? And should these systems be viewed or treated any differently from conventional aircraft? The latter question is part of a larger ongoing debate about whether drone technology is transformative. That is, does the technology have the capability to revolutionize the way nations conduct war?

V. Drones and Revolutions in Military Affairs

In his influential book *Wired for War*, Singer said that revolutions in military affairs (RMAs) "typically involve the introduction of a new technology or organization, which in turn creates a whole new model of fighting and winning wars."[189] Singer suggests that this can happen in a couple of different ways: "[a] new weapon is introduced that makes obsolete all the previous best weapons . . . [o]r it may be that a military figures out how to organize itself in a new way around an already known weapon, which makes all the old ways of fighting futile."[190] A number of commentators, policymakers, and scholars observing the progression of drone technology have described it as revolutionizing "the way nations conduct war,"[191] often citing the advantages drones possess. Zenko and Kreps, for example, point to three "unique properties" of drones that show that they should be treated as a distinct class of weapons: (1) the ability to loiter over a target for extended periods of time without being refueled; (2) being able to immediately fire at time-sensitive targets (while also being able to divert the missile at the last moment); and the fact that (3) drones do not place human pilots or ground forces at risk of being killed or captured.[192] However, it is debatable whether these "unique properties" and the overall capabilities of drones are enough to place the technology in the same category as tanks and aircraft carriers, or tactics such as *blitzkrieg*.[193]

So the key question is whether drones will "revolutionize" the way that war is conducted. Scholars examining this question have offered some interesting suggestions. In a short brief for the European Union Institute for Security Studies, Andrea Gilli wrote that "combat drones will reshape—if not completely revolutionise—air warfare."[194] Brimley, Sayler, and FitzGerald identified a number of potential "game-changing" technologies that they defined as technology that "radically alters the symmetry of military power between competitors," and when the technology "immediately outdates the policies, doctrines and organizations of all actors."[195] Among these emerging technologies, which include 3-D printers and cyber capabilities, was a discussion of drones with a particular focus on their autonomous potential.

According to Brimley, Sayler, and FitzGerald, the introduction of drones has opened the door for a variety of other autonomous systems "that are smaller, cheaper and able to operate in swarms to overwhelm adversary defenses."[196] Singer and Thomas Wright (director of the Project on International Order and Strategy at the Brookings Institution) have also described drones as game changers due to their ability to move "the point of critical human decision, both geographically off the battlefield and also, increasingly, chronologically away from the time of kinetic action."[197] Michael O'Hanlon, a defense policy expert at the Brookings Institution, made an even bolder claim by declaring that "the era of manned airplanes should be seen as over."[198]

Not everyone has been convinced of the anachronism of manned aircraft, however. The RAND Corporation claimed that armed drones are not revolutionary weapons, though they offer states some significant advantages against enemies that lack air defenses. The 2014 RAND report laid out several reasons why armed drones are not "transformative." First, many of the capabilities of armed drones can be found in other weapon systems. As the report said, "[h]elicopters, cruise and ballistic missiles, and manned aircraft can perform many, if not most, armed UAV functions."[199] Second, the RAND Corporation factored in the cost and ease of use. As discussed before, the complete system architecture required to carry out strikes is complex and costly, which means that only a small number of countries are capable of duplicating it. This also led to the third, and perhaps the most important, point: drones are highly vulnerable. Due to the fact it is relatively easy to shoot down a drone, and that some of them need a radio link (which is vulnerable to jamming), they can only be effectively used in rare circumstances and are otherwise easy to avoid or counter.[200] More broadly, the RAND Corporation pointed out that armed drones "do not win wars, and wars can be won without them."[201] Furthermore, the only time drones are able to decisively tilt the battle is when deployed against insurgent movements, or others that lack even basic air defenses.[202]

An exchange between Asa Kasher (professor at Tel Aviv University and author of the *Israel Defense Forces Code of Conduct*) and Avery Plaw provides an illustrative example of the divergent views expressed. Due to the novelty of using drones in combat, Kasher suggested that "a need for new concepts and principles may arise and is perhaps even expected," referring to the ethical norms that currently regulate the conduct of war.[203] His lines of argument encapsulate many of the key ideas of those describing drones as being revolutionary. For instance, Kasher stressed that one importantly distinctive feature of a drone is that "the operator and the weapon are far from each other, as are the weapon and the target," a point also stressed by Singer and

Wright.[204] In regard to tactics potentially permitted by drones, Kasher followed Brimley et al. by noting the possibility of drones being used in "swarms" or "clouds."

By contrast, Plaw argued that the usage of drones is not as "new" as many are led to believe, suggesting that drones mark more of an incremental rather than radical change in the technology of war. Plaw demonstrated this view by comparing the similarities drones have with cruise and smart missiles. In regard to the distance between the operator and weapon (and the weapon and target), for example, Plaw pointed out that it is not so different from guided missiles. Countering the new tactical possibilities drones provide, Plaw noted that swarm tactics are not "terribly unique," as missiles can be similarly deployed in a swarm, "albeit usually only once."[205] To supplement his claims, Plaw cited Steven Zaloga, a military historian specializing in aerospace technology: "Guided missiles differ from UAVs in [only] one crucial respect: UAVs are designed to return to base after their mission, while guided missiles explode when they impact their target."[206]

In conclusion, though many seem captivated by the inherent advantages of drones (e.g., eliminating pilot casualties), alternative systems with many of the same capabilities do exist. Furthermore, the possession of drones has not yet made "all the previous best weapons" obsolete, as several alternatives to drones, such as cruise missiles, airstrikes by fixed-wing aircraft and helicopters, and special operations forces raids, have been employed at various times against the same targets (al-Qaeda–linked terrorists and Taliban insurgents). At the same time, many of those describing drones as revolutionary are not talking about what the technology is today but what it could be tomorrow. If this is the case, it could mean one of two things. First, Singer said that RMAs take a while to bear fruit, so drones could be an RMA that won't be recognized "until after the fact."[207] On the other hand, it could be that the long-term impact of drone technologies is overpromised and the expected breakthroughs will never come to fruition. In the final case study we will examine the use of drone strikes by other countries, with a particular focus on Israel's drone campaigns.

Case Study: Non-U.S. Drone Strikes

In the middle of January 2009, agents from Mossad, Israel's legendary spy agency, received intelligence that containers packed with rockets and explosives from Iran were being loaded onto the backs of trucks in Sudan that were destined for the Egypt-Gaza border.[208] According to the tipoff, the containers were holding 120 tons of weaponry, including Iranian Fajr-5 artillery rockets. Furthermore, the rockets had a range capable of striking Tel Aviv[209] and Israel's nuclear reactor at Dimona[210] from Gaza. The planned shipment occurred at the height of Israel's assault on Gaza, and the Israelis were intent on striking before the twenty-three-truck convoy crossed the Egyptian border. The decision ultimately made by Israel Air Force (IAF) commander Major General Ido Nehushtan was to use a drone, the Heron TP (Eitan), to provide surveillance, and to use another drone, the Hermes 450, to strike.[211]

The *Sunday Times*, a British newspaper citing an Israeli security source, reported that at least fifty smugglers and their Iranian escorts were killed in the resulting drone strike.[212] According to the state *Suna* news agency, Sudan's defense minister Abdel Rahim Mohamed Hussein made a report to Parliament saying the attack on a suspected smuggling convoy killed fifty-six smugglers and sixty-three smuggled persons from Ethiopia, Somalia, and other countries.[213] Israeli officials have repeatedly refused to confirm or deny this incident.[214] However, Israeli Prime Minister Ehud Olmert's response when asked about the Sudan incident was striking:

> We operate everywhere we can hit terrorist infrastructure—in nearby places, in places further away, anywhere we can strike them in a way that increases deterrence . . . everyone can use their imagination. Those who need to know, know there is no place where Israel cannot operate. Such a place doesn't exist.[215]

This strike would not be the last reported drone strike in the region. On April 5, 2011, a U.S.-made Hellfire missile launched by an Israeli drone targeted the car of Abdel Latif al-Ashkar, who allegedly replaced Mahmoud al Mabhouh as director of Hamas's arms smuggling operation, following Mabhouh's killing in January 2010.[216] Israeli officials once again declined to publicly comment on the incident, but in private a senior military official told *Time* magazine, "It's not our first time there."[217]

Israel's Drone Campaigns

Israel is certainly a unique case, as it became involved in targeted killings soon after its creation in 1948, including the killing in 1956 of Egyptian and Jordanian army officers who were encouraging Fedayeen incursions across Israeli borders. Perhaps even more well known were the Wrath of God operations in the mid-1970s against Palestinian Black September militants. However, it was only with the beginning of the Second Intifada in September 2000 that the Israelis began to employ these tactics openly and systematically. More importantly, as the incidents above show, Israel has carried out drone strikes on the territory of another state outside of conventional armed conflict. It is the only country other than the United States known to have done so. Moreover, Israel's drone operations have not been limited to Sudan. On August 9, 2013, an Israeli drone entered Egyptian airspace over Sinai and targeted a rocket-launching station (aiming at Israel), killing at least four militants with alleged links to al-Qaeda.[218] As the *New York Times* reported at the time, "[a]n Israeli attack of this kind inside Egyptian territory would be extremely rare, if not unprecedented since the two countries signed a peace treaty in 1979."[219] There were conflicting reports on whether the Israeli strike had Egyptian government approval, with neither side asserting responsibility for the attack. Egyptian security officials speaking to the *Associated Press* said Egypt cooperated with Israel, while others disagreed:[220] "It is not true, either in form nor substance, that there were any attacks from the Israeli side inside Egyptian territory," said an Egyptian army spokesman who denied any Israeli role in the incident. "Likewise, the claim that there exists coordination between the Egyptian and the Israeli side in this matter is a matter completely void of truth."[221]

On January 18, 2015, it was reported that an Israeli drone strike in southern Syria left six Hezbollah and Iranian Revolutionary Guard Corps personnel dead, including Revolutionary Guard Commander Mohammed Allahdadi, and Jihad Mughniyeh, the son of late senior Hezbollah leader Imad Mughniyeh.[222] United Nations peacekeepers in the Golan Heights have reported that the attack against the Hezbollah convoy in the Quneitra region was carried out by two Israeli drones and not a helicopter, as initially reported. UN spokesman Farhan Haq told reporters that "[t]his incident is a violation of the 1974 Agreement on Disengagement between Israeli and Syrian forces."[223]

As Israel does not officially admit that it has ever used armed drones, piecing together details of how they are being used, in or outside of declared wars, is difficult. The problem is best described in a statement by Yaakov Katz of the *Jerusalem Post*: "While Jerusalem does not admit to possessing armed UAVs, it has been reported in the rest of the world that Israel has been using them for nearly a decade."[224] There have also been accounts of Israel employing armed drones in the context of conventional war zones. For instance, Israel is believed to have used armed drones during the Second Lebanese War (or July War) in 2006.[225] However, the most widespread and systematic use of drones has been in the Gaza Strip, with the first recorded incident occurring in 2004 when a drone struck two members of Hamas as they were planting explosives near an Israeli military position, killing both of them.[226] Israel's use of armed drones stepped up during Operation Cast Lead, Israel's twenty-two-day offensive in the Gaza Strip between December 27, 2008, and January 18, 2009. Michele Esposito, a senior research associate at the Institute of Palestine Studies, described Operation Cast Lead as having two operational phases. The initial phase began with a "'shock and awe' campaign involving 64 warplanes hitting more than 50 Hamas-related security targets across the Gaza Strip."[227] This was then followed by "more than 100 tons of explosives [that were] dropped in the first 9 hours of combat alone," as the IDF worked through a list of predetermined targets.[228] The second phase began on January 3 with ground troops entering Gaza after the IDF had done all it could to strike preselected targets from the air.[229] During this phase, drones "were used to clear the area ahead (firing antitank and antipersonnel weapons as needed) and to guide troops by relaying advice regarding safe routes of entry and advancement."[230] According to Esposito:

> During phases 1 and 2 of OCL, Israel relied heavily on unmanned aerial vehicles (UAVs or drones) to provide critical surveillance and remote strike capability. While UAVs primarily provided support to other IDF units, they were frequently also the primary tools for executing strikes.[231]

Esposito went on to point out that Operation Cast Lead "marked the first time that infantry commanders on the ground were allowed to direct UAVs, helicopters, and warplanes independently, without having to run operational orders through air force command."[232]

Using drones in this way is reported to have resulted in a significant number of civilian casualties, although there was some uncertainty over the exact number. Human Rights Watch summarized the controversy surrounding how many civilians were killed by Israeli drones strikes as follows:

> The total number of Gazan civilians killed by drone-launched missiles remains unclear. Israeli and Palestinian human rights organizations—B'Tselem, the Palestinian Centre for Human Rights, and the Al-Mezan Center for Human Rights—together reported 42 drone attacks that killed 87 civilians. Amnesty International told the media that it documented 48 civilian deaths from drones, and this does not represent the full number.[233]

A few years later, in November 2012, Israel launched another aggressive campaign against Hamas code-named Operation Pillar of Defense, and unlike previous military campaigns, Israel did not put a single boot on the ground.[234] Operation Pillar of Defense officially began when a drone struck a car traveling in Gaza City, killing Ahmed Jabari, the commander of the Hamas armed wing, on November 14.[235] The extensive use of drone technology during this campaign has been described as "unprecedented" by Israeli sources.[236] In researching a piece on the campaign for *Fight Global*, Arie Egozi was told by Israeli sources that "the type of warfare fought over Gaza could

not have been performed without the massive use of unmanned platforms."[237] At the time Egozi made the following comment about the campaign:

> In the history of combat involving massive use of unmanned air systems (UAS),
> Israel's Operation Pillar of Defence in Gaza last week is without doubt a mile-
> stone, not only for Israel but for any other UAS user.[238]

Journalist Peter Layton provided a detailed account of how armed drones
were employed in Israel's military offensive:

> Operation Pillar of Defense began with a precision attack on a car in the middle
> of Gaza by an armed IAF Hermes 450 Unmanned Air Vehicle (UAV) that fired
> a Spike anti-tank missile. Ahmed Jabari, chief of Hamas's military wing, and
> considered responsible for the rapid development of Hamas's formidable rocket
> forces was killed. A wave of manned aircraft attacks immediately followed that
> focussed [*sic*] on destroying the long-range rockets, especially the Fajars. . . .
> Armed Hermes UAVs also are reported to have continued with leadership
> attacks and in quickly responding to pop-up rocket launches by the mobile
> missile teams.[239]

Human Rights Watch investigated some of the attacks and found that at
least eighteen Israeli airstrikes during the fighting "were in apparent violation
of the laws of war."[240] Furthermore, at least seven of the airstrikes investigated were conducted by drones.[241] The report went on to provide more
details on specific incidents:

> Human Rights Watch investigations found that Israeli drone strikes on Novem-
> ber 19 killed three men in a truck carrying tomatoes in Deir al-Balah, and a
> science teacher who was sitting in his front yard with his 3-year-old son on his
> lap, talking to an acquaintance—only the toddler survived, but was seriously
> wounded.
>   Other drone-launched missile attacks killed a 79-year-old man and his 14-
> year-old granddaughter in the family's olive grove in Abasan; a farmer and his
> nephew as they were walking on a road near their olive trees in the Khan Yunis
> area; and a 28-year-old woman carrying a blanket in the yard of her home in
> the town of Khuza'a.[242]

Despite Operation Pillar of Defense ending on November 21, 2012, drone
operations in the region continued. On April 30, 2013, the *Financial Times*
reported that an Israeli drone strike killed Haitham al-Meshal, a militant
who was involved in the April 17 rocket attack on Eilat from the Sinai, as he
rode a motorcycle, at around 10 a.m.[243] This would be the first targeted
killing since the cease-fire.

As the case study illustrates, throughout the years Israel has carried out a number of drone strikes, in and outside of recognized war zones, and with each conflict drones took on a greater role in combat. Operation Cast Lead was the first time that the Israeli army integrated drones into its frontline attack force while also allowing infantry commanders to have more control in directing them. The next massive campaign launched by Israel, Operation Pillar of Defence, was the first operation in which there were no Israeli "boots on the ground" in Gaza. With both the United States and Israel engaging in controversial drone campaigns, many are concerned that emerging drone powers may mimic their actions. In fact, there is already an instance in which deployment of armed drones was reportedly contemplated by another country.

Cross-Border Use of Force against Individuals

In 2013, reports emerged of China contemplating the idea of conducting a drone strike in the mountains of Myanmar to assassinate Naw Kham, a drug trafficker who had murdered thirteen Chinese nationals.[244] "One plan was to use an unmanned aircraft to carry 20 kilograms of TNT to bomb the area, but the plan was rejected, because the order was to catch him alive," Liu Yuejin, the director of the Ministry of Public Security's antidrug bureau, told the *Global Times* in an exclusive interview.[245] As Andrew Erickson (professor at the U.S. Naval War College) and Austin Strange (at the time a researcher at the Naval War College's China Maritime Studies Institute) observed: "The fact that a Chinese official acknowledged that Beijing had considered using drones to eliminate the Burmese drug trafficker, Naw Kham, made clear that it would not be out of the question for China to launch a drone strike in a security operation against a nonstate actor."[246] While the Chinese government ultimately decided against launching a drone strike, contemplating the tactic as a possible solution highlights China's willingness to carry out such operations. As a CNN blog post warned, "[t]oday, it's Myanmar. Tomorrow, it could very well be some other place in Asia or beyond."[247]

China's control over Tibet and Xinjiang also continues to provoke domestic unrest in the region. According to Zenko and Kreps, states like China "already designate individuals from these groups [e.g., Tibetans and Uighurs] as 'terrorists,' and reserve the right to use force against them."[248] This may raise some valid concerns, given that China has already deployed drones within its borders for counterterrorism operations. For example, in August 2014, China deployed drones for domestic surveillance in Xinjiang three days after an eruption of violence left nearly one hundred people dead.[249] According to reports, thirty-seven civilians, including thirty-five ethnic Hans and two Uighurs, were killed, and fifty-nine people described as terrorists had been shot dead by the police, while another 215 were arrested.[250] During this incident, drones were deployed in order to provide "important intelligence in tracking down and arresting terrorists."[251]

As already explained, Israel has repeatedly deployed armed drones outside of conventional war zones, while others, like China, have at least contemplated doing the same. This is not entirely surprising. After all, drone strikes are really just one of many forms of lethal force available to some states. In recent years, a number of countries have carried out lethal operations against terrorist groups abroad using means other than drones. In addition, other states have asserted the right to carry out such strikes but have not yet done so. As Christian J. Tams, a professor of International Law at the University of Glasgow, put it, "The number of states which claim a right to take forcible anti-terrorist measures has markedly increased, while the willingness of other states to condemn such measures has decreased."[252] Moreover, this shift in attitude has occurred during the last two decades.

To illustrate this point further, consider the following cases of states resorting to lethal force against nonstate actors. Since the 1990s, Turkish troops have repeatedly crossed into northern Iraq in an attempt to deny the Kurdistan Workers' Party (PKK) a sanctuary in an enclave carved out of Iraq. In 2007, Russia conducted airstrikes against Chechen militants of the Pankisi Gorge in Georgian territory.[253] In another case, Russian agents killed Zelimkhan Yandarbiyev, an active leader of Chechnyan resistance groups, in Doha, Qatar, on February 13, 2004, by planting a car bomb in his Land Rover.[254] Colombia has also launched cross-border attacks against nonstate groups. On March 1, 2008, shortly after midnight, a Colombian air strike targeted Luis Edgar Devia Silva, better known by his nom de guerre, Raúl Reyes, inside Ecuadorian territory.[255]

Terrorism in other regions of the world has also pushed states to use lethal force across international borders, either by invoking self-defense or for humanitarian purposes. In Africa, terrorist organizations like Boko Haram and Lord's Resistance Army (LRA) have repeatedly launched cross-border attacks, pushing states to respond with military force. For instance, Chad, Cameroon, and Niger have all launched airstrikes and sent troops into Nigeria in efforts to defeat Boko Haram.[256] In March 2002, Uganda launched a massive military offensive, named "Operation Iron Fist," against the LRA bases in southern Sudan.[257] In the Middle East, a U.S.-led coalition has launched an air campaign in Iraq and Syria in an attempt to "degrade and defeat" the Islamic State of Iraq and the Levant (ISIL). As of May 7, 2015, the coalition has launched 3,731 airstrikes against ISIL, killing around 8,500 militants.[258] During these operations, American drones have undertaken both surveillance and strike missions for "force protection reasons."[259] Britain is also known to have launched drone strikes against ISIL fighters in Iraq.[260]

The crucial point demonstrated here is that there is growing evidence of countries—including the United States—willing to take forcible action against terrorists operating abroad. Furthermore, the claim that they have the right to do so when the host state is either "unwilling or unable" to take measures to stop terrorists from operating within their borders "has become a standard formula of modern debates."[261] When viewed this way, "the debate about drones," as Tams and James G. Devaney (researcher at the University of Glasgow) rightly pointed out, "is part of a wider challenge to the *jus ad bellum* [i.e., rules for going to war] which began well before the advent of drone policies."[262] Overall, there appears to be evidence that drone strikes are proliferating, as are targeted killing operations more generally. Whether this proliferation of strikes is due to the technology itself, or to an increase in terrorist activities (with the rise of drones just being a symptom of the new threat), is not yet entirely clear.

Notes

1. Peter Bergen and Emily Schneider, "Hezbollah Armed Drone? Militants' New Weapon," *CNN*, September 22, 2014, accessed June 7, 2015, http://edition.cnn.com/2014/09/22/opinion/bergen-schneider-armed-drone-hezbollah/; Adiv Sterman, "Hezbollah Drones Wreak Havoc on Syrian Rebel Bases," *The Times of Israel*, September 21, 2014, accessed June 7, 2015, http://www.timesofisrael.com/hezbollah-drones-wreak-havoc-on-syrian-rebel-bases/.

2. Bergen and Schneider, "Hezbollah Armed Drone?"

3. Shawn Brimley, Kelley Sayler, and Ben FitzGerald, *Game Changers: Disruptive Technology and U.S. Defense Strategy* (Washington, DC: CNAS, 2013), 9.

4. T. X. Hammes, "Droning America: The Tech Our Enemies Can Buy," *War on the Rocks*, October 8, 2013, accessed March 15, 2015, http://warontherocks.com/2013/10/droning-america-the-tech-our-enemies-can-buy/.

5. *Unmanned Systems Integrated Roadmap FY2013–2038* (U.S. Department of Defense, 2013), 5.

6. John Horgan, "Unmanned Flight," *National Geographic*, March 2013, accessed March 15, 2015, http://ngm.nationalgeographic.com/2013/03/unmanned-flight/horgan-text.

7. Samuel J. Brennan, Ethan Griffin, and Rhys McCormick, *Sustaining the U.S. Lead in Unmanned Systems* (Washington, DC: Center for Strategic and International Studies, 2014), 4.

8. *Unmanned Systems Integrated Roadmap FY2013–2038*, 5.

9. *Unmanned Systems Integrated Roadmap FY2013–2038*, 5.

10. Spencer Ackerman, "Navy's Historic Drone Launch from an Aircraft Carrier Has an Asterisk," *Wired*, May 14, 2013, accessed March 10, 2015, http://www.wired.com/2013/05/drone-carrier/; Allen McDuffee, "U.S. Navy Gets in on Drone Action

with First Real Aircraft Carrier Landing," *Wired*, July 25, 2013, accessed March 10, 2015, http://www.wired.com/2013/07/navy-drone/.

11. Michael C. Horowitz and Matthew Fuhrmann, *Droning on: Explaining the Proliferation of Unmanned Aerial Vehicles* (October 24, 2014): 3, http://dx.doi.org/10.2139/ssrn.2514339.

12. Konstantin Kakaes, "From Orville Wright to September 11: What the History of Drone Technology Says About Its Future," in *Drone Wars: Transforming Conflict, Law, and Policy*, edited by Peter L. Bergen and Daniel Rothenberg (Cambridge: Cambridge University Press, 2014), 371–74.

13. Harriet Sherwood, "Israel Is World's Largest Drone Exporter," *The Guardian*, May 20, 2013, accessed March 15, 2015, http://www.theguardian.com/world/2013/may/20/israel-worlds-largest-drone-exporter.

14. Arie Egozi, "UAS War over Africa," *Flightglobal*, October 9, 2012, accessed March 15, 2015, http://www.flightglobal.com/blogs/ariel-view/2012/10/uas-war-over-africa/.

15. Jefferson Morley, "Israel's Drone Dominance," *Salon*, May 15, 2012, accessed March 15, 2015, http://www.salon.com/2012/05/15/israels_drone_dominance/.

16. Government Accountability Office, *Nonproliferation: Agencies Could Improve Information Sharing and End-Use Monitoring on Unmanned Aerial Vehicle Exports* (Washington, DC: GAO, 2012), 9; Peter Bergen and Jennifer Rowland, "World of Drones: The Global Proliferation of Drone Technology," in *Drone Wars: Transforming Conflict, Law and Policy*, edited by Peter Bergen and Daniel Rothenberg (Cambridge: Cambridge University Press, 2015), 300, 304–27.

17. Kelley Sayler, *A World of Proliferated Drones: A Technology Primer* (Washington, DC: CNAS, 2015), 5.

18. Lynn E. Davis, Michael J. McNerney, James Chow, Thomas Hamilton, Sarah Harting, and Daniel Byman, *Armed and Dangerous?: UAVs and U.S. Security* (Santa Monica: RAND Corporation, 2014), 9.

19. Dan Parsons, "Worldwide, Drones Are in High Demand," *National Defense Magazine*, May 2013, accessed March 15, 2015, http://www.nationaldefensemagazine.org/archive/2013/May/Pages/Worldwide,DronesAreinHighDemand.aspx.

20. Patrick Tucker, "Every Country Will Have Armed Drones within 10 Years," *Defense One*, May 6, 2014, accessed March 15, 2015, http://www.defenseone.com/technology/2014/05/every-country-will-have-armed-drones-within-ten-years/83878/.

21. Andreas Lorenz, Juliane von Mittelstaedt, and Gregor Peter Schmitz, "Messengers of Death: Are Drones Creating a New Global Arms Race?," *Spiegel*, October 21, 2011, accessed March 19, 2015, http://www.spiegel.de/international/world/messengers-of-death-are-drones-creating-a-new-global-arms-race-a-792590.html.

22. Davis et al., *Armed and Dangerous?*, 7.

23. Press Report, "Teal Group Predicts Worldwide UAV Market Will Total $91 Billion in Its 2014 UAV Market Profile and Forecast," *PR Newswire*, July 17, 2014, accessed March 15, 2015, http://www.tealgroup.com/index.php/about-teal-group-corporation/press-releases/118-2014-uav-press-release.

24. Press Report, "Teal Group Predicts Worldwide UAV Market."

25. Glennon J. Harrison, *Unmanned Aircraft Systems (UAS): Manufacturing Trends* (Washington, DC: Congressional Research Service, 2013), 2.

26. Cited in Michael C. Horowitz, "The Looming Robotics Gap: Why America's Global Dominance in Military Technology Is Starting to Crumble," *Foreign Policy*, May 2014, accessed March 15, 2015, http://foreignpolicy.com/2014/05/05/the-looming-robotics-gap/.

27. Robert Karniol, "Unmanned Aircraft Poised to Fill Asian Skies," *Asian News Network*, May 28, 2012, accessed March 15, 2015, http://www.asianewsnet.net/news-31229.html.

28. UAV Round Up, *Aerospace America* (Reston, VA: American Institute of Aeronautics and Astronautics, 2013), 32.

29. Adam Entous, "NATO to Acquire First Fleet of Unarmed Drones," *Wall Street Journal*, February 3, 2012, accessed March 15, 2015, http://online.wsj.com/news/articles/SB10001424052970203711104577201913461250618; also see Brian Williams, *Predator: The CIA's Drone War on al-Qaeda* (Washington, DC: Potomac Books, 2013), 235–36.

30. Entous, "NATO to Acquire First Fleet of Unarmed Drones."

31. "nEUROn Unmanned Combat Air Vehicle (UCAV) Demonstrator, France," *Airforce-Technology*, http://www.airforce-technology.com/projects/neuron/.

32. Adam Entous, "U.S. Plans to Arm Italy's Drones," *Wall Street Journal*, May 29, 2012, accessed March 15, 2015, http://www.wsj.com/articles/SB10001424052702303395604577432323658176792.

33. European Commission, "Towards a European Strategy for the Development of Civil Applications of Remotely Piloted Aircraft Systems (RPAS)," Commission Staff Working Document, 2012, 8.

34. "British Drone Taranis Completed Secret Test Flight, Officials Confirm," *Huffington Post*, February 7, 2014, accessed March 15, 2015, http://www.huffingtonpost.com/2014/02/07/british-drone-taranis-test-flight_n _4747267.html.

35. Timur Moon, "British 'Superdrone' Robot Plane Could Fly 'Within Weeks,'" *International Business Times*, January 27, 2013, accessed July 13, 2015, http://www.ibtimes.co.uk/taranis-bae-drone-mod-robot-plane-fighter-428334.

36. Nick Hopkins, "Afghan Civilians Killed by RAF Drone," *The Guardian*, July 5, 2011, accessed March 15, 2015, http://www.theguardian.com/uk/2011/jul/05/afghanistan-raf-drone-civilian-deaths.

37. Written evidence from James Earle on behalf of the Association of Military Court Advocates, "Droning for Britain: Legal and Ethical Issues Arising from the Use of Remotely Piloted Air Systems," *HC 772 Defence Committee*, September 9, 2013, accessed March 18, 2015, http://www.publications.parliament.uk/pa/cm201314/cmselect/cmdfence/772/772vw07.htm.

38. Micah Zenko and Sarah Kreps, "Limiting Armed Drone Proliferation," *Council Special Report* no. 69 (New York: Council on Foreign Relations, 2014): 3.

39. Ian M. Easton and L. C. Russell Hsiao, *The Chinese People's Liberation Army's Unmanned Aerial Vehicle Project: Organizational Capacities and Operational Capabilities* (Arlington: Project 2049 Institute, 2013), 2.

40. Government Accountability Office, *Nonproliferation: Agencies Could Improve Information Sharing and End-Use Monitoring on Unmanned Aerial Vehicle Exports*, 13.

41. Edward Wong, "Hacking U.S. Secrets, China Pushes for Drones," *New York Times*, September 20, 2013, accessed March 15, 2015, http://www.nytimes.com/2013/

09/21/world/asia/hacking-us-secrets-china-pushes-for-drones.html?pagewanted =
all&_r = 0; also see Easton and Hsiao, *The Chinese People's Liberation Army's Unmanned Aerial Vehicle Project*, 11.

42. Wong, "Hacking U.S. Secrets, China Pushes for Drones."

43. Defense Science Board, *The Role of Autonomy in DOD Systems: Task Force Report* (Washington, DC: Department of Defense, 2012), 69.

44. "Russia May Begin Constructing Advanced Military Drones in 2014—Defense Ministry," *Ria Novosti*, May 29, 2014, accessed March 15, 2015, http://sput niknews.com/military/20140529/190223169/Russia-May-Begin-Constructing-Ad vanced-Military-Drones-in-2014-.html.

45. "Russia May Begin Constructing Advanced Military Drones in 2014—Defense Ministry."

46. Damien Sharkov, "Russia to Open Arctic Military Drone Base 420 Miles Off the Alaskan Coast," *Newsweek*, November 13, 2014, accessed March 15, 2015, http://www.newsweek.com/russia-open-arctic-military-drone-base-420-miles-alaskan-coast -284240.

47. Rob O'Gorman and Chris Abbott, *Remote Control War: Unmanned Combat Air Vehicles in China, India, Iran, Israel, Russia and Turkey* (London: Open Briefing, 2013), 13.

48. Emre Soncan, "Turkey to Manufacture Armed Version of National Drone," *Today's Zaman*, July 18, 2012, accessed March 15, 2015, http://www.todayszaman.com /national_turkey-to-manufacture-armed-version-of-national-drone_286926.html.

49. "Turkey Prepares to Launch First Domestically Made Drones," *Turkish Weekly*, January 15, 2014, accessed March 15, 2015, http://www.turkishweekly.net/ news/161521/turkey-prepares-to-launch-first-domestically-made-drones.html.

50. O'Gorman and Abbott, *Remote Control War*, 15.

51. "UAVs Capable of Launching Weapons Soon: DRDO Chief," *The Hindu*, August 27, 2013, accessed March 15, 2015, http://www.thehindu.com/news/cities/ Hyderabad/uavs-capable-of-launching-weapons-soon-drdo-chief/article5062289.ece.

52. Tim Craig and Haq Nawaz Khan, "Pakistan Unveils Its Own Military Drones, as Protests Continue against U.S. Attacks," *Washington Post*, November 25, 2013, accessed March 15, 2015, http://www.washingtonpost.com/world/asia_pacific/paki stan-unveils-its-own-military-drones-as-protests-continue-against-us-attacks/2013/ 11/25/fae691cc-5607-11e3-bdbf-097ab2a3dc2b_story.html.

53. Tim Craig, "Pakistan Says It Will Deploy Its Own Armed Drone against Terrorists," *Washington Post*, March 13, 2015, accessed March 19, 2015, http://www .washingtonpost.com/world/pakistan-says-it-will-deploy-its-own-armed-drone-against -terrorists/2015/03/13/ac0a9008-c98d-11e4-bea5-b893e7ac3fb3_story.html.

54. Craig, "Pakistan Says It Will Deploy Its Own Armed Drone against Terrorists."

55. "Iran Unveils 'Ambassador of Death' Unmanned Drone Bomber," *Associated Press*, August 22, 2010, accessed March 15, 2015, http://www.foxnews.com/world/ 2010/08/22/ahmadinejad-inaugurates-irans-unmanned-bomber/.

56. "Iran Unveils 'Indigenous' Drone with 2,000km Range," *BBC News*, September 26, 2012, accessed March 19, 2015, http://www.bbc.com/news/world-middle -east-19725990.

57. "Iran Unveils New Drone Sarir H-110 Armed with Air-to-Air Missiles during Military Parade in Tehran," *Army Recognition*, April 19, 2013, accessed March 19, 2015, http://www.armyrecognition.com/april_2013_news_defence_army_military_industry_uk/iran_unveils_new_drone_sarir_h-110_armed_air-to-air_missiles_during_military_parade_tehran_1904131.html; "Photos: First Iranian Air-to-Air Combat Drone," *The Iran Project*, May 13, 2013, accessed March 19, 2015, http://theiranproject.com/blog/2013/05/13/photos-first-iranian-air-to-air-combat-drone/.

58. "Iran Says It Has Gleaned Data from U.S. Spy Drone," *Associated Press*, April 23, 2012, accessed March 19, 2015, http://www.sfgate.com/world/article/Iran-says-it-has-gleaned-data-from-U-S-spy-drone-3501847.php.

59. Mark Hosenball, "Iran Helping Assad to Put Down Protests: Officials," Reuters, March 23, 2012, accessed March 19, 2015, http://www.reuters.com/article/2012/03/23/us-iran-syria-crackdown-idUSBRE82M18220120323.

60. Keir Simmons and Gil Aegerter, "The Race Is On: Manufacturer Sets Sights on Market for Armed Drones," *NBC News*, May 28, 2013, accessed March 19, 2015, http://investigations.nbcnews.com/_news/2013/05/28/18472665-the-race-is-on-manufacturer-sets-sights-on-market-for-armed-drones.

61. Simmons and Aegerter, "The Race Is On."

62. International Human Rights and Conflict Resolution Clinic and Global Justice Clinic, *Living Under Drones: Death, Injury and Trauma to Civilians from US Drone Practices in Pakistan* (New York and Palo Alto: NYU School of Law and Stanford Law School, 2012), 140.

63. Defense Science Board, *The Role of Autonomy in DOD Systems*, 13.

64. U.S. Government Accountability Office, *Nonproliferation: Agencies Could Improve Information Sharing*, 13.

65. Horowitz, "The Looming Robotics Gap."

66. Robert O. Work and Shawn Brimley, *20yy Preparing for War in the Robotic Age* (Washington, DC: CNAS, 2014), 35.

67. Work and Brimley, *20yy Preparing for War in the Robotic Age*, 35.

68. Daniel Byman, "Why Drones Work: The Case for Washington's Weapon of Choice, *Foreign Affairs* (2013): 41.

69. Byman, "Why Drones Work," 41.

70. Scott Shane, "Coming Soon: The Drone Arms Race," *New York Times*, October 8 2011, accessed March 19, 2015, http://www.nytimes.com/2011/10/09/sunday-review/coming-soon-the-drone-arms-race.html?pagewanted=all&_r=0.

71. Peter W. Singer, "The Global Swarm," *Foreign Policy*, March 11 2013, accessed March 19, 2015, http://foreignpolicy.com/2013/03/11/the-global-swarm/.

72. Shawn Brimley, Ben FitzGerald, and Ely Ratner, "The Drone War Comes to Asia," *Foreign Policy*, September 17, 2013, accessed March 19, 2015, http://foreignpolicy.com/2013/09/17/the-drone-war-comes-to-asia/.

73. Patrick Tucker, "Every Country Will Have Armed Drones Within 10 Years," *DefenseOne.com*, May 6, 2014, http://www.defenseone.com/technology/2014/05/every-country-will-have-armed-drones-within-ten-years/83878/.

74. Tucker, "Every Country Will Have Armed Drones Within 10 Years."

75. Dennis M. Gormley, "Limiting the Unintended Consequences of Unmanned Air System Proliferation," *Whitehead Journal of Diplomacy and International Relations* 14, no. 1 (2013): 70.

76. Micah Zenko and Sarah Kreps, "The Drone Invasion Has Been Greatly Exaggerated," *Foreign Policy*, March 10, 2014, accessed March 19, 2015, http://foreignpoli cy.com/2014/03/10/the-drone-invasion-has-been-greatly-exaggerated/.

77. Davis et al., *Armed and Dangerous?*, 3.

78. Government Accountability Office, *Nonproliferation: Agencies Could Improve Information Sharing and End-Use Monitoring on Unmanned Aerial Vehicle Exports*, 14.

79. Andrea Gilli and Mauro Gilli, "The Diffusion of Drone Warfare? Industrial, Organizational and Infrastructural Constraints: Military Innovations and Ecosystem Challenge," *Security Studies* (forthcoming), http://ssrn.com/abstract=2425750.

80. Gilli and Gilli define combat-effective drones as those that grant armed forces a significant and enduring military advantage at the tactical and operation level and that can thus deeply affect international affairs. See Gilli and Gilli, "The Diffusion of Drone Warfare?," 45.

81. Gilli and Gilli, "The Diffusion of Drone Warfare?," 47.

82. Gilli and Gilli, "The Diffusion of Drone Warfare?," 4.

83. Gilli and Gilli, "The Diffusion of Drone Warfare?," 36.

84. Gilli and Gilli, "The Diffusion of Drone Warfare?," 37.

85. Gilli and Gilli, "The Diffusion of Drone Warfare?," 35–36.

86. Defense Science Board, *The Role of Autonomy in DOD Systems*, 30.

87. Gilli and Gilli, "The Diffusion of Drone Warfare?," 36.

88. Gilli and Gilli, "The Diffusion of Drone Warfare?," 4.

89. Micah Zenko, "Reforming U.S. Drone Strike Policies," *Council on Foreign Relations Special Report* 65 (New York: Council on Foreign Affairs, 2013), 20.

90. Davis et al., *Armed and Dangerous?*, 13.

91. Singer, "The Global Swarm."

92. Zenko and Kreps, "Limiting Armed Drone Proliferation," 8–9; Davis et al., *Armed and Dangerous?*, 11–12.

93. Zenko and Kreps, "Limiting Armed Drone Proliferation," 9–10.

94. Michael J. Boyle, "The Costs and Consequences of Drone Warfare," *International Affairs* 89, no. 1 (2013): 24.

95. Zenko and Kreps, "Limiting Armed Drone Proliferation," 12.

96. Zenko and Kreps, "Limiting Armed Drone Proliferation," 12.

97. "ASDF Confirms Unidentified Drone Flying over East China Sea," *Asahi Shimbun*, September 10, 2013, accessed March 17, 2015, http://ajw.asahi.com/article/asia/china/AJ201309100069.

98. ASDF Confirms Unidentified Drone Flying over East China Sea."

99. "Japan to Shoot Down Foreign Drones That Invade Its Airspace," *Japan Times*, October 20, 2013, accessed March 5, 2015, http://www.japantimes.co.jp/news/2013/10/20/national/japan-to-shoot-down-foreign-drones-that-invade-its-airspace/#.VY92_0Y6zIX.

100. "China Warns Japan against Shooting Down Drones over Islands," *Times of India*, October 27, 2013, accessed March 5, 2015, http://timesofindia.indiatimes.com/world/china/China-warns-Japan-against-shooting-down-drones-over-islands/articleshow/24779422.cms?referral=PM.

101. Brimley, FitzGerald, and Ratner, "The Drone War Comes to Asia."

102. Shane, "Coming Soon: The Drone Arms Race."

103. "Statement of U.N. Special Rapporteur on U.S. Targeted Killings without Due Process," ACLU, August 3, 2010, accessed March 19, 2015, https://www.aclu.org/national-security/statement-un-special-rapporteur-us-targeted-killings-without-due-process.

104. Jeremy Waldron, "Justifying Targeted Killing with a Neutral Principle?," in *Targeted Killing: Law and Morality in an Asymmetrical World*, edited by C. Finkelstein, J. Ohlin, and A. Altman (Oxford: Oxford University Press, 2012), 130.

105. Zenko, "Reforming U.S. Drone Strike Policies," 24.

106. Davis et al., *Armed and Dangerous?*, 17.

107. General John P. Abizaid and Rosa Brooks, *Recommendations and Report of the Task Force on US Drone Policy* (Washington, DC: Stimson Center, 2014), 11.

108. Government Accountability Office, *Nonproliferation: Agencies Could Improve Information Sharing*, 17.

109. Government Accountability Office, *Nonproliferation: Agencies Could Improve Information Sharing*, 17.

110. Singer, "The Global Swarm."

111. Horowitz, "The Looming Robotics Gap."

112. David Cortright, "The Scary Prospect of Global Drone Warfare," *CNN*, October 19, 2011, accessed March 19, 2015, http://www.cnn.com/2011/10/19/opinion/cortright-drones/.

113. Zenia Karam, "Hezbollah Says It Sent Drone over Israel," *Associated Press*, October 11, 2012, accessed March 19, 2015, http://bigstory.ap.org/article/israeli-leader-accuses-lebanese-hezbollah-group-launching-drone-aircraft-israeli-skies.

114. David Barnett, "Hezbollah Takes Responsibility for Last Week's Drone over Israel," The Long War Journal, October 11, 2012, accessed July 14, 2015, http://www.longwarjournal.org/archives/2012/10/netanyahu_hezbollah.php.

115. "Israel Shoots Down 'Suspicious Flying Object' Near Dimona Nuclear Reactor," *Haaretz*, December 16, 2010, accessed March 19, 2015, http://www.haaretz.com/news/diplomacy-defense/israel-shoots-down-suspicious-flying-object-near-dimona-nuclear-reactor-1.330959.

116. Anna Mulrine, "Drones in the Hands of Hamas: How Worrisome Is That?" *Christian Science Monitor*, July 18, 2014, accessed March 19, 2015, http://www.csmonitor.com/USA/Military/2014/0718/Drones-in-the-hands-of-Hamas-How-worrisome-is-that-video.

117. Alexander Marquardt and Martha Raddatz, "Israel Says It Downed Drone as Gaza Death Toll Climbs," *ABC News*, July 14, 2014, accessed March 10, 2015, http://abcnews.go.com/International/israel-downed-drone-gaza-death-toll-climbs/story?id=24548970.

118. Marquardt and Raddatz, "Israel Says It Downed Drone as Gaza Death Toll Climbs."

119. Mulrine, "Drones in the Hands of Hamas."

120. Alex Brandon, "FBI: Man Plotted to Fly Drone-Like Toy Planes with Bombs into School," *Associated Press*, April 8, 2014, accessed March 20, 2015, http://www.cbsnews.com/news/fbi-man-in-connecticut-plotted-to-fly-drone-like-toy-planes-with-bombs-into-school/.

121. Jess Bidgood, "Massachusetts Man Gets 17 Years in Terrorist Plot," *New York Times*, November 2, 2012, accessed March 19, 2015, http://www.nytimes.com/2012/11/02/us/rezwan-ferdaus-of-massachusetts-gets-17-years-in-terrorist-plot.html?_r=0.

122. Zenko, "Reforming U.S. Drone Strike Policies," 21.

123. Jack Nicas, "Criminals, Terrorists Find Uses for Drones, Raising Concerns," *Wall Street Journal*, January 28, 2015, accessed March 19, 2015, http://www.wsj.com/articles/criminals-terrorists-find-uses-for-drones-raising-concerns-1422494268.

124. Zenko and Kreps, "Limiting Armed Drone Proliferation," 12.

125. Government Accountability Office, *Nonproliferation*, 11.

126. Shane, "Coming Soon: The Drone Arms Race."

127. Davis et al., *Armed and Dangerous?*, 6.

128. Davis et al., *Armed and Dangerous?*, 7.

129. Singer, "The Global Swarm."

130. Simmons and Aegerter, "The Race Is On."

131. Davis et al., *Armed and Dangerous?*, 4.

132. Sayler, *A World of Proliferated Drones*, 5.

133. Michael S. Schmidt and Michael D. Shear, "A Drone, Too Small for Radar to Detect, Rattles the White House," *New York Times*, January 26, 2015, accessed March 19, 2015, http://www.nytimes.com/2015/01/27/us/white-house-drone.html?_r=0.

134. Schmidt and Shear, "A Drone, Too Small for Radar to Detect, Rattles the White House."

135. Eric Bradner, "Spy Drone Operator Was Drinking," *CNN*, January 28, 2015, accessed March 19, 2015, http://www.cnn.com/2015/01/27/politics/drone-white-house-crash-secret-service/.

136. Mulrine, "Drones in the Hands of Hamas."

137. Government Accountability Office, *Nonproliferation: Agencies Could Improve Information Sharing*, 18.

138. Government Accountability Office, *Nonproliferation: Agencies Could Improve Information Sharing*, 19.

139. Davis et al., *Armed and Dangerous?*, 4.

140. Sayler, *A World of Proliferated Drones*, 29.

141. Horowitz and Fuhrmann, *Droning on*, 13.

142. Horowitz and Fuhrmann, *Droning on*, 13.

143. Avery Plaw and João Reis, "Learning to Live with Drones: Answering Jeremy Waldron and the Neutralist Critique," *Journal of Military Ethics* (forthcoming).

144. Government Accountability Office, *Nonproliferation: Agencies Could Improve Information Sharing*, 4.

145. Mary Beth Nikitin, Paul Kerr, and Steven Hildreth, *Proliferation Control Regime: Background and Status* (Washington, DC: Congressional Research Service, 2010), 33.

146. Nikitin, Kerr, and Hildreth, *Proliferation Control Regime: Background and Status*, 34.

147. *MTCR Annex Handbook* (2010), iii.

148. "Missile Control: An Interview with Deputy Assistant Secretary of State Vann Van Diepen," *Arms Control Today*, July/August 2012, accessed March 19, 2015, https://www.armscontrol.org/2012_07-08/Interview_With_Deputy_Assistant_Secretary_Of_State_Vann_Van_Diepen.

149. "The Missile Technology Control Regime at a Glance," *Arms Control Association*, last modified December 2012, accessed March 19, 2015, http://www.armscontrol.org/factsheets/mtcr.

150. Government Accountability Office, *Nonproliferation: Agencies Could Improve Information Sharing*, 14.

151. "The Wassenaar Arrangement at a Glance," *Arms Control Association*, last modified on October 2012, accessed March 19, 2015, http://www.armscontrol.org/factsheets/wassenaar; Davis et al., *Armed and Dangerous?*, 14.

152. NTI, "Wassenaar Arrangement," accessed March 19, 2015, http://www.nti.org/treaties-and-regimes/wassenaar-arrangement/.

153. "The Wassenaar Arrangement at a Glance."

154. Zenko and Kreps, "Limiting Armed Drone Proliferation," 17.

155. Davis et al., *Armed and Dangerous?*, 16.

156. The United States has exported a limited number of Category I drone systems, sending Reapers and Predators to Italy, Reapers to the United Kingdom, and Global Hawk airframes to Germany and NATO as part of joint UAV development programs. See Government Accountability Office, *Nonproliferation: Agencies Could Improve Information Sharing*, 11.

157. Government Accountability Office, *Nonproliferation: Agencies Could Improve Information Sharing*, 21.

158. Government Accountability Office, *Nonproliferation: Agencies Could Improve Information Sharing*, 21.

159. Government Accountability Office, *Nonproliferation: Agencies Could Improve Information Sharing*, 21.

160. Davis et al., *Armed and Dangerous?*, 10.

161. For instance, the GAO reported that an Israeli manufacturer is marketing the Heron TP, a drone that would fall under Category I. See: Government Accountability Office, *Nonproliferation: Agencies Could Improve Information Sharing*, 12.

162. William Wan and Peter Finn, "Global Race On to Match U.S. Drone Capabilities," *Washington Post*, July 4, 2011, accessed March 19, 2015, http://www.washingtonpost.com/world/national-security/global-race-on-to-match-us-drone-capabilities/2011/06/30/gHQACWdmxH_story.html.

163. Josh Meyer, "Why Israel Dominates Global Drone Exports," *Quartz*, July 10, 2013, accessed March 19, 2015, http://qz.com/102200/why-israel-dominates-global-drone-exports/; Sherwood, "Israel Is World's Largest Drone Exporter."

164. Meyer, "Why Israel Dominates Global Drone Exports"; Sherwood, "Israel Is World's Largest Drone Exporter."

165. John Kaag and Sarah Kreps, *Drone Warfare* (Cambridge: Polity Press, 2014), 153.

166. Robert Karniol, "Unmanned Aircraft Poised to Fill Asian Skies," *Asian News Network*, May 28, 2012, accessed March 19, 2015, http://www.asianewsnet.net/news-31229.html.

167. Bill Gertz, "Red Dawn: Communist China Stepping up Drone Deployment," *Washington Times*, March 26, 2013, accessed March 19, 2015, http://www.washingtontimes.com/news/2013/mar/26/china-stepping-drone-deployment/?page=all.

168. Gormley, "Limiting the Unintended Consequences of Unmanned Air System Proliferation," 79.

169. Adam Entous and Julian E. Barnes, "U.S. Pursues Sale of Armed Drones," *Wall Street Journal*, December 15, 2011, accessed March 15, 2015, http://online.wsj .com/article/SB10001424052970204844504577098583174059746.html.

170. Jeremiah Gertler, *U.S. Unmanned Aerial Systems* (Washington, DC: Congressional Research Service, 2012), 28.

171. Lieutenant Colonel Ken Callahan, "Enhancing National Security Cooperation Policy with Remotely Piloted Aircraft," *DISAM Journal*, November 7, 2012, accessed March 20, 2015, http://www.disamjournal.org/articles/enhancing-national -security-cooperation-policy-with-remotely-piloted-aircraft-786.

172. Gormley, "Limiting the Unintended Consequences of Unmanned Air System Proliferation," 77.

173. Gormley, "Limiting the Unintended Consequences of Unmanned Air System Proliferation," 77.

174. Zenko and Kreps, "Limiting Armed Drone Proliferation," 18.

175. Zenko and Kreps, "Limiting Armed Drone Proliferation," 23.

176. Zenko and Kreps, "Limiting Armed Drone Proliferation," 24.

177. Kaag and Kreps, *Drone Warfare*, 151.

178. Kaag and Kreps, *Drone Warfare*, 153.

179. Kaag and Kreps, *Drone Warfare*, 153.

180. Missy Ryan, "Obama Administration to Allow Sales of Armed Drones to Allies," *Washington Post*, February 17, 2015, accessed March 19, 2015, http://www .washingtonpost.com/world/national-security/us-cracks-open-door-to-the-export -of-armed-drones-to-allied-nations/2015/02/17/c5595988-b6b2-11e4-9423-f3d0a1 ec335c_story.html.

181. "U.S. Export Policy for Military Unmanned Aerial Systems," *U.S. Department of State*, February 17, 2015, accessed April 25, 2015, http://www.state.gov/r/pa/ prs/ps/2015/02/237541.htm.

182. Scott Shane, "New Rules Set on Armed Drone Exports," *New York Times*, February 17, 2015, accessed April 25, 2015, http://www.nytimes.com/2015/02/18/ world/new-rules-set-on-armed-drone-exports.html?_r = 0.

183. Gilli and Gilli, "The Diffusion of Drone Warfare?," 48.

184. Gilli and Gilli, "The Diffusion of Drone Warfare?," 48.

185. Gilli and Gilli, "The Diffusion of Drone Warfare?," 48–49.

186. Gilli and Gilli, "The Diffusion of Drone Warfare?," 49.

187. Zenko, "Reforming U.S. Drone Strike Policies," vii.

188. Zenko and Kreps, "Limiting Armed Drone Proliferation," 13, 24.

189. Peter W. Singer, *Wired for War: The Robotic Revolution and Conflict in the Twenty-first Century* (New York: The Penguin Press, 2009), 181.

190. Singer, *Wired for War*, 181.

191. Peter Bergen and Jennifer Rowland, "A Dangerous New World of Drones," *CNN*, October 8, 2012, accessed March 20, 2015, http://www.cnn.com/2012/10/01/ opinion/bergen-world-of-drones.

192. Zenko and Kreps, "Limiting Armed Drone Proliferation," 8–9.

193. Davis et al., *Armed and Dangerous?*, 11.

194. Andrea Gilli, *Drones for Europe* (Paris: EUISS, 2013), 1.

195. Brimley, Sayler, and FitzGerald, *Game Changers*, 11.

196. Brimley, Sayler, and FitzGerald, *Game Changers*, 15.

197. Peter W. Singer and Thomas Wright, "Memorandum to the President: An Obama Doctrine on New Rules of War," *Brookings Institution*, January 17, 2013, accessed March 20, 2015, http://www.brookings.edu/research/papers/2013/01/an -obama-doctrine-on-new-rules-of-war.

198. Jonathan Fahey, "A Golden Decade for Defense Companies Is Ending," *Associated Press*, August 16, 2011, accessed March 19, 2015, http://news.yahoo.com/ golden-decade-defense-companies-ending-195617808.html.

199. Davis et al., *Armed and Dangerous?*, 13.

200. Davis et al., *Armed and Dangerous?*, 13.

201. Davis et al., *Armed and Dangerous?*, 15.

202. Davis et al., *Armed and Dangerous?*, 15.

203. Avery Plaw and Asa Kasher, "Distinguishing Drones," in *Killing by Remote Control*, edited by B. J. Strawser (Oxford: Oxford University Press, 2013), 48.

204. Plaw and Kasher, "Distinguishing Drones," 47.

205. Plaw and Kasher, "Distinguishing Drones," 54.

206. Steven Zaloga, *Unmanned Aerial Vehicles: Robotic Air Warfare 1917–2007* (New York: Osprey Press, 2008), 4, 7–8, 40.

207. Singer, *Wired for War*, 183–84.

208. Yaakov Katz, "Israel's Eye in the Sky," *Jerusalem Post*, October 7, 2011, accessed March 20, 2015, http://www.jpost.com/Magazine/Features/Israels-eye-in -the-sky.

209. Katz, "Israel's Eye in the Sky."

210. Uzi Mahnaimi, "Israeli Drones Destroy Rocket-Smuggling Convoys in Sudan," *Sunday Times*, March 29, 2009, accessed March 20, 2015, http://www.the sundaytimes.co.uk/sto/news/world_news/article158293.ece.

211. Katz, "Israel's Eye in the Sky."

212. Mahnaimi, "Israeli Drones Destroy Rocket-Smuggling Convoys in Sudan."

213. "Air Strike on Sudan Convoy Killed 119: State Media," *Reuters*, May 25, 2009, http://www.reuters.com/article/2009/05/25/us-sudan-attack-idUSTRE54O4 FA20090525.

214. It is also worth noting that while the majority of press reports described the incident as a drone attack, *Time* magazine provided a different account. In its reporting, drones were used for surveillance while the attack was launched by Israeli F-16 bombers escorted by F-15 fighters. See *Time* Staff, "How Israel Foiled an Arms Convoy Bound for Hamas," *Time*, March 30, 2009, accessed July 14, 2015, http://content-.time.com/time/world/article/0,8599,1888352,00.html.

215. Amos Harel, Yoav Stern, and Barak Ravid, "Sudan Strike Targeted Weapons Believed Capable of Hitting Tel Aviv," *Haaretz*, March 27, 2009, accessed March 20, 2015, http://www.haaretz.com/print-edition/news/sudan-strike-targeted-weapons -believed-capable-of-hitting-tel-aviv-1.273003.

216. Uzi Mahnaimi, "Israeli Drone Kills Hamas Arms Chief in Sudan," *Sunday Times*, April 17, 2011, accessed March 20, 2015, http://www.thesundaytimes.co.uk/ sto/news/world_news/Middle_East/article606445.ece; Sheera Frenkel, "Israeli Operations in Sudan Aimed at Disrupting Gaza Arms Trade, Officials Say," *McClatchy DC*, October 25, 2012, accessed March 20, 2015, http://www.mcclatchydc.com/2012/10/ 25/172602/israeli-operations-in-sudan-aimed.html.

217. Karl Vick, "Were the Israelis Behind the 'Mystery' Air Strike in Sudan?," *Time*, April 06, 2011, accessed March 20, 2015, http://world.time.com/2011/04/06/were-the-israelis-behind-the-mystery-air-strike-in-sudan/.

218. William Booth and Sharaf al-Hourani, "Militant Group in Sinai Accuses Israel of Deadly Drone Strike," *Washington Post*, August 10, 2013, accessed March 20, 2015, http://www.washingtonpost.com/world/militant-group-in-sinai-accuses-israel-of-deadly-drone-strike/2013/08/10/21ff7340-0203-11e3-8294-0ee5075b840d_story.html.

219. Ben Hubbard and Isabel Kershner, "Sinai Blasts Kill Up to 5 Thought to Be Militants," *New York Times*, August 9, 2013, accessed March 20, 2015, http://www.nytimes.com/2013/08/10/world/middleeast/sinai-blasts-kill-up-to-5-islamic-militants.html?_r=1&.

220. Booth and al-Hourani, "Militant Group in Sinai Accuses Israel of Deadly Drone Strike."

221. "Four Islamist Militants Killed in Egypt Near Israel: Sources," *Reuters*, August 9, 2013, accessed March 19, 2015, http://www.reuters.com/article/2013/08/09/us-egypt-explosions-idUSBRE9780TB20130809.

222. Steven Simon, "What Was Behind Israel's Strike in Syria That Killed an Iranian General? *Reuters*, January 23, 2015, accessed March 19, 2015, http://blogs.reuters.com/great-debate/2015/01/23/what-was-behind-israels-strike-in-syria/; "Iran General Died in 'Israeli Strike' in Syrian Golan," *BBC News*, January 19, 2015, accessed June 19, 2015, http://www.bbc.com/news/world-middle-east-30882935.

223. Barak Ravid, "UN Observers: Syria Strike Carried Out by Two Drones That Crossed from Israel," *Haaretz*, January 19, 2015, accessed March 19, 2015, http://www.haaretz.com/news/diplomacy-defense/.premium-1.637958.

224. Yaakov Katz, "IDF Believed to Be Using Armed UAVs," *Jerusalem Post*, August 8, 2012, accessed March 20, 2015, http://www.jpost.com/Defense/IDF-believed-to-be-using-armed-UAVs.

225. Katz, "IDF Believed to Be Using Armed UAVs"; Peter La Franchi, "Israel Fields Armed UAVs in Lebanon," *Flight Global*, August 6, 2006, accessed March 20, 2015, http://www.flightglobal.com/news/articles/israel-fields-armed-uavs-in-lebanon-208315/.

226. Steven Erlanger, "3 Palestinians Are Killed in Gaza; Candidate Pays a Visit," *New York Times*, January 1, 2005, accessed March 20, 2015, http://www.nytimes.com/2005/01/01/international/middleeast/01mideast.html?_r=0.

227. Michele K. Esposito, "Military Dimensions: The Israeli Arsenal Deployed against Gaza," *Journal of Palestine Studies* 38, no. 3 (2009): 175.

228. Esposito, "Military Dimensions," 175.

229. Esposito, "Military Dimensions," 175.

230. Esposito, "Military Dimensions," 176.

231. Esposito, "Military Dimensions," 176.

232. Esposito, "Military Dimensions," 176.

233. "Precisely Wrong," *Human Rights Watch*, June 30, 2009, accessed March 20, 2015, http://www.hrw.org/node/84077/section/3.

234. Gabriele Barbati, "Drones, Warriors or Robots? Israel Debates Tomorrow's Conflicts," *International Business Times*, July 5, 2013, accessed March 20, 2015, http://

www.ibtimes.com/drones-warriors-or-robots-israel-debates-tomorrows-conflicts-1326949.

235. Ben Hartman, "2012 Story of the Year: Operation Pillar of Defense," *The Jerusalem Post*, January, 2, 2013, accessed March 20, 2015, http://www.jpost.com/Features/In-Thespotlight/2012-story-of-the-year-Operation-Pillar-of-Defense; Peter Layton, "War in the Air over Gaza," *Defence Today*, February 16, 2013, accessed March 20, 2015, http://www.defence-today.com.au/war-in-the-air-over-gaza.

236. Arie Egozi, "Operation 'Pillar of Defence' a Milestone in UAS Combat Participation," *Flight Global*, November 26, 2012, accessed March 20, 2015, http://www.flightglobal.com/blogs/ariel-view/2012/11/operation-pillar-of-defence-a-milestone-in-uas-combat-participation/.

237. Egozi, "Operation 'Pillar of Defence' a Milestone in UAS Combat Participation."

238. Egozi, "Operation 'Pillar of Defence' a Milestone in UAS Combat Participation."

239. Layton, "War in the Air over Gaza."

240. "Israel: Gaza Airstrikes Violated Laws of War," *Human Rights Watch*, February 12, 2013, accessed March 20, 2015, http://www.hrw.org/news/2013/02/12/israel-gaza-airstrikes-violated-laws-war.

241. "Israel: Gaza Airstrikes Violated Laws of War."

242. "Israel: Gaza Airstrikes Violated Laws of War."

243. John Reed, "Israeli Forces Kill Militant in Gaza Strike," *Financial Times*, April 30, 2013, accessed March 20, 2015, http://www.ft.com/intl/cms/s/0/a1cc1b84-b175-11e2-b324-00144feabdc0.html#axzz3T4VpW3nw; David Barnett, "MSC in Jerusalem Member Targeted by Israeli Air Force," The Long War Journal, April 30, 2013, accessed March 20, 2015, http://www.longwarjournal.org/archives/2013/04/msc_in_jerusalem_mem.php.

244. Jane Perlez, "Chinese Plan to Kill Drug Lord with Drone Highlights Military Advances," *New York Times*, February 20, 2013, accessed March 20, 2015, http://www.nytimes.com/2013/02/21/world/asia/chinese-plan-to-use-drone-highlights-military-advances.html?_r=4&.

245. Liu Chang, "Manhunt for Deadly Drug Kingpin," *Global Times*, February 19, 2013, accessed March 20, 2015, http://www.globaltimes.cn/content/762449.shtml.

246. Andrew S. Erickson and Austin Strange, "China Has Drones. Now What?" *Foreign Affairs*, November 24, 2014, accessed March 20, 2015, http://www.foreignaffairs.com/articles/139405/andrew-s-erickson-and-austin-strange/china-has-drones-now-what.

247. Global Public Square staff, "The Trouble with U.S. Drone Policy," *CNN*, March 12, 2013, accessed March 20, 2015, http://globalpublicsquare.blogs.cnn.com/2013/03/12/the-trouble-with-u-s-drone-policy/.

248. Zenko and Kreps, "Limiting Armed Drone Proliferation," 11.

249. Didi K. Tatlow, "China Said to Deploy Drones After Unrest in Xinjiang," *New York Times*, August 19, 2014, http://sinosphere.blogs.nytimes.com/2014/08/19/china-said-to-deploy-drones-after-unrest-in-xinjiang/.

250. Bai Tiantian, "Xinjiang Vows Unceasing Terror Crackdown," *People Daily*, August 5, 2014, http://english.peopledaily.com.cn/n/2014/0805/c90882-8765210.html.

251. Tatlow, "China Said to Deploy Drones After Unrest in Xinjiang."

252. Christian J. Tams, "The Use of Force against Terrorists," *European Journal of International Law* 20, no. 2 (2009): 378.

253. Tams, "The Use of Force against Terrorists," 380.

254. "Blast Kills Exiled Chechen Leader," *CNN*, February 13, 2004, accessed July 14, 2015, http://edition.cnn.com/2004/WORLD/meast/02/13/qatar.chechen/index .html.

255. Jeremy McDermott, "Farc Aura of Invincibility Shattered," *BBC News*, March 1, 2008, accessed July 14, 2015, http://news.bbc.co.uk/2/hi/americas/7273 320.stm.

256. "Cameroon Launches Air Strikes Against Nigerian Extremists," *New York Times*, December 29, 2014, http://www.nytimes.com/aponline/2014/12/29/world/ africa/ap-af-cameroon-nigeria.html?_r = 0; Eugene Nforngwa, "Cameroon Launches First Strike against Boko Haram inside Nigeria," *Standard-Tribune*, March 17, 2015, http://www.standard-tribune.com/?p = 2594; Madjiasra Neko and Abdoulaye Massa-laki, "Chad, Niger Launch Joint Offensive against Boko Haram in Nigeria," *Reuters*, March 8, 2015, http://uk.reuters.com/article/2015/03/08/uk-nigeria-violence-niger -idUKKBN0M40LF20150308.

257. "LRA Conflict in Northern Uganda and Southern Sudan, 2002," *Human Rights Watch*, October 29, 2002, accessed July 14, 2015, http://www.hrw.org/legacy/ press/2002/10/uganda1029-bck.htm.

258. Micah Zenko, "Nine Months of Coalition Air Strikes Against the Islamic State," *Council on Foreign Relations*, May 8, 2015, accessed July 14, 2015, http:// blogs.cfr.org/zenko/2015/05/08/nine-months-of-coalition-air-strikes-against-the-is lamic-state/comment-page-1/.

259. "US Flying Armed Drones in Iraq," *The Guardian*, June 28, 2014, http:// www.theguardian.com/world/2014/jun/28/us-flying-armed-drones-in-iraq.

260. Ben Farmer, "British Drones Carry Out First Strikes against Isil in Iraq," *The Telegraph*, November 10, 2014, http://www.telegraph.co.uk/news/worldnews/mid dleeast/iraq/11221048/British-drones-carry-out-first-strikes-against-Isil-in-Iraq.html.

261. Tams, "The Use of Force against Terrorists," 393.

262. Christian J. Tams and James G. Devaney, "*Jus ad Bellum*: Crossing Borders to Wage War against Individuals," in *Legitimacy and Drones: Investigating the Legality, Morality and Efficacy of UCAVs*, edited by Steven J. Barela (Burlington: Ashgate Press, 2015), 33.

Conclusion

The Age of Drones?

I N THIS CONCLUDING CHAPTER, we offer some general observations on the drone debate described in the previous chapters. Since we haven't engaged critically with the arguments we've outlined, but have sought instead to provide a general overview—a roadmap—of the debate, we don't have anything to say about who is winning or losing specific points. We hope that the book so far has put readers in a better position to make this assessment for themselves. We can, however, offer some ideas about the character and evolving dynamics of the debate.

I. Unrecognized Agreement

To begin with, there is probably more agreement among participants on all sides of the drone debate than is commonly recognized. The arguments among participants tend to focus, understandably, on the most fiercely contested points and practices (such as the numbers of civilians being killed, or the strategic impact of drone strikes on targeted groups). These are the areas that tend to most interest potential readers and where there is the greatest opportunity to score debating points against opponents. And it must be acknowledged that the U.S. drone campaigns involve a lot of novel and controversial elements that provide ammunition to partisans on all sides. But we think that, at times, the back and forth barrages mask deeper agreement. For example, we suggest that a careful examination of the positions taken by the great majority of contributors of the debate will reveal broad agreement on the following points:

1. Armed drones have proven to be *tactically* effective in neutralizing suspected terrorists and especially leaders (by killing them) both within and outside of conventional combat.
2. Armed drones are permissible weapons in conventional armed conflict.
3. There are circumstances under which their use outside of conventional combat may be justifiable—for example, to disrupt a terrorist attack in progress that could not otherwise be prevented and where civilians are not endangered.
4. The use of drones outside of conventional armed conflict, and especially the aggressive way that they are being used by the United States today, has worrying implications for how armed force will be used in the future, especially as drones and particularly armed drones proliferate among states and even nonstate actors.

These very basic points of agreement already help to explain some of the interest and controversy that drones have attracted, for we would suggest that accepting point 3 (about the permissibility of disrupting attacks in progress) makes at least some of the serious worries raised in point 4 (about eroding restraints on force) inescapable. To put it another way, the serious worries entailed in point 4 cannot be resolved without prohibiting some of the justifiable use of force in self-defense (which could potentially save innocent lives) acknowledged in point 3. This suggests that some moral conflict over the use of armed drones is felt by most participants in the debate, and may be irreducible without some radical alteration of the facts at hand (such as the successful ratification of an enforceable international convention limiting the preemptive use of drones narrowly to an agreed set of cases justified under point 3).

II. Sources of Dispute

Of course, the views of most contributors to the drone debate go far beyond these four basic points outlined above, but we suggest that a good deal of controversy can still be traced back to how broadly the third point is construed and how significant its impacts on the fourth are thought likely to be—that is, how widely contributors interpret the justification for drone use in "circumstances outside of conventional combat" (point 3), and the degree to which they think such uses will undermine norms constraining the use of force by actors in the international system (point 4).

In other words, while we think that there is broad agreement that drone strikes may be narrowly permissible in the circumstances outlined in point

3, there is also a continuum of increasingly controversial circumstances in which drone strikes may be thought justified and about which people disagree. A range of considerations may come into play, including the following:

- Which terrorist organizations can legitimately be targeted (only those who have carried out major attacks, like al-Qaeda, or any one that threatens even small attacks)?
- How imminent must the threat be (an attack in progress or anticipated in the foreseeable future)?
- Who counts as a combatant (only suspected terrorist leaders or any members of targeted organizations?
- What evidence is required to establish combatant status (the identity and function and history of each individual or a pattern of behavior exhibiting certain signatures)?
- How much endangerment of civilians is permissible (none or whatever is not disproportionate to the legitimate military goals of the operation)?
- What permission is required from the state on whose territory the operation is taking place (explicit and public authorization of the specific operation or effective noninterference)?
- What evidence of effectiveness is required to warrant the continuation of such operations (tactical or strategic or both)?

All of these considerations obviously generate controversy, especially when they are combined. We suggest that part of the reason is that they engage not only moral and legal issues about how far it should be permissible for countries to go in hunting down threats to civilians but also the very different question (in point 4) of what the long-term consequences of these new precedents are likely to be for the use of armed force in the future. Disagreements are likely not only over both questions, but also how they should be balanced at each point on the continuum suggested above. Part of the reason for the great furor over U.S. drone strikes is that individual U.S. operations have ranged across the continuum, including toward the controversial end. Critics tend to focus on the cases that range out furthest on the controversial extreme, while defenders emphasize the least controversial. For this reason, among others, there is a tendency to talk past one another and to obscure the points over which there may actually be some agreement. But each of the questions listed above seems to us genuinely both difficult and important. Each involves its own distinctive problems that warrant individual attention as well as discussion in combination with the others.

Nonetheless, to us there also seems to be one question that is especially central, and that tends to shape responses to all of the foregoing questions:

Do the attacks by transnational terrorist networks warrant an aggressive military response against the terrorist groups themselves (rather than strictly against state sponsors)? If the answer is yes, then the use of drones will seem justified, and the key question will be how to adapt the rules governing military operations to the use of this new technology against unconventional targets. If the answer is no, then the use of drones outside conventional combat will seem generally unjustified, except perhaps for a very narrow set of cases in which terrorists are actually in the act of threatening the lives of civilians and there is no other means to protect them. Those who embrace a military response tend to look to Just War Theory as a framework for guiding counterterrorism, and focus on showing a just cause and making sure that other *jus ad bellum* and *jus in bello* requirements are met. Those who reject the resort to military force, by contrast, focus on the other instruments of policy (like law enforcement, intelligence cooperation, diplomacy, economic sanctions, etc.), which might prove effective over time but are prone to be eclipsed by a military response. Those who favor a military response emphasize a strategic goal of degrading and destroying terrorist groups, while those who reject this option focus on containment, violence reduction, and the gradual reintegration of at least parts of terrorist groups into the official political, economic, and social systems. So this basic distinction over whether military force is warranted helps to explain many aspects of the drone debate.

III. The Intractability of Drone Disputes

The basic distinction between military and nonmilitary responses to terrorist groups may also help to illuminate why these debates about drones are both so passionate on both sides and are as yet unresolved. We suggest three specific reasons. The first is that, on this basic question over whether military force is warranted, we just simply don't know who is right yet. This is partly because the threat—or at least the degree of threat—posed by transnational terrorist networks is relatively new. At the same time, it is partly because long-range drones armed with laser-guided missiles are new weapons, and we don't know how effective they are likely to be against these transnational terrorist networks over time (and indeed the answer may be different for al-Qaeda Central, the TTP, AQAP, and al-Shabaab, according to the distinctive features of the groups and the cultures and societies in which they operate).

The second reason is that the partial evidence that is available at this point gives comfort to both sides, particularly in the areas that each sees as most important. For example, the databases on drone strikes referenced throughout this book support the view that drone strikes are effective in killing suspected militants, including terrorist leaders. At the same time, there is ample evidence that these strikes may be strategically counterproductive. For example, they are associated with high levels of popular antagonism to the United States, and in some cases with growth in the terrorist groups targeted. Both sides, in short, can claim to be winning the debate in their own terms. We hope that the force of the arguments on both sides is captured in this book.

The third reason for the intractability of the drone debate is that drones are implicated in two broader debates, both with their own controversies. One of those broader debates concerns the idea of targeted killing. Nils Melzer, the former legal adviser to the International Committee of the Red Cross, aptly defined "targeted killing" as "the use of lethal force attributable to a subject of international law, with the intent, premeditation and deliberation to kill individually selected persons who are not in the physical custody of those targeting them."[1] Drone strikes, or at least "personality strikes" aimed at specifically identified individuals on "kill lists," like the disposition matrix, are really just one among many forms of targeted killing.

A second broad debate that involves drones is over asymmetrical warfare. Colonel Robert Shaw, the first commanding officer of the U.S. Army's Asymmetric Warfare Group, defines *asymmetric warfare* as follows: "Warfare in which the two or more belligerents are mismatched in their military capabilities or accustomed methods of engagement," as is the case, for example, between the United States and al-Qaeda and its affiliates.[2] In such a conflict, Shaw notes, "the militarily disadvantaged power must press its special advantages or . . . its enemy's particular weaknesses if they are to prevail"—for example, by striking soft targets like civilians, and by making its militants difficult to distinguish from civilians so as to evade the other side's superior forces.[3] By contrast, the more powerful belligerent must find ways to overcome these unconventional tactics by developing measures to identify and engage groups of enemy militants before they hit soft targets. This is the aim of signature strikes, which are probably best understood as a tactic of asymmetrical warfare.[4] The key distinction here is that signature strikes target on the basis of a status (i.e., observed patterns of life that suggest active participation in targeted organizations), whereas personality strikes target a specific individual on the basis of his known history of action and the future threat that he personally poses. Status-based targeting is characteristic of armed conflict, whereas targeting a specific individual in the light of a known threat that he poses is more compatible with self-defense operations or even potentially, in the case of an immediate threat with no other means of neutralizing it, law enforcement operations.

Both targeted killing and asymmetrical warfare are practices to which states are turning with growing frequency, including, in many cases, operations that do not involve drones. The killing of Hezbollah commander Imad Mughniyeh in 2008 by the CIA and Mossad by putting a bomb in his SUV, and the killing of Osama bin Laden by a SEAL team in 2011, offer examples of recent targeted killings that did not rely primarily on drones.[5] Likewise, strikes by manned aircraft against ISIL in Syria and Iraq provide obvious examples of asymmetric warfare using weapons other than drones.[6] An increasing number of countries—including Australia, Russia, Israel, and Turkey—have asserted the right to carry out targeted killings and/or to conduct limited forms of warfare against terrorist groups that attempt to execute attacks against their nationals (see the case study in chapter 6 for details). And there is growing scholarly and legal debate over these practices and whether at least certain forms may be permissible and prudent under certain circumstances.[7] Indeed, in a widely debated decision in 2006, the Israeli High Court of Justice affirmed that targeted killing of active members of terrorist groups might be legal if certain conditions were met.[8]

Many of the arguments deployed in the drone debate are ultimately arguments for or against targeted killing and/or over the resort to asymmetrical warfare against terrorist groups outside of a state's own territory. To see this, consider for a moment whether critics of drone strikes would be less opposed if targeted killings were carried out by blowing up victim's cars with pipe bombs, or if asymmetrical warfare were conducted by means of cruise missiles rather than drones. In other words, the issue at stake often goes far beyond drones themselves, despite what sometimes seems to be a narrow focus on them.

Four Reasons Why the Focus Has Been on Drones

Drones, in effect, have often become a proxy for talking about targeted killing and/or asymmetric warfare with terrorist groups for at least four reasons. In the first place, they have become, in the apt phrase of Syracuse University law professor William Banks, "the counterterrorism weapons of choice for the United States."[9] In short, this is the weapon the United States has used for the vast majority of its military operations outside of conventional battlefields in the last fourteen years, and these strikes have attracted enormous worldwide attention.

A second explanation for the focus on drones is that it seems that they are likely to remain the weapon of choice for the foreseeable future for two reasons. First, like commando raids, drone strikes may be seen as military operations, especially since they are generally flown by U.S. Air Force personnel. This is significant because lethal actions are easier to justify in the context of a military operation than outside of one. Second, unlike commando raids, drone strikes do not generally endanger military personnel. As President Obama put it in his May 23, 2013, speech at the National Defense University, commando raids, like "our operation in Pakistan against Osama bin Laden[,] cannot be the norm. The risks in that case were immense. The fact that we did not find ourselves confronted with civilian casualties, or embroiled in an extended firefight, was a testament to the meticulous planning and professionalism of our Special Forces, but it also depended on some luck."[10] If the United States is going to carry out targeted killings and/or conduct asymmetric warfare against al-Qaeda and its affiliates, it will often have to be by the use of drones.

A third reason why drones have become the "poster child" for targeted killing and/or asymmetric warfare is because drones are just plain spooky, and the idea of states using lethal force outside of conventional combat is scary, and together they have formed an indelible image on the public consciousness. Because drones seem to be the focus when discussing these issues, debates over targeted killing, asymmetrical warfare, and drone strikes have all become deeply entangled.

A fourth and final reason for the tendency to focus on drones is that the swift rise in their use and their rapid proliferation make them seem at times like an almost irresistible and transformative phenomenon. The effect of this seemingly unstoppable rise can be to make objections to states using them, including outside of conventional battlefields, seem quaint. However, it is worth bearing in mind that if the current foray into asymmetrical warfare and targeted killing turns out to be a momentary detour, and the next war is between major military powers with advanced air defenses (for example, between the United States and Russia or China), then it may be the drones that end up looking quaint, since they only function effectively in permissive air space. Indeed, in this scenario of great power conflict, it could even be the aggressive use of drones to collect data across borders or in disputed territory that could trigger the escalation that draws the United States into conflict with Russia or China (as in Russian drones in Ukraine or the Baltics, or Chinese drones in the Senkaku Islands, or U.S. drones in Russian or Chinese airspace). So here again the justification for drone strikes is at least partially entangled with another debate, in this case over the trajectory of military development. And just as it is difficult to forecast the next conflict based on past or current ones, it is correspondingly difficult to know whether drones will be a transformative or tangential military technology based on operations to date.

IV. The Drone Stands Alone

Yet even if the drone debate is complicated by its entanglements with a range of other complex issues and debates, there are still ample features that are unique to drones and deserve careful attention. The drone's capacity to hover in place for over a day and its extraordinarily precise visual surveillance capacity set it apart from virtually any other system. The facts that it can often carry out surveillance surreptitiously and its crews can be changed without returning to base also stand out and reinforce its unique ISR capacity. When we add laser-guided munitions and the fact that they do not put pilots in danger, it's clear that drones are a weapons platform with unique capabilities for tracking and, where appropriate, killing targets in remote territories that are seeking opportunities to evade and attack. And so it is not surprising that the vast majority of lethal U.S. unconventional counterterrorist operations have been carried out by means of this particular platform. In this light, drones do give dramatic shape and context to the central question that confronts U.S. counterterrorism efforts today and perhaps that of many other countries tomorrow: Should terrorists be pursued by armed force outside of conventional battlefields?

This question of the justifiability of counterterrorist drone strikes outside of conventional battlefields is not just a matter of whether this or that particular strike can be justified. It is also the broader question of whether U.S. policies regarding drone strikes are the best available option and/or can reliably be made so. The evaluation of these policies is not only crucial for the United States but also for other countries that are confronting unconventional security threats today or that will do so in the future. To assess the policies and to move toward answering the big question of whether terrorist groups should be pursued with lethal force outside of conventional combat, we need to know as much as we can, not only about what the procedures and rules are for carrying out drone strikes today but also about the capabilities of the platform and how it has performed (and with what effect and consequences). We need to listen to what their defenders say about the precision and effectiveness of drones, and what their critics say about their tragic impacts on the ground and their strategic counterproductivity. We need to compare both sets of claims to the facts as they are most credibly reported in order to critically assess the best arguments and to render an informed judgment. This is not only a matter of prudence. It is also, for Americans at least, a moral and civic obligation when our country carries out lethal military operations abroad in our name. It is owed not only to ourselves but also to the innocents who are killed and their families who are left bereft. It is our hope that this book will contribute to that process.

Notes

1. Nils Melzer, *Targeted Killing in International Law* (Oxford: Oxford University Press, 2008), 5.
2. David L. Buffaloe, "Defining Asymmetric Warfare," The Institute of Land Warfare, Land Warfare Papers, no. 58, 2006, 13, accessed July 19, 2015, https://www.ausa.org/SiteCollectionDocuments/ILW%20Web-ExclusivePubs/Land%20Warfare%20Papers/LWP_58.pdf.
3. Buffaloe, "Defining Asymmetric Warfare," 13.
4. For an illuminating discussion of the way drone strikes contribute to non-international armed conflicts between states and nonstate actors like terrorist groups, see Daniel Rothenberg, "Drones and the Emergence of Data-Driven Warfare," in *Drone Wars: Transforming Conflict, Law, and Policy*, edited by Peter Bergen and Daniel Rothenberg, 450–55 (Cambridge: Cambridge University Press, 2014).
5. Adam Goldman and Ellen Nakashima, "CIA and Mossad Killed Senior Hezbollah Figure in Car Bombing," *Washington Post*, January 30, 2015, accessed July 17, 2015, https://www.washingtonpost.com/world/national-security/cia-and-mossad-killed-senior-hezbollah-figure-in-car-bombing/2015/01/30/ebb88682-968a-11e4-8005-1924ede3e54a_story.html.
6. Ned Resnkioff, "More U.S. Airstrikes in Iraq and Syria Destroy ISIS Targets," *MSNBC*, October 4, 3014, accessed July 19, 2015, http://www.msnbc.com/msnbc/more-us-airstrikes-iraq-and-syria-destroy-isis-targets; Walter Pincus, *Washington Post*, "Strikes from Manned Aircraft Draw Much Less Scrutiny Than Drones," May 4, 2015, https://www.washingtonpost.com/world/national-security/strikes-from-manned-aircraft-draw-much-less-scrutiny-than-drones/2015/05/04/997a3672-f1ac-11e4-b2f3-af5479e6bbdd_story.html.
7. See, for example, Melzer, *Targeted Killing in International Law*; Claire Finkelstein, David Ohlin, and Andrew Altman, *Targeted Killings: Law and Morality in an Asymmetrical World* (New York: Oxford University Press, 2012); Kenneth Himes, *Drones and the Ethics of Targeted Killing* (Plymouth: Rowman & Littlefield, 2015); Matthew Machon, *Targeted Killing as an Element of U.S. Foreign Policy in the War on Terror* (War College Series, 2015); Pauline Kaurin, *The Warrior, Military Ethics and Contemporary Warfare: Achilles Goes Asymmetrical* (Burlington: Ashgate, 2014); Michael Gross, *Moral Dilemmas of Modern Warfare: Torture, Assassination, and Blackmail in an Age of Asymmetric Conflict* (Cambridge: Cambridge University Press, 2010); Rod Thornton, *Asymmetric Warfare* (Cambridge: Polity Press, 2007); Ivan Arreguin-Toft, *How the Weak Win Wars: A Theory of Asymmetric Conflict* (Cambridge: Cambridge University Press, 2005).
8. *The Public Against Torture in Israel v. the Government of Israel*, HC 769/02, December 14, 2006, accessed July 19, 2015, http://elyon1.court.gov.il/files_eng/02/690/007/A34/02007690.a34.pdf.
9. William C. Banks, "Regulating Drones: Are Targeted Killings by Drones Outside Traditional Battlefields Legal?" in *Drone Wars: Transforming Conflict, Law, and Policy*, edited by Peter L. Bergen and Daniel Rothenberg (Cambridge: Cambridge University Press, 2014), 152.
10. Barack Obama, "Remarks by the President at the National Defense University," speech, National Defense University, Fort McNair, Washington, DC, May 23, 2013.

Index

Abdulmutallab, Umar Farouk, 88
accountability, 3–4, 44, 200–201, 203–205, 207–213
Afghanistan, 8–9, 20–23, 25, 27, 34, 43–45, 49–50, 67–8, 74, 81, 86, 95, 112, 115, 120, 129, 131–133, 134–137, 140, 148, 151, 156n21, 170, 172, 175, 177, 185–186, 193, 195, 208, 229n1, 236, 251, 258, 285
al-Awlaki, Abdulrahman, 91
al-Awlaki, Anwar, 89–91, 141, 179, 208, 263
al-Harithi, Ali Qaed Sunian, 22, 86–89, 138
al-Qaeda, 3, 20, 32–34, 40, 50, 65–74, 80, 83, 85–89, 92, 94–96, 115–117, 119–124, 144, 151-2, 172, 175–182, 187–190, 208, 234, 236–237, 239, 255, 261, 295, 306, 308, 329–331, 333; leader(s), 22, 37, 45, 50, 68, 70, 86, 181–182, 227, 239; war (or armed conflict) with, 8, 41, 71, 112, 115, 119, 128–140, 177, 264; training camp/compound, 20, 86, 94, 120, 147, 151, 236
al-Qaeda in the Arabian Peninsula (AQAP), 65–66, 71, 76, 83, 88–92, 94–97, 139–140,152, 177–178, 244, 261, 263, 330
al-Shabaab, 70, 139–140, 176, 178, 182, 244, 261, 330

al-Wuhayshi, Nasir, 88, 90, 92, 94–95
Alston, Phillip, v, 128, 140–141, 170, 182, 203–213, 293
al-Wuhayshi, Nasir, 88, 90, 92, 94–95
Amnesty International, 60n192, 183, 309
Anderson, Kenneth, 112, 127–128, 144, 227, 242
anticipatory self-defense, see self-defense
AQAP, see al- Qaeda in the Arabian Peninsula, 65–66, 71, 76, 83, 88–97, 139–140, 152, 177–178, 244, 261, 263, 330
Article 51, see self-defense
assassination, 1, 4, 6, 112, 114, 116–117, 171, 173, 243–244, 311, see also targeted killings
asymmetric warfare, 171–172, 187, 196, 281, 331–333
Atef, Mohammed, 22
AUMF, see Authorization for Use of Military Force
Authorization for Use of Military Force (AUMF), 114–116, 129, 139, 141, 177, 252
autonomous technology/systems/drones/robots, 2, 4, 168–169, 199–203, 304–305

Beauchamp, Zack, 196–198
bin Laden, Osama, 20–21, 35, 50, 69–72, 88, 116, 129, 175, 227, 332–333

RQ-170 sentinel drone, 286
RQ-4 Global Hawk, *see* Global Hawk
Russia, 194, 247, 254, 285, 290, 293, 300, 302, 312, 332, 333

Saleh, Ali Abdullah, 22, 87–90
Schultz, Kenneth, 249
self-defense, 4, 113, 119–128, 137–138, 175, 187–188, 194, 201, 234, 251, 293, 312, 328, 331
Shane, Scott, 153–154, 293
Sharkey, Noel, 199–201, 288
signature strikes, 3–4, 67–68, 78, 89, 91, 145, 147–154, 179, 182–183, 233, 235–236, 250–252, 331
Singer, Peter W., 7, 19, 170, 173, 195, 198, 288, 291, 294, 296, 303, 304–306
Somalia, 1, 3, 9, 14, 28–30, 37, 39, 41–42, 46, 62n216, 68–70, 86, 112, 131, 137, 141–142, 148, 167, 174, 195, 197, 231, 243–244, 254, 307
South Asia, 80, 137–138
sovereignty, 45, 81–82, 131, 139–143
Sparrow, Robert, 198–200
State Department, 152, 205, 234, 303
Steinhoff, Uwe, 168, 174, 198
Strawser, Bradley J., 167–174, 202
swarms, 297, 305–306
Swift, Christopher, 66, 69, 94–97

tactical drones, 7, 8, 17, 291, 297, 299
Taliban, 8, 21–22, 28–29, 32–35, 37, 45, 49–50, 65, 67, 69, 71, 73–74, 77, 79, 83–84, 112–113, 114–116, 129, 133, 136–137, 140, 153–154, 175–176, 178, 188, 239, 257, 260, 286, 306
targeted killings, 1, 3, 6, 21–22, 28–29, 42, 46, 89–91, 167, 204–205, 208–210, 213, 298, 313, 331–333; ethics of targeted killing, 170–171, 187–189, 194–195; Israeli targeted killings, 76, 307–310; issues over the effectiveness of targeted killing, 66–67, 72–75, 78; legal status targeted killings, 112–113, 115, 116–117, 127–128, 141; targeted killing of

American, *see* targeting Americans; U.S. politics of targeted killing, 227–228, 241–242, 244, 259
targeting Americans, 4, 86, 91; Department of Justice Memorandum on the legality of targeting Anwar al-Awlaki, 118–119, 132, 141, 239; U.S. criticism of targeting an American, 236–239; targeting Anwar al-Awlaki, 90–91; White Paper on lawfulness of targeting an American, 118, 124,126, 234, 242–243, 250
terrorism, 1, 76, 80–81, 84, 86, 129–130, 135, 137–138, 148, 168, 177, 180, 196, 225, 227, 237, 239, 242, 252, 255, 312; terrorist(s), 2, 29, 33, 66–70, 75, 77, 80–82, 84, 86, 88, 90, 96–97, 116, 120, 122–123, 125, 128–129, 139, 143–144, 148–149, 151–152, 154, 176,179, 184–185, 190, 192, 194, 201, 227–228, 234, 239, 241–243, 245, 248–249, 251–253, 262, 264, 266–267, 286, 295–296, 298, 306–307, 311–313, 330, 334; terrorist leaders/leadership, 3, 9, 66, 69, 73, 176, 226, 241, 247, 329, 331; suspected terrorist/terrorist suspects, 4, 27, 72, 111, 118, 125, 128, 228, 231–232, 237, 241–242, 244, 263, 266, 328; terrorist attack(s), 2, 35, 72, 74, 88, 114, 120, 122, 124, 139, 147–148, 151, 169, 179, 190, 194, 248–250, 266, 295–296, 328; terrorist network(s), 9, 68–69, 71, 80, 125, 330; terrorist organization(s)/group(s), 3, 66, 68, 72–74, 82, 85, 94, 96–97, 115, 117, 121–123, 126, 130, 133–134, 140–141, 177–179, 187, 189–190, 194, 291, 293–296, 312, 329–332, 334; (global) war on terror, 1, 13, 111–112, 115–116, 129–130, 140, 156n17, 243
transparency, 28, 43–45, 203–204, 254, 259, 293, 299
Turkey, 256, 285–286, 288, 290, 294, 300, 332

About the Authors

At the time of this writing, *Avery Plaw* was associate professor of political science at the University of Massachusetts Dartmouth and is now professor of political science at the same institution. His research focuses on political theory and international relations, and he has a particular interest in strategic studies. He received his PhD from McGill University in 2002, taught at Concordia University in Montreal, and was a visiting professor at New York University before joining the University of Massachusetts in 2006.

Matthew S. Fricker is a co-founder of the Center for the Study of Targeted Killing and holds a masters degree in nonproliferation and terrorism studies from the Monterey Institute of International Studies. He is passionate about computers and other technology and enjoys problem-solving.

Carlos R. Colon is a co-founder and analyst at the Center for the Study of Targeted Killing at the University of Massachusetts Dartmouth. He worked as a research intern at the National Consortium for the Study of Terrorism and Responses to Terrorism (START) in the summer of 2014. Prior to that he interned at the International Center for Terrorism Studies at the Potomac Institute for Policy Studies Fall 2012. He was also awarded a Terrorism Studies certificate by the Inter-University Center for Terrorism Studies and the International Law Institute in 2012.